TCP/IP
Clearly
Explained

THIRD EDITION

TCP/IP
Clearly
Explained

THIRD EDITION

Pete Loshin
BYTE Magazine

Morgan Kaufmann

ACADEMIC PRESS, A Harcourt Science and Technology Company

San Diego   San Francisco   New York   Boston
London   Sydney   Tokyo

ACADEMIC PRESS
A Harcourt Science and Technology Company
525 B Street, Suite 1900, San Diego, CA 92101-4495 USA
http://www.academicpress.com

Academic Press
Harcourt Place, 32 Jamestown Road, London, NW1 7BY, UK

Morgan Kaufmann
340 Pine Street, Sixth Floor, San Francisco, CA 94104-3205
http://www.mkp.com

Library of Congress Catalog Number: 99-62309
International Standard Book Number: 0-12-455826-7

Printed in the United States of America
00 01 02 03 04 VH 7 6 5 4 3 2

Contents

Acknowledgments

No book gets published without the help of a lot of different people. The people at AP Professional have all done wonderful jobs of taking my raw manuscripts and turning them into readable, attractive, and useful texts. First, thanks to Ken Morton, acquisitions editor. Editorial assistant Gabrielle Billeter helped keep me on track and on schedule.

Jan Harrington made many helpful comments that helped keep me on track while writing this, third, edition. Frank Klatil of Johns Hopkins University and Buck Graham, author of *TCP/IP Addressing* (AP Professional, 1996), provided insightful comments and invaluable assistance in creating the second edition of this book.

There was a time when I wasn't sure that I would be able to finish writing the first edition of this book. From the very beginning, Lisa Wolfe, then my girlfriend and now my wife, has given me the unconditional love and support necessary to keep me going despite self-doubt—as well as Jacy, our special little boy. And Zoom, too.

Feedback and Comments

Thank you for picking up this book. I hope you buy it; if you've already bought it, I hope you read it. And if you read it, I hope you let me know what you thought of it. The best part of my day is hearing from people who have read my books and have questions or comments.

Questions and comments from readers have shaped this book and, I hope, made it better and more clear in this, its third edition. If you find this book useful, please let me know. If you need clarification of any part of this book, please let me know this, too—by answering your question I can also make the next revision of this book more useful for others.

Feel free to contact me by e-mail at:

pete@loshin.com

Introduction

Research on packet switched networks, financed by the U.S. Department of Defense, produced in 1969 the network connecting a handful of systems that eventually became the Internet. By the close of 1998, the number of machines connected to the Internet was on the order of 100 million (10^8); in 1994, when the first edition of this book was written, there were on the order of 10 million (10^7), most of them still in universities, research organizations, and vendors of computer and networking products. In less than 30 years, the Internet protocol suite, also known as TCP/IP, has fueled the growth of a global network over eight orders of magnitude.

1969 was the year that humankind first stepped on the moon, also fueled by Department of Defense expenditures. To put the Internet's success in perspective, if the moon program were as successful as TCP/IP, tens of millions of people would now be living and working there and generating enormous new wealth from industries previously unimagined.

This book provides an introduction to the TCP/IP protocol suite, and how it is currently being used. First, some basic definitions are in order.

- A **node** is a system or device that is connected to a network. Most nodes are computers, but any device capable of receiving and transmitting data to the network can be a node.
- A **protocol** is the set of rules that governs how nodes communicate.
- A **network** is a system in which two or more nodes can use a shared medium to communicate. The medium may be a physical one, like a wire cable, or it can use radio waves for wireless communication.
- An **internetwork** is a network of networks. There was a time when the word **internet** was an abbreviated form of internetwork, and meant the same thing: two or more networks connected through intermediary systems. This usage is now mostly obsolete, replaced by the term **intranet**. Internetworks usually use open networking protocols—standards that are not owned or controlled by any single organization, and that can be used freely by anyone able to implement them in a software or hardware product.
- The **Internet** with a capital "I" is the global internetwork that links businesses, educational institutions, other organizations of all types, and individuals.
- All data transmitted across the Internet uses the **Internet Protocol (IP)**. A large part of that data also uses the **Transmission Control Protocol (TCP)**.
- **TCP/IP**, the pairing of the two most important Internet protocols, is also the name given to the suite of protocols that make the Internet run. The TCP/IP protocol suite includes quite a few additional related protocols.

The TCP/IP protocol suite allows any two nodes connected to the same internetwork to seamlessly interoperate with no more information than the source and destination node addresses. This bears clarification: My computer can communicate with your computer, no matter whether I'm using an IBM mainframe computer connected to a token-ring network and you're using a Macintosh connected to a dialup connection. My computer doesn't need to know anything about your computer or network, and your computer doesn't need to know anything about my computer or network—just the address.

Seamless interoperability is what makes TCP/IP so powerful.

This bears repeating: TCP/IP internetworks let any connected host communicate with any other connected host, without knowing any details about the other host or about the intervening network topology.

Interoperability is the ability to communicate with other hosts regardless of hardware, operating system, physical location, network medium, or method of connecting to the internetwork, and interoperability is what makes or breaks an internetworking protocol suite.

As shown in Figure I-1, users (as well as network engineers) can usually more profitably view an internetwork as a cloud obscuring the sordid details of the intervening network architecture(s). It is possible to fairly completely illustrate a link between two hosts across an internetwork just by showing how each host is connected to the internetwork. Although more information about the path taken by data between the two hosts might help, that information usually isn't available or applicable.

TCP/IP internetworking protocols define the way data is passed along the networks and links between the networks in such a way as to assure that:

- ♦ Destination and source addresses are discernable at any point in the journey from host to host
- ♦ Data passed from one network medium to another is handled correctly
- ♦ Routing can be done dynamically to maximize efficiency, and without requiring the originating host to define the route

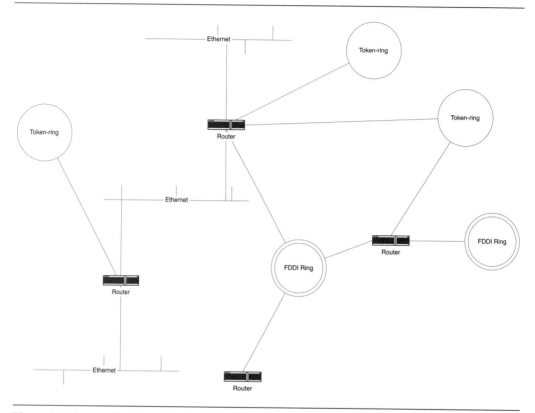

Figure I-1: Even a simple network of networks, or internetwork, starts to look complicated.

TCP/IP has been a phenomenally successful protocol suite:

♦ It is implemented on virtually every hardware platform and under virtually every operating system in general use today

♦ The number of networks, systems, and users using TCP/IP continues to double roughly every year as it has since 1988, with little sign of slowing growth

♦ At current growth rates and the growth of new markets, TCP/IP users will likely hit the one-billion mark soon after the millenium

- Every network software of importance, including Microsoft, IBM, Apple, Novell, Sun MicroSystems, and many, many others support TCP/IP

TCP/IP continues to be spectacularly successful for three reasons:

- It is an open set of protocols
- Proposed changes and additions go through iterative design and live testing before codification
- Protocol developments must help support the goal of interoperability among all systems and networks

The Internet and IP

IP offers a complete and robust solution for enterprise internetwork interoperability; the Internet is simply the largest arena in which you can implement an IP network. It is not necessary to be connected to the Internet if you are using TCP/IP, and many organizations concerned about the security risks inherent in exposing their networks to the public use TCP/IP on intranets with limited or no Internet access.

Likewise, it isn't necessary to be connected to a corporate TCP/IP intranet to connect to the Internet, as millions of new users, drawn by increasingly easy-to-use interfaces and an avalanche of easily accessible content on the World Wide Web, are finding out. Until the mid-1990s, most Internet access was from institutional or corporate sites, using high-speed links between Internet backbones and large organizational networks. As the Internet gained popularity among a mass consumer market in the mid- to late-1990s, the number of individuals, working both from homes and offices connecting to the Internet using serial links to Internet service providers (ISPs) over their telephone lines, increased dramatically. And as we enter the next millenium, broadband, satellite, digital subscriber line, and other high-bandwidth solutions will start to predominate.

TCP/IP network software vendors continually improve and simplify their offerings, particularly in the personal computer market. Vendors of all types, ranging from personal computer makers to telephone companies are bundling Internet access with their products, another important step in making Internet access accessible. Practically everyone in the business, from software vendors to content providers to hardware manufacturers to ISPs are looking for ways to make the Internet accessible to the masses.

Whether connected through a corporate link on an Ethernet network or a serial connection over a home phone line to a local ISP, TCP/IP connections require that certain basic software and hardware installation and configuration be done, and that TCP/IP software be running. As vendors continue to refine their network offerings, more and more of the installation and configuration process is being taken out of the hands of end users. Users won't have to be able to install, configure, and manage their Internet link, but understanding how that link works will still be important to many.

Requests for Comments

Internet protocols are usually described in documents called Requests for Comments (RFCs). These documents are published by the Internet Engineering Task Force (IETF), and provide an excellent resource for anyone who wants to learn more about TCP/IP. At the end of each chapter of this book, I have included a table of RFCs, including number, title, and description of all RFC documents that are relevant to that chapter.

The RFCs are available in many forms, including several Web sites. The interested reader can find many of these sites on the web using a preferred search site and searching on the words "RFC" and "archive." My favorite source is the Internet Standards Archive hosted at the Swiss SunSITE:

http://sunsite.cnlab-switch.ch/cgi-bin/search/standard/nph-findstd

SunSITE Switzerland is a collaborative effort of cnlab (Content provider), SWITCH (System/ Network Management), and Sun Microsystems (Schweiz) AG.

What's in This Book

This book introduces TCP/IP networking to anyone interested, from the curious end user to the prospective TCP/IP network engineer. Though a handful of excellent texts cover the technical details of every TCP/IP protocol, and an avalanche of books introduce the general reader to using applications from the TCP/IP suite on the Internet, this book offers an introduction to the concepts and use of TCP/IP network protocols and applications for everyone with an interest in how things work.

Internetworking concepts and methods are introduced gradually, starting with a general introduction to internetworking and TCP/IP applications in Part One. Internetwork addressing and namespace, internetwork architecture, and data flow from host to host and network to network are introduced. The most important internetwork protocols are introduced, as are the most common internetwork applications.

Part Two delves more deeply into the workings of the TCP/IP protocols themselves, the rules that specify how network traffic gets from one system to another—how it moves within the internetwork clouds. The actual protocols that make up TCP/IP—the Internet Protocol, which moves data across internetworks; the Transmission Control Protocol, which reliably connects hosts across internetworks; and the other lower-level protocols that make it possible for users to communicate with computers across vast distances—are explained in Part Two. Also in Part Two are an overview to IP multicasting and an introduction to the long-awaited upgrade to the Internet Protocol, IP version 6.

Although the network protocols are the underpinnings of any internetwork, the applications are what make it useful. Part Three

examines the most important TCP/IP applications, including
Internet commerce and the World Wide Web, distributed computing and network computing, as well as more traditional applications like remote terminal sessions, file transfers, communication
services, data publication, and resource sharing. This section not
only explains how to use these applications, but also explains how
these applications use the TCP/IP networking protocols.

Part Four addresses internetwork implementation and management issues, including configuration protocols, internetwork security, intranets and extranets, troubleshooting, and network
management with TCP/IP protocols.

Part Five includes appendices and pointers to other important
information sources. Appendix A gives a brief overview of Internet
history and organizations. Appendix B is an annotated bibliogra-
phy and pointer to various TCP/IP and Internet resources, both
online and in print. Appendix C is a glossary and compendium of
network acronymns.

A Note to the Reader

This book is not for dummies, but for regular people who need to
know more about TCP/IP internetworking. If you are entirely new
to networking, don't expect to "get it" in a single reading. Even if
you understand LANs, you'll find a lot that is new and different
here. To truly understand how TCP/IP works, you need to understand many different things, all at once. Unfortunately, you can
read about only one thing at a time, so sometimes a term or concept will crop up before I've had a chance to explain it. At those
times, be patient and read on.

Learning TCP/IP was, for me, very much like learning how to play
bridge. It took me several years' worth of attempts to learn to play
bridge and it took me close to a year to truly "get" TCP/IP.
Whenever someone tried to teach me bridge, he or she would start

out saying something like, "Bridge is simple. First, there's a round of bidding to see who thinks will get the most tricks... ." At that point, I'd interrupt and ask, "What's a trick?" The answer usually would be something like "Don't worry about tricks yet, we'll get to them later."

So as you read through the chapters, if you come across an unfamiliar term try to hold onto the question until you've read a little bit further.

Part One

Introduction to TCP/IP Internetworking

1

Internetworking Models and Conceptual Tools

The mighty Internet—linking systems, networks, and services around the world and across organizational and national boundaries—is nothing more than an assembly of much simpler building blocks. By examining these building blocks and using some basic networking models, it is possible to understand how TCP/IP networking works. Starting with the most basic concepts of networking, this chapter introduces network reference models, the TCP/IP protocol suite, encapsulation, and network addressing issues.

Building a Network from Scratch

The simplest network imaginable is a single computer connected to a network medium. A personal computer with a network interface and network software installed can be considered a single-node network. On a trivial network like this one, the single host

3

would transmit data to itself: data would be processed by the network software, transmitted across the host's network interface, and then received through the same interface and processed in again by the networking software.

Perhaps surprisingly, this type of network actually has value as a production system or testbed for developing or testing network software and applications. However, this type of network has little value for end users who need access to network services. There are no services accessible over the network to this lone host that are not accessible to it directly through its own operating system.

Some networking terms were defined in the Introduction (see page xiv). Another term, **host**, now appears. A kind of node, a host is simply a system that can have one or more users. Another kind of node, a **server**, is a system that provides services to other nodes (servers can provide services to hosts as well as to other servers). The term **client** refers to a system that gets services from a server. A server can also act as a client when it gets services from some other kind of server.

Finally, a network **service** is anything that a server provides to other nodes. Clients request something from the server, and the server provides a response. A service can be as simple as a time service, where clients ask for the current time and the server responds with that information. Other types of services provide access to different kinds of data. Web servers, for example, simply respond to requests from clients (browser software) for access to files and data. Still other types of servers allow clients to share access to network devices like shared printers or disk storage.

Any computer or device connected to a network is a node on that network; other things, which aren't normally considered computers, can also be nodes, as long as they communicate over the network by sending and receiving data to other nodes.

The whole point of building a network is to foster communication among connected nodes. Data passed from one computer to another is carried by some kind of network medium. Ethernet is a very common network medium, but others include token ring, FDDI (Fiber Distributed Data Interface, a term referring to a fiber-optic network medium), and Apple's LocalTalk. Nodes connect to the network medium through a network interface that transmits signals from the computer to the wire, fiber strand, or other network medium, and receives signals from the medium intended for the computer.

Gedanken-Net: A Nontrivial Example

Consider the trivial network of one node that we just created, with its single node and network interface. Add a second computer with its own network interface and network software and connect both computers to the same network medium. As shown in Figure 1–1, each of these two computers can now communicate with the other. Any resemblance to actual network hardware or software is purely coincidental, so we shall call this thought-experiment network *Gedanken-Net*, after Einstein's *gedanken* ("thought") experiments that use logic and reasoning instead of physical experiments to work out theories in physics.

Let's assume that both these systems are running the same operating system and using the same networking protocols. However,

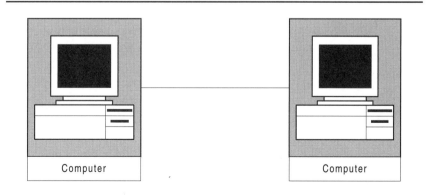

Figure 1–1: The simplest possible nontrivial network, connecting two hosts.

on any network with more than one node there must be some way to distinguish nodes. A host can communicate with another host only if there is some way for the source node to address its message to a destination node. Because this is a simple network with only two nodes, it is quite simple to assign numbers to each of the nodes: we'll call the first system number 1 and the second system number 2.

Since numbers are so impersonal and sometimes hard to remember, the hosts can also be given special host names; in this example we'll call system 1 *Dick* and system 2, *Jane*.

Network traffic for either host can be addressed to that host using the host number; we can also use some kind of mechanism to keep track of the names we use instead of numbers. In general, people use the host names because names are easier to remember, whereas computers usually use the host numbers because numbers are easier for computers to manipulate. When a name is used, the computers look up the associated network address in a database, somewhere, so the computer can find the proper network address number.

In our Gedanken-Net, when a node starts up it identifies itself to the network by telling all the other hosts on the wire that it is up and running and will be listening to the network for traffic addressed to its host number. Each computer on the network has its network interface device wait for network traffic addressed to it. When it receives traffic from another host, the network interface device sends that traffic up to the computer to determine what response to make. This is similar to the way Ethernet networks can work, but not the only way that networks can work.

Clients, Servers, and Peers

Two models for providing network services are the client/server model and the peer-to-peer model. We've already mentioned clients and servers, but a **peer** is a node that acts as both client and server to all other nodes on the network. And in the peer model, all other connected hosts can also offer services on the network to other peers and take services from other peers. This model works in smaller networks because it minimizes the need to invest in special network nodes to offer services and it maximizes available system resources by sharing them throughout the network. However, it stops being attractive once the network gets too big because (a) it can disrupt work on a single, "popular" peer that has often-used resources on it, and (b) managing network resources (setting up accounts for individual users as well as restricting or allowing access to various resources) can be a problem in larger networks with many users.

If the Gedanken-Net used peer-to-peer network software, node Dick might send a message saying that it needed a file stored on Jane. Assuming that Dick was authorized to access that file, Jane responds by sending that file to Dick, which might in turn respond by acknowledging that the file has been received.

However, once more nodes are added to the network—say, Sally, Tim, and a few dozen others—the client/server model becomes more attractive. Rather than letting every node act as both a user of services and a provider of services, client/server networks separate the providers of services from the users of those services. Special servers are set up to offer services like file storage space or the use of peripherals like printers, fax machines, or modems over the network. Some servers provide access to data and files, applications, and interactive terminal sessions with larger computers. The nodes using these services are called **clients**. As shown in Figure 1–2, the clients all access the larger server systems to work with shared data. In this example, the servers are dedicated systems with lots of disk storage, fast processors, and lots of memory, so many clients can access each resource at the same time without degradation of performance.

Although clients and servers use the same underlying network software to communicate with the network (and with each other), the server uses a special application program that offers its service

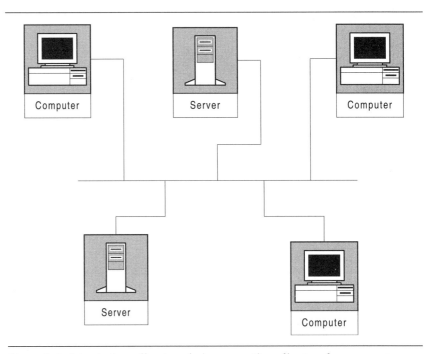

Figure 1–2: A typical small network, incorporating client and server systems.

to the network, called a **server program**. The client uses a special application, called a **client program**, to communicate with the server program on the server computer.

Advantages to this type of arrangement are many, but include

- ◆ Economies of scale from using a powerful dedicated server to support many users
- ◆ Ease of administration (a single system to manage user accounts)
- ◆ Simpler resource management (a single system to back-up for emergencies)

Most important to the users is that they no longer need to share their workstation resources, which tends to degrade their system performance as well as use up their resources. The users are also relieved of security concerns and responsibility for other people's data.

It Isn't All or Nothing

Commercial vendors at times have chosen one model and enforced it strictly. For example, Microsoft Windows for Workgroups networks used the peer model, with each connected Windows workstation being able to use or offer network services. Novell's commercial NetWare products use the client/server model, requiring a dedicated server to administer and offer any type of network services.

However, there is no rule requiring network hosts to be either peers or client/server. In fact, even Novell NetWare servers can use network services from other Novell NetWare (or other) servers, so it is possible for a server to act as a client, too. This may seem contradictory, but it simply means that a Novell NetWare server can act as a client, connecting to another NetWare server as a client to get access to data stored on that server—but NetWare client computers can still act only as clients.

TCP/IP networks use a client/server model that in practice does not limit servers to being dedicated servers, nor does it prohibit systems acting as clients to act only as clients. In general, a TCP/IP server is defined more by the fact that a host is running software that allows it to offer a service than by whether or not it is a dedicated server. Likewise, a client is any host running client software. A user logged onto a mainframe can run a client program on that system to access a service provided by a personal computer—as long as the personal computer is running the appropriate server program.

Gedanken-Net Limitations

Gedanken-Net is an imaginary network, so it uses an imaginary (and proprietary) set of network protocols, the details of which are unimportant. As long as we take care to assign unique network numbers (1, 2, etc.) and names (Dick, Jane, etc.) to each newly connected computer, there won't be any problems when nodes try to figure out where to send requests for information or replies to those requests. Every network, even this imaginary one, uses some kind of network medium. The network medium manifests itself through the action of the physical world, whether it carries bits over a metal wire, a fiber-optic cable, or a radio transmission. Being a physical manifestation, networks are subject to physical laws—which means that networks are subject to physical limitations on their size and performance.

These physical factors can limit the number of network nodes that are practical on any particular network. For instance, the **bandwidth** (maximum amount of data that the network medium can handle at one time) may cause an upper limit based on the amount of traffic generated by a network with some number of nodes. In practice, bandwidth and other physical restrictions generally keep networks well under 1,000 nodes.

There are also logical limitations on networks. For example, the numbering scheme will have an implicit maximum number of nodes depending on how high host numbers can go: if only 1 byte (8 bits) is set aside for a host number, then 256 hosts is the absolute maximum: from binary number 00000000 through binary 11111111. This can also be represented in hexadecimal as 0x00 through 0xFF (the 0x prefix identifies a number as hexadecimal). Increasing address size to 2 bytes (16 bits) would allow up to 65,536 hosts on a single network (though this would be well above the physical limitations of the network medium in most cases). Host addresses could be represented in hexadecimal as 0x0000 through 0xFFFF.

The use of unlimited, variable-length host numbers would remove the logical limit on the number of hosts in a network. However, variable-length network addresses make network processing far more complicated than fixed-length addresses. And variable-length addresses do nothing toward addressing the physical limits on network size.

In our Gedanken-Net, however, the network is well within all limits: there is a foolproof method of uniquely naming and numbering all network nodes and there is plenty of room for network expansion both in the network address space and on the physical wire. The imaginary network's peak traffic load is well below the point at which network performance is affected by the number of hosts transmitting on the local network.

> NOTE: *Although these problems are under control in our thought experiment, in real life the problems of assigning unique names and addresses to hosts, keeping local networks the right size to maximize performance, and expanding network size, are all real issues. These topics will be addressed later.*

Implementing this imaginary network, at least in our imagination, is not terribly difficult. We can easily imagine away all the real-world issues that would complicate matters, like keeping track of host addresses, network cabling, traffic management, and software installation and configuration. If all networking could be done in the imagination, there would be no need to develop any more complicated networking technologies. However, this is clearly not the case.

Gedanken-Net Deployment Issues

To continue the experiment, assume an organizational rather than technical development. The company operating Gedanken-Net (Company A) merges with another company (Company B), which has its own network. Both networks use the same protocols, the same network medium, are about the same size, and just happen to be right next door to each other in the same building. The newly merged company decides to merge the two networks, and the trouble begins.

That both networks use the same protocols and the same medium is encouraging, because it means network resources will be freely available to all users on both nets after the merger, without any need for installing new software for either clients or servers, or new hardware to convert hosts on either network from one type of medium to another. The physical closeness of the networks may also be a plus—unless the sum of the lengths of the two networks exceeds the maximum allowable network length. In that case, the resulting merged network would not be able to support transmission of data from one end to the other. The same problem occurs if the networks were too far away, creating a need for an extension between them.

For this example, assume the cables are sufficiently short and sufficiently close to allow a simple connector, called a **bridge**, between the two networks. Assume also that the merged network doesn't exceed limits on network address space nor will it generate enough traffic to disrupt performance on the network. The resulting merged network should now work correctly, but it will not (unless management was extremely lucky) because network names and addresses that are unique on each of the two nets individually are likely to be duplicated within the merged network. Assuming that each network was set up with the same software and the same rules used earlier, both nets will have numbered their hosts starting with 1, 2, and so forth, using host names that correspond to common human given names like Dick and Jane.

At this point it is clear that the network managers of the merged net must somehow create a new scheme for assigning network names and numbers, and then implement that new scheme by reconfiguring some or all of the merged network nodes.

Even supposing that an organization is willing to go through this kind of reconfiguration once, considering how frequently companies merge, reorganize, expand, contract, and spin off business units, most organizations quickly will see the benefit of using some other method. And remember that in this example, the two networks being merged were exactly compatible in every way: using the same network medium, using the same network software. In real life, there are many different choices and flavors of network wiring, as well as many different choices and flavors of network software.

Some Good Reasons to Network Networks

The obvious and simple answer to the problem is to use a network scheme that accommodates the seamless linking of networks. Although this example eliminates many of the more pressing reasons that network managers link different networks in the real world, it demonstrates the desirability of creating a universal network framework that allows unforeseen future expansion.

The imaginary network described here masked many of the important reasons why the ability to network individual networks together should be a part of the definition of the network protocols. Explicitly, here are some of the reasons networks should be networked together:

◆ For interconnection of dissimilar network media
◆ For interconnection of dissimilar network protocols
◆ To allow fragmentation of networks to support growth
◆ To allow fragmentation of networks to manage network performance
◆ To support frequent organizational changes

A network of networks, also known as an **internetwork**, solves many of the problems implicit in the attempt to provide data communications across large, dynamic organizations. Internetworking uses a uniform set of rules, or protocols, to define behavior on an internet for all nodes, using any supported network media.

Interoperability with Gedanken-Net

The Gedanken-Net example is simply a tool for examining some of the practical reasons for internetworking. Most network users will want to be able to do certain things with an internet:

Permit any two internet-connected hosts to interoperate seamlessly across network boundaries (different physical networks and network media) transparently to the user.

The TCP/IP protocol suite, when completely and correctly implemented, provides just this type of network functionality, as shown in Figure 1–3. The next section addresses the formal networking reference model used as the framework for implementation of the TCP/IP protocols and moves from hypothetical networks to the world of real TCP/IP internetworks.

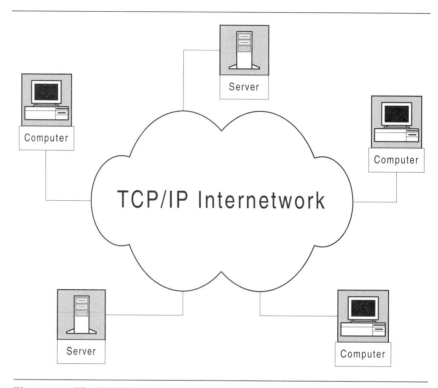

Figure 1–3: The TCP/IP protocol suite helps hide the details of network connections from users, so they have universal connectivity no matter where the
remote hosts are.

Network Reference Models

Network engineers and researchers find that a layered reference
model helps to model data communciations across internetworks.
One of the most widely accepted reference models is the OSI
(Open Systems Interconnection) seven-layer model, whereas
TCP/IP internetworks use a four-layer model (sometimes
described as five layers, depending on how the layers are count-
ed). These models assign certain functions to each layer, as illustrated in Figure 1–4. The upper layers handle the network
application session, representation of data, and interaction

between application and user; the lower layers are concerned with the movement of data through the internetwork. The upper layers pass only the most necessary information to lower layers, in particular, where to send the data and how to handle that data. The lower layers generally pass on to the higher layers only information that concerns the status of the connection.

It's not important right now to understand exactly what happens at each layer so much as it is useful to think about what a layer is and how entities can communicate across networks at different layers.

To illustrate, consider the *application layer*. For now, let's imagine that this is where a user and a remote application interact. The user wants to see a file, and the remote server sends that file to the requesting user. The user doesn't need or want to know anything about ports or network addresses, so these things are hidden and handled at lower layers. By the same token, when data is being passed across an Ethernet network, the entities operating there (the software driving network interface cards, actually) don't need or want to know anything about what's happening at the application layer—all they are interested in is knowing where the data is coming from and where it is going to.

If it's confusing, don't worry about it—yet. It should all become much clearer as you read on.

The OSI Model

In Figure 1–4, look at the seven layers of the OSI internetworking model. At the bottom, the physical layer refers to the handling of the transmission and reception of electrical impulses (or another appropriate signal like light for fiber optic networks). In an Ethernet network the physical layer is represented by the network itself. Here, the data is passed physically from one interface to another, and the physical layer provides the wherewithal to create links between data link entities.

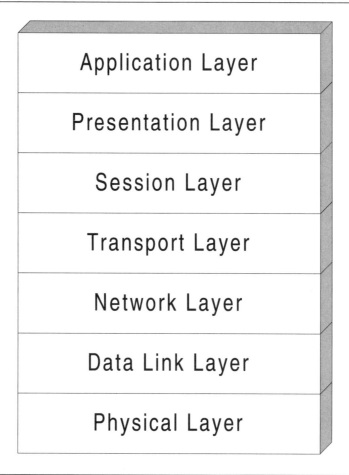

Figure 1–4: Network interactions can be mapped to seven different layers using the OSI model.

The data link layer adds reliability and retransmission functions, is defined by the firmware and software that drive the network interface. For example Ethernet specifies how electrical impulses are encoded with data, and supports the connection of network layer entities.

The network layer is defined by the actual physical systems that are being connected. At this layer, the network is concerned with actually delivering bits of data between physically connected nodes on the network. The network layer supports the connection of transport layer processes.

It should be noted that at the network layer and below, network entities are not concerned with the contents of the packages of data being moved around the network. These contents are often referred to as a **payload**. At the physical, data link, and network layers, the entities are concerned simply with moving bits of data from one place to another. However, above the network layer the emphasis is on the data being moved rather than how that data is to be moved. This means that at the transport layer and higher, the data being moved is actually being passed between programs (or processes) running on communicating hosts.

The transport layer is where the actual processes on communicating hosts communicate with each other. The transport layer handles the interaction between processes on the destination and source hosts, mediating how the data is being sent, often doing error detection and correction on data being sent and received, and determining whether data has been lost and needs to be retransmitted.

The session layer manages the flow and timing of a connection, determining whether data is being sent and received by the processes. The presentation layer is where communicating systems can translate data from possibly proprietary system representations into data that all networked hosts can correctly interpret. At the top, the application layer manages the interaction between the user and the network application itself, taking commands from the user, returning error codes to the user, and passing along information retrieved from across the internetwork.

The TCP/IP Model

Mention of the OSI reference model is mandatory in any introduction to TCP/IP, but it is most useful as a base of comparison to the TCP/IP reference model. Whereas the OSI model came from work done by standards committees, the TCP/IP model came out of practical work done by researchers who were building an actual network architecture. The four TCP/IP layers, built on top of a hardware layer, have to date proven sufficient for all practical purposes. The session and presentation layer functions defined in the OSI model are omitted from the TCP/IP model, and the functions are fulfilled as needed by different TCP/IP protocols (these functions are usually either performed at the application layer or the transport layer). Figure 1–5 shows the TCP/IP model layers.

From the top down, the TCP/IP layers are as follows:

Application Layer: As with the OSI model, this is where the user interacts with the network application. Data is received as commands from the user and as data from the network application on the other end of the connection. TCP/IP applications communicate in client/server pairs at this layer.

Transport Layer: This layer manages the flow of data between two internetwork hosts. TCP/IP relies on two transport protocols, TCP (Transmission Control Protocol) for reliable data flow, and UDP (User Datagram Protocol), a much simpler protocol that offers no reliability guarantees.

Network Layer: Data is moved around the internetwork at this layer. The Internet Protocol (IP) operates at this layer to route packets across networks independent of network medium.

Data Link Layer: At this layer, also known as the *network interface layer*, data is transmitted across a single network. Data from the network layer, which has been routed appropriately, has arrived at (or has never left) the local network and is transmitted to its destination.

While of considerable importance to network programmers, the reference models are also helpful in understanding the way TCP/IP internetnetworks offer seamless and transparent interoperation between hosts. And they are also important in understanding how the different protocols in the TCP/IP protocol suite work individually and together.

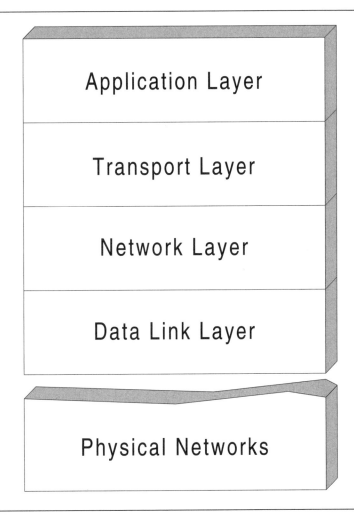

Figure 1–5: TCP/IP networks use only four network layers to map network interactions and let the physical networks manage themselves.

TCP/IP Protocols

There are many TCP/IP protocols. No universal TCP/IP protocol is available at the data link layer, since it handles local network transmission exclusively. ARP and RARP (Address Resolution

Protocol and Reverse Address Resolution Protocol, respectively) operate at the data link layer where they are used on any networks that need to convert internetwork addresses to physical addresses, which may be hard-coded in the network interface hardware. Although ARP and RARP are concerned mostly with issues at the data link layer, they are sometimes depicted as being part of the network layer, operating in parallel to the Internet Protocol. See Chapter 7 for more about ARP and RARP.

At the network layer, IP is the dominant protocol used for inter-network routing of data between hosts and across network links. ICMP (Internet Control Message Protocol) is a kind of helper pro-tocol that works with IP to pass error and status information between hosts and routers (see Chapter 7 for more about IP and ICMP). IGMP (Internet Group Management Protocol) helps to route data to multiple hosts for multicasting (see Chapter 13 for more about multicasting). Both ICMP and IGMP are carried with-in IP traffic, so they are sometimes depicted as operating one layer above IP, but their function is strictly related to the network layer, as opposed to the transport layer.

Internet routing, the set of methods for making sure that network traffic is passed between hosts and networks efficiently, calls for its own set of protocols. These routing protocols ensure that the spe-cial systems that connect networks, called routers, are able to detect changes in internetwork routes and to keep data flowing across the internetwork.

At the transport layer are two major, and very different, transport protocols: TCP (Chapter 10) and UDP (Chapter 9). Each supports applications with different requirements and expectations as to performance and reliability of data transmission. Although UDP supports "request/reply" transactions with no added reliability or guarantee of delivery, TCP offers a connection-oriented, reliable, and guaranteed-delivery service to applications that need a link that behaves like a circuit between two hosts. TCP is arguably more important to TCP/IP than UDP, but we discuss UDP prior to TCP simply because UDP is a more straightforward protocol.

Protocols proliferate at the application level, with each application defined both from the client side (how the client software is expected to interact with the remote server and the local user) and from the server side (how the server software interacts with the client software, and what functions it provides to the client user). Application protocols include FTP for file transfers, Telnet for remote terminal sessions, SMTP for electronic mail, and SNMP for network management. See Table 1–1 for a partial listing of TCP/IP protocols, what they mean, and what they do. (References to relevant RFCs are available in later chapters where each of these protocols is discussed in more detail.)

We'll cover how the different network protocols relate to each other in greater detail throughout the book; in the meantime, the next set of tools for understanding internetworking relate to locating hosts and networks with a uniform and universal scheme.

Networks, Data, and Communication

Communication between networked computers means one computer (or host) is transmitting user or application data to some other computer. This wouldn't work if the originating computer did nothing but dump raw data onto a network: it has to add enough network data to the application data so that the payload can make it to its destination. For example, one vitally important item to add is the destination address of the system for which the data is intended; other bits of information are equally necessary for data to be moved from one computer to another.

A user initiating a terminal session between a local host and a remote host must specify a valid user ID and password. At the highest layer (the application layer), the network protocols handle the collection of this information from the user and formats the user ID and password in a manner suitable and acceptable to be sent over the network. Lower down in the network architecture, transport layer protocols add information about the process

Protocol	Stands for	Purpose
ARP	Address Resolution Protocol	To match hardware network addresses to TCP/IP network addresses
BGP	Border Gateway Protocol	To pass routing information across internetworks
BOOTP	Boot Protocol	To boot and configure systems to the network remotely
DHCP	Dynamic Host Configuration Protocol	To boot and configure systems to the network remotely
DNS	Domain Name System	To associate host and network names with host and network addresses
EGP	Exterior Gateway Protocol	To pass routing information across internetworks
FTP	File Transfer Protocol	To copy files between hosts
HTML	Hypertext Markup Language	To create internetworked hypertext documents
HTTP	Hypertext Transfer Protocol	To publish and read hypertext documents across the World Wide Web
ICMP	Internet Control Message Protocol	To carry internetwork routing control messages between networked systems
IGMP	Internet Group Management Protocol	To manage transmission of data to selected groups of hosts
IP	Internet Protocol	To move network traffic across internetworks
MIME	Multipurpose Internet Mail Extensions	To attach multiple data files of any sort (text, graphics, audio, etc.) to electronic mail

(continued)

Table 1–1: There are a lot of TCP/IP protocols, but these are some of the most common and important ones.

Protocol	Stands for	Purpose
NFS	Network File System	To share files across networks
NTP	Network Time Protocol	To keep system clocks synchronized across internetworks
OSPF	Open Shortest Path First	To pass routing information across internetworks
PPP	Point-to-Point Protocol	For direct links between a host and a network (point-to-point)
RARP	Reverse Address Resolution Protocol	To match TCP/IP network addresses to hardware network addresses
RIP	Routing Information Protocol	To pass routing information between internetworked systems
SLIP	Serial Line Internet Protocol	For serial links between a host and an IP network
SMTP	Simple Mail Transfer Protocol	To transfer electronic mail between hosts and networks
SNMP	Simple Network Management Protocol	To provide basic network management functions of networked devices
TCP	Transmission Control Protocol	To connect applications on two internetworked hosts (connection oriented, reliable)
Telnet	Telecommunications Network Protocol	To log onto remote hosts and run terminal sessions
TFTP	Trivial File Transfer Protocol	A minimal implementation of a file transfer protocol
UDP	User Datagram Protocol	To connect applications on internetworked hosts (connectionless, unreliable)
WWW	World Wide Web	Graphically oriented internetwork hypertext browsing service

Table 1–1 continued.

running on the source host and the process running on the destination host, so that the data is delivered to the right process.

Still lower down in the stack, the network layer protocols make sure the data is addressed and delivered to the specified host. At the very lowest layers the data is coded and transformed into electrical impulses and physically delivered to the specified destination host.

Information moves in two dimensions. From the application layer down to the physical layer, network information is added to the raw data so that it can be transported across the internetwork (and removed, so the data can be delivered to the appropriate program for further processing). The other dimension is the movement of actual nuggets of information that are passing between two communicating hosts across an internetwork.

Encapsulation

The result of this two-dimensional, compartmentalized model of data movement is that data becomes "encapsulated," or enclosed, in the headers. Each succeeding network layer wraps a header around the data that is to be delivered, so that the data can be handled properly by the layer below. Each network layer is concerned primarily with the data in the header, and the rest of the data packages are, basically, the payload to be handled as indicated by the header.

For instance, at the application layer, network application data creates messages or streams. These units are simply data, but data with a destination: a process running on some networked computer (the destination process is usually running on a different computer from the source process, but the destination and source processes can also be running on the same computer). At the transport layer, headers are added to these parcels of data to create TCP segments or UDP datagrams. The headers include information linking the enclosed data to specific processes; the data within, including the application headers, is largely ignored. Figure 1–6 shows how application data gets "wrapped" with additional addressing information as it goes deeper into the network protocols.

The application layer collects data to be sent across the network

Host adds TCP segment headers to point the traffic at a remote application process

Host adds IP datagram header to point the TCP segment at the remote host

Host frames the IP datagram to be sent out on the local area network

Figure 1–6: Network traffic gets encapsulated by headers that contain different network information at each network protocol layer.

IP headers are added at the network layer to create IP datagrams. IP headers include destination and source host addresses, so at this point the data is being directed at a specific process running on a specific computer on a specific network.

At the data link layer, when the data has been delivered to the destination network, additional information is added to point the data at the desired network interface on that wire, resulting in a network frame. For example, on Ethernet LANs, an Ethernet header and trailer are added to create Ethernet frames. The header includes LAN destination and source addresses, as well as frame type, which identifies it as one containing an IP datagram.

Network host destinations and sources often differ from IP destinations and sources. This is because the data link layer is concerned with physical delivery of network traffic from one host to another on the same physical network. When data must traverse more than one physical network, it gets transferred from one network host to another as it passes across those networks. At the same time, the IP destination and source remain unchanged—the data is always heading for its IP destination.

The result is that, at each step down, the network adds additional information to network data, wrapping the previous layer's chunk with destination and other information like a mail package. At each layer the only important part of the data chunk is the header instructing that layer what to do with the data.

Demultiplexing

Encapsulation, as we just described, is a method for enclosing data chunks with delivery wrappers for efficient processing and delivery across an internetwork. The process of encapsulation begins when an application creates a piece of data to be transmitted across the internetwork. Of course, the process reverses as that piece of data is delivered. As the data is moved from one place to another the headers are stripped away until the raw data is output to the destination program.

Figure 1–7 illustrates this. When an Ethernet frame arrives at a host, the network software starts by removing the Ethernet header and trailer. The destination host was monitoring the Ethernet for frames addressed to its own Ethernet network interface card MAC (Media Access Control) address. Once the frame is received, removing the Ethernet headers reveals an IP datagram. The network software on the destination host strips off the IP header to reveal either a TCP segment or a UDP datagram, and it passes that

Network frame (raw network data from LAN)

IP datagram (network frame stripped of IP header)

TCP segment (IP datagram stripped of IP header)

Application data (TCP segment stripped of TCP header)

Figure 1–7: Encapsulation makes it possible for network traffic to be transported easily across internetwork boundaries.

unit of network traffic up to the appropriate protocol. The transport layer protocol strips off its header to reveal data destined for some process running on the local host, which it then passes to the appropriate program. The network application program then takes that data and presents it to the person (or program) using the application.

Hardware Addresses, Network Addresses, Ports, and Sockets

As Figures 1–6 and 1–7 show, the actual data being sent across an internetwork gets wrapped and unwrapped as it gets passed along its path. For instance, data being sent from a computer on an Ethernet network to another computer across an internetwork would get wrapped up all the way down to the data link layer (Ethernet headers) and then sent on. An intervening host, called a **router**, has to take that traffic and send it down some other kind of network connection—which means that although the Ethernet frame was addressed to the router, the router has to forward (send along down another network to some other host or router) the data. However, this forwarding will happen on some other network, not the original Ethernet where the data originated.

As a result, the router will strip away the Ethernet frame header, check the IP datagram header to figure out where to direct that datagram, and then rewrap the IP datagram in a network frame (perhaps an FDDI frame), which will be sent on to the next hop in the route of the datagram. Although the router does not know (or care) what the contents of the IP datagram are, it does have to unwrap the original Ethernet frame to figure out what to do with the contents (to see if the Ethernet frame is traffic directed at the router or if it is intended for some other destination).

The Ethernet frame itself is directed to some other host, which (as demonstrated previously) may or may not be the address of the ultimate destination host.

Once the Ethernet frame's header is stripped away, an IP datagram is revealed. IP network addresses of the source and destination hosts are included in the datagram's header. These addresses help define the connection between two hosts and refer to the two actual systems being connected across the internetwork. The destination address of an IP datagram does not get altered, no matter to how many intervening routers it is passed along.

Once the IP datagram is delivered to its final destination, the IP header is removed to reveal a TCP **segment** (the unit of data that the TCP protocol deals with) or a UDP **datagram** (the unit of data that UDP handles). In either case, the headers of the resulting segment or datagram point to **ports**. A port number refers to a particular process on a networked computer and helps the computer maintain one or more virtual connections with one or more hosts simultaneously. However, a pair of source and destination port numbers, combined with a pair of source and destination internetwork addresses, define the connection between two individual hosts: this is called a **circuit**. As we'll see in Chapter 10, this creates a virtual circuit—there is no fixed wiring involved. The transport layer protocols (TCP and UDP) generally are unconcerned with which host they are connecting to, beyond knowing that data is flowing between the correct hosts, since that is the task of the network layer protocol (IP). Similarly, the network layer protocol (IP) doesn't care which processes are involved in the transfer, since that is the concern of the transport layer protocols.

Specifying circuits between two specific host/program pairs is not important to an unreliable, connectionless transport protocol like UDP. Since UDP supports transmission of the same data to many different destinations at once (broadcasting), it is not even practical to consider keeping track of whether specific hosts received transmitted data. On the other hand, TCP offers reliable, connection-oriented transport service. Not only does TCP require connections to be between only two hosts, it also must be able to keep track of what data has been transmitted to which host, and which host has received what data.

TCP uses the combined specifier of internetwork address and port number, called a **socket**, to uniquely identify internetwork virtual circuits. With a socket on one host, defining the host itself (its internetwork address) and the program running on that host, combined with the same information for the other host, a unique network link can be defined. For example, a link between Host A, using Client Application X, and Host B, using Server Application Y, is defined by the internetworking addresses of the two hosts (Host A–Host B) and the port numbers of the applications (Client X–Server Y).

Multiple virtual circuits are easily managed because each chunk of data arriving at a host can be linked to a specific virtual circuit in this way. If Host A is connected to several servers, using the same client application, all the servers will be sending data back using the same port number. However, since each server has a unique internetwork address, the sockets for each virtual circuit are different. As a result, Host A is able to sort out the incoming data into the appropriate client session correctly.

Chapter Summary and References

In this chapter, we started out by introducing some basic networking concepts using a thought-experiment network testbed, Gedanken-Net. This experiment helped to pinpoint some of the most basic challenges in networking: whether to use a client/server or peer-to-peer model, how to identify nodes, how to interoperate between dissimilar systems, and how to interoperate across dissimilar networks.

From there, we introduced the concept of a network reference model, looking at both the OSI and the TCP/IP reference models. From there, a brief overview of the protocols that make up the TCP/IP protocol suite was followed by an introduction to network encapsulation and demultiplexing.

Table 1–2 lists a useful RFC to read in conjunction with this chapter.

RFC	Title	Description
1594	FYI on Questions and Answers—Answers to Commonly Asked "New Internet User" Questions	This document, though a bit dated (published in 1994), provides answers to many basic questions about the Internet and TCP/IP.

Table 1–2. Useful RFC for Chapter 1.

2

Network Addresses, Network Names

The explicit function of networking is to provide communication between and among computers linked through the network. Networks outwardly seem to do this by providing network services like file storage, interactive terminal sessions, and data retrieval and presentation applications. However, in TCP/IP networks, the network and the underlying protocols serve simply as a means of delivering data, whether it is a command from a user or a file being transferred from a remote site or an image to be viewed with a World Wide Web browser. As explained in Chapter 1, the virtual circuits between networked hosts are created by chopping up, sending, and receiving data in packages. Network names and addresses were introduced in Chapter 1; Chapter 2 explains some of the actual network addressing and naming conventions that enable accurate data delivery across complex internetworks.

Identifying Hosts on a Network

Two hosts connecting across an internetwork have much in common with two people carrying on a transcontinental conversation over a telephone connection. There is a circuit between two individuals who are talking on the telephone. Neither participant in the phone conversation needs to be concerned with what type of equipment the other is using, nor does either of them have to be aware of the route the phone company is using to create that circuit. In fact, it is possible that quite different technologies are being used at each end and anywhere in between, but those details are irrelevant to the people on the phone. It is even possible that some or all of the conversation is actually being transmitted across TCP/IP networks.

On an internetwork, two hosts can communicate in the same way. The interaction begins when the hosts set up a virtual circuit, or connection. This can occur when a user initiates a remote terminal session on a supercomputer, or when a browser program requests a web page from a web server. Although some applications (like a remote terminal program) may require additional authorization information, the hosts need only the most basic of information to set up the virtual circuit (as we will see in Chapter 10, where TCP virtual circuits are discussed). Neither host need be concerned with what type of equipment the other is using, nor do they care which route the data is traveling between the two hosts.

When setting up a virtual circuit a unique identifier for the destination telephone/host is required from the initiator of the circuit. When dialed, any telephone number, with its associated country and area codes, will connect the dialer to a particular telephone instrument (except where the calls are taken by a special switch that can route them to different instruments; in those cases, the calls are always handled by the same telephone switch). The same is true on an internetwork where each node has a unique identifier used to make connections with that node. Let any other connected host invoke that network address when starting a network application program, and data will be transmitted to exactly the same host—as long as that host is accessible over the inter-network.

Actual Circuits, Virtual Circuits, and Packet Switching

TCP/IP internetworks are very much like telephone networks in many ways, but they differ from traditional telephone networks in one important way. Traditional telephone networks create circuits between two parties by actually building an electrical circuit between the two phones through physical wires and cables strung above, under, and across the landscape. This type of network is vulnerable to any interruption: if any wire or connection should fail, the phone call circuit would be broken. The phone call itself can be visualized as a stream of electrons that is poured through pipes and hoses to get to its destination. If the circuit is broken, the electrons just gush out all over the floor.

TCP/IP networks are packet switched, meaning that data is sent not as raw streams of electrons but packaged up into **packets** that are handled individually. Each packet gets sent by the best route available, so if a connection to the best route is broken, a router will send the packet to the next best route. When a link is broken, packets may start falling on the floor but TCP/IP network protocols guarantee that such problems can be detected and worked around.

Although communicating hosts may appear to users as if they are connecting by a circuit, data is being transported from one host to the other in discrete packets. Each packet may take the same route, or alternate routes may be necessary as intermediate links fail or experience high demand. Large packets may need to be broken into smaller pieces to meet transmission requirements of interme-diate carriers and have to be reassembled at the destination.

So, while networks may appear to function at a high level like tele-phone networks, they also function at a lower level like postal or delivery services. The network delivers packages of data from a sender to a recipient host. The destination address is used to target a uniquely identified host, and the return address is used by the destination host to respond to requests (or used by an intermediary host to notify the sender when there is a problem reaching the desired destination). As we'll see later, internetwork addresses are used to help "sort" data being transmitted, so that local traffic is handled locally and other traffic is routed to the appropriate place.

TCP/IP Network Identifiers

Every node on a TCP/IP network must have a valid IP address, and should have a valid name. Each name and address must be unique on the network, and every link on a network must have an address.

IP network addresses and names actually identify the link—network interface—of connected nodes. In other words, a node with more than one network interface would have as many addresses and names as it has network interfaces.

> NOTE: Some computers have more than one network link; for instance, computers that are connected to two or more different networks through two or more hardware connections. Each network interface requires its own network address and name, so some individual computers will have multiple addresses—these are called **multihomed** hosts. The most commonly encountered type of multihomed host is the router, which we have already mentioned informally and will discuss in greater detail in Chapters 3 and 8.

The Internet Protocol Address Space

We speak of network address spaces as being defined by the length of the network address itself and by rules for allocating addresses within the space. A network protocol that mandated 16-bit addresses would have an upper limit of 2^{16} (65,536) available network addresses. However, that protocol might have certain rules about network addresses; for example, the "all-ones" address (all the bits are equal to 1) and "all-zeroes" address (all the bits are equal to 0) might have special uses. This reduces the number of available addresses by 2. Another rule might set aside all the addresses whose most significant (first from the left) bit was equal to 1, in which case the available addresses would be cut in half.

In fact, IP network addresses are four bytes or 32 bits, normally represented in "dotted decimal" or "dotted quad" format. That is, addresses are expressed with decimal digits, each byte separated by a "dot" or period. For example,

```
0.0.0.0
255.255.255.255
```

are, respectively, the lowest and highest decimal numerical values that can be assigned to IP addresses, but since these two addresses both have special meaning (to be discussed later), they would never refer to actual hosts. Addresses can also be thought of as 32-bit binary numbers, so these two addresses are sometimes referred to as all-zeroes and all-ones, respectively.

IP addresses may also be represented as hexadecimal (base 16) numbers, with each byte separated by a dot. For example, the decimal address 178.76.50.253 could also be represented in hexadecimal as:

```
B2.4C.32.FD
```

Hexadecimal notation is useful for many computer applications because it is easier for people to deal with than binary digits but is still directly related to binary notation. For example, the binary represenation of the number 9 is 1001; the hexadecimal representation is 9. Table 2–1 shows the decimal, binary, and hexadecimal representations of values from 0 to 16.

IP addresses are assigned through national registries that distribute network addresses (see Appendix A for more information about Internet organizations). Network addresses are distributed to organizations, which in turn are responsible for making sure that all attached hosts are properly numbered.

Decimal	Binary	Hexadecimal
0	0000	0
1	0001	1
2	0010	2
3	0011	3
4	0100	4
5	0101	5
6	0110	6
7	0111	7
8	1000	8
9	1001	9
10	1010	A
11	1011	B
12	1100	C
13	1101	D
14	1110	E
15	1111	F

Table 2–1: Decimal, binary, and hexadecimal numerical representations.

The network address is an IP address in which the least significant (rightmost) bits are set to zero. Depending on the type of address being assigned, as many as 24 bits or as few as 8 bits are set to zero. The most significant bits identify the network itself, while the least significant bits are used within the network to identify individual nodes.

A total of five types of IP network addresses were originally defined: Class A, B, C, D, and E. Table 2–2 shows the different network classes, the number of each type available, and the potential size of networks using each class. The idea was that only a few very, very large organizations (national governments and huge

Network class	Address range	Maximum networks in class	Maximum hosts in network
Class A	0.0.0.0 to 127.255.255.255	126 $(2^7 - 2)$	Over 16 million $(2^{24} - 2)$
Class B	128.0.0.0 to 191.255.255.255	16,384 (2^{14})	65,534 $(2^{16} - 2)$
Class C	192.0.0.0 to 223.255.255.255	2,097,152 (2^{21})	254 $(2^8 - 2)$
Class D	224.0.0.0 to 239.255.255.255	Reserved for multicasting	N/A
Class E	240.0.0.0 to 247.255.255.255	Reserved for future use	N/A

Table 2–2: IP network address classes.

multinational companies, for example) would need more than 65,000 hosts, as allowed by a Class A network. More (but still not that many) organizations would support between 256 and 65,534 hosts that a Class B network allows, and 2 million Class C networks would be enough to cover the rest of the smaller organizations and offices with fewer than 254 nodes.

> NOTE: The address space was apportioned before ubiquitously networked personal computers were even imagined; by the late 1980s it became clear that the IP address space might be exhausted as early as the mid-1990s. Chapter 14 offers the latest information about the replacement Internet Protocol, IPv6 (for more in-depth coverage, see **IPv6 Clearly Explained**, Morgan Kaufmann 1999). Vendors began implementing IPv6 by the middle of 1996, but implementers promise there will be no "drop-dead" date for conversion, so users of current products won't need to make any changes. A condition of the protocol upgrade is that existing networks and nodes be able to continue interoperating without upgrading.

Distinguishing which class a network belongs to is simple: check the first byte (also called an octet, since it refers to 8 bits). Table 2-2 shows the permissible IP address ranges for each network class.

RFC 791, Internet Protocol, laid out the IPv4 address space apportionment. The most significant bit of Class A network addresses is always 0, thus the first octet of Class A addresses ranges from 1 to 126. The two most significant bits of Class B addresses are always 10, thus the first octet of Class B addresses range from 128 to 191. And the three most significant bits of Class C addresses are always 110, thus the first octet of Class C addresses range from 192 to 223.

Special Addresses

As mentioned earlier, IP addresses with all ones (255.255.255.255) and all zeros (0.0.0.0) are not valid IP addresses for individual hosts or networks. Broadcast addresses will be discussed shortly, but in the meantime it is worthwhile noting that this reduces the maximum number of available host addresses in each network class by two, since host addresses of all ones or all zeros are also not valid.

There is one more special address worth talking about. Though the address 127.0.0.0 is in the Class A address space, it is reserved for special duty as the loopback address for use when a host needs to communicate with itself through its network interface. This will be discussed in greater detail in Chapter 6.

Subnetting

Just as the protocol imposes order on the IP address space by dividing it into different classes by network size, network managers can impose their own order on their own networks. Although it would be possible (in theory) for a Class B network to consist of a single wire, with all attached hosts assigned IP addresses purely in order of their connection to the network, this is highly unlikely. More often, networks (especially very large networks) are segmented into smaller **subnetworks** or **subnets**.

All IP addresses can be divided into two parts: the network portion of the address, which is the same for all hosts on the same network, and the host portion of the address, which is different and unique for every host on any given network. Remember that network addresses leave the least significant bits set to zero, and those bits are assigned by network managers to nodes on the network.

Class B network host addresses are split exactly evenly between the network portion of the address (the first two bytes) and the host portion (the second two bytes). As many as 65,534 hosts can be connected to this network (host addresses of all zeroes or all ones are not allowed), but managing the delivery of data to each host would be difficult or impossible if all 65,534 hosts were connected to a single wire.

The accepted solution is to organize the larger internetwork hierarchically by dividing it into subnetworks, each of which has its own prefix in addition to the Class B network address prefix. Each host is still identified in two bytes, but the first of those two bytes refers to the host's subnet and the second identifies the host. The first two bytes of the network address refer to the Class B network, the third byte refers to the subnet, and the last byte is reserved for the host address. All hosts on the network share the first two bytes as before, but now all hosts on each subnet have the same third byte as well.

The IP addresses can now be split into three sections: the first part refers to the network address, the middle part to the subnet address, and the last part to the host address. The result is shown in Figure 2–1. The main network in this example is represented by the Class B address 172.16.0.0. There are two subnets, 172.16.1.0 and 172.16.2.0. All the hosts on the first subnet (and only these hosts) have addresses whose third byte is 1, like this:

```
172.16.1.1
172.16.1.2
172.16.1.3
...
172.16.1.146
172.16.1.147
```

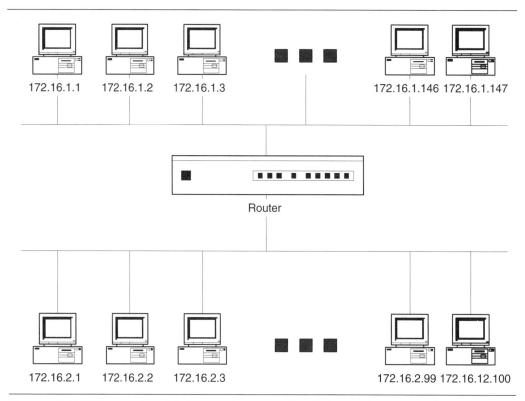

Figure 2–1: Splitting a network into subnets can result in better performance and improved use of limited network address space.

and hosts on the second subnet all share the third byte value of 2, like this:

```
172.16.2.1
172.16.2.2
...
172.16.2.100
```

Each host is uniquely identified on its own subnet. Each subnet can have no more than 254 nodes, and there can be up to 254 different subnets within a Class B network (host addresses and subnets cannot be all zeroes or all ones).

Because of various performance and network media limitations (all dependent on the type of traffic being carried and the network medium in use), some maximum number of hosts will be permitted on each network segment. Subnetting helps manage network traffic as well as maximize the efficient use of allotted network space.

Subnet Masking

Most TCP/IP software assumes Class A and Class B networks are subnetted, but network managers can choose a nonstandard subnet scheme rather than the default eight-bit subnet mask (that is, the third network address octet is used entirely to designate a subnet). Some sites need to have more hosts on each individual subnet so they might allow only seven bits to designate the subnet (permitting only 126 subnets, each having up to 510 hosts, instead of 254 subnets, each with 254 hosts, when using eight bits). Other sites require more subnets and don't allow as many hosts on each subnet, so these sites could use nine-bit subnet addresses, permitting up to 510 subnets, but with no more than 126 hosts on each subnet.

In practice, because there are so few Class A and Class B addresses, Class C networks increasingly are being subnetted. This is especially true at Internet service providers (ISPs) who are assigned blocks of Class C addresses and who then distribute them to their customers. Since many of those customers may need only a handful of IP addresses, a Class C network may be subnetted into 14 subnets, each serving a customer with 14 or fewer nodes, for example. Network addresses cannot be all zeroes or all ones; network managers subnetting Class C networks must use at least two bits of the host address to get two subnets, and each subnet could have no more than 62 hosts attached. Using three bits results in up to six subnets with no more than 30 hosts on each.

Subnet masks are expressed either in the standard IP address format (dotted decimal) or as the number of bits being taken from the host part of the address to designate the subnet. The "normal" subnet mask for a Class B address would be represented as

```
11111111111111111111111100000000
```

In this case, the representation is binary, but it demonstrates how the term **subnet mask** came about. If you were to overlay this value on top of the network address in question, you would in effect block out the first two bytes of the address (the Class B portion) as well as the third byte (the subnet identifier), leaving you with the least significant eight bits, which identify the host. This subnet mask may also be expressed as

```
255.255.255.0
```

or as "8 bits." A 7-bit subnet mask could also be represented as

```
11111111111111111111111110000000
```

or as

```
255.255.254.0
```

The subnet mask "masks out" certain parts of the host portion of the IP address along with the entire network portion of the address with ones and leaves the portion available to host addressing as zeroes. A subnet mask of zero bits, or no subnet at all, for a Class B network would be expressed as

```
255.255.0.0
```

Broadcast Addresses

The maximum numbers of hosts and networks is always two fewer than you might imagine: 254 hosts on an eight-bit subnet instead of 256. This is because a host or network address of 0 is used to designate "this" host or network, whereas the host or network address that contains all ones (e.g., X.Y.255.255, for a Class B network) is a **broadcast address** interpreted as addressing all the hosts on that Class B network.

Networked hosts use broadcast addresses to transmit to all the hosts on a network. A host may need to broadcast a request for information; for instance, diskless workstations use broadcasts to locate boot services from boot servers. Likewise, a host that discovers a new gateway on the local network may broadcast that information to other hosts on the network.

Broadcasts originally seemed to be a very good idea, but over the years they have been recognized as sources of many problems, most to do with excessive network traffic. Applications that use broadcasts tend to saturate networks with their broadcasts, especially applications that use broadcasts to advertise system availability or unavailability.

IPv6 does away with broadcasts entirely (see Chapter 14), and IPv4 implementers are increasingly looking to IP multicast (Chapter 13) to solve some of the problems raised by broadcasts.

Multicast and Reserved Addresses

Table 2–2 showed five different classes of network address and only three have been explained so far. Class D addresses have been set aside for use with **multicast**, and the Class E addresses have simply been reserved for some unspecified future use (unlikely because the next revision of IP, IPv6, is already available in commercial products).

Multicast addresses act as alias addresses for data that is intended for more than one host. Chapter 13 covers multicast in more detail, but the most visible application of multicasting is the transmission of live audio and video to dispersed audiences. There are many other applications of this method of transmitting data to dispersed members of a group of networked hosts. Normal TCP/IP transmissions intended for a single node are called **unicast**, and are transmitted from one point to a single destination; broadcasts to all hosts on a network or an internetwork are made for various purposes (to share information with other hosts on a local network or to search for a particular TCP/IP service).

Multicasting, as the name implies, transmits the same set of data to multiple hosts, but not to all possible hosts. Hosts that are members of a multicast group receive the data sent to the group's multicast address. Group members may be receiving video or audio transmissions, but a more important function for multicasting is to distribute routing information to Internet routers (see Chapter 8 for more information about Internet routing protocols). By limiting transmissions to members of a group, multicasting is less costly than broadcasting for the hosts that don't need to respond, since broadcasts take up bandwidth and must be dealt with by all hosts within earshot of the broadcast. Because members of a multicast host group can be on different networks, multicasting works better than broadcasting (which would flood networks with traffic intended for only the members of the group).

Because of its importance to real-time audio and video transmissions, multicasting issues are being addressed in the IPv6 implementation. See Chapter 14 for further discussion of IPv6.

Network Names

Numerical network addresses are fine for computers and are especially useful when they can include implicit information about network architecture as well as a unique address for a host, as IP addresses do. However, people do better with names than numbers, and although TCP/IP requires only that hosts have unique addresses, people like to identify network hosts by their names as well as by their addresses. IP networks are also named, and the resulting system is embodied in the distributed database called the **Domain Name System** (DNS) used by TCP/IP network software to link network and host names and addresses. DNS is discussed at greater length in Chapter 11.

A **domain name** is a hierarchical name registered for an organization's network. Each name level gives increasing information about the domain. For example, the original seven three-character root domains (shown in Figure 2–2) are usually used for networks

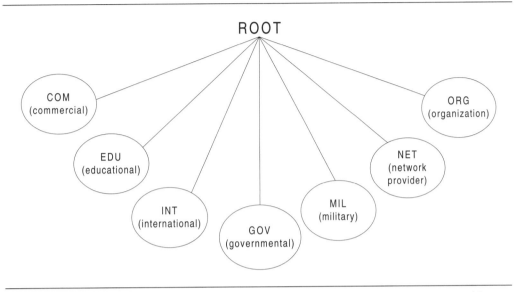

Figure 2–2: The seven highest level Internet domain names are augmented by a geographic hierarchy.

located within the United States. Another set of domains is taken from a list of two-character country codes defined by an ISO standard, called **geographic** or **country domains**. Some networks in the United States use the .us domain, while .fr is used in France, .uk in the United Kingdom, and so on. Working backward from the top level domains it is possible to uniquely identify each network domain in any given domain name.

As the Internet has grown in popularity, demand for domain names has increased. Users and organizations have been clamoring for new domains for years, and soon we should see some new three-letter root domains (they are not available as of this writing).

Within each root (or top-level) domain, second-level domains are assigned based on some other criteria. For example, network service providers might be listed by their company name under the .net domain (for example, ibm.net). See Figure 2–3 for another example: networks located in Massachusetts using the top-level

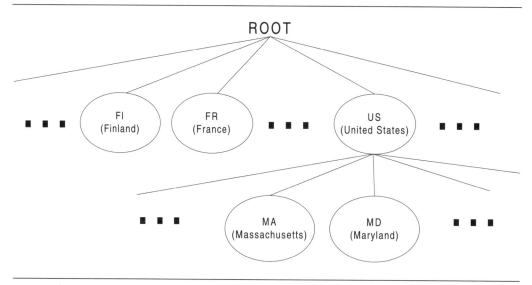

Figure 2–3: Geographical entities can also be used to create Internet domains.

domain .us might have .ma.us as part of their domain name, and universities in the United Kingdom might use .ac.uk (for academic institution).

The result is that some network domain names can be several units long (for example, a network in an Australian university has the domain name itd.adelaide.edu.au) or just two units long (whitehouse.gov or mit.edu for example). At each level, a domain can have "children" that are linked to the parent; for example, an lcs.mit.edu domain for the Lab for Computer Science at MIT, listed under .mit.edu.

Host Names

Just as domain names for each organization are unique, each host on a particular network must have a unique name—within its domain. Just as there may be matches on some portion of any two domain names (for example, acme.net, acme.com, and acme.org can all coexist) host names can also be duplicated on different networks, under different network domains. So, there can be a host named *pete.lcs.mit.edu* and a host named *pete.microsoft.com* without any problem.

A **fully qualified domain name** (also called an *absolute domain name*) includes the complete domain name with the host name. So the fully qualified domain name of any particular host will uniquely identify that host, first, on its own network, and second, throughout the entire internetwork (Internet). A host on a network within a department of a subsidiary of a large international conglomerate might have a fully qualified domain name something like

```
bonzo.mailroom.littleco.bigco.com.
```

This host name is pronounced "bonzo dot mailroom dot littleco dot bigco dot com"—the periods are necessary to differentiate names like littleco.com from names like little.co.com.

Note that the name ends in a period: this is how network software denotes a fully qualified domain name. The extra dot indicates that the top-level domain (in this case, com) is appended off a "tippy-top" level domain that includes everything and is unnamed. This convention is useful for connecting to hosts in the same network domain by just the host name. When a user connects to a host called *hostname* (when the host is on the same domain as user), the DNS software will append something like *users.network.dom* (substituting the local network domain name), saving the user some typing.

Note also that working from right to left, starting with the final period, the network is increasingly identified: the last dot indicates the domain is fully qualified, and is part of the universe of network domains; the *com* indicates a commercial organization; the *bigco* indicates the name of the large conglomerate, the *littleco* indicates the subsidiary name, and *mailroom* indicates the department where the network is located. Finally, the host name, *bonzo*, identifies a specific host.

Domain Name System

The Domain Name System uses distributed servers to keep track of all the different network domains and host names used in an internetwork (in particular, the Internet). DNS is the mechanism that lets people use host names instead of host IP addresses: it translates host names and network domain names into IP addresses, and IP addresses into host name and network domain names. No single DNS server can contain all this information: hosts and network domains are added, changed, and deleted constantly around the world, and there are millions of hosts to keep track of.

DNS distributes the task of keeping up with domains and hosts across the internetwork. Each organizational network must have at least two DNS servers, or name servers. The network administrator updates a list of the IP addresses and associated host names of all the hosts on the network in a file on the primary name server. The secondary name servers periodically check the primary name server to get a copy of the name and address list, and to offer name service in the event that the primary name server is unavailable.

Hosts needing name service can get the IP address for another host on the local internetwork by querying the local DNS server. When a host needs an IP address for a host not on the local internetwork, the local DNS server contacts a root name server, depending on the top-level domain of the fully qualified domain name being queried. These root name servers correspond to the top level domain names (.org, .com, etc.) and each one keeps track of all the second-level domains registered under that top-level domain name. The process continues until a domain name server is found that can point directly at the specified host.

Figure 2–4 illustrates this. Attempting to connect to a host called

```
somehost.program.bigdept.biguniv.edu
```

results in the local name server requesting information from the root name server for the .edu domain. The root server responds with the IP address of a name server serving the .biguniv.edu

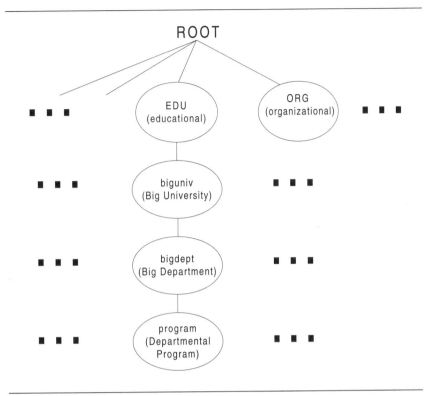

Figure 2–4: Following the DNS tree results in tracking down whatever host is being sought.

domain, maintained at Big University. The local name server queries that name server and gets the IP address of the name server serving the domain .bigdept.biguniv.edu, maintained at the Big Department. This server sends along the IP address of the name server for the complete network domain name, program.bigdept.biguniv.edu, which will, when queried, return the IP address of the specified host, somehost, so the original requesting host can communicate with it.

At each level, DNS servers are responsible for keeping track of only the address information for the level below. By distributing network address resolution responsibilities to local authorities,

DNS makes it possible to get reliable, complete, and up-to-date information about host names and network addresses.

Host Files

Domain name service is not always necessary or available. For example, smaller internetworks, with fewer hosts and networks attached (and also with fewer available resources) may be able to dispense with DNS and rely on host files for each networked host. Where there are relatively few hosts and relatively slow change to the network structure, keeping a simple list of all locally internetworked computers by host name and IP address can be sufficient for all practical purposes.

Hosts that are off the network need to be added to the host file or else specified by IP address when trying to connect to them.

Chapter Summary and References

In this chapter, we moved to the real world of networking and examined how nodes are identified on a network. Starting with the concepts of virtual circuits and packet switching, we introduced the concept of network addressing and the network address space. Moving to IP addressing of nodes, networks, and subnets, we looked at the mechanics of expressing IP addresses and the mechanisms behind IP network subnetting.

We also introduced three types of IP addresses: broadcast, multicast, and unicast addresses, and considered how these are used. Rounding out the chapter was an introduction to Internet Protocol host and domain naming. The Domain Name System (DNS) and simple host files were described as being two important mechanisms for linking names to network addresses.

Table 2–3 lists useful RFCs for this chapter.

RFC	Title	Description
791	Internet Protocol	This is the original specification for the Internet Protocol, and it includes discussion of IP addressing.
1122	Requirements for Internet hosts—Communication Layers	Everything that an Internet host must support at the lower layers of the network reference model are explained in this document.
1034	Domain Names—Concepts and Facilities	With RFC 1035, this is a good introduction to the Domain Name System.
1035	Domain Names—Implementation and Specification	This is a good introduction to the implementation of the Domain Name System.
950	Internet Standard Subnetting Procedure	A good discussion of both the need for subnetting and the way subnetting is done.

Table 2–3: Useful RFCs for Chapter 2.

3

Internetwork Architecture: Bridges, Routers, Gateways

The last two chapters have made clear some of the reasons why individual networks somehow must be connected to create internetworks, rather than just hooking them all up together into a large or even a very large network:

- Physical limitations on the length of the wire
- Performance limitations implicit in networking large numbers of hosts on one wire
- Logical limitations on the number of permitted hosts on a single wire
- Different types of network media
- Different network topologies
- Different hardware and software implementations

It is simply easier to deal with lots of smaller networks than with one huge network. The technology is simpler, the logistics are simpler, and overall network reliability is higher when you remove single points of failure that can affect every connected system. Understanding how networks with such wide variation can be connected together requires a brief discussion of the different network types.

Network Architecture

Though some may argue the metaphysics of this characterization, three network topologies are in general use: bus, star (also called hub), and ring. Each has its own characteristics, but the bus and star topologies that are common with Ethernet have been hugely successful for creating internetworks.

Bus Topology

The bus network shown in Figure 3–1 is very common in Ethernet networks. In Ethernet bus networks, a single wire serves as the medium over which data is transmitted. Electrical signals travel down the wire and all connected computers receive all signals transmitted on the wire, but pay attention only to those signals addressed to them. Each end of the Ethernet has a special terminator, and computers connect through special taps into the Ethernet, which connect to the Ethernet network interface card.

Note: This type of Ethernet network is rarely encountered today. Most modern Ethernets are switched through hubs.

Network data is propagated along the entire wire so any break in that wire will break the network. When cabling an Ethernet bus, most installers provide drops of some kind throughout the wire to support the addition of new nodes later on. These may be extra barrel connectors or specially cabled plugs into which an Ethernet interface card can be plugged without breaking the network.

Bus Ethernets are passive; that is, the connected systems do all the sending and receiving and the coaxial wire simply acts as a signal

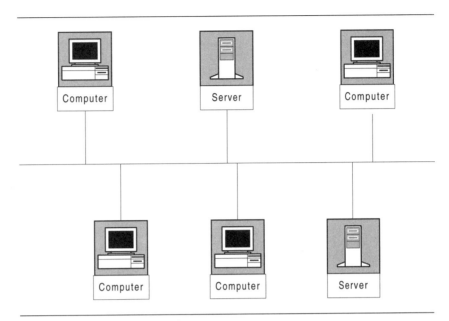

Figure 3–1: Bus network topology.

carrier. Each Ethernet cable is limited in size (for example, single coaxial cables can't exceed 500 meters), but an Ethernet can be expanded by adding **repeaters** between Ethernets. A repeater simply repeats signals from one Ethernet on the other connected Ethernet, so that hosts on both Ethernets behave as if connected to a single LAN.

Repeaters are useful for extending the length of an Ethernet, but add a point of failure to the network that didn't exist previously, since they must be up and running to work. However, when a repeater fails, it affects only communication between the connected networks—traffic within each network will be unaffected.

Two Ethernets can also be connected by linking them with **bridges** (also more commonly referred to as *switches*) that pass traffic from one network to another, like repeaters. Switches differ from repeaters in that they don't simply repeat the signals being sent on one wire but actually receive all those signals, process them, and retransmit them. The result is that only valid Ethernet frames are transmitted by the switch, rather than the raw electrical signals sent by repeaters. Switches are single-purpose computers, with a network interface card on each linked network, that read and retransmit Ethernet frames. This means that bad packets don't get propagated across networks, thus reducing to some extent the overall network traffic.

Learning or adaptive switches further refine the concept: instead of indiscriminately retransmitting all data from both attached networks onto both attached networks, these switches keep track of the sources of the data being transmitted. As Figure 3–2 shows, the switch listens to traffic on both networks. When a host on Network 1 sends data anywhere, the switch listens and adds that host to its list of systems that are on Network 1. Then, when a host on Network 2 transmits a message for the host on Network 1, the switch will retransmit that message. If the switch detects a transmission for the first host on Network 1, however, the switch is smart enough to ignore the message since it does not have to be retransmitted to reach the message's destination.

Ring Topology

Ring networks, as you might expect, arrange connected computers in a ring, as shown in Figure 3–3. Each node connects logically to the node in front and the node behind it; data is passed along the network in one direction. In token ring networks each node takes a turn using the network.

IBM threw its weight behind **token ring** network technology during the 1980s while most other hardware vendors chose Ethernet. As a result, many true-blue MIS shops opted to implement token ring. In this scheme, each connected host takes turns using the network to transmit by passing a "token." The system with the token can send data across the network; other systems simply pick up data transmitted on the ring, examine it to see if it is addressed to them, and either pass it down the ring (if it is intended for another host) or pass the data into memory if it is intended for that host.

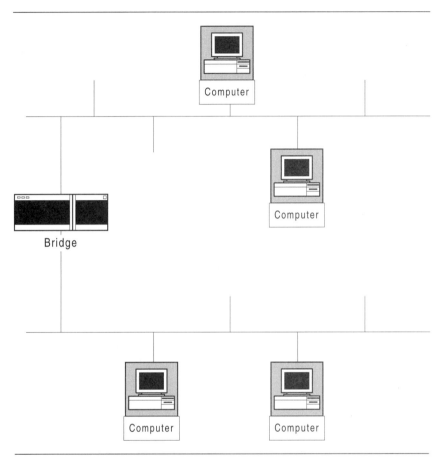

Figure 3–2: A bridged bus network.

Star or Hub Topology

The schematic of a star (or hub) network looks like a star—a central hub with wires radiating out to each connected host, as you can see in Figure 3–4. The hub of a star network either actually uses a bus or ring network architecture, but the hosts connect to the hub through dedicated wires, collapsing the network structure inside a single piece of equipment.

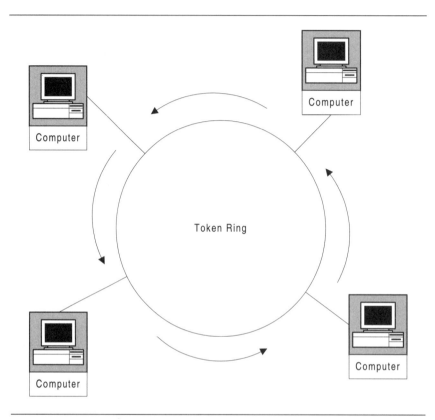

Figure 3–3: Ring network topology.

Stars are useful for implementing either bus or ring topologies for a number of reasons. For one thing, they simplify cabling: each node must have a single strand of wire leading to the hub. Although this sometimes means more wire overall, it also means that a broken wire affects only a single node. When an Ethernet bus cable is broken, all connected nodes lose connectivity. Clearly, using a hub topology helps to isolate the point of failure by allowing network administrators to keep the actual hub in a protected environment. Likewise, administrators can add or remove nodes from ring-based networks built on a star topology without having to break the ring and affect other users' connectivity.

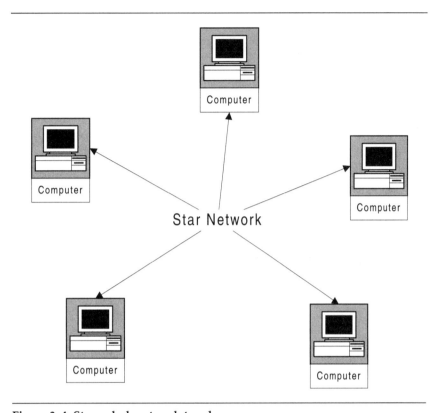

Figure 3–4: Star or hub network topology.

Star network topologies reduce the vulnerability of the entire net to any single break in a cable, as in bus or ring networks. If a wire connecting a single host is damaged or disconnected (as can often happen in a busy office), only that host will lose network access, whereas severing a bus or opening a ring will bring down the entire network.

For this discussion of internetworking, the specific network topology of any individual network is relatively unimportant. As shown in Figure 3–5, a single Ethernet might include two repeaters and a bridge, but the topology of the connection is irrelevant to two hosts on that network. For all practical purposes, those two

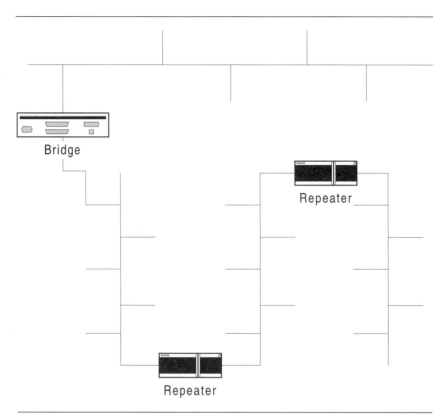

Figure 3–5: A repeated and bridged Ethernet.

hosts are simply both connected to a single network cloud that passes data from one to the other.

Bridges, Routers, and Gateways

We have seen that bridges can extend the size of networks by connecting together two same-protocol networks. They use the hardware network address of the source and destination hosts to determine whether to send a frame on to a connected network. On an Ethernet network they examine only the Ethernet hardware addresses, ignoring everything else in the Ethernet frame being transmitted. Recalling our discussion of network layers in Chapter 2, bridges operate only at the data link layer.

However, internetworks must link different kinds of networks, any of which may be using different link layer protocols. At the data link layer, network frames are aimed at the hardware interface of the individual hosts. On Ethernet networks, this is the six-byte hardware-encoded Ethernet **media access control** (MAC) address burned into the Ethernet network interface card. Other network media may be using some other hardware-encoded interface number. At the next layer up, the network layer, IP datagrams are directed at IP addresses. This permits a host on an Ethernet LAN in Topeka, Kansas, to interoperate with a host on an ATM network in Kobe, Japan, with neither having to know any details of the others' local network interface.

Routing in an internetwork is the process of directing the transmission of data across two connected networks. Switches seem to do this function as they route data from one network to a destination host on another network, but this type of routing is based solely on the link layer address. The switch does not need to understand TCP/IP networking, just as long as it understands the network protocol being used. Routers and gateways (terms sometimes used interchangeably) connect networks of different types at the network layer.

> NOTE: A great deal of confusion exists in the TCP/IP vocabulary about **routers** and **gateways**. Both terms are often used to mean the same thing: a computer connected to at least two networks, which is configured to direct network traffic between those networks. When a distinction is drawn, it is usually to indicate that gateways pass network traffic between protocols and routers pass network traffic between networks. The distinction is that a gateway might pass traffic between IPX and IP, but a router might pass IP traffic between an Ethernet and a token ring network. For the most part, the term router will be used in this book to refer to systems that route IP network traffic from one physcial network to another. The term **gateway** may also be used, when that term is included in a protocol name.

Routers are **multihomed hosts**, connected to at least two different networks. As shown in Figure 3-6, a router can connect different

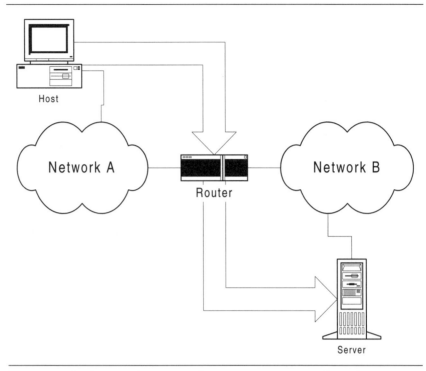

Figure 3–6: An IP router is connected to two or more networks and moves network traffic from one network to another, where required.

network types (but not necessarily) to allow interoperation between hosts on dissimilar networks. A host on Network A trying to connect to a host on Network B would transmit data directly to the router, which would read the link layer frame, determine the frame was addressed to the router, and at that point strip off the link layer headers (demultiplexes) and read the IP (network layer) datagram, which contains the destination host's IP address.

Static and Dynamic Routing

TCP/IP network nodes can use two general methods to determine where to send off-network traffic: static and dynamic routing. **Static routing**, as the name implies, means that a system is configured to route traffic to a specific, predefined router. **Dynamic routing**, on the other hand, uses a family of routing protocols to determine the appropriate routes for different network traffic.

Static routing is simple for small networks. Installers preconfigure each host with a default router address, and when the host generates nonlocal network traffic it just sends that traffic to the router. However, static routing can be inadequate as networks grow and additional internetwork connections between networks are made.

When there is sufficient traffic to support multiple routers on a single network or when several different networks are internetworked together, deciding on which router to send off-LAN traffic to is no longer a trivial problem. Routing protocols (to be examined in greater detail in Chapter 8) support dynamic routing, allowing hosts and routers to determine the best route for network traffic, based on to which networks each router has direct access and where the traffic is being directed.

Protocol Switches

By 1996, the networking industry was buzzing about new IP switches. Intended as replacements for routers, the IP switches were also known as layer 2 switches, referring to the OSI data link layer. They worked by keeping lists of IP network addresses and their associated data link layer addresses, and then forwarding data without worrying too much about doing any more complicated routing tasks.

These switches were touted as being much faster as well as less expensive than routers. They did the job by building the routing intelligence into hardware using ASICs (application specific integrated circuits) to make their layer 2 switches fast: instead of building router software, the switching smarts are burned into silicon.

Ultimately, interest in layer 2 switching waned as it became apparent that many of the benefits of layer 2 switching could be transferred to existing router technologies simply by building routers with ASICs. At the same time, some of the drawbacks of switches could be avoided. In particular, switches tend not to be as capable of dealing with routing problems as routers. By the end of 1998, most network router vendors were quietly deploying layer 2 switching technologies in their mainstream router offerings, while downplaying their layer 2 switches as the solution to all routing problems.

Routing Network Traffic

In a TCP/IP network, host configuration makes available certain information to the network software, including

- Its own IP address
- Its own network IP address
- The local router's IP address

Because each host knows what network it is on, it will also be aware of when it is trying to connect to a host that isn't on the local network. It can know this by comparing its own network address with the network address of the destination. This is where the default router comes in handy, since it is usually the designated place to send data that is going off the local network. The default router gets traffic destined for the "unknown outside" from local hosts and passes along this traffic to the appropriate network, based on the network address of the destination host.

Routing in a network with only one router can be fairly simple. The network traffic is either destined for the local network, in which case the router ignores it, or the traffic is meant for some other network, in which case it will be sent to the router for forwarding. When more than one router is on a local network, routing becomes more interesting, as Chapters 7 and 8 make clear.

In the example shown in Figure 3–6, the router could choose to forward the data either from Network B to Network A or from Network A to Network B. Real internetworks are generally much larger and more complex than this, with several different routes to

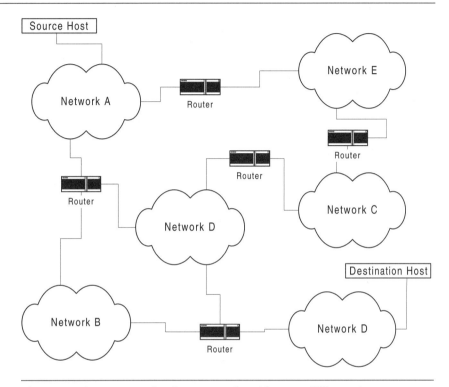

Figure 3–7: A more complex internetwork, with many different inter-connections.

any given network, as shown in Figure 3–7. The source host shown in that figure is connected to Network A, and the destination host is connected to Network F. Although the most direct routes between these two hosts would be either through Network D or Network B, an alternate route could send data from Network E to Network C to Network D and finally to Network F and the destination host.

Internetwork routing depends on each router being able to make what is essentially a binary decision: traffic either goes to a local destination (a host on a directly connected network) or it goes somewhere else. If the traffic is local, meaning destined for one of the networks directly attached to the router, the router will transmit that traffic directly onto the appropriate network. But if the traffic is meant for some other more distant network, the router sends it to the appropriate next-hop router. Just as each TCP/IP host configuration includes an address to send traffic outside the local network, so each router passes along more distant traffic to another router.

Routing and Deliveries

It should now be clear why the different network layers, as described in Chapter 1, add headers with addresses of the source and destination. A network frame containing traffic from one host to another can actually be addressed (at the data link layer) to an entirely different host (an intermediate router) and from a different host (another intermediate router).

The application and transport layers function as end-to-end protocols, since they specify communications between the end systems. The client application needs to communicate with the server application, and neither should care what route the network traffic between them takes. Likewise, the transport layer specifies processes as sources and destinations; it too is unconcerned with the route the traffic takes.

However, at the data link and network layers the protocols are concerned with the actual delivery routes that traffic takes. Moving down the protocol stack, the network layer represented by the IP network protocol is responsible for delivering datagrams from one host to another. Whereas the transport layer is concerned with the end systems and TCP addresses its segments to end systems, the network layer is concerned with the route those segments must take to arrive at the end system. At the IP layer, datagrams are still addressed to the ultimate source host, but intermediate routers examine that destination address and route the traffic locally in whatever way necessary.

It isn't until data gets to the data link layer that the local network addressing becomes important. It is only at the data link layer that it becomes necessary even to consider host hardware addresses on the same physical wire. Consider an Ethernet frame being passed from one intermediate router to another in the middle of a transmission from one host to another. The application, transport, and network (IP) layers will all point to the original source and ultimate destination information specifying the programs, processes, and hosts being linked—but the data link layer shows source and destination addresses of the two intermediate routers.

By delegating different functions to different network layers, it is possible to route traffic across the global Internet. Only the intervening routers need to maintain any significant amount of information about the internetwork structure. Individual hosts need to know nothing about the structure of any part of the internetwork. The host needs to know only which traffic is local and which is not. This can be determined by the host's own network and IP address; the rest is taken care of by the default (and any other available) routers.

Delivery and Reliability

Reliable service is characterized by use of acknowledgments of receipt, requests for retransmission, and use of timeouts. Perhaps counterintuitively, reliable service is not necessary at every network layer—if it were, overhead for these guarantees would hurt performance, particularly across wide internetworks. At the data link layer on Ethernets for example, the CRC (Cyclic Redundancy Check) can help detect transmission errors, but some network medium protocols don't implement any kind of error detection method. Similarly, moving up the protocol stack, IP offers best effort delivery only, with a checksum to flag transmission errors but no mechanisms to track end-to-end transmission delivery.

Best effort delivery means that the protocol makes every effort possible to deliver the network traffic, but does not have provision for confirming that delivery has been made or that the traffic has been delivered accurately. Part of the reason IP can dispense with delivery guarantees is that these functions are usually handled at some higher layer (usually at the transport layer) or can be dispensed with to cut down on network overhead for certain applications or for less important applications.

IP offers an unreliable, connectionless service, but the Transmission Control Protocol (TCP) provides reliable end-to-end transmission, with timeout and retransmission services and end-to-end acknowledgments of receipt of transmissions. The User Datagram Protocol (UDP) on the other hand, is an unreliable transport protocol and is used where reliability of service is not needed (for services that can easily be provided with unreliable transmissions) or is undesirable (where reliability adds network overhead that cannot be supported).

Chapter Summary and References

This chapter provided an introduction to the building blocks of networks and internetworks. Starting with a discussion of the topologies used to build local area networks, including the bus, ring, and hub (or star) topologies, we moved along to the devices that are used to connect local area networks together.

The building blocks of internetwork connectivity—bridges, routers, gateways, and protocol switches—were all introduced and put into perspective. The topic of internetwork routing was also introduced along with a basic overview of the way that routing occurs in TCP/IP networks.

Some useful RFCs to read in conjunction with this chapter include those listed in Table 3–1.

RFC	Title	Description
875	Gateways, Architectures, and Heffalumps	An interesting early (1982) discussion of the concept of protocol gateway as it applies to linking dissimilar network protocols.
1812	Requirements for IP Version 4 Routers	A very lengthy document that explains what an IP router is supposed to do, and how. Not easy reading—I'll refer to this one again in Chapter 8.

Table 3–1: Useful RFCs for Chapter 3.

4

Network Implementation Issues

As shown in the preceding chapters, every net-connected node must be uniquely identifiable by address and should be uniquely identifiable by name, all within the context of a larger network (which must also be identified by an address). Even more variables must be configured in practice when actually connecting a computer to an internetwork. These variables may be determined by issues that occur below the data layer such as hardware settings for the network interface, up to the application layer such as default servers for applications. The host must also be pointed at servers and services for various network purposes ranging from internetwork name services to e-mail and news, and network options may be configurable for the intervening layers as well. Other configuration options, usually called advanced options, can help the system administrator optimize the network link.

This chapter explains the different configuration options and requirements in a general way. We'll look at configuration and implementation issues from the bottom layer, the actual hardware, up to the application layer. Most networks will have a network administrator, engineer, or support person who can provide all the network configuration information you need to configure a network node. If you are that person, you may need to research the setup procedures for various systems and servers, and research your network's overall architecture and protocols before being able to complete a TCP/IP network node configuration.

The Hardware/Link Layer

This is an overview of the issues involved at the network hardware and data link layers. The issues raised here will be discussed in greater detail in Chapter 6.

The hardware portion of a network connection consists of some sort of network interface device. This may be as simple as the computer's serial port, with or without a modem connected to it; it may be a network interface card; it may be a device capable of sending and receiving radio transmissions. Corporate networks usually have a cabled network, very often an Ethernet, which all systems connect to through their own network interface cards. Links created over telephone lines are still probably most common for offsite users doing remote network access to an organizational internetwork and for individuals using Internet services from homes or small offices, although high-speed alternatives like cable modems, satellites, and digital subscriber lines (DSLs) are becoming increasingly important for the home and small office/home office user.

TCP/IP protocols generally stay away from the bottom-level hardware implementations instead letting the hardware take care of the raw communications. However, if the hardware is not properly installed and configured, you will not be able to do any networking over it.

It is most important to configure the networking software for the appropriate hardware interface correctly. The procedure depends on the type of network interface, the type of system on which it is installed, and the operating system being used on that system. For many years, configuring hardware could prove a major obstacle to installing a network. However, Microsoft has improved its Windows software, adding plug-and-play capability for devices including network devices. Similarly, installing network devices on Linux and other operating systems related to Unix has also become much easier with auto-detecting installation software.

Whether or not the process is automated, there must be some mechanism by which the signals received on the network interface can be converted into data that can be processed by the computer to which it is attached.

Generally some sort of driver is available for a direct interface with the network interface, which passes traffic up the stack to a standard interface. For example, NDIS (Network Device Interface Specification), developed by Microsoft and 3Com, permits the user to identify the network interface card in a special configuration file. ODI (Open Data-Link Interface) was developed by Novell to let the network interface card communicate to a standardized interface used by different protocols. Packet driver is another standard interface in common use: a special program initializes the network connection and passes traffic from the network interface card to a generalized interface used by any supported protocol.

Network interfaces are specified through a combination of the hardware and the software being used to manage the interface. ODI, NDIS, and packet drivers are usually used with Ethernet and other types of cabled networks; serial connections (over telephone links) interface with the network software through other mechanisms like SLIP (Serial Line Internet Protocol) and PPP (Point-to-Point Protocol), both covered later in this chapter.

Although TCP/IP is widely implemented on a wide range of different network media, examples in this book focus on the Ethernet implementations and the serial or point-to-point implementations. Ethernet, in its various flavors, is probably the most important network medium for corporate networking; point-to-point networking is central both to serial connections over modems as well as to high-speed connections over media like **Asynchronous Transfer Mode** (ATM), to be discussed in Chapter 6.

Ethernet Media Types

Ethernet comes in several different flavors, which means that Ethernet adapter cards, cable, and connector hardware can vary from network to network and still be Ethernet. Currently, the most popular type of Ethernets use twisted-pair cable: copper telephone-style wiring and modular (phone-jack) type connectors.

Ethernet first gained popularity as a 10 megabit per second (Mbps) medium. Fast Ethernet, offering 100 Mbps throughput, is now widely available and deployed, and gigabit Ethernet products are becoming increasingly common.

Ethernets are usually denominated by throughput and network cabling method. For example, the most common type of cabling is twisted pair Category 5 wire; 10 Mbps Ethernet using twisted pair cabling is called *10baseT;* 100 Mbps Ethernet over twisted pair cables is denoted *100baseT.* A less common type of cable is known as thin-wire coaxial cable, used for *10base2* Ethernets. These use coaxial cables with barrel-connectors (also called *BNC connectors*). Neither of these cabling methods requires a separate Ethernet transceiver, as thick-wire Ethernets do. Thick Ethernet connections used a small hardware device to link the Ethernet to the computer. These transceivers usually have an array of lights, which are useful for troubleshooting; when they are flashing, network traffic is being detected.

Twisted pair wiring has certain advantages, including low cost and a hub-style implementation. The actual Ethernet bus, as descibed in Chapter 3, is implemented entirely within the hub, so cabling to each node is independent and the failure of a cable linking one node will not affect other nodes on the network. The cable itself is easy to connect with its modular jacks, and the cable is relatively inexpensive and often already installed in modern office buildings. On the down side, the special hubs add to the expense of the network (Ethernets built on coaxial cables require no hubs), and there are limits on the distance a node can be from a hub. Also, the hubs are powered, so if the hub loses power the entire network goes down; coaxial Ethernets remain in service even if some nodes lose power.

Except for the fact that it is obsolete, thin-wire Ethernet can be more robust, since it requires no active electronics other than that in the networked nodes themselves. It is not uncommon for end users to bring down a network by disconnecting a barrel connector and inadvertently splitting an Ethernet cable. This can be avoided by cabling Ethernet connections through a special socket and using special cables with a barrel on one end and a special plug on the other.

Another set of choices is to be made when using Ethernet, and that involves the actual standard being used. Ethernet refers to the standards defined for this type of network hardware by Xerox, DEC, and Intel; a very similar, but more comprehensive, set of standards was codified by the IEEE (Institute of Electrical and Electronics Engineers) called the IEEE 802 standards. These two sets of standards will be examined in greater detail in Chapter 6, but the implementer often needs to know which standard is in use on the local network.

Hardware and Memory Issues

Ethernet and other network interface cards must be properly configured for all systems, although this is another area where autosensing and plug-and-play have simplified things for network engineers. The network interface cards may have jumpers and dip switches configured to set the IRQ (interrupt level) and memory used. However, almost all modern network cards can be configured through software interfaces. Physical configuration of the network cards, coupled with the need to exclude the memory addresses used by the cards manually, probably caused more problems with new TCP/IP network installations than any other single problem before the advent of software-configurable cards.

Increasingly, vendors have been eliminating physical configuration, or at least offering it only as an option, with software configuration of the cards done through special programs included with an installation/diagnostic diskette. Of course, software configuration will cause problems when the installation diskette is not available—as when a user discards it or the diskette is lost.

As for memory issues, until 1995 users had to modify DOS and Windows system files manually to properly exclude hexadecimal memory addresses and also often had to configure the network software to point it at the appropriate internal hardware interrupts. Some network software vendors had already begun to automate parts of this process, but for the most part users needed to turn to systems support staff to properly configure (or troubleshoot) their systems. Although network interface card vendors have already gone a long way toward making their products software configurable (as opposed to requiring physical hardware configuration using jumper switches), Microsoft effectively solved the problem with plug-and-play configuration starting with Windows 95.

Ethernet Address Resolution

On bus networks, like Ethernet, data is transmitted on the bus and each connected node listens in for traffic directed at it; all the rest is ignored. Ethernet frames use the hardware interface address to direct traffic: this is a six-byte address hard-coded into each network adapter by the vendor. Each vendor gets its own address range, so it is possible to identify the maker of a network card by its address. At the interface between the network layer (IP) and the link layer (Ethernet), a mechanism is needed to translate IP addresses into Ethernet MAC addresses, and vice versa.

ARP (Address Resolution Protocol) and RARP (Reverse Address Resolution Protocol) are used to associate network hardware addresses (like those used by Ethernet) with IP addresses. ARP simply links an IP address with a physical address. The requesting host sends out a broadcast to all the nodes on the local network asking for a response from the owner of the IP address in question. The host that owns the IP address in question answers with its own hardware address, and the original requesting host can continue with its transmission, sending data directly to that host. All the other hosts ignore the request.

Whereas ARP is handy when the transmitting host knows the IP address of the destination host, RARP is useful when a host knows a hardware address but does not know the IP address it desires. The most common situation where this occurs is booting a diskless workstation. The workstation reads its own MAC address, but needs to send a request to a RARP server to map an IP address to itself. We will examine ARP and RARP more comprehensively in Chapter 7, where we will see how IP uses these protocols to figure out how to get data from source to destination.

Point-to-Point Links

When commercial access to the Internet first started, most Internet service providers focused on offering high-speed, high-bandwidth connections to the Internet for larger organizations. Serial connections were offered to individuals wishing to connect to internetworks from off-site (usually their homes), but providers often offered this type of service only as a supplement to full, on-site service. By the mid-1990s, however, Internet service providers offer connections to the Internet both as a business service to small business people and to individuals and families for educational and entertainment purposes. Previously, modem-connected internetwork users were a minority; they are now far and away the greater portion of the internetworked population. The Point to Point Protocol (PPP) will be examined in greater detail in Chapter 6, but this section offers an introduction to the use of modems and other devices for small office/home office and home connections to the Internet.

Serial and Point-to-Point Hardware

Most commonly, users connect to their internetwork through a POTS (plain old telephone service) wire and a serial modem. A correctly installed and configured modem is all the hardware required for a remote internetwork connection, at least from the client side.

The client must have a properly configured server to dial into and start a remote link. Remote network access services are usually provided by a modem pool to answer the incoming calls, and a system connected on one side to the modems and on the other to the connecting internetwork. These servers can act as routers, passing along traffic from the internetwork to each attached remote node, and passing traffic from remote nodes on to the attached internetwork.

ISDN (Integrated Services Digital Networks) is an integrated digital telephone service for delivering all traffic, including voice, video, and data, over a digital network. Local telephone companies are offering it as a replacement for POTS, but it is largely being ignored by most consumers due to its high cost and marginal improvement in network bandwidth over high-speed modems. At best, ISDN offers throughput of 128 thousand bits per second (Kbps), with 64 Kbps being the more usual case. The typical modem currently can support throughput as high as 56 Kbps.

Other alternatives for consumer connectivity include cable modems, which are actually very simple routers that can connect to an Ethernet card in the consumer's PC and route data through cable TV coaxial links to the Internet. Similar setups, connecting a box to an Ethernet card on a PC, are used for other high-speed services like satellite. Digital subscriber line (DSL) technologies can use special hardware that connects to a telephone line; telephone companies are just starting to offer these services to the public.

Serial and Point-to-Point Protocols

SLIP, or Serial Line Internet Protocol, was the first widely used protocol for connecting a node to a network over a serial connection. SLIP is little more than a slightly modified version of IP. Routing is simplified, since all "other" hosts are on the other side of the phone link; IP datagrams carried over a SLIP link have a special END character appended before and after the datagram. If the END character appears within the datagram, SLIP inserts a special ESCAPE character. Compressed SLIP, or CSLIP, takes advantage of the fact that there are only two directly connected hosts in the link (SLIP server and SLIP client) and reduces some of the overhead required by an IP connection. SLIP and CSLIP have both been widely supported both in client and server software, and the term *SLIP* usually encompasses both implementations.

However, SLIP has been losing importance over the past five years as PPP, or Point-to-Point Protocol, was developed to rectify some of SLIP's problems. Notably, SLIP supports only TCP/IP transmissions. PPP links can be shared simultaneously by different network protocols, including the common IPX (Internetwork Packet eXchange) still used by early versions of Novell's NetWare. Organizations are moving to PPP for their remote network access needs, particularly in mixed-network environments that require support for different protocols.

The Network Layer

Configuring a network node to work in a TCP/IP environment requires certain IP-level configuration, specifically, host and network identification, routing information and options, and other choices. Characterizing network configuration issues by their associated network layers is a convention here, rather than a hard and fast set of rules: the boundaries can be blurred between any two layers, and often are, as with setting the broadcast address and IP address of any particular host. These two configuration items relate directly to the link layer, particularly in relation to the use of ARP, but they also help the host to interoperate in a well-behaved fashion and identify the host within any IP network.

The IP identifiers include the network domain name, host name, network IP address, and host IP address, as discussed in Chapter

2. Routing information includes the address of the default gateway to other networks, as well as options for specifying the maximum transmission unit (MTU) size and the time to live (TTL) value of IP datagrams. Both these concepts will be explained below. Many more IP configuration variables may or may not be allowed in any particular TCP/IP implementation; in general personal computer implementations support configuration of some subset of protocol tuning parameters, but otherwise they depend on some default values that are not configurable.

Identification Issues

Host name, network domain name, subnet mask, host, and network IP addresses all must be entered correctly in some central configuration file, preferably entered through the action of the TCP/IP network software. These and other configuration items may be collected by installation and configuration software on Microsoft Windows 95/98, but implementations of TCP/IP under earlier versions of Windows, DOS, and many other operating systems, the system administrator must configure special files by hand.

Host and domain names are not case sensitive, but are usually spelled out in lowercase characters only. The network IP address is implicit in the host IP address (depending on the range in which the first octet of the address falls), so it is not usually required. Some software products have required a separate entry for both the network domain name and the fully qualified domain name (FQDN), though usually the software is able to extrapolate the proper FQDN from the domain and host names. Of course, the primary requirement for both the name and address of a host is that they be unique.

Routing Variables

The default router, or gateway, is the most obvious of routing variables that must be configured on any node. Some software offers the choice of using a dynamic routing protocol. The subnet mask helps determine which traffic actually is local to the host, and the broadcast address identifies how broadly to broadcast. Routing, broadcasting, and multicasting are discussed in greater detail in Chapters 7 and 8.

Time to Live

There are circumstances under which a packet can be caught in a loop (see Figure 4–1), where data can be passed along from one router to the next without ever arriving at its destination, which has lost its only link to the rest of the internetwork. A **time to live**, or **TTL**, field remedies this situation by setting a limit on the amount of time network traffic can remain in the internetwork before it is discarded. The IP TTL field is discussed in more detail in Chapter 7. Many TCP/IP implementations use different TTL defaults for different transport layer protocols, depending on whether there is a need for reliable or guaranteed delivery.

Transmission Unit Sizes

Though we have not yet touched on the specifics of protocol data packaging, there are maximum and minimum sizes for the various chunks of data being passed around an internetwork. Minimum sizes are generally decreed by the need for certain specific information about the packet, frame or datagram, but the **maximum transmission unit** (**MTU**) size of a network medium is generally determined by the **bandwidth** (amount of data that can be handled in a given time) of the medium and the reliability of the infrastructure. Network media that can move large volumes of data quickly can afford to pack the data up in big chunks, but media that move data more slowly may need to break it up into smaller chunks to keep it moving smoothly across the network.

MTUs (exclusive of headers) for different network media range from as high as 65,535 bytes for Hyperchannel, a high-speed medium, down to 4,352 for FDDI (fiber optic), 1,500 bytes for Ethernet,

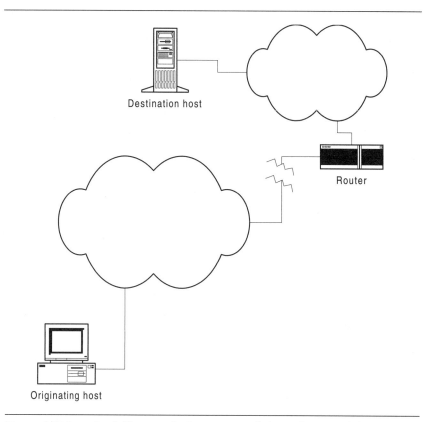

Destination host

Router

Originating host

Figure 4–1: A router failing can isolate a network from the rest of the internet-work, and cause network traffic to loop.

1006 bytes for SLIP, 576 bytes for X.25 networks (a WAN technolo-gy), to as low as 296 bytes for point-to-point links with low delay. These figures come from RFC 1191, Path MTU Discovery, which discusses how to handle setting path MTUs across routes that pass through LANs that use wildly different network media. Not men-tioned is **Asynchronous Transfer Mode (ATM)**, which transmits data in chunks called cells, each of which is only 53 bytes. ATM will be discussed at greater length in Chapter 6.

It is important to understand that the MTU of a network medium may be affected by the physical characteristics of the medium but that these are not the only factors involved. Setting an appropriate

MTU for a PPP link depends on determining the optimal size. The MTU should be large enough to get a meaningful amount of data into each frame, but not so large that it takes too long to transmit each frame.

As part of the routing configuration, it is sometimes possible to specify an MTU. This permits the TCP/IP networking software to optimize the size of outgoing datagrams to avoid fragmenting. For example, FDDI supports a larger MTU than Ethernet. Since FDDI networks are customarily used for aggregating traffic from some number of local networks, traffic originating on an Ethernet can use an MTU of 1,500 bytes without fear of fragmentation, even if it is being directed across a FDDI backbone and routed to another Ethernet network. However, users connected together in a FDDI LAN who regularly send traffic to Ethernet networks across an internetwork might want to reduce their MTU to 1,500 bytes, since any datagrams larger than that will be fragmented by the FDDI/Ethernet router. IP fragmentation is discussed in greater detail in Chapter 7.

The Transport and Application Layers

Network administrators can use many different options to tune network software implementing protocols at the transport layer. As with the IP fine-tuning options, many TCP/IP implementations simply set the values to defaults.

Application configuration usually consists of configuring default servers for the various application clients. The most commonly configured servers are for e-mail and network news; printer and file services, network time servers, WWW servers, and others are also frequently configured.

One of the most important upper layer configuration items is the method of network name resolution. There are two basic choices: use a stored host file or the Domain Name System (DNS). DNS will be discussed at greater length in Chapter 11.

Transport Protocol Options

Most TCP/IP network software permits configuration of the number of sockets available to network applications (see Chapter 2 for an introduction to sockets, or Chapter 10 for more in-depth coverage). As explained earlier, each network application uses the port number of a process to which it is connecting, along with the IP address of the host to which it is connecting, to create a unique identifier: a socket. The maximum number of available sockets can be modified if desired, usually by increasing them to allow more network applications to run concurrently.

Since TCP is a reliable transport, it needs to send acknowledgments and retransmission requests back and forth between connected hosts. If every segment had to be acknowledged individually, it would hurt performance badly. TCP options will be discussed at greater length in Chapter 10, but for now suffice it to say that the network administrator can often configure how long the node should wait before retransmitting data, how long it should wait before checking that an idle connection is still alive, and others.

Although UDP, as an unreliable protocol, does not need mechanisms for acknowledgment of receipt, some implementations allow the choices like whether to use a checksum for outgoing UDP datagrams, and what the default value for UDP TTL should be. UDP options will be discussed in Chapter 9.

Application Server Configuration

Configuring application servers for a workstation is usually a matter of getting the host names of the desired servers and entering them in a configuration file (more common when using a command line interface like DOS or Unix), or entering them in a dialog box (more common when using a graphical user interface like Windows, X Windows, OS/2, or Macintosh).

Host names are usually preferred to IP addresses, although some implementations do allow configuration of servers with IP addresses. Because network managers often have to shift servers from one network or host to another, the use of server names is preferred. This is particularly true in larger networks where system upgrades and transfers of servers to more powerful systems are common strategies to deal with increased or changed service demands. Although the actual IP address of the system offering a service may change from time to time, network managers strive to maintain the same server host names. This ensures that end users can connect to the service, no matter where the service originates.

Name Resolution

Where DNS is implemented, the IP address of a primary name server is required, and one or two backup name servers can often be added. Name server host names are never necessary, since the name server itself would have to be queried to get the correct IP address. Every Internet-connected network must have at least one DNS server.

Hosts can avoid using DNS if they have a **hosts file** listing all the hosts with which they communicate. This file is just a simple list of host name and host IP addresses. When a connection is being made, the host looks up the name of the destination host in the hosts file and finds its IP address. Both DNS and hosts files will be covered in greater detail in Chapter 11.

Other Configuration Items

Information like the name, computer user ID (for remote systems), location, and phone number of the user/owner of the workstation is often requested by TCP/IP configuration software, as is the time zone, whether daylight savings is used, and other identifying information.

Chapter Summary and References

In this chapter, we previewed some of the things that need to be done to deploy a host on a TCP/IP network. Examining configuration issues at each of the TCP/IP network reference models, we took an advance look at many of the issues that will be covered in the chapters to come.

Starting at the hardware and link layers, we introduced some of the issues involved with connecting a computer to a network, notably how electronic signals are converted into digital data that the computer can process. Point-to-point connections were introduced, as were some of the issues involved with mapping link layer addresses to network layer addresses using ARP and RARP.

At the network layer, where IP operates, we dealt with host identification and some topics related to routing including maximum transmission unit size and time to live values.

Moving up to the transport and application layers, we introduced the notions of transport layer protocol tuning and application layer configuration, with special attention given to the Domain Name System that is so important to the TCP/IP suite.

A useful RFC to read in conjunction with this chapter is listed in Table 4–1.

RFC	Title	Description
1191	Path MTU Discovery	Explains why path MTU discovery is helpful, and how it works.

Table 4–1: Useful RFC for Chapter 4.

5

TCP/IP Applications

Assuming everyone involved in the technology has done his or her job well, the only thing users want to know about are the applications they can use with their networked systems. The most important TCP/IP applications now in use are probably the World Wide Web (or simply the web) and electronic mail. But there are many other applications available in the TCP/IP protocol suite. Some of them were designed for use by network managers and administrators, and others were designed to be used by end users. Most are described in RFCs, and the ones deemed useful have been implemented on different platforms and improved over time.

Applications are usually implemented in pairs: the client side and the server side. To be useful, an application must be widely implemented both by network managers as a service on network servers and by users as a client program running on networked workstations.

This chapter introduces the most popular and widely implemented applications and explains how they are used. Later chapters take a closer look at each of the more important application protocols, examining the way the applications work both at the user level and within the framework of TCP/IP protocols.

Categories of Service

To provide an organizational framework for this book, traditional internetwork applications are placed into one of the following categories:

- ◆ Remote computing
- ◆ File transfer
- ◆ Resource sharing
- ◆ Communication
- ◆ Data publication
- ◆ Network management

Applications in the last category, network management, are discussed separately in Chapter 23. Network management applications are used either by network engineers or by the other network applications themselves to support internetworking. This chapter introduces the applications used by end users.

Network applications evolved over time with the changing demands of the user population. When most networked computers were larger multiuser systems, accessing other systems through a terminal session was an important function. Many organizations and their systems still depend on remote terminal emulation and raw file transfer to move information between two or more points. However, systems professionals are using the Internet and its applications as a development platform on which to build their systems. It is no longer necessary to mandate the use of terminal emulation for remote users to connect to mainframe applications. Now, developers can build applications that allow remote users to access information from those mainframes without specifying the mechanisms those remote users use to access the data.

Nevertheless, the mechanisms by which terminal emulation, file transfer, resource sharing, and the rest of the TCP/IP suite applications work are still basic to most of the things that developers are doing with networked applications. Before we cover topics like the World Wide Web, Java, and network computing, it is helpful to understand the basic application building blocks. The ability to send commands and responses across an internetwork is a fundamental function, often used to develop other network applications. Likewise, file transfer protocols are long-standing necessities for internetworks: sending files across an internetwork is one of the basic building blocks necessary for other internetwork applications.

Remote computing applications let networked users run software on remote systems. File transfer protocols let users transfer data files between local and remote systems. Resource sharing lets users access remote system resources like disk storage space or printers as if they were directly connected to the user's local system. The difference between resource sharing and file transfer is not always readily apparent. Shared network resources can be used directly, without any intervening step (beyond making the initial connection). Files on a remote system accessed with a file transfer program must be completely transferred from the remote system before they can be used, whereas files on a shared network drive can be used without taking any intermediate steps. A user can send a print job to a shared networked printer directly from a word processing program; the same printer may also be accessible to a user running a terminal session on the print server, but only for files that reside on the server system.

Communication functions like electronic mail and network news also continue to be important. News and e-mail, both within an organizational internetwork and across the Internet, provide vital links for their users. Unlike the other applications already mentioned, e-mail and news are asynchronous communication applications since participants in e-mail exchanges or news contributors read and reply to messages on their own schedules, without any coordination needed between participants.

Data publication applications, notably World Wide Web, use a combination of techniques to allow organizations and individuals to publish their data to anyone with a connection to the Internet (or to a local intranet) and the appropriate client software.

Remote Computing

The **telnet** (short for Telecommunications Network) protocol defines the dominant protocol for raw remote computing over the Internet. Remote users use their telnet client application to connect to hosts running a telnet server application. The telnet client converts input from the local keyboard into standardized "virtual keystrokes" on a **network virtual terminal** (NVT), which are interpreted by the telnet server software on the host. Data passed by the host to the client is translated for the NVT so the local client application can convert it into the appropriate screen output. Figure 5–1 shows a sample terminal session running between a Windows workstation and a remote host.

The **r-utilities** offer another method of doing remote computing, but these applications are not as universally implemented. There are several, some of which issue single commands, like rcp (remote copy) and rexec (remote execute of a command). Rlogin does roughly the same thing as telnet, offering a way to log into remote hosts.

The r-utilities, originally developed for use on networked Unix workstations, use system identifiers for security purposes instead of user ID/password combinations. Although this was reasonably secure for closed networks with Unix systems (or other platforms with better defined security), r-utilities can be unsecure in more open networks where personal computers are in use. Telnet and the r-utilities are discussed in Chapter 15.

```
# delete deletes and ^C interrupts
stty dec

# Set for your terminal type...
# you can change "vt100" to the name of the terminal you use
#set noglob; eval `tset -s -m ':?vt100''
#unset noglob
setenv TERM vt100
# Avoid nasty core files
limit coredumpsize 0k

# Print announcements of note,
msgs
# a random adage,
/usr/games/fortune
# show what mail you have
#subj
# and whois logged in
# f
~
~
~
~
".login" 19 lines, 391 characters
```

Figure 5–1: Connecting to a remote host with Telnet is like being connected through any other type of terminal; all functions are available.

NOTE: This issue will come up again in discussion of the Network File System (NFS) in Chapter 18. NFS was originally developed by Sun MicroSystems for resource sharing among networked Unix workstations.

File Transfer

One of the most basic network applications is the ability to manage files on remote systems. The ability to copy, delete, and move such files continues to be important despite the growing popularity of other applications. Two file transfer protocols are in general use: **FTP** (File Transfer Protocol) provides high performance file transfer functions robustly and reasonably securely. **TFTP** (Trivial File Transfer Protocol) offers a bare-bones protocol for file transfers, usually implemented in a small application program running under a minimal underlying protocol stack. Used almost exclusively for remote booting of diskless workstations, TFTP pays the price for low overhead in reduced reliability and security. As we will explain in Chapter 16, the difference between these two file transfer applications lies in the use of different transport protocols. FTP uses TCP for reliability and robustness and TFTP uses UDP for performance and simplicity of implementation.

FTP moves data between any two hosts independent of operating system and file type or character representation. Data files on an IBM mainframe, using the EBCDIC character set, can be transferred to a Windows PC, Macintosh, or Unix workstation as ASCII files, without any special treatment or need for conversion.

File management tools are provided in the basic FTP implementation, but files on a remote system must be transferred before they can be used in any way on the local system. So, although an FTP client can be used to display directory listings, including file name, size, type, and creation date, the contents of that file can't be examined until it has been transferred to the local host.

As with all TCP/IP applications, a set of commands are defined by the FTP protocol specifications. Any FTP client must offer a minimal selection of these commands, and any FTP server must be able to respond to any of the supported commands. If you are familiar with FTP commands on one system, you can use the same commands on any other system that implements FTP. A typical command-line ses-

```
-rw-r—r—  1 root         daemon      285814 Mar 27 09:00 ls-ltR
-rw-r—r—  1 root         daemon       63829 Mar 27 09:00 ls-ltR.Z
drwxr-xr-x  3 root       daemon         512 Jun 22  1994 mac
drwxr-xr-x  2 root       daemon         512 Feb 15 18:39 outgoing
dr-xr-x—- 12 root        private        512 Feb  6 21:26 private
drwxr-xr-x  2 root       daemon         512 Mar  3 22:28 pub
drwxr-xr-x  2 root       daemon         512 Aug 31  1994 tmp
drwxr-xr-x  5 root       daemon         512 Jan 12 22:36 unix
dr-xr-xr-x  3 root       daemon         512 May  5  1994 usr
drwxr-xr-x  4 root       daemon         512 Mar 10 18:39 vendor
drwxrwxr-x  2 root       101            512 Mar  3 22:30 web
226 Transfer complete.
ftp> get ls-ltR.Z
local: ls-ltR.Z remote: ls-ltR.Z
200 PORT command successful.
150 Opening BINARY mode data connection for ls-ltR.Z (63829 bytes).
226 Transfer complete.
63829 bytes received in 35.23 seconds (1.77 Kbytes/s)
ftp>
```

Figure 5–2: FTP using a character-based system.

sion is shown in Figure 5–2; the same commands will work on any system running a command-line interface FTP client program. However, there may be slight cosmetic differences; for example, command line prompt may be different. FTP does not have to be implemented as a command-line program, and graphical implementations can provide the exact same functionality but with an easier to use graphical user interface, as shown in Figure 5–3.

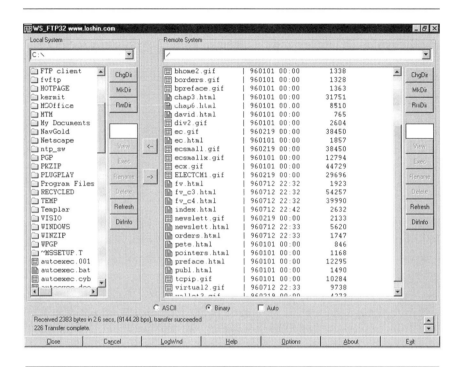

Figure 5–3: A graphical user interface version of FTP.

Resource Sharing

Perhaps the most compelling reason for installing a local area network is the ability to share computer resources. In practice, this
means shared disk space. This is the function personal computer
LAN users are most familiar with and this is the function that
Novell's highly successful NetWare network operating system
supports. You can share virtually any computer resource over a
network or an internetwork: printers, plotters, CD-ROM drives,
fax machines, modems, and virtually any other peripheral device
that produces output or stores data.

Although resource sharing is usually a local network function,
TCP/IP does offer sharing functions. NFS, Sun's Network File

System, is widely implemented for the personal computer world; client software for PCs is common and server programs that allow other NFS clients to share data from a PC's hard drive are not hard to find. Another (usually) Unix-based program, lpr, shares printers across a network.

Other types of resource sharing can be done in parallel with TCP/IP. In fact, leading LAN operating systems such as Novell's NetWare and Microsoft's NT Server can use IP as their basic network layer protocol.

These resource sharing applications function as "redirectors," with the network software integrating with the client operating system to map logical names onto network resources. The client system then displays the network resources as if they were connected locally to the client. For example, a network storage volume might be redirected to the logical drive name, E:\, on a client PC system. Someone using that system would be able to treat that volume as if it were attached to the system directly, managing files, running programs, and storing data on it. Network resources can also be protected, so volumes can be restricted to authorized users or available as read-only resources.

Communication

This category of applications supports communication between and among users. The most important application here is electronic mail, or e-mail. Applications like electronic mail and network news (Usenet news) support interpersonal communication—people send messages to other individuals (e-mail) or to groups of people sharing an interest (news). Other communication protocols, like Internet Relay Chat and various "talk" applications, allow direct, real-time interaction between two or more individuals. A new category of workgroup communication applications is becoming increasingly common. These allow individuals to exchange business card as well as schedule information, permitting widely dispersed users to coordinate meetings across the Internet.

E-mail is usually supported through the Simple Mail Transfer Protocol (SMTP) or the third version of the Post Office Protocol (POP3). The user runs an e-mail application on the local host, which checks the e-mail server periodically to see if messages have been received or to send new messages. The Internet Message Access Protocol (IMAP) is a rising e-mail protocol that allows users to read and manipulate their e-mail on a remote server.

Electronic mail has been important to organizations for many years, starting with internal e-mail systems running on large time-shared computers. In the past, e-mail service providers, such as MCI Mail, offered important communication links to users world-wide. Internet mail gateways make it possible to link people no matter where their e-mail originates.

By the mid-1990s, free e-mail services were making their appearance on the Internet. Juno, one of the first, offered free e-mail using their proprietary e-mail client. Users paid nothing for the service, but had to view paid advertising that appeared with each message. Alternatives quickly sprang up, with many of them using Web-based interfaces to allow users access to their mail from any system with a browser. Yahoo! and other Web portals now offer free e-mail.

Network news uses the Network News Transfer Protocol (NNTP) and operates similarly to e-mail in many ways—in fact, it is not uncommon to see combined e-mail and news readers. News, like mail, is distributed from a server that can receive network news feeds from the Internet or that uses internally provided news content on a private internetwork. News readers can be strictly ASCII based, looking much like the e-mail reader as shown in Figure 5–4, although graphical interfaces, like that shown in Figure 5–5, are more common in Windows implementations.

News and e-mail are fairly self-explanatory applications, though many options are available to the savvy user and administrator in various implementations. For example, you can screen mail and news to ignore material originating from certain individuals or on certain topics. In general, Unix implementations will give you the

```
PINE 3.89    MAIN MENU                    Folder: INBOX   0 Messages


        ?    HELP                  -  Get help using Pine

        C    COMPOSE MESSAGE       -  Compose and send a message

        I    FOLDER INDEX          -  View messages in current folder

        L    FOLDER LIST           -  Select a folder to view

        A    ADDRESS BOOK          -  Update address book

        S    SETUP                 -  Configure or update Pine

        Q    QUIT                  -  Exit the Pine program



Copyright 1989-1993. PINE is a trademark of the University of Washington.
                [Folder "INBOX" opened with 0 messages]
? Help                    P PrevCmd                    R RelNotes
O OTHER CMDS L [ListFldrs] N NextCmd                   K KBLock
```

Figure 5–4: A character-based electronic mail reader.

greatest amount of flexibility, whereas personal computer implementations may be less flexible.

Data Publication

The **World Wide Web** (WWW) makes possible the publication of data across the Internet (or within a private intranet). Publishing information over a Web server has greater immediacy and accessibility than files that must be transferred from an FTP server; it also has more permanence than information posted to a network news

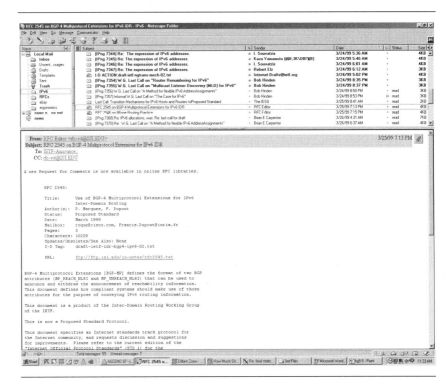

Figure 5–5: A graphical user interface version of an electronic mail reader.

group. Figure 5–6 shows a sample Web page, which, with attractive graphics, point-and-click navigation within each site and across the Internet to other Web sites and to integrated hypertext document links, makes an excellent vehicle for publishing information to users.

Gopher, a precursor publishing application to the Web, provides a front end to various TCP/IP services, focusing on anonymous FTP and information search services. The Web more properly describes the global implementation of servers and clients supporting the **Hypertext Transfer Protocol** (HTTP). Each Web document can include live references to other Web documents. This includes local documents maintained by the same person or group as well as documents maintained by other people and groups, anywhere in the world. By encouraging publishers of

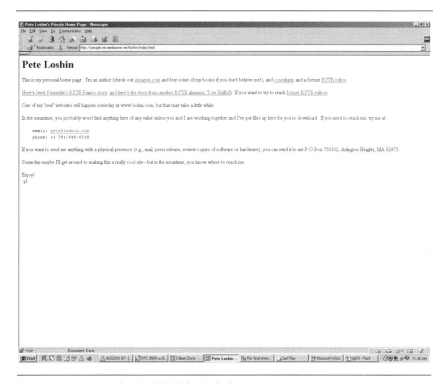

Figure 5–6: A sample World Wide Web document.

Web pages to link their documents with other documents, what appears to be a web starts to form, with strands of the web being links between different servers on the Internet, as shown in Figure 5–7.

Gopher, a predecessor to WWW, is less ambitious but also is accessible to a much wider audience since it relies less on graphics and graphical linkages and more on ASCII text menus. Though the result is less flashy, as illustrated in Figure 5–8, users who don't have access to high-quality graphics and to the high-speed network connections that transfers of large graphics files require still sometimes use Gopher.

The fact remains that web clients and servers have been distributed so widely, particularly outside the traditional Internet com-

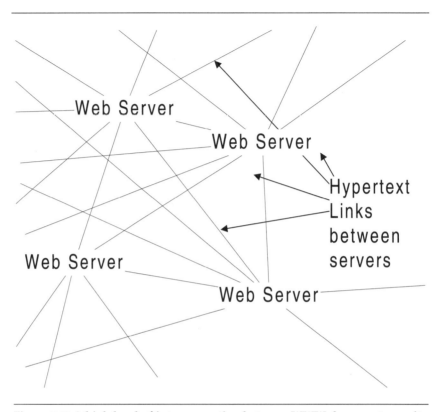

Figure 5–7: A high level of interconnection between WWW documents results in a kind of "information web."

munity, that for many users the Web and the Internet are perceived as the same entities. This movement toward a single standard for data publication forced private on-line services like America Online to migrate their business from a members-only, private service into an Internet service provider/public Internet model. Likewise the Microsoft Network, which was originally launched in parallel with Windows 95 as a private dial-in network but which, through disuse, was turned into an Internet resource in less than a year. Internet service providers and managers of corporate intranets connected to the Internet have all been equally exuberant in their embrace of the Web by offering HTTP services.

```
Internet Gopher Information Client v1.13

                  Root gopher server: gopher.std.com

-->    1.  Information About The World Public Access UNIX/
       2.  The World's ClariNews AP Online Newswire Index/
       3.  OBI The Online Book Initiative/
       4.  Internet and USENET Phone Books/
       5.  Shops on The World/
       6.  Commercial Services via the Internet/
       7.  Book Sellers/
       8.  Bulletin Boards via the Internet/
       9.  Consultants/
      10.  FTP/
      11.  Government Information/
      12.  Internet Information and Resources/
      13.  Libraries/
      14.  Membership and Professional Associations/
      15.  Metropolitan and Community News/
      16.  News and Weather/
      17.  Non-Profit Organizations/
      18.  Other Gopher and Information Servers/

Press ? for Help, q to Quit, u to go up a menu        Page: 1/2
```

Figure 5–8: Gopher, though less flashy than the World Wide Web, still offers value for publishing data across the Internet to users who lack high-speed links to support high-resolution graphics.

Other Services and Applications

These are the principle user-oriented network applications implemented on TCP/IP networks. All these applications are discussed in greater detail in Part Three.

Network management and administrative functions are discussed throughout Part Four. The Domain Name System is discussed in Chapter 11.

Chapter Summary and References

This chapter introduced the most important feature of TCP/IP networking: the applications. Unless there is something compelling to do with a network, there is no reason to bother with that network. TCP/IP applications include simple things like remote computing, file transfer, and resource sharing. These applications were indispensible once users realized that they could be used to communicate interoperably with any other computer.

E-mail and the World Wide Web have emerged as the most important two TCP/IP applications, and are likely to continue to fuel the growth of the Internet.

A useful RFC to read in conjunction with this chapter is listed in Table 5–1.

RFC	Title	Description
2151	A Primer On Internet and TCP/IP Tools and Utilities	This document provides an introduction to the Internet and TCP/IP in general.

Table 5–1: Useful RFC for Chapter 5.

Part Two

TCP/IP Networking Protocols

6

The Data Link Layer

Strictly speaking, TCP/IP should not be concerned with the data link layer. Networked hosts use the data link layer to move data between the network interfaces of two different computers on the same physical network. At this level, network traffic is just one level above the physical signal: whether the signal is a variation in current on a conducting medium, a variation in light signals on a fiber optic medium, or a variation in sound on an analog telephone wire. The data link layer is concerned with properly sending and receiving these signals between communicating hosts through their network interfaces.

Although IP works at the layer above the data link layer, it still must interact with protocols at the data link layer. This interaction is usually related to the task of mapping an IP address to a link layer network address—in other words, figuring out what network address should be associated with a particular IP address. This issue of address resolution will be taken up again in Chapter 11.

TCP/IP runs over just about any conceivable network medium, but two methods dominate network connections made by end users' computers: most are either connected to an organizational Ethernet network or they connect to an internetwork across a telephone connection. Ethernet connections use the Ethernet frame standard, and telephone links generally use the Point-to-Point Protocol (PPP).

Although Ethernet and dialup connections predominate for end-user connectivity, backbones—the networks over which the bulk of all Internet and intranet traffic passes en route to its destination—increasingly rely on the Asynchronous Transfer Mode (ATM). ATM is capable of very high throughput, but it differs from Ethernet in one important respect: it is a nonbroadcast medium. On Ethernets, all connected nodes can listen to a single transmission; on ATM, all nodes are connected through virtual circuits. Functions like address resolution and multicast are made far more complicated under ATM, but they can be accomplished, as we'll see later.

In this chapter, we look at Ethernet frame formats as well as ATM and how it can be used for TCP/IP networking. We continue by examining serial links and a discussion of relative performance issues and frame formats. Finally, we will discuss the loopback interface, a mechanism that allows a host to communicate with itself through its own network interface.

Protocol Data Units

As explained in Chapter 1, chunks of network traffic get "wrapped up" or encapsulated in lower level protocols as they pass down the protocol stack on a host. As they get passed back up the protocol stack on destination (or intermediate) hosts, the lower level encapsulation is stripped away to reveal actual network data.

These encapsulated chunks of data have different names depending on what protocols have been doing the wrapping. Chunks of data that are encapsulated inside IP headers are called **packets** or **datagrams**. Chunks of data that are wrapped up in Ethernet headers are called **frames**. The generic term that describes a chunk of data for a particular protocol is **protocol data unit** or **PDU**.

At the lowest layer above the actual hardware, the data link layer, PDUs are often referred to as *network frames*. Frames are what get transmitted on an Ethernet, for example. On ATM, the PDU is a **cell**. Unwrap a frame or a cell and you may find an IP datagram, the name for the PDU in IP (datagrams are also often called packets). Unwrap an IP datagram, and you're likely to find a TCP segment (the TCP PDU) or a UDP datagram (UDP's PDU).

Knowing that different protocols have different names for their units of data transmission can help reduce confusion when working with a multilayer network reference model.

Ethernet

Ethernet is actually a set of standards specifications that define network MAC addresses, frame formats, and transmission standards. Ethernet took its basic form in the mid-1970s and took its modern form by 1982, although the IEEE published a set of standards that, though mostly similar to Ethernet, differ sufficiently to cause difficulty on occasion. TCP/IP is generally associated with Ethernet, and although TCP/IP implementations are required to be able to send and receive Ethernet frames, they are not required to handle IEEE frames—though the ability to handle these frames is highly recommended to implementers.

Ethernet originated at Xerox PARC (Palo Alto Research Center), and later became standardized through efforts of Xerox, Digital Equipment Corporation, and Intel Corporation. Hence, the name DIX (Digital-Intel-Xerox) Ethernet. DIX Ethernet 2.0, also known as Ethernet II, was the result of the 1982 revision.

IEEE standard	Area standardized
IEEE 802.2	Logical Link Control (LLC)
IEEE 802.3	Standardization for Ethernet (CSMA/CD baseband networks)
IEEE 802.4	Token bus network standards
IEEE 802.5	Token ring network standards

Table 6–1: The IEEE 802 standards apply to various types of networks, with the 802.2 standard applicable to all of them; 802.3 relates to Ethernet-type networks.

The IEEE called their Ethernet standards group *Project 802* because it was started in February 1980, and they came up with several sets of standards relating to the standard networks of that time (see Table 6–1).

CSMA/CD is an acronym for **Carrier Sense Multiple Access/ Collision Detection**. This little phrase sums up the most important characteristics of Ethernet as we know it. In Ethernets, all connected nodes have to share the same network medium. This means that only one node can transmit at any given time. Carrier Sense Multiple Access means that each node shares the same medium. Collision Detection means that each node has to check to make sure that no other node is transmitting before it can send any data onto the medium—and if it detects a collision, it will back off and wait until attempting to resend.

The IEEE standard numbers aren't version numbers, as one might think; they simply differentiate the standards. The 802.2 standard provides transparency to the physical layers for all the 802 network standards (802.3, 802.4, and 802.5). So, if a CSMA/CD baseband network runs IEEE 802.2, it generates 802.3 frames and uses the 802.2 Logical Link Control (LLC) specifications within those frames. Likewise, if a network uses the IEEE 802.3 standard, one should expect that it uses the 802.2 extensions (but this is not always the case).

Network Frame Functions

The Ethernet frame, which is discussed in more detail later, consists of header fields and a field for a **payload**, which is the actual data being carried across the Ethernet network. The frame's payload is itself network traffic relating to a higher layer. In TCP/IP internetworks the payload is invariably an IP datagram, though in heterogenous networks IP datagrams can coexist with other types of network traffic. The nodes that process the frame are unconcerned with the payload: the frame's function is to act as a container in which to deliver the payload to the correct destination host on the local network.

The source and destination hosts may or may not be the source and destination hosts for the frame's payload. Consider Figure 6–1, a simple internetwork. Host A is sending a piece of data to Host C across an internetwork. Host A begins (at the application layer) collecting the application data, adds TCP headers to address it to a specific remote process (at the transport layer), then adds IP network addressing to address it to a particular host (at the network layer). Before the resulting IP datagram can be sent out on the Ethernet, the originating host adds network link layer information to create an Ethernet frame.

There are three different PDUs involved here:

- A transport layer PDU, which in this case is a TCP segment addressed to a particular process running on the destination node
- A network layer PDU, which in this case is an IP datagram addressed to a particular host's IP address somewhere on the internetwork pictured
- A link layer PDU, which in this case is an Ethernet frame addressed to a specific network interface directly connected to the same network as the source

Host A knows the ultimate destination for the IP datagram is off the local network. (The next section discusses frame headers; Chapters 7 and 8 discuss IP routing issues in greater detail.)

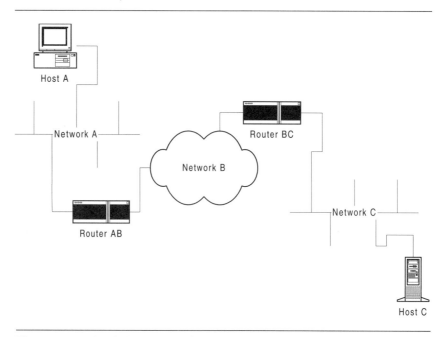

Figure 6–1: A simple internetwork with heterogenous network media.

Therefore, the originating source host addresses an Ethernet frame to the local router. Even though the IP datagram is addressed to Host C, the Ethernet frame sent by the originating host is addressed to Router AB.

Although Network A and Network C in our example are both Ethernets, the intermediate internetwork, Network B, could just as easily be a high-speed ATM backbone, a token ring network, or something else. Once the frame is received by Router AB, it strips away the Ethernet frame headers, checks the IP destination address, and determines that the IP datagram is intended for a host on a different network.

Since Router AB is configured to send all packets destined for Network C to Router BC, it creates a new network frame (perhaps an Ethernet frame, perhaps not) containing the IP datagram (from Host A to Host C). The new network frame, traveling from Router

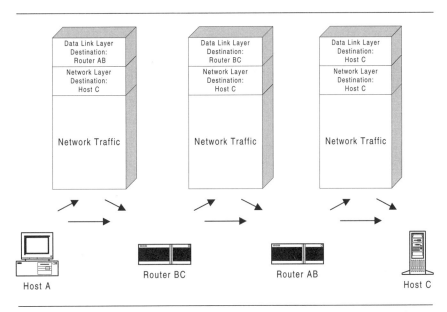

Figure 6–2: The data link layer addresses on a network frame change as they move from one network to another, but the IP destination stays the same.

AB to Router BC, will have Router AB as the source and Router BC as the destination—but the IP datagram will remain unchanged, and the destination address of that datagram will also remain unchanged. Figure 6–2 shows that the headers are stripped off and the router converts the frame into the proper format for Network B; Router BC in turn must accept the resulting frame, determine the local network address of the destination host, Host C, and create a new Ethernet frame for Network C. The final network frame in this example will show Router BC as the source and Host C as the destination—but, the IP datagram again remains unchanged, with the IP destination still Host C.

Ethernet Frame Formats

Network frames literally "frame" the data being sent, with header fields (and often with trailer fields). The network data fits in a data field. Figure 6–3 shows the structure of an Ethernet frame, and

Figure 6–4 shows the IEEE 802.2/802.3 frame. Ethernet and IEEE headers start out looking pretty much the same. They both start with the destination's **media access control** or **MAC** address. A MAC address is a six-byte value hard-coded into the network interface card. The source address, also a six-byte MAC address, follows the destination address. A four-byte Cyclic Redundancy Check (CRC) trails each frame. The CRC is generated by the Ethernet hardware and is also present in both standards.

Differences between Ethernet and IEEE standards become apparent when you look at Ethernet's two-byte entry in the "type" field that identifies the type of network data contained within the frame. This field identifies the network protocol used by the enclosed datagram and could be TCP/IP traffic, NetWare traffic, or

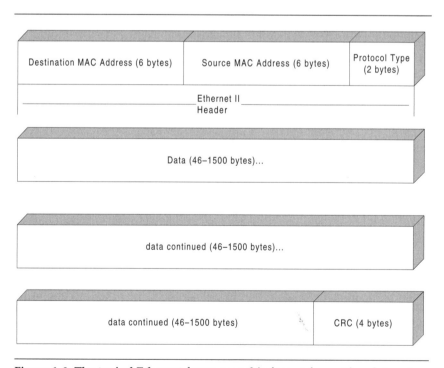

Figure 6–3: The typical Ethernet frame uses this format for putting data out on the physical network.

any other kind of valid network protocol. By indicating protocol type in this way, any individual host can send and receive network traffic from two or more different protocols, as long as the appropriate protocol stacks are running on that host. This has long been found in enterprise networks that use Novell's NetWare network operating system or other protocols such as DECnet or Apple's AppleTalk.

When the host is initialized, it starts up software that handles the interface between the network interface and the host. Running on top of that program are the network protocol stacks, with one stack for each different protocol being used. In a NetWare environment it was not uncommon for a host to run one protocol stack to handle NetWare IPX (Internetwork Packet eXchange) datagrams and

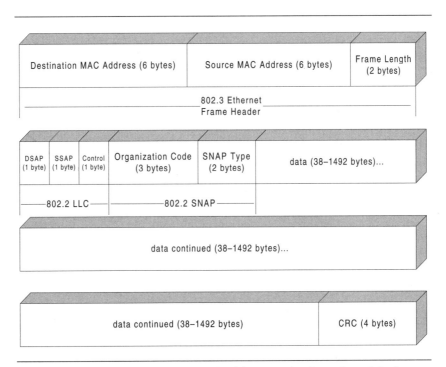

Figure 6–4: The IEEE 802.2/802.2 standard frame varies from the original Ethernet standards, but is still largely compatible with it.

another protocol stack to handle IP datagrams. When it receives a network frame, the interface driver determines to which protocol stack the unwrapped datagram should be sent by checking the type field. As frames are received by the host through the network interface card, the interface software deals the frame to the protocol stack based on what the protocol type field indicates. For example, IPX is indicated by a value of 8137 or 8138, and IP datagrams are indicated by the value of 0800.

The IEEE frame uses the two bytes following the source and destination addresses as a length field, indicating the length of the data portion of the frame. Ethernet frames identify the contents with a simple two-byte type field; the IEEE standards permit much further refinement through the Logical Link Control and Subnetwork Access Protocol (SNAP) fields.

Since valid Ethernet type values are all higher than 1,500 (the maximum number of bytes for the data portion of the network frame), IEEE 802 frames are distinguished from Ethernet frames simply by checking the two bytes that follow the destination and source addresses: if the value is larger than the hexadecimal for 1,500, the frame is an Ethernet frame (and the value defines a protocol type); if it is 1,500 or less, it's an IEEE frame.

The important part of the frame, the actual payload, differs between Ethernet and IEEE in the first eight bytes, assigned by IEEE to LLC and SNAP functions. As a result, an Ethernet data field can be no longer than 1,500 bytes and no smaller than 46 bytes; valid IEEE data fields range from 38 bytes to 1,492 bytes.

The minimum sizes are important because sometimes there isn't enough data to fill a frame; for example, during a remote host session a user command, password, or user ID may be only a few bytes long. Even though the IP datagram within the frame has its own header, which is encapsulated in the frame, the package may still be smaller than 46 bytes (or 38 bytes for IEEE); "padding" is added to data fields that aren't long enough.

Asynchronous Transfer Mode

Unlike Ethernet, Asynchronous Transfer Mode (ATM) technology was devised to be independent of the physical layer, and to be used for transmission of any kind of digital information—voice as well as network data. The objective was to build a technology capable of handling a lot of data at very high speed. ATM networks consist of nodes with ATM network interface cards that are all connected directly to ATM switches or routers.

ATM differs from Ethernet in two very important ways:

◆ ATM networks use a small, fixed-length PDU. ATM cells are limited to 53 bytes, of which 5 bytes are for network headers and the rest is payload.

◆ ATM networks use a true star topology and belong to the category of networks described as Non-Broadcast, Multi-Access (NBMA). This means that a message intended for more than one node on an ATM network must be repeated for each destination node. There are no such things as broadcasts or multicasts.

Although high-speed networks can handle large PDUs, because only one node can transmit at any given time these big PDUs can also sometimes cause problems, especially when the network carries voice as well as data.

During a telephone conversation, voice signals are digitized and packaged into packets and transmitted to their destination. We are accustomed to hearing voice transmission in a continuous stream, so voice would have to packaged into small units and transmitted quickly, in order, to its destination—otherwise, telephone calls would sound very jerky.

If voice is transmitted over the same network as data, you run into problems. A computer wants to send big chunks of data over the network because it can process those big chunks more easily and because it (usually) doesn't care if its interaction is jerky or smooth.

Now, I answer the phone by saying "Hello, this is Pete Loshin." If I share the network with computers, after the word "hello" is digitized and sent, a computer might start sending a very large packet causing an interruption in my transmission. The person calling me would hear "hello," then a pause, and then "… this is Pete Loshin."

The solution is to make all packets very small so that you can't hog bandwidth by sending big packets. Thus, even though ATM is usually used in very high-capacity networks, it uses a small PDU.

The other major and obvious difference between ATM and Ethernet is that although Ethernet permits broadcasts and multicasts, ATM does without. Because ATM nodes are all directly connected to an ATM switching or routing device—and not directly connected to any other device or medium—there is no simple way to deliver a message to more than one node at a time. This also means that it can be very difficult to send a cell to another node unless you already know that node's addressing information.

ATM Cells

ATM cell headers are depicted in Figure 6–5. The user node interface (from individual nodes to the ATM network device) is shown on the left, and the network to network interface (an ATM network device to another network device) is shown on the right. ATM header fields include the following.

- ◆ The Generic Flow Control (GFC) is a four-bit field that contains information relating to the way traffic flows across the interface. The GFC field can be used to indicate that an interface should slow down on transmissions. ATM provides no mechanisms for buffering cells, so it uses the GFC field to control traffic.
- ◆ The Virtual Path Identifier (VPI) is either eight bits (for user-network interface links) or twelve bits (for network to network interface links), and identifies the cell's path—its source and destination.

♦ The Virtual Channel Identifier (VCI) is 8 bits and when taken together with the VPI, it is used to route the cell.

♦ Payload Type (PT) is a three-bit field that identifies what kind of data is being carried in the cell. This is useful for distinguishing data that may require special handling or that may be necessary for maintaining the network.

♦ Cell Loss Priority (CLP) is a single-bit flag that indicates whether the cell can be discarded or additional network resources must be allocated to guarantee delivery of the cell.

♦ Header Error Control (HEC) is essentially an eight-bit data integrity field that is used by the physical layer to verify that the cell has not been damaged in transit.

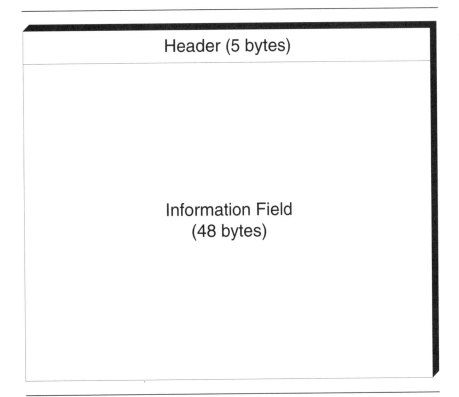

Figure 6–5: ATM header structures.

ATM and IP

Things like address resolution and delivery of IP multicast packets in ATM networks depends on building some kind of mechanism to emulate a LAN. One approach is the LAN Emulation (LANE) method; another is Classical IP over ATM. With LANE, one or more LAN emulation servers act as the LAN for all member nodes. These nodes send their broadcast or multicast messages, or other transmissions intended for more than one destination, to these servers. With Classical IP over ATM (see RFC 2225 for more details), special servers are set up to act on behalf of the network for IP-related function.

IP over ATM faces another problem: that of encapsulation. Normally, IP headers are encapsulated in each link layer PDU. However, with only 48 bytes available in an ATM cell, IP headers (which we'll discuss at great length in Chapter 7) can pose a problem. IP headers are at least 20 bytes long, which means a lot of extra processing and a big cut in bandwidth available. Unlike most other link layer protocols, ATM does not unwrap each cell for routing, but rather simply switches each cell through to its destination. The virtual circuits defined in the cell's header are enough to get the data to its destination, and once there the encapsulated IP datagram is reconstructed.

Dialup IP

Originally, the idea of internetworking required connections between networks, and connections between hosts were of much less importance. Connecting networks together across organizational borders, preferably with several links for each organizational network, ensured that each organization would be able to both receive the benefits of connectivity and provide connectivity services to other organizations. Individuals who were not physically located at a connected organization dialed into a connected host using a modem and a terminal from their homes or remote sites.

This arrangement was satisfactory, for the most part, as long as remote users had a terminal and a larger host (minicomputer or mainframe) to which they could connect. They used no more network resources than they might have had they been working on site.

Two trends made this model obsolete: the rise of personal computing and the rise of TCP/IP internetworking through the commercialization of the Internet. As users moved away from large computer command-line interfaces and "unfriendly" user interfaces to personal computers, they became less likely to have an account on a multiuser system (or even to want one). Furthermore, actual host or network connections to the Internet were expected to give (through routing services) as much as they got (through connectivity), but as the Internet grew it became increasingly useful for single-user hosts (like home and satellite office computers) to connect as fully privileged Internet hosts.

The response has been implementation of protocols intended to connect two hosts over a direct link, most often a telephone connection. Originally patched together as a stopgap measure, the Serial Line IP (SLIP) protocol came into use during the mid-1980s. SLIP simply defined a method for using the Internet Protocol over a serial phone line. Compressed SLIP (CSLIP), the form now most commonly implemented, was specified in 1990 and improves SLIP performance. However, the Point-to-Point Protocol defined in 1992 addresses most of SLIP's shortcomings and now is the preferred method for dialup access to TCP/IP networks.

This section describes SLIP first, to provide a historical reference point, followed by a discussion of PPP. In addition to the obvious value of understanding the two successive solutions to the same problem, this discussion should also clarify how Internet standards are built over time. Part of the reason for SLIP's success over the years is that it did the job well enough to make the task of improving it less important.

How SLIP Works

The remote host makes a connection to a SLIP server, a system directly connected to the internetwork that accepts telephone calls from off-site. That server behaves like a router for TCP/IP traffic, passing traffic between the remote hosts and the internetwork. Remote users are either assigned their own IP addresses or they may request an available IP address from the SLIP server, but in either case it must be done explicitly—the protocol does not support any type of "discovery" for IP addresses of either the remote host or the SLIP gateway. The dial-in host must know the IP address of the system being dialed, and it must also know its own IP address.

The remote host usually initiates the link, usually through simple dialing software, to the remote network. Once the connection is made with the remote network, the dial-up program is no longer necessary (as long as the serial link remains active) and the rest of the TCP/IP network stack can be loaded on the SLIP host. The SLIP interface does minimal encapsulation of IP datagrams, as explained in the next section.

Once connected, the properly configured off-site SLIP host sends all network traffic to the remote network over the serial interface. Network traffic is exchanged over the telephone link, so performance is an issue for bandwidth-intensive applications: applications with lots of graphics, file sharing, or hypermedia. Character-based applications like terminal sessions often perform almost as well as when connected directly to a LAN.

SLIP Data Formats

SLIP adds little to the standard IP datagram before sending it off to the other end of the link. There are two special characters, as shown in Table 6–2.

As shown in Figure 6–6, SLIP encapsulation starts out simply with an END character, to ensure that any previous line noise is not interpreted as a datagram. If the END character is encountered within the datagram as data (not as a SLIP END indicator), SLIP converts the c0 into a two-character sequence: db dc (in hexadecimal). Likewise, if the ESC character appears within the datagram,

Character	Function	Decimal	Hex
END	Bounds each IP datagram sent over SLIP link	192	c0
SLIP ESC	To avoid interpreting data being transmitted over the SLIP link as SLIP control characters	219	db

Table 6–2: SLIP adds minimally to the IP datagram before sending it on along the serial connection.

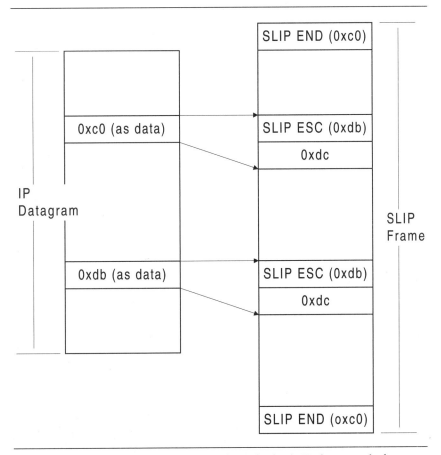

Figure 6–6: SLIP encapsulation adds little to the basic IP datagram before sending it across the serial link.

it is replaced with another two-character sequence: db dd (hexa-decimal). The datagram ends with the END character.

Compressed SLIP

As we will see, there can be a fair amount of overhead to a TCP/IP connection, specifically in the headers required for IP and TCP connections. TCP/IP headers can use 40 bytes (or more)—20 for IP and 20 for TCP—even though the datagram payload is consider-ably less. For example, during an interactive session where the user enters short commands or single keystrokes, the data portion of the datagram can be as little as a single byte.

With standard SLIP, the amount of time required to transmit this extra baggage can visibly slow the connection, especially on slow-er links. This was particularly problematic before the advent of fast modems. For instance, on a 2400 bps link, it can take over one tenth of a second; when characters are being echoed directly to the remote host this becomes a painfully slow process. Even on faster links, this can still present a problem.

Compressed SLIP (CSLIP) addresses this problem by compressing the TCP/IP headers to as few as three to five bytes. Also called *Van Jacobson compression,* after the author of the specification, CSLIP takes advantage of the fact that the content of the headers doesn't vary too much after the initial connection is made. As a result, it is possible to keep track of up to 16 TCP sessions under CSLIP, while minimizing the overhead needed to properly route those sessions.

SLIP Drawbacks

SLIP was originally an interim solution to the remote host internet-work connection problem rather than an actual proposed standard. It supports only IP network traffic (there is no accommodation for other network types, unlike Ethernet and most other network media). It doesn't include any type of error correction, compression, or even checksums, and depends on higher layers for error detection and handling, and on hardware (through the modem) for compression.

In large part to address these issues, the Point-to-Point Protocol was developed by the early 1990s. SLIP is still widely supported, but PPP offers significant improvements, and as it continues to gain in acceptance and popularity it will eventually supplant SLIP as the protocol of choice for serial connections.

Point-to-Point Protocol

PPP addresses SLIP's deficiencies. It uses a frame format that includes a protocol field, so the remote host can connect to the network and use IP (or any other supported) network protocols. It includes a protocol to control the actual link, and it can negotiate connection parameters as well as compression. And it includes a CRC to protect against transmission errors.

PPP defines a network frame with a five-byte header and a three-byte trailer. As shown in Figure 6–7, the PPP frame starts and ends with the control byte, *7e* hex (126 decimal). The address (*ff* hex) and control (03 hex) bytes are constant, and many implementations drop these bytes upon negotiation.

The two-byte protocol field indicates the contents of the PPP frame. This field may indicate whether the data portion of the frame contains an IP or an IPX datagram or it may indicate that the frame is carrying information relating to the link itself.

PPP uses the Link Control Protocol (LCP) to control the data link layer connection: starting and ending the actual serial connection and negotiating line parameters are done through this protocol.

Likewise, various sets of protocols are defined for controlling the network layer. Called **Network Control Protocols** (NCPs) these are · defined for different network protocols, including NetWare/IPX, DECnet, AppleTalk, and others. For example, header compression options (like Van Jacobson compression) may be negotiated through these protocols.

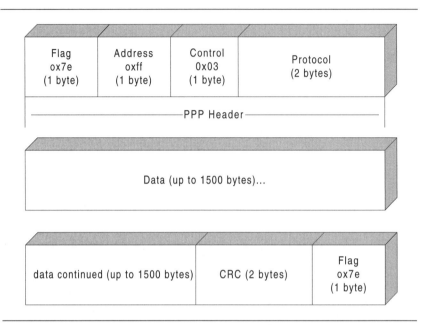

Figure 6–7: PPP network frame format.

The Loopback Interface

The Class A network address 127.0.0.0 (noted earlier) is reserved for use as a "loopback" interface. Any host address on this network is interpreted to mean "this" host—most often, the loopback address 127.0.0.1 is used. The host name associated with this address is "localhost" and the entry:

```
localhost 127.0.0.1
```

should appear in the hosts file on just about every system. The loopback driver operates at the link layer of the protocol stack. When a host sends to its loopback address, the loopback driver behaves as if it were a network driver that has received network traffic and sends that data up to the host as if it were received from the network.

Every host uses the loopback interface to send network traffic to itself, most particularly when the host broadcasts network traffic. Broadcasts, by definition, are intended for all the hosts on a given network or wire, and since network interfaces are designed *not* to read data on the network that has originated from an interface, the loopback driver checks for broadcasts from the local host. When it detects one, it passes it back to the local host. Figure 6–8 demonstrates how the loopback driver operates with the network hardware driver.

The loopback interface is useful for testing: when network traffic is directed at the loopback address, it is not sent out onto the network medium. Instead, it is passed down through the protocol stack, interpreted by the loopback driver as if it were received over the

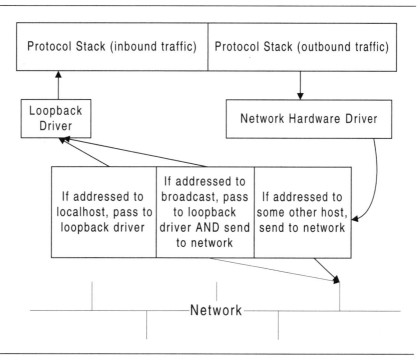

Figure 6–8: Network traffic destined for the sending host, which includes broadcasts as well as data sent directly to the localhost, flow back to the host through the loopback driver.

network, and passed back up to the higher protocols. As a result, network engineers use it to check that network software has been installed properly.

When there are connectivity problems with a workstation, attempting to send a ping (see Chapter 8) to localhost can be useful in determining whether the TCP/IP software has been installed correctly. If the workstation responds correctly to the ping it means that the software has probably been installed correctly and the problem is either in the software configuration or with the actual network interface (improperly installed or configured network card).

Chapter Summary and References

In this chapter we introduced four important data link layer media: Ethernet, ATM, serial (modem) and other point-to-point connections, and the loopback interface. We explained how these network media work, and how IP fits in.

Some useful RFCs to read in conjunction with this chapter include those listed in Table 6–3.

RFC	Title	Description
894	Standard for the Transmission of IP Datagrams over Ethernet Networks	A very brief but useful document, explaining how IP and Ethernet work together.
1661	The Point-to-Point Protocol (PPP)	Describes the current preferred method of doing point-to-point IP networking.
2225	Classical IP and ARP over ATM	Good documentation of ATM and IP issues and solutions.
2226	IP Broadcast over ATM Networks	Explains how IP broadcasts can be emulated over ATM networks.
1055	Nonstandard for Transmission of IP Datagrams over Serial Lines: SLIP	Explains where SLIP came from and how it works.

Table 6–3: Useful RFCs for Chapter 6.

7

The Internet Protocol

When data moves across a single physical network, from one network interface to another, that movement is managed through the data link layer. The last chapter discussed how different network media protocols get chunks of data from one point to another. The content of these chunks is unimportant at the data link layer, but very important at the network layer—which is where the Internet Protocol operates.

The contents of an Ethernet frame or an ATM cell become very important when they are destined for a node that is not directly connected to the source node's network. Once the network attempts to move data across network boundaries it is the job of the network layer to manage the movement of that data.

When a host receives a network frame it must demultiplex (or unwrap headers from) the frame. In doing so, the host determines whether or not to pass the contents of the frame up its protocol stack.

If the contents of the frame are intended for the receiving node, then the frame is unwrapped and the payload passed up the protocol stack. If the contents of the frame are intended for some other node, then the receiving node repackages and forwards the payload to its intended destination—if the receiving node is a router.

The Internet Protocol (IP) defines the rules for packaging network traffic into IP datagrams, and it defines the rules for moving these datagrams across network boundaries.

IP uses various tools to insure that messages arrive at their destination: datagrams can be fragmented, or broken up into small enough pieces to fit on intervening networks; there are mechanisms for making datagrams disappear if they haven't been delivered to their destinations after a certain amount of time; there are mechanisms for securing access and authenticating IP datagrams to prevent tampering or snooping.

Despite all these functions, IP service is connectionless and unreliable. Each datagram is sent across the internetwork independent of every other datagram and with no guarantee that it will be delivered in any particular order and no guarantee that it will be delivered at all.

The data link layer may provide minimal error detection mechanisms (for example Ethernet's Cyclic Redundancy Check), but delivery and reliability guarantees are largely absent from the lower network layers and have traditionally been left to the transport and application layers. Protocol designers like to put reliability and security functions at higher rather than lower levels. Putting those services at the data link layer, for example, would require every single node to be able to process them. Leaving security and reliability to the higher levels means they can be implemented as end-to-end services that need to be processed only by the originating node and the destination node. Performance at the lower layers will not be affected.

This chapter examines the IP datagram format and the mechanisms used to ensure that datagrams are routed properly across internetworks. These mechanisms include direct routing through Address Resolution Protocol (ARP) and Reverse Address Resolution Protocol (RARP), and routing tables on IP routers. We will also discuss how broadcasts and multicasts are routed.

IP Datagram Structure

As explained in the previous chapter, network frames consist of headers containing addresses and some identifying information about the frame—and a payload of data. At the internet layer IP datagrams also consist of headers and data, but the headers now contain much more detailed and extensive information. Figure 7–1 shows how the IP header fields describe routing information for the datagram.

IP headers are all at least 20 bytes long. All IP headers are organized into four-byte words, for ease of processing (nodes and routers process four bytes at a time).

The fields in the first word identify the datagram as far as version of IP, header length, how the datagram is to be handled (Type of Service) and datagram length. The next word includes information about fragmentation: a unique ID number for the datagram, flags for fragmentation control, and the fragment offset. The third word includes time to live, the originating transport protocol of the content being carried, and a checksum for the header itself. The fourth and fifth words are the source and destination IP addresses, and an optional options field can be added when IP options are needed.

IP Datagram Fields

By looking at the meanings of the different IP datagram header fields, it is possible to get a good idea of how datagrams are created and routed through internetworks.

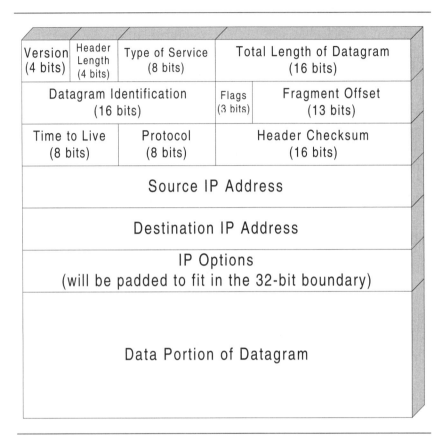

Version (4 bits)	Header Length (4 bits)	Type of Service (8 bits)	Total Length of Datagram (16 bits)	
Datagram Identification (16 bits)			Flags (3 bits)	Fragment Offset (13 bits)
Time to Live (8 bits)		Protocol (8 bits)	Header Checksum (16 bits)	
Source IP Address				
Destination IP Address				
IP Options (will be padded to fit in the 32-bit boundary)				
Data Portion of Datagram				

Figure 7–1: IP datagram headers include at least five four-byte words and may include separate additional options relating to routing options.

Version: This four-bit field indicates the version of IP being used. The current version of IP is v4, although the latest version, IPv6, has been specified and has been deployed experimentally for some time. IPv6 will become increasingly important as more products are rolled out and more organizations upgrade. IPv6 is discussed in Chapter 14. For a more complete treatment, see *IPv6 Clearly Explained*, Morgan Kaufmann 1999.

Header Length: This four-bit field indicates the length of the header. The maximum value is 15 ($2^4 - 1$). The value of this field specifies the length of the header in four-byte words. Thus, the maximum length of an IP header is 60 bytes (15 four-byte words). Since all IP headers are at least 20 bytes (5 four-byte words) long, this allows as many as 40 bytes for IP options.

Type of Service: This field is eight bits long but only four bits are used to make Type of Service requests of IP routers. Type of Service (ToS) options for IP allow routers to handle IP datagrams differently depending on what option is selected. For example, the ToS bits specify how the datagram is to be processed: to minimize delay, minimize cost, maximize throughput, or maximixe reliability. Since there may often be no choice as to the route taken, these are considered suggestions. The bits are set automatically to appropriate values by the higher level application protocol (for instance, remote network sessions request minimized delay, and file transfers request maximized throughput).

Datagram Length: This value represents the entire datagram length, including the header, in units of single bytes. At 16 bits, this limits IP datagrams to a maximum size of 65,535 bytes long ($2^{16}-1$). Since there is no "end of datagram" character or sequence, network hosts use value to figure out when the datagram ends and other network data begins.

Datagram Identification: This is a unique 16-bit identifier assigned to a datagram by the originating host. At the source, there is a one-to-one relation between datagrams and datagram identifiers; however, as the datagrams pass through an internetwork, they may become fragmented. This can happen when datagrams cross network boundaries between higher speed networks (like 100 Mbps Ethernets) and slower networks (like serial links). When datagrams are split, the identification field contains the same identifier for all of the resulting datagrams. This helps the host at the receiving end to reassemble the orginal datagram.

Flags: The first of the three flag bits is unused; the other two are used to control the way the datagram is fragmented. The Don't Fragment (DF) bit, when set to 1, means that the datagram must not be fragmented. If the datagram has to be fragmented in order to be routed (it must be forwarded to a network that cannot handle the datagram without breaking it up into smaller pieces), the router will throw it away and send an error message back to the originating host. When the More Fragments (MF) bit is set to 1, it means the datagram is one of two or more fragments, but not the last of the fragments. If the MF bit is set to 0, it means there are no more fragments (or that the datagram was not fragmented). Receiving hosts use the More Fragments flag and the fragment offset to reassemble fragmented datagrams.

Fragment Offset: This number tells the receiving host how many units from the start of the original datagram the current datagram is. This value represents units of eight bytes; with 13 bits, the maximum value is $2^{13} - 1$, or 8191. Thus, the furthest from the start of the original datagram that a fragment can begin is 65,528 bytes. For example, let's say that a datagram is 64,000 bytes long, and is being divided into eight fragments of 8,000 bytes each. The fragment offset value for the first fragment datagram will be 0 because the fragment begins at the start of the original datagram. The fragment offset for the second fragment will be 1,000 because the second fragment starts after the first 8,000 bytes of the original datagram.

Time to Live: This eight-bit field indicates how long the datagram should be allowed to exist after entering the internetwork, measured in seconds (maximum TTL is 255). Time to live was originally intended to be a measure of the number of seconds a datagram was to be allowed to exist in transit across an internetwork. The intent was for each router to calculate how long it took to process each datagram, and then decrement the TTL by that number of seconds. In practice, however, datagrams traverse routers in less than a second, so router vendors implemented this as a simple decrement. As a datagram is forwarded, its TTL is decremented by one. This means that in practice TTL actually represents the maximum number of hops that a datagram can make before being discarded, and IPv6 formalizes this by discarding the TTL entirely and replacing it with a hop count—see Chapter 14 for a more detailed account.

Protocol: This field identifies the protocol of the next higher layer data being carried in the datagram. This field might indicate that the payload data is a TCP segment or a UDP datagram.

Header Checksum: This field contains a checksum on the IP header only. The header is treated like a series of 16-bit binary numbers with the checksum field itself set to zero. These values are added together and then ones-complemented. This ensures that the datagram header is not corrupted, but as noted earlier, does not add any transmission reliability or error detection to the Internet Protocol itself.

Source/Destination: These are the actual 32-bit (four byte) IP addresses of the originating host and the destination host.

Datagram Fragmentation

One of the most controversial features of IP is its fragmentation feature. Fragmentation is a messy feature: it takes up a lot of the IP header real estate, it is troublesome to implement, and it puts a large computational burden on nodes and routers. The datagram ID, fragmentation flags, and fragment offset fields together account for 20 percent of the basic IP header.

However, it was decided to allow fragmentation because the alternatives were less appealing. One option was to put an upper limit on the size of IP datagrams that was lower than the smallest allowed PDU on any network medium using IP. This would put an unreasonable limit on PDU size for media that can handle very large chunks of data efficiently. Some proposals would limit the size of IP datagrams to no larger than 1,500 bytes (the maximum size for Ethernet frames) or to 576 bytes (the maximum transmission unit for the X.25 wide area network protocol).

Another alternative would be to put a lower limit on the size of PDU of any network medium using IP. Rather than limiting IP packets to some maximum size, this option would require that all network media support some minimum PDU size determined by the IETF. Mandating that a network medium could carry IP traffic only if it can handle datagrams that are at least 1,500 bytes long would unnecessarily restrict the types of media capable of carrying IP. Since one of the most basic tenets of IP networking is that it is a universally interoperable protocol, this option is also not acceptable.

A datagram can be fragmented any time it is forwarded across different types of network media. For example, an IP datagram that is 1,492 bytes (just long enough to fit inside an Ethernet frame) would have to be fragmented if it passed across an X.25 network, which can handle only datagrams as large as 576 bytes.

The originating host generates datagrams based on its own MTU. IP has an inherent maximum datagram size of 65,535 bytes since the IP header field for datagram length is 16 bits long, but most common network media have much smaller limits on network frame sizes, as discussed in the previous chapter. When there are several different networks across which network traffic passes, there will be a **path MTU**. This is the largest size unit that can pass unfragmented across all the intervening networks in a datagram's route; in other words, the smallest MTU of any of those networks.

Figure 7–2 shows an internetwork consisting of an FDDI network (Network A), an Ethernet (Network B), and a 16 Mbps IBM token ring network (Network C). Traffic staying entirely on Network C could maintain an MTU of 17,756 bytes because the high-speed token ring network allows frames to carry that much data. However, traffic going from Network C to Network B would be limited to the much smaller Ethernet MTU of 1,500 bytes. Each of the token ring frames (assuming they used that MTU) would be broken into a dozen or so smaller Ethernet frames as they are processed by the router between the two networks.

Traffic moving from Network C to Network A would also have a Path MTU of 1,500 bytes, even though the FDDI network can sustain an MTU of 4,352 bytes—since datagrams would have to traverse the Ethernet before arriving at the FDDI network, they would already be fragmented.

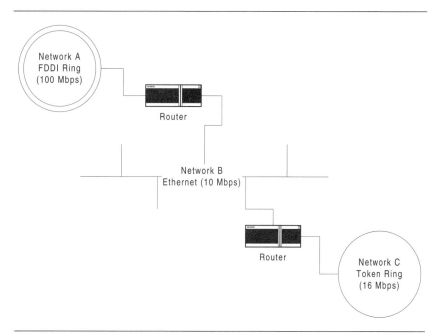

Figure 7–2: An internetwork with different MTUs for each local network will result in different path MTUs for internetwork traffic depending on where it originates and which network it must pass through to arrive at its destination.

Intermediate routers do not bother reassembling fragmented datagrams. Since each datagram is routed independently over the internetwork, not all intermediate routers could be certain of processing all fragments of any particular datagram. And since datagram fragments may be delivered out of order with considerable delays between fragments, reassembling datagrams at every intermediate router would hurt overall performance.

A router fragments a datagram only if it is too large for the next-hop network. Most of the original datagram's header fields are simply copied, though the router modifies the fragmentation-related fields. The datagram length is recomputed for the datagram fragment, though the datagram identifier remains the same. The router sets the MF bit to 1 for all the fragments except the last one, and computes the fragment offset value for each fragment.

The router decrements the TTL counter and recalculates the header checskum for each fragment header, but other fields remain the same and each fragment is forwarded onto the next leg of its route.

It is possible for datagrams to be fragmented more than once: moving from a high-speed network to a medium-speed network might call for one level of fragmentation, and moving to a slower network would call for another round of fragmentation. In such a case, the destination node first would have to reconstruct the twice-fragmented fragments, then take those fragments and reconstruct the original IP datagram.

IP Options

IP options, as the name implies, are strictly optional. Implementers and applications developers tend not to use IPv4 options. Routers tend to be optimized for the general case of IP datagrams, which means nonoptioned packets. Packets with options must get special treatment, which means that routers often shunt such packets off until enough processing resources are free to handle the IP options properly. Using options with IPv4 often means that performance will suffer. IP options are commonly used for application debugging and testing.

IP options were intended to be the way the protocol handled certain special functions. The original specifications left these options undefined, but eventually options for things like security as well as certain routing functions were added. The record route option causes every router that handles the optioned packet to record its address. The timestamp option causes each router to record its own address as well as the time it handles the optioned packet. There are two source routing options available: Loose source routing specifies a list of routers through which the packet must pass on its way to the packet's destination. Strict source routing specifies a list of routers through which the packet must pass—and requires that no other routers be used by that packet on its way to the packet's destination.

Options cause problems because they are special cases. Most IP datagrams have no options, and vendors optimize their routers to handle standard IP datagrams. The IP header without options is always 20 bytes long and is easy to process when the router design is optimized to process 20-byte headers. Network managers prefer faster routers and because most traffic does not use IP options the routers tend to handle those packets as exceptions, shunting them off to the side to be handled when it is convenient—and when it won't affect the router's overall performance.

Despite the benefits of using IPv4 options, the cost in terms of performance has been enough to keep them from being used very often.

When used, IP options are strung together without any delimiting characters, and if they do not end on a word boundary (number of bytes is not evenly divisible by four) padding characters are added. As noted in the description of the header length field, the options field cannot contain more than 40 bytes of options and options data.

IP Routing Issues

Understanding IP routing means understanding how the IP addressing scheme and the IP datagram header fields work. An IP node originates a datagram and creates an IP header for that datagram using its own address as the source and the IP address of the destination host as the destination. When this datagram is passed down the network protocol stack to the link layer, the network software must figure out where to actually send the data on the local network interface. The datagram must be sent to a host connected to the same network that the sending host is connected to, even if the destination is on a different network.

When the sending and destination hosts are on the same network, IP routing is done directly by the source node. The source node simply encapsulates the IP datagram encapsulated in a network frame and sends it directly to the destination host. All IP routing ultimately involves the actual delivery of IP datagrams between two machines (two hosts or a host and a router) on the same network. This is called **direct routing**.

Direct routing happens when the source node checks the destination address and determines that it is on the same IP network, the same subnet, and the same physical network. In that case, the host uses the Address Resolution Protocol (ARP) to send a broadcast to the local network and map the IP address to a link layer (for example, Ethernet) address. The node then encapsulates the datagram into a link layer frame and sends it directly to the datagram's destination. However, if the destination address is on a different subnet or different IP network entirely, the sender must figure out where to send the datagram so it will be forwarded to the right network.

All networked systems that do IP routing maintain routing tables to point IP traffic sent from each host in the appropriate direction. Although a router is usually a special-purpose computer with network connections on two or more networks, it can also behave as a general-purpose host. Likewise, a multihomed host (which is simply a host with connections on two or more networks) can be configured to act as a router; however, a host behaves differently than a router would when dealing with network traffic not directly addressed to it.

When a datagram must be forwarded through an intermediary (a router), another type of routing is being used. **Indirect routing** relies on routers to forward datagrams from one network to another so that they eventually reach their destinations. Nodes keep a list of nodes and routers that are local to them. Usually at least one or two routers on each subnet are available to forward datagrams as **default routers**. A router is a default router if a node uses it as a default router—any router can be a default router, but only if some other node is using it as such.

The sending host encapsulates the IP datagram (addressed to its final destination and from the original sender) into a link layer frame that goes directly to the default router, which then opens up that frame and examines the IP datagram header. It processes the header fields, decrementing the time-to-live field and recalculating the header checksum.

The router looks at the datagram's destination address to determine whether it is a local address on any network to which the router is directly connected. If the destination address is on a local network, the router then uses ARP to determine the destination's link layer address and then delivers the datagram encapsulated in a link layer frame. If the destination address is not local to any network to which the router is connected, then the router will continue to forward that datagram along to another router. This continues until the datagram reaches its destination network.

Each router updates the time-to-live value as well as the header checksum; intermediate routers also modify values for the datagram ID and fragment offsets if it is necessary to fragment a datagram between the sender and the recipient.

Routers must exchange information to be able to figure out where to send datagrams. Several protocols specific to or supporting routing will be discussed in the next chapter, including the Internet Control Message Protocol (ICMP), Exterior Gateway Protocol (EGP), Routing Information Protocol (RIP), Open Shortest Path First (OSPF), Classless Inter-Domain Routing (CIDR), and Border Gateway Protocol (BGP).

Direct Routing

You can do direct routing only if you can correlate data link layer network addresses with Internet layer IP addresses. Some network media permit network engineers to assign link layer addresses to networked workstations that relate directly to the workstation's IP address, simplifying direct routing—the network drivers are able to derive a destination network address based on the IP destination address.

However, Ethernet/IEEE (and many other) networks use MAC addresses encoded in the network interface hardware. At 48 bits, Ethernet MAC addresses can hardly be collapsed into a 32-bit IP address, even if network engineers were able to assign specific hardware addresses in these networks.

The Address Resolution Protocol (ARP) offers a different approach to direct routing on Ethernet and other networks with hardware addresses. When a host determines that a datagram is destined for a host on the same network, it broadcasts an ARP request to all hosts on the network, asking for the MAC address of the destination host. We will discuss ARP and its partner the Reverse Address Resolution Protocol (RARP) later.

Indirect Routing

Any datagram sent to a node on a different network than the sending node must be routed indirectly at least once. The source node cannot send the datagram directly to the destination node because it is not on the same network. The source node must send the datagram to a router, which has to forward the datagram to another network. The datagram may need to be forwarded more than once, passing through many different routers before it arrives at the network to which the destination node is connected.

How do the routers know where to forward the datagram? Using a "universal map" to keep track of every node would be overwhelmingly difficult. Nodes are moved, added, and removed from networks constantly. Imagine trying to keep track of the many millions of nodes around the world connected to the Internet. Maintaining a central map would reduce routing efficiency: determining a proper route in that case would be very computationally intensive. Even though host IP addresses imply the host's network address, storing and accessing network addresses and routes would be only slightly less difficult.

Usually, intranets link local networks to one another through local routers, and the local networks link to the Internet through a sin-

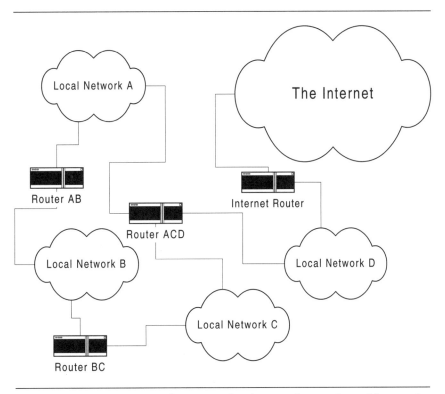

Figure 7–3: Most internetworks connect local networks together with several different routers, but with only one route to the Internet.

gle main Internet router. Figure 7–3 shows the typical layout. IP routing relies on different routing protocols to handle different configurations as well as to insure that routers are notified of router connectivity changes, as we will discuss in Chapter 8.

Source Routing

Source routing provides an alternative to relying on the intranet/Internet routing infrastructure to deliver datagrams to their destinations. Implemented as an option within the IP header, with source routing the originating host specifies the route IP datagrams are to take. Unlike other routing methods, source routing requires that the sender have knowledge of the internetwork archi-tecture; otherwise, it couldn't specify a correct route to the desti-nation host. Source routing is useful for testing different routes between two hosts.

Two types of source routing are defined: strict source routing and loose source routing. When strict source routing is used it means that the datagram can be routed through the specified routers only— no routers other than those listed in the options header are allowed. Loose source routing requires that all the routers specified in the list must be traversed, but other routers may be used if necessary.

Source routing is invoked by the originating host adding an option to the IP header. The option includes a code to indicate whether strict or loose source routing is to be used, a length field indicating how long the options field is, and a pointer field that points to the currently relevant address in the options field. Of course, the options header also includes a list of IP addresses of routers spec-ified for the route.

Routers, Hosts, and Routing Tables

A host is any computer connected to an internetwork that can send and receive network traffic to and from any other system connect-ed to the internetwork. A multihomed host is simply a host with two or more network connections within the internetwork. The multihomed host could be a system with connections to two or more different Ethernet networks, a connection to an Ethernet and a PPP link to another network, or any other combination of links.

A host listens for network traffic addressed to it on its network interface. Network frames addressed to the host are demulti-plexed, and if the destination IP address of the enclosed datagram does not match the IP address for its network interface, the data-gram is discarded.

A multihomed host listens for network traffic addressed to it on all of its network interfaces. Network frames addressed to the host are demultiplexed and if the destination IP address of the enclosed datagram does not match the IP address for the network address on which it was received, the datagram is discarded.

A router is a special-purpose multihomed host that forwards datagrams. Routers act as normal hosts when processing datagrams addressed to them. But instead of discarding datagrams that are not specifically addressed to it, the router examines the IP addresses of those datagrams and forwards the datagram. If the destination is a node on a network to which the router is directly connected, the router will resend the datagram directly to its destination. If the destination is not on a directly connected network, the router uses some routing protocol to figure out where to send the datagram so that it can be delivered by some other router.

Whether a system is a host or a router, it uses a special process to make decisions about where and how to send IP traffic. The first step for any system is to examine the IP address of the destination host and compare it to its own network IP address. If the destination and source IP addresses are on the same network, then the datagram can be routed directly to the destination host.

If the destination is not on the same local network, then the routing table is consulted. The routing table is a list of destinations that IP software maintains on each host and router. Individual host addresses (including the loopback address) are listed here. A specific router can be linked with a particular node or network address, in which case any datagrams intended for that node or network will be sent to the listed router for forwarding. The routing table also holds an entry for a default router. Datagrams destined off the local network and whose addresses are not listed elsewhere are sent to the default router for proper forwarding.

Looking at Figure 7–3 again, a host attached to Network D would list itself (loopback) and a default router, Router ACD, for all traffic destined off Network D.

Router BC is able to directly route IP datagrams from Network B to Network C and vice versa, but it would still have a more complicated routing table, listing

♦ Router ACD for traffic destined for Network D
♦ Router AB for traffic destined for Network A
♦ Router ACD for all traffic outside the local internetwork (Networks A, B, C, D)

The result is that routers in general need to be aware of only neighboring networks for routing purposes (the local intranet), and anything that is "far away" (the Internet, for example) is usually routed through a default gateway that attaches the local intranet to the rest of the world.

Receiving IP Datagrams

Hosts and routers both receive datagrams, but only routers are permitted to forward datagrams to other systems. If a host receives a network frame addressed to it, but containing an IP datagram addressed to some other host, the host ignores that datagram. However, a router must determine the correct route for that datagram, re-encapsulate it for its next-hop destination network, and retransmit it.

Hosts don't have to do anything about incorrectly addressed frames, just ignore them. If hosts were obliged to respond somehow to such bad frames, the resulting traffic could adversely affect network performance. Routers, on the other hand, use a special protocol specifically for exchanging information about routing issues like delivery failures, timeouts, and unexpected circumstances like gateway failures: it's called the Internet Control Message Protocol (ICMP) and will be discussed in Chapter 8.

Network Address Translation

There are times when it is preferable for packets not to be forwarded directly from inside an internetwork. Network address translation (NAT) is an approach used for those instances. There are two common reasons for using NAT: for security, and for mapping a large network on a small IP address space.

NAT works by allocating three sets of IP addresses for use by any-one who wants to use them, as long as those networks are never directly connected to the Internet. The address ranges are

```
10.0.0.0          10.255.255.255
172.16.0.0        172.31.255.255
192.168.0.0       192.168.255.255
```

IP routers are not supposed to forward datagrams addressed in these ranges outside the local internetwork. If a backbone router receives a datagram bound for one of these addresses, it is sup-posed to drop it. However, these addresses can be used within an organizational internetwork.

Allowing outsiders access to information about a network's host names and IP addresses can expose that network to security risks. Some network administrators prefer to put their entire network behind a network address translator, which accepts datagrams from outside the internetwork and translates them to the NAT addresses used by the hosts inside the private network.

Perhaps more common is the use of NATs to preserve IP address space. As the IP address space is depleted, more and more organi-zations have been denied Class B or even Class C networks. One solution is to use the private network space allocation to set up a private network with a Class A, B, or C network address. Routers within the private network can route packets within the network, and packets destined for the global Internet are passed through a network address translator that acts on behalf of the internal sys-tems when interacting with Internet hosts.

Direct Routing: ARP and RARP

If you could make IP addresses and network addresses match, linking an IP adress to a network address becomes trivial. Unfortunately, this is not feasible for the most common network media. MAC addresses are six bytes long, and cannot be mapped directly onto four-byte IP addresses. You could try padding the IP addresses and inserting them into the MAC address, but MAC addresses are hard-coded into network interface cards.

You could also try copying all the network addresses of hosts on the local Ethernet into a file and associating them with the hosts' IP addresses. However, this approach is flawed. Although the IP addresses are associated with specific hosts, the network addresses are bound to the network interface cards. When a card fails or a new card is installed, that network/IP address list becomes useless. A more dynamic approach is required.

When a host determines that an IP datagram is destined for a node on the local network, it uses the Address Resolution Protocol (ARP) to get that address. Reverse Address Resolution Protocol (RARP) takes a similar approach to allow hosts to find out their own IP address on the basis of their network address.

ARP is simple. The host that wishes to send the IP datagram broadcasts an ARP request to the local network. The request is for the system assigned to the specified IP address to respond with its local network address. All the systems on the network process the request, but only the host with the specified IP address responds. The system originating the ARP request then uses the network address supplied to address the local network frames.

A few elaborations make ARP less unwieldy than it appears at first glance. The first is the ARP cache: each system maintains a list of network address and IP address pairings. The next is that ARP requests include the network address/IP address of the requesting system—if host A needs a network address to direct traffic to host B, chances are good that host B will soon be sending some kind of traffic to host A. Finally, even though only the requesting and responding hosts generate any traffic on the local network, all the hosts on that network listen in and update their own ARP caches with the network address/IP address pairs being exchanged.

ARP Format

Most often, ARP is used to correlate six-byte link layer addresses with four-byte network layer addresses, but ARP can be used to link any size network addresses with any size link layer addresses. ARP operates at the data link layer, so ARP messages are carried in network frames rather than in IP datagrams. Figure 7–4 shows a typical Ethernet ARP frame. To conform with the standard Ethernet frame, the Ethernet destination will be either all ones or the Ethernet broadcast address. Every host on the network will receive the frame. The Ethernet source address is the originating host's Ethernet address, and the Ethernet frame protocol type value is 0x0806, indicating the frame carries an ARP message.

The first two fields within the Ethernet frame indicate the kind of network hardware address (Ethernet) that must be located to match the address of the network protocol type (IP). The next two fields, hardware length and protocol length, indicate in bytes how long the hardware and protocol addresses are. These four fields may vary for different network and protocol types, but for IP over Ethernet they specify that the ARP packet will be 28 bytes long: 8 bytes for the header fields, 10 bytes for the originating host's IP address (4 bytes) and Ethernet address (6 bytes), and 10 bytes for the target host's IP address and Ethernet address (which the originating host leaves blank when it sends the ARP request).

Finally, the operation field indicates the function the ARP packet is fulfilling. An ARP request has the value of 1 here, and an ARP reply has the value 2. RARP requests are indicated by the value 3, and RARP replies by the value 4. The requests have all the fields filled in except for the address being sought: the network address of the host with the specified IP address, for ARP requests, or the IP address of the host with the specified network address, for RARP requests.

ARP requests and ARP replies look pretty much the same, except that the operation field is different and the requested address field will have the requested address in it.

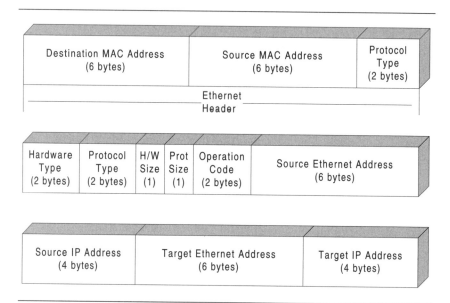

Figure 7–4: An ARP packet, as encapsulated in an Ethernet frame, will be 28 bytes long, with 14 bytes of Ethernet header.

ARP Cache

ARPs are broadcasts, and broadcasts are a nuisance to almost all hosts that receive them. We try to keep broadcasts to a minimum because they can really cut into network performance. So, to keep the number of broadcast ARP requests to a minimum, hosts store the addresses they receive from ARP replies in an **ARP cache**. When a host needs to send an IP datagram, it first looks in the ARP cache to see if it has a data link layer address for that datagram. If it does, the host can forego sending out an ARP request.

Hosts build up their ARP caches in several ways. First, whenever a host gets an ARP reply, the addresses are stored in the cache. Next, whenever a host receives an ARP request, that host puts the requesting host's addresses in its own cache. Also, all the hosts on the network receive broadcast requests and make note of the network and IP addresses of the requesting system in their ARP caches.

Finally, **gratuitous ARP** also enhances ARP cache efficiency. Every host, as it boots, sends itself an ARP request. The purpose is not to try to determine its own address so much as to get its IP/network address pair recorded in the ARP caches of the other hosts on the network.

Proxy ARP

Proxy ARP is a method used when two parts of the same network are divided by a router. Hosts on one side need to be able to address Ethernet frames that encapsulate IP datagrams for hosts on the other side. Although the originating host thinks the remote host is on the same physical network, network traffic is actually being directed through the router. Addressing the network frame to the remote host would not work, since it isn't on the same physical network, so the router performs the proxy ARP service, filling in its own Ethernet address in response to ARP requests for hosts on opposite sides of the network.

This is also the approach to ARP used in nonbroadcast networks like ATM. An ARP server keeps track of all connected nodes and maintains a list of data link layer and network layer addresses. When a node needs a data link layer address, it sends out an ARP request to the ARP server, which responds on behalf of all connected nodes.

Reverse ARP

As the name implies, RARP is simply the reverse of ARP. Used by diskless workstations to get their assigned IP addresses, RARP requires that at least one host on the network be designated a RARP server. The RARP source fills its own network address in both the source and target network address fields, and the RARP servers to the requester with the required IP address.

RARP packets use a different set of values for the operations field and use the value 0x0835 for Ethernet frame type (instead of the value 0x0806 used by ARP).

Inverse ARP

Inverse ARP, or **InARP**, was first described in RFC 1293 in 1992 and updated in RFC 2390, in 1998. InARP lets a node find the IP address of another node to which it already has a data link layer connection. ARP and RARP are used to determine an IP address to link to a data link layer address through the use of broadcasts. In contrast, InARP is used in networks where broadcasts must be replicated across all virtual circuits. Instead of sending the request to all connected nodes, the requesting node can just send a single request down a single virtual circuit to ask the node at the other end what its IP address is.

InARP adds two values to the ARP operation type. The InARP request uses the value 8, and the InARP response uses the value 9. Other than this and their use of unicast rather than broadcast to make requests, InARP messages are identical to ARP messages.

IP Broadcast

Network broadcasts occur when every host connected to the network gets a copy of the broadcast traffic. In a network medium like Ethernet, where all network traffic is broadcast along the wire, network broadcasts are received and processed by all connected hosts. In other network types that use separate connections or virtual circuits to link nodes, broadcast data must be replicated for each connected host.

In general, network broadcast addresses are addresses consisting of "all ones," meaning "all the hosts on this network." This applies at the hardware level, where an Ethernet broadcast is ad-dressed to the six-byte MAC address (as shown here in standard hexadecimal notation):

```
ff:ff:ff:ff:ff:ff
```

Hosts on an Ethernet listen to all network traffic and check the Ethernet address; if it is addressed to the listening host or if it is

addressed to the hardware broadcast address, the network interface passes the Ethernet frame further up the protocol stack for
processing.

Broadcasts are also used at the IP level, and again, all ones indicates every host on the network should get a copy of the message.
However, there are some variations, since there are different ways
to express "this network." For example, filling the entire four-byte
IP address with ones:

255.255.255.255

creates a limited broadcast address. Although it could be interpreted to mean "every host on the entire Internet," the assumption
is made that the host simply may not know what network it is on,
and therefore the message being broadcast is passed along only to
hosts on the same physical network. If routers were to pass these
broadcasts across network borders, the Internet would be quickly
flooded.

More common is the network-directed broadcast, which specifies
a network on which to broadcast the message. For example, a **net-
directed broadcast** on a Class B network looks like this:

172.16.255.255

resulting in the broadcast message being routed to every host on
the entire Class B network. This kind of broadcast, particularly on
a large, subnetted internetwork, can still be disruptive, so **subnet-
directed broadcasts** are more commonly used. For example, a
subnet-directed broadcast on a Class A, subnetted internetwork
would look like this:

10.1.255.255

Even though this looks very much like a network-directed broadcast on an unsubnetted Class B network, it can be differentiated
because network addresses whose first octet value is anything less
than 127 are Class A nets.

Broadcast messages are most relevant to hosts on the same physical or logical network, and use up a lot of network resources. They tax individual hosts because most broadcasts won't be relevant to many hosts, but must still be processed. And broadcasts tax the networks because the broadcasts use bandwidth and may require routing services.

When a process on a host determines that a message must be broadcast, the network software uses the appropriate broadcast address. As the network traffic moves down the protocol stack to the network interface, the hardware broadcast address is appended to the network frame, and all other hosts on the network will receive the frame. In the event that a broadcast is intended for more than one network, the router (or bridge) would simply repeat the broadcast on the appropriate network interface.

Although it may seem obvious, it is worth noting that a broadcast address cannot be used as source address. There are cases where a host may not (yet) know its IP address, but in those cases it can use the all zeroes address, to indicate "this host":

```
0.0.0.0
```

Or it may know its host number, but may not (yet) know its network address, so it could use all zeroes for the network address and its proper host number,

```
0.0.0.7
```

for host number 7, for example.

Why Use Broadcasts?

Network applications use broadcasts for two purposes: to get information from "somewhere" on the network, and to publish network information to interested parties (other hosts on the network). Network nodes that boot from remote boot servers may not know where those servers are, so protocols for remote booting (like BOOTP) may use broadcasts to solicit responses from an appropriate server.

A more important broadcast function is the publication of relevant information to interested parties. Routing information, like the availability of a new router, is distributed by broadcasts using the Internet Control Message Protocol (discussed in Chapter 8). Likewise, local network routing information is available to hosts on a network through ARP and RARP, as discussed earlier in this chapter.

Broadcasts are not always an effective method of disseminating information: they use resources on every connected host, as well as network bandwidth. As we discuss in the next section and in Chapter 13, multicasting, a type of selective broadcast, can be more effective. And although broadcast will remain an important feature of IPv4, IPv6 replaces the broadcast message type entirely, as we'll see in Chapter 14.

IP Multicast

Broadcasting has its uses: the originating host need not specify individual recipients, and each piece of network traffic is generated once by the originating host. Multicast uses these advantages while attempting to minimize the disadvantages by making sure that only "interested" nodes receive the multicasts and by directing traffic across an intranet without flooding it.

Like broadcasting, multicasting is often implemented at the data link layer. In Ethernet networks, for example, special Ethernet MAC addresses are reserved for multicasts. Ethernet multicast addresses have the last bit of the first byte of the MAC address set to 1. The Ethernet broadcast address is, therefore, a special multicast address to which every host on the Ethernet subscribes (since the Ethernet broadcast address is "all ones"). However, an Ethernet multicast address would look like

```
01:00:00:172.16.144
```

The first octet could be any number, as long as it is odd (the low-order byte is 1).

Network nodes subscribe to a multicast group. With hardware multicast, the subscribing node is configured to listen for network frames addressed to the multicast address.

IP multicasting is an extension of hardware multicasting. Instead of special hardware addresses reserved for multicasts, IP reserves special IP addresses: the Class D network addresses (see Chapter 2). Individual hosts can join multicast groups by notifying a multicast router (using the Internet Group Management Protocol described next) that it wishes to join a particular group.

The multicast routers then forward multicasts for groups that they know are subscribed on attached networks, using the hardware multicast addresses. In Ethernets it is possible to map multicast addresses to hardware addresses by using a special range of hardware multicast addresses. These addresses use the last three octets of the six-byte MAC address that match the last three octets of the multicast group address. Multicast is a bit more difficult in non-broadcast networks like ATM. The solution usually involves some kind of proxying, and we discuss at greater length in Chapter 13.

A router, which can receive multicast traffic on any of its network interfaces, needs to choose a single interface to receive traffic for any given multicast group. If the router did try to listen for traffic on more than one interface, it would likely receive traffic more than once and get confused.

Multicasting is an ideal solution for applications that would like to include some indeterminate number of participating hosts in high-volume applications. For example, audio and video conferencing are possible over the M-Bone (Multicast Backbone). Hosts can join groups to get copies of the transmissions.

Internet Group Management Protocol

The Internet Group Management Protocol (IGMP) sends multicast group information across the internetwork through IP datagrams. Hosts can join a multicast group by sending the appropriate IGMP message to a multicast router. When a host joins a group, it simply needs to notify a router to make sure that the group multicasts are propagated on its network. The multicast router uses IGMP to make sure that multicast group members are still active and interested in the multicasts. The multicast router also keeps track internally of groups it subscribes to and group members on its connected networks.

As with broadcasts, a multicast address can never be a valid source address for a network datagram.

Chapter Summary and References

In this chapter we got into the guts of the Internet Protocol, examining the IP datagram structure, IP headers, and the mechanics of datagram fragmentation. We also discussed IP routing issues, paying special attention to the differences between routers and hosts, and between direct and indirect routing. The IP source routing options were also introduced.

This chapter examined the Address Resolution Protocol (ARP) and its relatives, Reverse ARP and Inverse ARP.

We finished up with a discussion of network and data link layer broadcasts and multicasts.

Some useful RFCs to read in conjunction with this chapter include those listed in Table 7–1.

RFC	Title	Description
791	Internet Protocol	The original specification for IP as we know it. Published in 1981, it has proven remarkably resilient and robust; only a few minor changes have been necessary for this standard to remain usable today.
1349	Type of Service in the Internet Protocol Suite	A discussion of the Type of Service field, and how it should work.
2101	IPv4 Address Behaviour Today	Almost 20 years after the Ipv4 addressing scheme was first deployed, this document reviews how it has been working.
1597	Address Allocation for Private Internets	Describes the IP address ranges that are reserved for private networks, and that are not to be forwarded into the public Internet.
826	An Ethernet Address Resolution Protocol—or—Converting Network Protocol Addresses to 48.bit Ethernet Address for Transmission on Ethernet Hardware	ARP over Ethernet, with enough information to allow ARP to be generalized to other network media.
903	A Reverse Address Resolution Protocol	This document explains how RARP works.
1735	NBMA Address Resolution Protocol (NARP)	Doing ARP over ATM and other nonbroadcast network media.
2390	Inverse Address Resolution Protocol	An update of RFC 1293, which describes InARP and how it can be used by nodes to find IP addresses of other nodes on nonbroadcast networks that use virtual circuits.
1112	Host Extensions for IP Multicasting	Explains how hosts should be extended to support multicast.
2236	Internet Group Management Protocol, Version 2	Describes how IGMP works to support multicast.

Table 7–1: Useful RFCs for Chapter 7.

8

Routing Protocols

Up to now, we've been avoiding the topic of how routers know where to send IP traffic. It is much more comforting to believe that every network device knows about local connectivity and sends any traffic outside its "known world" to some default gateway that somehow knows the right place to send it. Things aren't so simple in the real world. Routing can be a complicated operation, particularly in a network with 100 million nodes or more, like the Internet. Routing works differently locally, within corporate internetworks; regionally, between organizational internetworks, and globally, among systems and networks worldwide.

The two basic routing tasks are, first, making sure that all networks within an organizational internetwork route traffic among them-selves, and second, making sure that all internetworks connected to a large internetwork (particularly the Internet) are able to route reliably between each other. We call the first task **interior routing** and the second task **exterior routing**.

Routing responsibilities are divided into these two classifications. Exterior routing happens at the level fo the Internet at large. Providers of Internet services, maintainers of Internet backbones, and the builders, managers, and owners of Internet routers have to worry about exterior routing. Exterior routing happens when a packet is sent from someone's home PC in Schenectady, NY, to a server in Mumbai, India, for example.

Interior routing happens within organizations. Network managers reponsible for organizational networks and intranets have to worry about interior routing. Interior routing happens when a packet is sent from a workstation in the accounting department to an intranet web server in the personnel department, or when e-mail is downloaded from an ISP mail server to someone's home PC, for example.

In this chapter we start by looking at the protocol designed to allow hosts and routers to exchange some routing-related information, the Internet Control Messaging Protocol (ICMP). We will examine related applications, **ping** and **traceroute**, which use ICMP for diagnostic purposes, and then turn to the issues of routing traffic on a large internetwork (like the Internet) as they have been addressed over the years through TCP/IP protocols like Gateway-to-Gateway Protocol, Exterior Gateway Protocol, and the latest version of the Border Gateway Protocol. We will also examine methods for efficient routing within organizational internetworks, like Routing Information Protocol and the Open Shortest Path First protocol. Finally, we will take a look at Classless Inter-Domain Routing, which lets routers work more efficiently in an environment of rapidly depleting IP network addresses. With it, routing uses "supernet" masks to allow aggregated Class C networks to appear together in a single routing table entry, thus allowing more efficient use of the Class C networks while keeping the resulting routing tables a manageable size.

Internet Control Message Protocol

Even though it is carried inside IP datagrams, the Internet Control Message Protocol is considered to be a parallel protocol running side by side with IP at the network layer. Routers use ICMP to notify hosts and other routers that a route is unreachable, that there is a problem with a particular path, or that a router is being overloaded. Although ICMP can also be used to provide certain information to hosts (like the current time or the subnet mask for a particular network), these functions are less vital and are often available in other ways.

ICMP has been a part of the STD-5 specification that includes the Internet Protocol, and it is documented in RFC 792. All IP hosts must implement ICMP.

Even though ICMP is valuable for making routing information available, it only fulfills that function for local networks, not for propagating routing information across gateways and to remote networks. Most commonly, ICMP is used to

- ◆ Send error messages about unreachable destinations
- ◆ Send error and status messages about routes and gateways
- ◆ Send echo requests and replies to indicate status of reachable hosts
- ◆ Send error messages about traffic that has timed out (the TTL value reaches 0)

As shown in Figure 8–1, ICMP messages have a simple structure: a one-byte type field, which indicates what function the message is fulfilling, and a one-byte code field, which may be used to further clarify the contents of the message. For example, the code field is not used with echo requests or replies (see the section on Ping), though there are many codes to go with "destination unreachable" error messages.

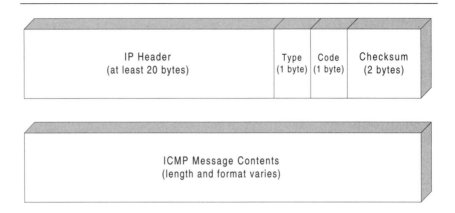

Figure 8–1: ICMP message encapsulated in IP datagram.

A two-byte checksum follows the type and code fields, and the contents of the ICMP message will vary, but will always include the header and the first eight bytes of the datagram that caused the error message to be sent. ICMP provides no error correction: it simply reports routing errors by sending error messages back to the source.

The message contents field contains the IP header and the first 64 bits of the original datagram that caused the ICMP message to be sent. This is enough to permit higher level protocols (like TCP) to examine their own headers and take corrective action based on the ICMP message. The message may also contain the IP addresses of intervening routers between systems or a list of available routers on a network with corresponding preference levels, depending on the ICMP message type.

Ground Rules for ICMP

Mostly to avoid having the cure be worse than the disease, ICMP has certain limitations built into the specification. For one thing, ICMP error messages cannot beget ICMP error messages. For another, broadcast or multicast messages also cannot beget ICMP error messages. Both these rules help avoid cascading errors which would result in "broadcast storms" that could easily flood a network.

Unreachability Messages

ICMP unreachability messages indicate there has been a failure somewhere in the process of addressing the datagram that triggers the message. For example, an incorrectly addressed datagram can cause an unreachable message to be sent to the host originaly sending the datagram. The message usually indicates that the host or the network is either unreachable or unknown. This happens when a host is turned off, when a network link is down, or even when the specified protocol is not available (for instance, attempting to connect to a network application port that is prohibited or restricted).

ICMP Routing Messages

The most obvious uses for ICMP routing messages are requests for lists of available routers and the replies that include lists of other available routers (each router listed with a priority level). Hosts often use ICMP to request a list of available routers when they boot up, to initialize their routing tables. Routers advertise gateways when they boot up, and they will also periodically broadcast this information.

These routing messages include a field to indicate how long to retain the enclosed information because sometimes routers fail, are taken down, become overloaded, or lose connectivity to remote networks. By periodically broadcasting the current routing preferences, routers ensure that hosts on their networks don't attempt to use a default router that is inappropriate.

Another type of routing message is generated when a router becomes overloaded. Routers can be overwhelmed by a high-volume of traffic from a single host or from a generally high load generated by many hosts on the network. Although routers attempt to process all network traffic as it is received, when volume is high this is not always possible. The use of memory buffers to store incoming traffic prior to processing can help, but it no longer takes a Cray or Thinking Machines supercomputer to saturate a typical 10 Mbps Ethernet wire—nor does it take that many video-conferencing sessions to saturate a 100 Mbps Fast Ethernet LAN.

Routers may send out **source quench messages** when they are overloaded (though this is not required). Each time the router receives a datagram it can't handle, it discards the datagram and sends back a source quench message, basically asking the fast transmitter to slow down. The originating host then drops its speed until it stops getting the error messages, slowly building up speed again until it starts getting the error messages again.

Another instance where an ICMP message may carry routing information occurs when a host sends traffic to one router when a different router advertises a better route (a route with fewer hops). This is called a **redirect**. This is a common occurrence on networks with more than one router, where the hosts start out with only a single default router in their routing tables.

Figure 8–2 demonstrates this situation. Host A is attempting to send a datagram to Host C and is using Router AB as a default gateway. Since Host A knows that the datagram is destined for a nonlocal network, it sends it to the default gateway. However, Router AB has to route that datagram to Router AC to get it to Host C, taking an extra step (the first step is from Host A to Router AB, then Router AB to Router AC, then Router AC to Host C; the optimal route is from Host A to Router AC to Host C).

Redirects occur when a router forwards a datagram onto the same network on which the datagram was received—to the router this means that the originating host could have sent the traffic directly to another router on the same network. Although the router still forwards the datagram, it also generates a message back to the originating host that there is a better route. The host can then incorporate the new, more efficient, route into its routing table.

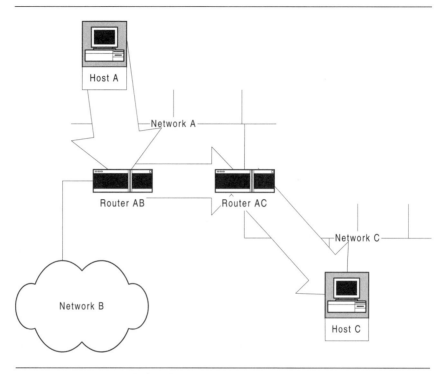

Figure 8–2: ICMP can help a host learn about optimal routes.

Ping and ICMP Echo Messages

Probably the most common explicit use of ICMP is the **ping** application. Ping (or PING) stands for **Packet InterNet Groper**, though it behaves like the "ping" sent out by warships using sonar. Ping sends an ICMP echo request out to a specific host, and the host responds to ICMP echo requests by sending out an ICMP echo reply. Ping's purpose is to see if anything is out there.

Ping represents the simplest level of connectivity possible between two hosts on an internetwork, so it is useful for testing whether a remote host is reachable or whether the network connection for a local host is properly configured and installed. Most ping applications use the command format

```
ping <IP host name | IP address>
```

By using the IP host name instead of the address, it is possible to verify not only that the two hosts have connectivity, but also that the local host is resolving names properly (see Chapter 11 for more on network name resolution).

Because organizations connected to the Internet are increasingly using firewall gateways (see Chapter 24 for more about network security issues) to protect against unauthorized use of their hosts, some hosts that may be visible to network applications won't respond to ICMP echo requests. However, ping continues to be useful as a diagnostic tool on unconnected internetworks as well as (usually) within organizational internetworks.

Ping implementations can vary a surprising amount, but all do the same task: send out at least one ICMP echo request and report back whether the host is reachable or not. Some implementations simply send a single ICMP request, and report whether the pinged host responds. Most implementations also report the amount of time it took between the request being sent and the response being received, which helps diagnose slow links between hosts.

Also fairly standard is the use of multiple pings for each invocation of the program, one request per second. In these cases, a sequence number is recorded for each request and is reported when the response is received. Again, this is useful for identifying links that are dropping traffic (there will be missing numbers in the responses received) or that are sending traffic out of order or with varying routes (replies will not be received in the same order the requests were sent out).

Ping implementations usually pad out the datagram with some amount of data to simulate actual traffic. Some implementations allow the user to modify the amount of padding, making the ping datagrams larger or smaller. Chapter 24 describes how this function can be subverted into a denial-of-service attack known as the "ping of death." Sending a ping datagram that is larger than it should be has been known to crash some systems.

Traceroute

Ping offers a tool to test connectivity between two individual hosts. IP's record route option (see Chapter 7) will report the route taken by any IP datagram, including an ICMP echo request. This option causes every system handling the request to add its own IP address to the IP options field. Although useful, record route is severely limited. It records every system, every time that system handles the message—which includes the destination host and every intervening router, every time the router is traversed. So a packet traveling from Host A to Router AB to Router CD to Router EF to Host N, and then back to Router EF, to Router CD, to Router AB, to Host A would have nine routing entires.

This would not be a problem except that the route must be stored in the IP header options field, which can be no longer than 40 bytes. Nine routing entries would take up 36 bytes (IP addresses are 4 bytes long each). A simple route like the one just described, with only three routers between source and destination, is as long a route as can be recorded by this option. A single byte of the options field identifies the option type, another indicates the length of the options field, and a third indicates where in the field the IP address of the next stop in the route is recorded—leaving room for a maximum of nine IP addresses.

Traceroute uses a different strategy to trace the route between hosts on an internetwork. Rather than attempting to collect all the intermediate routers in a single pass, traceroute takes advantage of rules about handling IP datagrams that are about to expire because their TTL (time-to-live) field is almost 0. Routers won't forward a datagram with a TTL of 0 or 1; the datagram is thrown away—but the router also sends an ICMP message back to the originating host. The message indicates that the offending datagram expired on the network.

ICMP messages are addressed from the router that discovered the error to the originating host, so that when the host gets the ICMP error message, it then can know where the original ICMP echo request was in its route when the TTL counter expired. Traceroute determines the route between hosts by sending out pings with varying TTL values. The first ping has a TTL field value set to 1. The first router receives the ping, throws it out (since the TTL is too low to pass it on), and generates an ICMP error message back to the originating host.

Traceroute stores the address of the first router, then pings the remote host again with the TTL counter set to 2. This time the echo request gets past the first router, but causes the second router to return an ICMP error message. Traceroute keeps this up until the TTL counter is just large enough to reach the remote host, which sends back an ICMP echo reply. The program then outputs the IP addresses of all the routers that sent ICMP error messages in the proper order.

Traceroute is not foolproof. Since IP provides no connections but simply delivers datagrams, it is possible that traffic between two hosts may be sent over more than one route. Over time it is likely that the route between any two hosts on the Internet will vary due to changes in internet connections, modification of routers, and changes in service. However, over the short term these changes will usually not be present, making traceroute a useful tool.

Interior and Exterior Routing

Routing between networks is quite straightforward as long as all the networks behave and all the networks interconnect simply. The simple routing formulas described in this chapter and the previous chapter are sufficient for internetworks that don't get too complicated. Simple routing strategies like default gateways and ICMP route advertising will be sufficient to move network traffic inside most intranets.

However, routing can get very sticky in the real world. Determining a route for traffic from a LAN onto the Internet is usually not too difficult, since the host itself knows that the traffic it generates either goes to a local host on the same LAN or else it goes to the host's default router. In a simple network, that router will be directly connected to an Internet service provider, who in turn connects to an Internet backbone. Routing outside the local network must be more dynamic to respond to the frequent changes in conditions and connectivity, and it is handled by someone else "out there" on the Internet somewhere.

The interface between the organizational internetwork and the Internet is where the two major routing tasks meet. Interior routing requires that participating gateways be able to exchange information about which networks they can reach and which networks they can't reach. In simple intranets, particularly those with only a couple of networks and routers, static routing tables can be maintained by hand. However, it doesn't take much complexity before this task can overwhelm the network managers, and dynamic routing protocols are required.

To illustrate, look at Figure 8–3. Before adding the new router between Network B and Network D, all the networks were reachable in just one way. Traffic from Network B destined for Network D all was routed to Router BC to Router CE to Router DE to the destination on Network D. With the new router in place, there are now two routes from Network B to Network E, both apparently equivalent—just as there are now two routes for traffic from Network A to Network E. Routing protocols allow routers to communicate network connectivity across network boundaries to other routers. Reachability data can be passed along, as well as changes in reachability: if the new router fails after being installed, routing protocols allow the other neighboring routers to report the failure to their neighbors.

Look at the same internetwork, as it relates to the rest of the Internet, as shown in Figure 8–4. For one thing, there is only a single point of contact between the local internetwork and the connected Internet—that is, the Internet router itself. This router knows directly about Networks A, B, C, and D—it is connected to Network B, just as Routers AB, BC, and the new router are, so it can exchange routing information with those routers. However, it

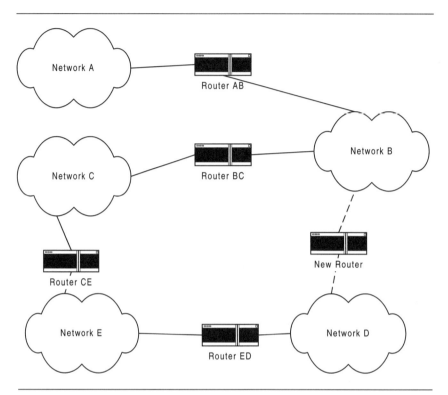

Figure 8–3: Putting in an extra router in a simple internetwork demonstrates why a mechanism for advertising reachability becomes very useful if one router fails or is overloaded; if there is a choice, routers need to know how to decide which choice to make.

may not know about Network E or other more remotely connected networks.

Rather than requiring that the Internet router in this example be able to notify other Internet routers of all internal routes automatically as well as keeping track of Internet routes, interior routing is assigned to the organization that runs the local internetwork and Internet routing is reserved for routing systems that run on the backbones of the Internet.

Exterior routing, on the other hand, is done externally to organizational internetworks. There are a number of issues, not the least of

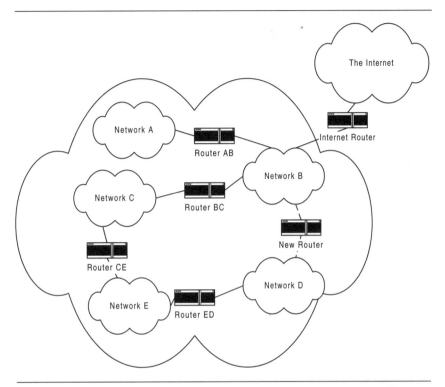

Figure 8–4: Routing internally in an autonomous system presents a different set of problems from routing across the Internet.

which is the number of different networks (and the rapid pace of change to the Internet overall) to track. You could require each organizational unit to arrange somehow for internal routes to be reported to its Internet router, but all core routers for the Internet would then have to communicate those routes to each other.

Figure 8–5 illustrates one of the main reasons why Internet-connected gateways need to be able to route traffic dynamically to the Internet. Each of the autonomous systems is actually an organizational internetwork, but for the purpose of the Internet, each autonomous system's router passes traffic from the interior out into the Internet and routes traffic in from the Internet. When there are few internetworks connected to the Internet and a single

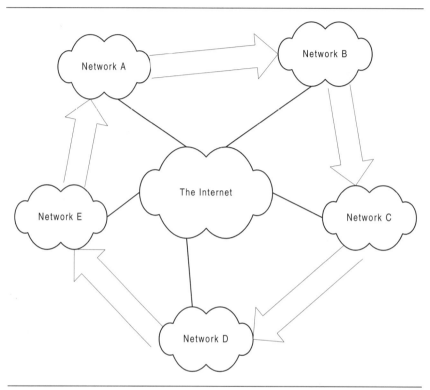

Figure 8–5: Organizational internetworks connected to an Internet backbone could route traffic using default gateways, but it would become tremendously inefficient quickly.

backbone to carry all Internet traffic, routing traffic by default gateways might almost make sense: give each Internet router another gateway to send Internet traffic to, as shown in Figure 8–5. If each unit routes to the right along the backbone (which is as reasonable a scheme as any), traffic intended for the neighbor on the left will have to transit the entire Internet before it arrives at its destination—a single hop away.

The problem is compounded as soon as more than one backbone appears; in today's Internet there are many different backbones and carriers to consider and special routing protocols have been introduced to handle this kind of exterior routing.

Vector/Distance vs Link State Routing

Routing protocols can use two basic methods to measure connectivity across internetworks, whether within organizational internetworks or across the Internet. The **vector/distance** approach calls for routers to share their routing tables and make additions and corrections based on reports from other routers. Routes are advertised as data pairs, with the router reporting each network it can reach along with the number of hops it takes to reach it. When a router receives new routing information from another router, it compares the new data with its current routing table: if there are any new networks, it adds them to the table; if there are networks shown as reachable with fewer hops than the current entry in the routing table, the router updates its entries, pointing to the closer router.

This approach has a major drawback for use in large internetworks: it quickly becomes cumbersome to implement. As routers must track connections to more networks, they must send, receive, and process larger and larger lists of network routes. There are also various errors that vector/distance routing may allow. Network A is reachable only through Router AB. Router AB advertises to the other routers that it can reach Network A in a single hop. Router BC receives this information and incorporates it into its routing table, indicating that it can reach Network A in two hops (one from Router BC, and one more from Router AB). If the link to Network A fails just before Router BC advertises its own routes, Router AB, knowing that its link to Network A is down, may add Router BC to its own routing table as the way to get to Network A—in three hops (the two that Router BC advertised and itself, again). This is shown in Figure 8–6.

With timers that expire advertised routes, Router BC may drop the link that (it thinks) gets it to Network A and may add it again when some other router advertises this three-hop link to Network A as a four-hop link. This could go on forever, but it is a well-known problem with vector/distance routing, and protocols based on vector/distance routing usually also include fixes that do things like put limits on the maximum number of hops allowed in a route.

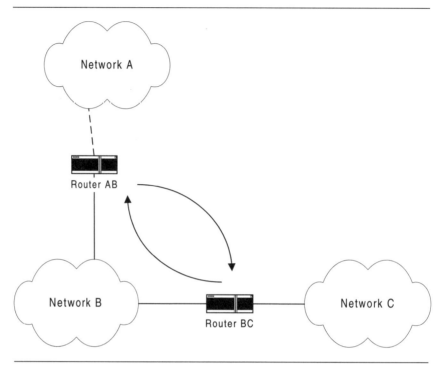

Figure 8–6: The interval between routing reports can cause a routing loop when the only link to a network fails.

The **link state** approach to routing keeps the volume of information passed along to other routers to a minimum. Each router periodically checks on the status of neighboring routers, reporting which links are alive to all other participating routers. With this information, each router can then create its own map of the internetwork, as shown in Figure 8–7.

Interior Routing Protocols

For a long time the Routing Information Protocol (RIP) was the closest thing we had to a standard routing protocol for interior routing. Implemented in the **routed** (routing daemon) program distributed with Unix systems, the RIP protocol specification RFC

Network A connects to Networks B and C

Network B connects to Networks A and D

Network C connects to Networks A and D

Network D connects to Networks B and C

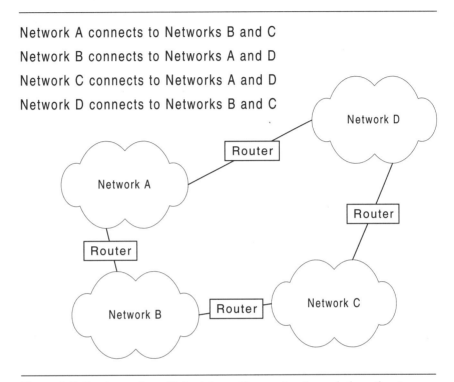

Figure 8–7: Routers using a link state routing protocol can deduce the structure of their internetwork.

was published after RIP had been implemented. Although long an Internet standard, RIP was finally replaced by RIP-2 in 1998. RIP-2 is backward compatible with RIP but adds the ability to transmit more routing information, support for multicasting, and improved security.

RIP relies on the vector/distance method to advertise routes within routing tables; another routing protocol, Open Shortest Path First (OSPF) uses the link-state method to let routers create their own internetwork maps. Developed partly in response to some of the shortcomings of RIP, OSPF propagates routing information more quickly and stably than RIP, handles subnets appropriately, can balance loads where equivalent routes are available, and uses multicasting—all advantages over RIP.

Despite RIP's flaws, development of RIP-2 continued for several reasons. RIP is widely implemented on many different platforms, partly because it is an easy protocol to implement. On small intranets, RIP can be a very efficient routing protocol making few demands on system overhead and bandwidth. Finally, RIP is relatively easy to configure and manage.

Routing Information Protocol

All systems on an internetwork can use RIP, but hosts generally are passive participants, listening to the routing information and updating their routing tables, whereas routers can both listen to routing broadcasts and transmit routing information. Routes can be propagated on request by a router that has just booted up, though routers typically broadcast their routes every 30 seconds.

Routes are broadcast as vector/distance pairs: a network and a hop count. Other routing protocols use the convention that a hop indicates a transmission to another router, so the hop count from a gateway to a network to which the gateway is connected directly would be 0. RIP counts that as one hop, so the lowest number of hops possible with RIP is one; with other protocols zero hops are possible.

The rules for RIP are fairly simple:

1. Active routers broadcast their routes every 30 seconds by default (though this may vary if the network administrator wishes).
2. All listening systems compare these broadcasts to their own routing tables and update their routing tables if

   ♦ there are routes to new networks previously unlisted,
   ♦ there are better (e.g., shorter) routes to existing networks,
   ♦ a route is reported unreachable (it should be removed).

3. A route is kept until a better route is reported.
4. If there are two equivalent routes (same hop count), the first received goes into the routing table.
5. Routes are timed out if they are not updated after three minutes; in other words, a route must be assumed down if it is not being reported.
6. Routers broadcast route changes as they occur, without waiting (triggered updates).
7. A hop count of 16 is considered unreachable (which means RIP is unusable in any intranet wider than 15 hops).

RIP tends not to propagate corrections to routing tables very quickly, although errors are passed along more quickly. RIP's relatively low maximum hop count and the use of triggered updates help minimize some of the inherent problems with the distance/vector method of sharing routing information as described in the next section. Finally, RIP does not send subnet mask information in routing updates, so there is the potential for routing problems in internetworks that are highly subnetted, particularly if more than one subnetworking scheme is being used in the internetwork. RIP-2 addresses many of the shortcomings of RIP, and adds support for subnets—something that the original RIP lacks simply because subnets had yet to be accepted as part of the IP networks at the time that RIP was first designed.

Slow Convergence and Router Loops

One common dynamic routing problem occurs when a router or network goes out of service. Consider the example in Figure 7–3. Assuming that all routers advertise all known routes to all other routers, if the Internet router goes down, it might take some time before all the other routers would become aware of the failure.

What happens is this: Router ACD would know that its one-hop link to the Internet was no longer available, but Router AB would be advertising a two-hop route to the Internet (actually via Router

ACD). Router ACD would then say to itself, "The direct route via the Internet router is down, but there is an indirect, two-hop route to the Internet via Router AB." It would then reset its own routing table to show a three-hop link to the Internet.

This problem is called slow convergence, since it means that it takes quite a few routing table updates before all the participating routers become aware of the fact that they are all actually routing through the failed link. There are several solutions to this problem, which is already limited by the maximum number of hops that the routing protocol allows (for example, RIP allows no more than 15 hops before it considers the route to be unreachable).

One solution is to use a **split-horizon update**. This method calls for routers to keep a record of each interface for which they received a route. When a router sends out routing information, it avoids sending information to any interface over which it originally heard about a particular route. In other words, it assumes that the routers on a particular interface already have more current information about routes reported over that interface. Routers thus are made aware of changes on connected networks without incorrectly propagating status about those connections.

Another solution to this problem is called **hold-down**. Instead of updating routing tables right away, any changes are ignored for a long enough time that the changes are likely to have been propagated to all participating routers. Usually, the hold-down period is twice as long as the normal reporting period, so if routers advertise routes every thirty seconds, the hold-down period would be 60 seconds.

Other methods can be used to resolve this problem. One is called **poison reverse**. This approach mandates that routers continue to advertise any failed routes, even after the link has been dropped, but advertise them as accessible only as unreachable (i.e., hop count of 16 for RIP) for a number of reporting periods. This is especially effective when used in conjunction with triggered updates, which require routers to broadcast a failed route as soon as they become aware of it.

Open Shortest Path First

Though widely implemented and distributed, RIP falls short in several areas as a routing protocol, particularly as even moderate-sized intranets increase in size and complexity. Because routers build their internetwork maps with link status rather than vector/distance pairings, OSPF remedies the problems inherent in the vector/distance method used by RIP. OSPF version 2 is currently an Internet standard.

OSPF solves most of RIP's problems, either through implementation of special features or by virtue of using a more efficient method of mapping network routes. For instance, link state routing protocols in general will have less impact on the network because they generate a lower volume of data and because that data is passed to neighboring routers, which pass it on to other routers. By virtue of being a link state protocol OSPF also makes changes propagate in a more orderly and reliable fashion. Since a link is either up or down, there is no reason for hosts to retain looped routes.

Also important are OSPF's added features. Routing decisions can be made explicitly in cases where there are equivalent alternate routes: load balancing. Under RIP, the first of any group of equivalent advertised routes is the route that will be recorded; OSPF allows network managers to distribute traffic across these equivalent routes.

Another feature that offers greater flexibility is the use of separate routes for different types of IP services. For example, it supports routing of FTP traffic over one route (perhaps a faster link, to give better overall file transfer performance) and Telnet over a different route (perhaps a link with lower latency or roundtrip time for better interactive response).

Support of subnet addressing is an important feature, as is the use of multicasting to routers. OSPF also includes authentication of routers to each other to avoid giving out routing information to unauthorized systems or users.

With the acceptance of RIP-2 as an Internet standard alongside OSPF, these two routing protocols will continue to coexist. Neither is likely to dominate TCP/IP interior routing any time soon.

Exterior Routing Protocols

In the early days of the Internet, routing that happened outside organizational networks—Internet routing—was accomplished through centrally managed routers called **core gateways**. Noncore gateways were controlled by the organizations connected to the Internet and needed some connection to core gateways for proper routing of Internet traffic. The connection from organization to core doesn't necessarily have to be direct, meaning that one organization can function as a gateway to the core gateway for other organizations. But there does have to be some connectivity between the organization and the core.

This was effective, but the mechanism did not scale well as the Internet grew. Tracking all possible routes rapidly increased in difficulty, especially as more organizations linked to the core indirectly. Finally, as the Internet grew more complex, with multiple, parallel backbones, the routing problem became more intractable. Figure 8–8 shows that with more choices there are more opportunities for making the wrong choices—and the right choice is often far from obvious. Choosing the right route between two networks separated by backbones can be considerably more efficient than choosing what might appear to be a slightly worse route.

Exterior Gateway Protocol

The Exterior Gateway Protocol (EGP) eventually replaced Gateway-to-Gateway Protocol (GGP), the protocol originally used within the Internet to communicate routes among core gateways. As the Internet gained in complexity, GGP, which was a fairly straightforward vector/distance routing protocol, was no longer up to the task. One of the biggest problems was that not every

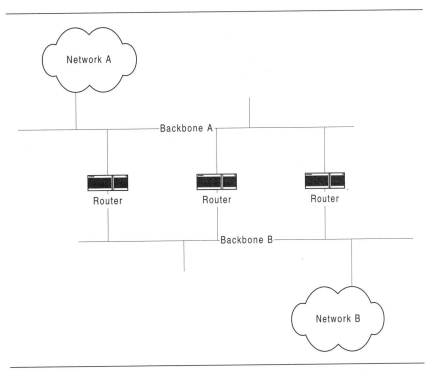

Figure 8–8: Routing between backbones can be quite direct, moving from one to the other once, or it could zigzag if routing tables are not properly maintained.

organizational internetwork could be connected directly to a core router, so extra hops were added when noncore routers sent Internet traffic to their default routers, which then forwarded the traffic to a more appropriate Internet router.

EGP added mechanisms to propagate routing information across the Internet to noncore routers as well as to core routers. Routers coming online attempt to acquire some other router to act as a peer; peers then exchange routing information about which networks they can reach. However, its major drawback was that it did not provide any way to determine whether any given advertised route was closer than another, equivalent, route. The result was that, whenever a router advertised that it had a route to a destination, that route was considered by the other participating routers as the only route to that destination.

Border Gateway Protocol

The Border Gateway Protocol (BGP) replaced EGP as the current solution to Internet routing. Routers pass along vector/distance reachability information, but instead of just including networks and distances, BGP includes the actual route needed to reach each destination. This allows the router to lay down the vector/distance routes into an actual map of the Internet and eliminate the routing loops to which vector/distance protocols are prone.

There are three different entities in the BGP scheme: organizational internetworks that connect to only one other internetwork and route traffic only locally; internetworks with connections to more than one other internetwork but don't carry traffic from any non-connected internetworks; and internetworks that carry both local and nonlocal traffic.

Classless Inter-Domain Routing

Exterior routing is sometimes also referred to as **inter-domain routing**—routing traffic between domains or organizational internetwork systems. **Classless Inter-Domain Routing** (CIDR), as the name suggests, determines routes to some networks without considering the network class involved.

As of 1999, the IP address space is still rapidly being depleted (see Chapter 14 for more details about the near future of TCP/IP). In particular, the larger Class B networks that most medium- to large-size companies need to accommodate their large networks of personal computers are being exhausted. Class C networks, being limited to 255 hosts or fewer, are inadequate to the task for many organizations. However, by assigning groups of consecutively numbered Class C networks, it is possible to get larger networks connected to the Internet.

The biggest problem this solution poses, however, is that adding a group of 16 Class C networks means adding 16 entries to routing tables. Even though the 16 networks actually compose a single internetwork, the routers wouldn't know that. A similar problem arises when a single Internet service provider offers Internet connectivity to many different, smaller, Class C networks—traffic for each one of those networks will be done through that service provider, using the same route, but routers across the Internet would have to add a single routing table entry for each Class C network.

CIDR, which is also called **supernetting**, addresses this problem by allowing the aggregation of Class C networks that have part of their network addresses in common. Routers can route traffic to any of a large number of aggregated Class C networks, simply by checking a single routing table entry.

Chapter Summary and References

In this chapter we took a bird's eye view of IP routing. Starting with the simplest routing-related protocol, ICMP, we looked at how routers and hosts can use ICMP to exchange routing information. We also examined two ICMP-based tools, ping and traceroute, which can be used to troubleshoot routing problems.

We continued by looking at some of the differences between exterior routing and interior routing, and how they present different problems to network developers. Here we introduced the concepts behind vector/distance routing and link state routing protocols.

The next section covered the most important protocols in use for interior routing: RIP and OSPF, and the following section introduced exterior routing protocols including GGP, EGP, and the current standard, BGP.

Some useful RFCs to read in conjunction with this chapter include those listed in Table 8–1.

RFC	Title	Description
792	Internet Control Message Protocol	The original ICMP specification, published at the same time as the original IP specification.
1256	ICMP Router Discovery Messages	Router advertisements and router solicitations are described here. These allow hosts to discover a router without having been pre-configured.
1054	Routing Information Protocol	Long part of Internet STD-34, RIP has been updated with RIP-2.
2453	RIP Version 2	Ten years after RIP was published as an RFC, its successor RIP-2 was finally accepted as an Internet standard.
2328	OSPF Version 2	Specification of the current standard for OSPF.
823	The DARPA Internet Gateway	This RFC describing the Gateway-Gateway Protocol (GGP) is now considered historical, and should be consulted purely for informational purposes—not to be implemented.
904	Exterior Gateway Protocol Formal Specification	EGP, described here, is also now considered an historical protocol.
1771	A Border Gateway Protocol 4 (BGP-4)	Documents the current draft standard for exterior routing on the Internet (see also RFC 1772).
1519	Classless Inter-Domain Routing (CIDR): an Address Assignment and Aggregation Strategy	Describes CIDR; see also RFCs 1517 and 1518 for related material.
1812	Requirements for IP Version 4 Routers	If you're interested in what a router is supposed to do, and how it is supposed to do it, this RFC may help.

Table 8–1: Useful RFCs for Chapter 8.

9

User Datagram Protocol

The transport layer lies between the applications layer, where real data is entered or viewed by a user, and the network layer, where IP routes the traffic from its source to its destination. It is at the transport layer that information from the application layer is packaged and routed from one process to another. The application layer enables interaction between a flesh-and-blood user and a mainframe computer. The transport layer enables interaction between the user's terminal emulation client program and the mainframe's terminal emulation server program, as well as interaction between a Web browser and Web server.

TCP/IP offers two choices for transport layer protocols: the Transmission Control Protocol (TCP) and the User Datagram Protocol (UDP). TCP is far and away the more important protocol, but it cannot stand alone. We look at UDP first because it is simpler than TCP and makes an easier transition to the examination of transport layer issues.

The User Datagram Protocl (UDP)

As we've seen at the network and data link layers, questions of network reliability are often deferred to the higher layers. The User Datagram Protocol (UDP) continues to defer reliability issues to the next higher layer. UDP is an elegantly simple protocol, providing no error detection, no error correction, no connection-oriented links, no handshaking, and no verification of delivery order. UDP offers basic datagram delivery and nothing more.

Applications based on UDP are often simple ones that don't need to maintain connections. UDP application may consist entirely of requests and replies to requests. UDP provides a connectionless delivery service between one host and another, offering a service over a particular protocol port. UDP delivers messages and responses. It provides no help as far as keeping track of the delivery order of datagrams, whether datagrams have been delivered, retransmission (or detection) of dropped datagrams, notification of duplicated datagrams, nor any kind of control over whether or not the link between the hosts is active.

A simple datagram delivery service like UDP, without any added features, is easy to implement and requires minimal overhead. UDP is often built into the limited memory of diskless workstations, where it is used for remote booting. UDP is also used for low-intensity tasks performed in the background, like resolving host names through the Domain Name Service (DNS, Chapter 11) or routine network monitoring through Simple Network Management Protocol (SNMP, Chapter 22). Applications that use UDP have to deal with reliability concerns at the application layer, if they are to be dealt with at all. Some UDP applications operate mostly over local networks that are usually reliable, and so don't need transport layer reliability. Other applications can trade the uncertainty of delivery for lower overhead, since retransmitting requests is easier and usually has minimal impact on network traffic.

UDP Datagrams

UDP datagrams each contain a single message. The message may be a request, or it may be a reply. UDP provides minimal transport layer functions, and it uses the minimal header structure, shown in Figure 9–1.

The UDP header itself is always eight bytes long, and consists of four two-byte fields. The first field is the Source Port Number and

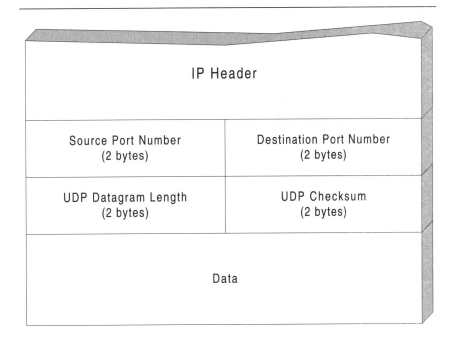

Figure 9–1: A UDP datagram is encapsulated in an IP datagram.

the second field is the Destination Port Number. The third field holds the length of the UDP datagram, and the fourth field contains a UDP checksum.

Port numbers refer to processes running on networked systems. Unlike at the data link and network layers, protocols at the transport layer no longer make any reference to specific nodes or network interfaces. Transport layer protocols identify source and destination processes. The systems on which those processes are running are specified by the lower layer protocols, and once you arrive at the transport layer it is no longer possible to identify in any way the source or destination systems simply by looking at the protocol headers.

Since a router may be forwarding the datagram, the MAC address at the link layer could as easily refer to a router's network interface to the actual source or destination hosts.

Well-Known Ports

The source port on any given UDP datagram (or on a TCP segment, as we will see in Chapter 10) is determined by the host originating the datagram (or segment, for TCP). However, the destination port poses a problem. By definition, the destination port specifies some particular program or process running on the destination host. If the destination port had to correspond exactly to whatever port number the destination host assigned, the initiating host would have no simple way to figure out that number—it would have to query the destination host and ask for the right port number before it could send out its datagram.

To avoid having to query a remote host for an appropriate port, there are special port numbers assigned to particular applications. Client hosts specify which application they want to connect to by addressing the datagram to the port associated with that application. These port numbers are called **well-known ports** because clients can depend on being able to address a UDP datagram to port 69, for example, when they run Trivial File Transfer Protocol.

All well-known ports are assigned within the range of 1 and 1023—ports with values higher than 1023 but lower than 5000 are called **ephemeral ports** (discussed in the next section), and port values higher than 5000 are reserved for servers that are not well-known across the Internet. For example, someone writing a specific client/server application for a corporate use might assign it a port value higher than 5000 rather than go through the long process of having the Internet Assigned Numbers Authority (IANA) assign it to a well-known port.

Ephemeral Ports

Even though it is necessary for server software to have a specific port number to "listen" to, client software does not need to operate out of the same port at all times. In fact, it is preferable to have each client session running on a unique port: that allows the same host to have multiple instances of, for example, telnet sessions or FTP sessions between the same two hosts. Ephemeral ports fulfill this purpose.

A server **daemon** listens for traffic coming in on the well-known ports assigned to that service. When a client initiates an interaction, the daemon assigns an ephemeral port to that client. In this way, the daemon can continue listening to the well-known port for new sessions, even new sessions from the same host. Interaction between the client and server is conducted using the ephemeral port rather than the well-known port. It's the computer equivalent to meeting someone in front of the big statue in the park and then going off to a coffee shop to continue a meeting.

UDP Datagram Format

Source and destination ports are 16 bits each; the source port is assigned by the originating host, and the destination port is usually the well-known port associated with the application using UDP. The UDP message length field is also 16 bits, and it indicates the length of the entire UDP datagram including header in bytes, giving an upper limit to UDP datagram size of 65,535 bytes.

The UDP checksum is a highly recommended option. It may not be strictly necessary on some LANs, especially Ethernets that already use a CRC on network frames, but in other circumstances, especially when the datagram is passing across unreliable links, it is advisable to use the checksum.

The checksum is calculated using a **pseudo-header** that uses IP addressing information taken from the IP header. As shown in Figure 9–2, the source and destination IP addresses, as well as the protocol code (17, for UDP) are added to the beginning of the UDP datagram, and a checksum is calculated on the entire datagram plus the pseudo-header.

Including the source and destination IP addresses adds to the usefulness of the checksum, since the destination host can verify not

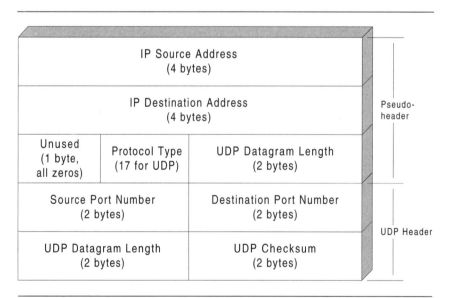

Figure 9–2: By creating a pseudo-header, UDP can calculate a checksum that helps to verify that datagrams have arrived at their proper destination.

only that the UDP datagram arrived uncorrupted but also that the UDP datagram arrived at the desired destination.

The rest of the datagram is simply data. Maximum datagram length can be configured, but is usually set to 8,192 bytes. Although the two-byte datagram length field sets the upper limit on the datagram size at 65,535 bytes, the maximum datagram length (8,192 bytes) generally implemented is determined more by other issues like programming interface and the way that TCP/IP is implemented. For example, application programs like NFS that use UDP by default use chunks of data that are 8,192 bytes long, so creating UDP datagrams any longer would add to the processing overhead without adding any benefits.

Another limiting factor is the requirement that computers running TCP/IP be able to handle IP datagrams that are at least 576 bytes long. This means that applications that use UDP and keep the data portion of each UDP datagram small enough can avoid IP fragmentation across any network.

UDP datagrams that are longer than the MTU for a given route get fragmented and encapsulated within IP datagrams and are reassembled on the receiving end. The maximum UDP datagram length shouldn't be too big or they won't all fit in buffers at the receiving end.

Where UDP Fits In

On first glance, UDP does not seem to be too useful: it adds no features on top of IP and pushes reliability functions up a layer to make the application responsible. Just as IP is connectionless and unreliable, so is UDP. However, UDP adds value by performing transport layer functions for applications that don't need or can't afford to allocate resources for making reliable connections between hosts.

As mentioned before, protocols relating to remote booting, like BOOTP (port number 67 for server; 68, for client) and TFTP (port number 69), use UDP because it reduces the amount of network software that must be implemented on diskless workstations prior to loading the bulk of the protocol stack from a boot server.

Likewise, request/reply applications are well suited to UDP. Domain Name Service (port 53) uses UDP, as does Network Time Protocol (port 123) and Quote of the Day (port 17). None of these applications is usually pressing in its urgency, nor does it require any significant interaction, thus making UDP a good choice for transport protocol. On the other hand, SNMP (Simple Network Management Protocol) handles more important data for network management, but still uses UDP to achieve a higher degree of efficiency for network management tasks (see Chapter 22).

UDP and Protocol Layering

Having described protocols at the data link layer in Chapter 6, the network layer in Chapters 7 and 8, and UDP, a transport layer protocol, it is now possible to envision TCP/IP network layering from the bottom to the top. Figure 9–3 shows graphically how the different layers are able to sort out network traffic handed up from lower layers and how to transmit network traffic coming down from higher layers. Once application protocols are discussed, the image will be complete.

Network applications produce or request information; the results of these actions are passed to the transport layer where the transport layer protocol encapsulates that data with a transport layer header. This header identifies the network traffic as coming from a particular process running on the local computer (source port number), and directs it to some other process running on some other nonlocal computer (destination port number).

The next layer down, the network layer, identifies the data by the source and destination addresses of the computers communicating. Again, the contents of the unit of data are enclosed with IP headers. The objective at this layer is to ensure that the traffic is directed at the correct host; in particular, at the correct host on the

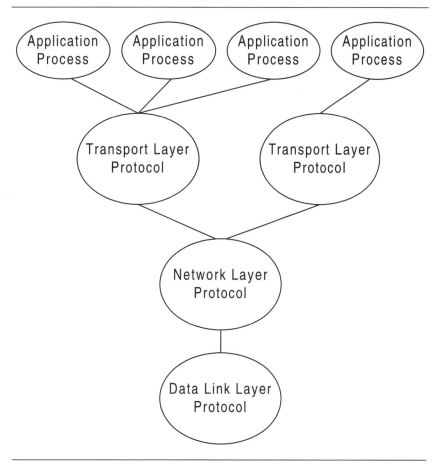

Figure 9–3: Applications can interact across an internetwork only through the cooperation of the lower network protocols, which link a process on one machine on one network to a process on another machine on another network.

correct network. At the bottom (link) layer, the protocols encapsulate the network traffic again to ensure that the data is delivered from one physical network interface to another network interface.

The process reverses on the receiving end: the link layer protocols unwrap the network frame, and determine to which network layer protocol to direct the traffic. The network layer protocol determines which transport layer protocol gets its datagram payload, which in turn passes the traffic up to the destination process on the destination computer.

Chapter Summary and References

This chapter covered the User Datagram Protocol, UDP, starting with an overview of the protocol itself and moving to a look at the UDP headers. A discussion of ports followed: well-known ports, ephemeral ports, and service ports that are not well known. We looked at the headers, especially the calculation of the UDP checksum, in more detail, and finished with a look at where UDP fits in to the TCP/IP protocol stack.

Some useful RFCs to read in conjunction with this chapter include those listed in Table 9–1.

RFC	Title	Description
768	User Datagram Protocol	Published in 1980, this RFC describes the Internet standard for UDP. It happens to be one of the shortest standards, at only three pages.
1700	Assigned Numbers	This RFC lists values that have relevance to Internet protocols. In particular, all well-known ports are listed here, along with values for many other fields in many other protocols.

Table 9–1: Useful RFCs for Chapter 9.

10

Transmission Control Protocol

The **Transmission Control Protocol** (TCP) is central to understanding TCP/IP networking. TCP dominates as a method to reliably and efficiently move network traffic between a client application on one host and a server application on another host. The keys are *reliability* and *efficiency*—TCP accepts the responsibility for maintaining reliable connections between hosts that lower protocols deferred to higher protocols, while managing the efficient packaging and transmission of network traffic that application protocols prefer to avoid handling.

TCP Properties

Like UDP, the Transmission Control Protocol is a transport layer protocol. However, whereas UDP offers little in the way of reliability or guarantees, TCP connects hosts across an internetwork reliably. TCP packages its data into segments containing both data and session control information that together comprise flows of information between the communicating hosts.

Whereas UDP is connectionless, TCP connections use virtual circuits. Each circuit behaves as if there is a direct, two-way connection between the communicating hosts. Whereas UDP is unreliable, TCP provides end-to-end reliability, requiring that communicating hosts coordinate and agree to make connections and acknowledge receipt of network traffic. Whereas each UDP datagram stands by itself as an individual message or reply, each TCP segment bears a relationship with the segment that came before and the segment that comes after. And that means the first and last segments in a sequence require special treatment. TCP also supports out-of-order delivery of segments, reassembling data streams from IP datagrams that have been delivered out of order.

TCP uses several techniques to tune connection performance. For example, TCP monitors the link to make sure that segments are neither too large nor too small and are being transmitted neither too fast nor too slow for the virtual circuit between the two systems. UDP interaction is in one direction only: a request goes from the requester to the network; the response comes from the responder back to the requester. TCP interaction is duplexed, allowing information to flow in both directions in each TCP segment. A host responds to a TCP segment requesting information by sending another TCP segment containing not only the information, but also control information about both the current segment being transmitted and about what segment it expects next from the remote host.

Finally, where UDP allows broadcasts and multicasts, transmitting data from one host to many hosts, TCP supports only host-to-host communication. TCP supports point-to-point circuits because each receipt of segment must be acknowledged. This means that the sending process must be listening for acknowledgment from the recipient and must at times wait for that acknowledgment before sending more segments.

TCP Features

So we see that TCP is differentiated from the other dominant transport protocol used in TCP/IP internetworks, UDP, in three very basic ways:

- ♦ Virtual circuits (TCP connections behave like live, two-way connections between hosts)
- ♦ Reliable connections (TCP guarantees delivery of data between hosts)
- ♦ Performance optimization (TCP includes mechanisms to modify transmission variables depending on current network conditions)

Whereas UDP provides a transport service "just good enough" for the applications that use it, TCP provides a more fully featured transport service for applications that need these amenities.

One interesting point about TCP is that each host in a connection has similar responsibilities for confirming receipt of transmissions and similar privileges for terminating the session. It doesn't matter who opened the link: both hosts must ackowledge receipt of all data sent by the other, and either host can terminate the session. Neither host acts as the master of the session; both are peers in the connection. For example, a file can be transferred from a host functioning as an FTP server to a host running an FTP client, but the client host has the option of transferring a file to the server, too.

The Virtual Circuit

TCP connections behave as if there were a hard-wired connection between processes on the two connected hosts. When a process initiates a TCP connection with another process, the two processes negotiate to open the connection. Each process must agree to participate. The TCP virtual circuit is similar to a telephone link: one person (process) initiates the telephone call (TCP circuit), but the person (process) at the other end has to answer the phone (agree to open the TCP circuit). A conversation (TCP circuit) ensues if both individuals (processes) agree to start and continue the conversation (TCP circuit).

Under certain circumstances, when a phone call is made a telephone conversation won't follow: a wrong number is dialed, the person being called is unavailable, there is a bad connection, the person being called can't talk. Similarly, there is no guarantee that a TCP circuit can be initiated and maintained: the requesting system wants a service that the other end does not provide, there is no connectivity between the two hosts, the server is unable to handle the request for service.

Each connection is identified uniquely with a combination of each host's IP address and port number for the connection. As with UDP, servers using TCP for their transport protocol use well-known port numbers for offering different network application services. The process specifies a port number to establish the connection, and the IP layer of the networking software indicates the host address. A client process attempting to connect to a Telnet server process specifies the Telnet port number (port 23). The port number and IP address of the host on which the process is running create a TCP socket. The client assigns some other TCP port number (not a well-known port) as its own TCP port, resulting in its own TCP socket: the client's IP address and TCP port number.

The combination of these two pairs of IP address and TCP port numbers, or two TCP sockets, uniquely identifies each TCP connection. A single host can maintain more than one TCP connection through a single TCP port because incoming TCP segments are differentiated by different source sockets. For example, a telnet server at address 10.0.0.1, listening to port 23, maintains any number of unique connections through the socket {10.0.0.1 | 23} because the other sockets (identifying the host IP addresses and port numbers of the client processes) are all unique.

In fact, a server can even maintain multiple connections made through a single client host. Consider what happens when several users of a mainframe system (10.0.0.1) all attempt to telnet to a remote mainframe (192.168.1.1). The server side socket will be {10.0.0.1 | 23} in all cases; the client side sockets will be of the form {192.168.1.1 | *nnnn*} where *nnnn* is some randomly selected port number. The server distinguishes incoming TCP segments not only by the IP addresses of the clients, but also by the port numbers so that the server can send the appropriate session data to the appropriate Telnet session.

TCP Reliability Features

The best reliability guarantee we've seen so far is a checksum calculated on the contents of the network transmission unit. UDP adds a pseudo-header to the UDP datagram prior to calculating the checksum, which helps the receiving system verify that the datagram arrived at the right address, without corruption. However, the UDP checksum itself is optional, and though it is widely implemented, not all implementations use it to verify received UDP datagrams. IP uses a header checksum, and even Ethernet includes a Cyclic Redundancy Check (CRC) field to do simple verification of data integrity.

With TCP you get more reliability. TCP implementations must include a checksum on the entire TCP segment as well as TCP header. TCP calculates the checksum on a pseudo-header that uses the same format as the UDP pseudo-header. The only difference is the value of the protocol type field—6 for TCP (see Figure 10–1). Calculating the checksum with the pseudo-header means the receiving host can verify that the TCP segment was received without any corruption at its intended destination.

However, TCP reliability features go well beyond checksumming all segments. There is a three-step handshaking routine required to initiate a TCP link, which will be described in more detail later in the chapter. Furthermore, every segment sent by either host must be acknowledged as received, and every segment includes information about the next segment to be sent. Both ends of the link keep track of what has already been sent, and both ends of the link keep track of what the other end is expected to be sending next.

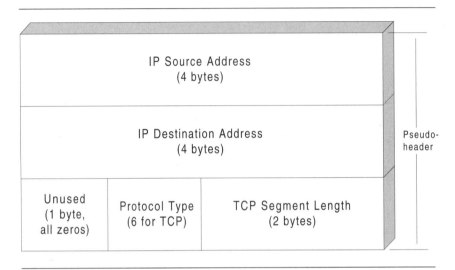

Figure 10–1: TCP uses a pseudo-header to calculate a mandatory checksum.

Recovery mechanisms at both ends deal with lost segments, duplicated segments, and segments sent out of order.

Though these features are necessary to create a reliable transport protocol, they add to the network overhead necessary to implement TCP. This could spell doom for any protocol that must operate over internetworks on a global scale: the smallest disruption in transmission between hosts could result in disaster to the connection. TCP includes features that allow it to adapt to changing transmission conditions, as well as to maximize performance, as we'll see later in the chapter.

TCP Segment Header Structure

The standard TCP header is 20 bytes long (but can be longer if options are used). As shown in Figure 10–2, the first two fields, source and destination port numbers, are each two bytes. The initiating host assigns itself an **ephemeral port number**, usually a randomly-assigned value greater than 1023. The destination port

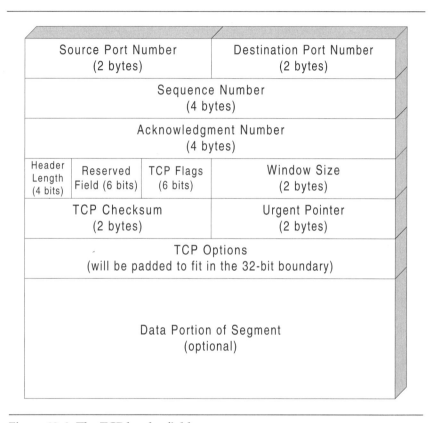

Figure 10–2: The TCP header fields.

number will be the well-known port associated with the service desired from the remote host.

Each byte in a TCP data stream is numbered, starting with an arbitrary number selected by the sending host. TCP connections are **duplex**, meaning data moves in both directions at the same time. Each host has its own data stream and each selects its own arbitrary starting point for numbering bytes in that data stream. The sequence number, a four-byte figure, is the number assigned by the sending host to the first byte in the current segment. The sequence starts at some arbitrary number between 0 and $2^{32}-1$ (about 4 billion), and wraps around to zero when the highest allowed value is exceeded. The next field is the acknowledgment number. This field contains the value of the next expected sequence number from the other side of the connection. In other words, if the last sequence number was 498 (see Figure 10–3), then the acknowledgment number will be 499, identifying by number the value of the next byte to be sent by the other side.

Figure 10–3 shows the three-way handshake protocol that opens all TCP connections. We'll come back to this figure several times as

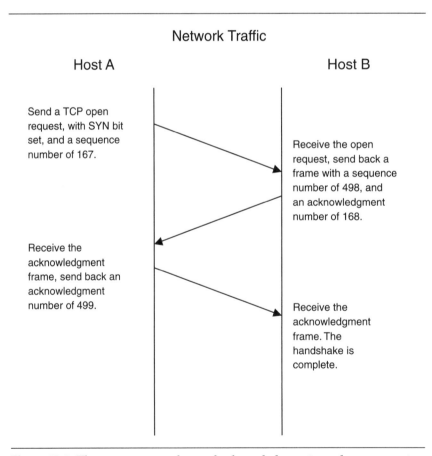

Figure 10–3: The sequence number and acknowledgment number represent byte counts in the streams of data being sent between two hosts connected using TCP.

we illustrate how TCP works. In this case, it demonstrates how the sequence number is related to the acknowledgment number, but we'll also be coming back to this figure when discussing the TCP flag bits and the three-way handshake.

In Figure 10–3, Host A sends a segment to Host B with the request to open a TCP connection. One of the TCP flag bits is named the SYN (for synchronization) bit, and when set indicates that the three-way TCP connection handshake is in process—that the two sides are synchronizing the connection.

Once Host B has received this initial message, it can send back a response, indicating two things: first, that it has received the initial message (also known as sending an ACK or acknowledgment), and second, it sends its own sequence number so that Host A can keep track of data sent from Host B. The acknowledgment is indicated by having the ACK bit set in the TCP flags, and the acknowledgment from Host B is actually Host A's sequence number plus one. Host A sent a sequence number of 167, and Host B acknowledges the message with the acknowledgment number of 168.

When Host A receives this message from Host B, it is able to verify that Host B got its initial message by comparing Host B's acknowledgment number with Host A's sequence number. It is also able to send off a third message to Host B with an acknowledgment of Host B's response: Host B's sequence number (498) plus one (499) is sent by Host A as an acknowledgment.

Sequence numbers are chosen arbitrarily, rather than always starting at some standard number (like 1), to avoid confusing the system when a host unexpectedly is turned off (or crashes). Fixing broken connections is much harder if all sequences began at 1 or 0. When the connection fails, one or both processes may be waiting for an ACK from the other. If a new connection is attempted, with the sequence number starting from 0 again, the receiving process may interpret that as a duplicate of a segment it already received. TCP would either have to add some facility to examine segments to determine which was a duplicate and which was a new transmission, or else time out connections relatively quickly.

Performance suffers in either case, so the arbitrary sequence numbers are preferred.

The four-bit header length measures the header in four-byte words, just like the IP header length field and for the same reason: TCP options may extend the header. As with the IP header, though, a four-bit field allows counts up to 15, setting the maximum header size at 60 bytes (15 four-byte words). The next six bits are reserved, followed by six TCP flag bits.

TCP flag bits are used to negotiate connections and manage the connection:

1. **URG:** indicates that the segment being sent should be considered urgent, and indicates that the urgent pointer field (see later) be used.
2. **ACK:** indicates that the acknowledgment number in the segment header is valid. In other words, when this flag is off, the value in the acknowledgment field must be ignored. This bit isn't set until a segment has been received from the other end, since there is no sequence number to acknowledge until then. However, this bit should always be on once a TCP connection has been established.
3. **PSH:** indicates that the data in the TCP segment should be pushed out to the application as soon as possible. This might be used during a Telnet session (or some other type of interaction) where the enclosed data will not be enough to fill up a receiving buffer but where the data should be processed immediately—like sending a carriage return or a short command to the remote server.
4. **RST:** indicates that the connection must be reset when turned on.
5. **SYN:** when the TCP connection is being negotiated, indicates that the synchronization process (of sequence and acknowledgment numbers) is taking place.
6. **FIN:** set to on when the sender has no more data to send.

The window size is a dynamic value that varies depending on how much data the process at either end of the circuit is willing to accept at any given time. The window size is specified as a number of bytes that the receiving host is willing to accept within its window. The process at either end can modify its window size at any given time while the TCP circuit is in use. When a window is large, it means the efficiency of the link is increasing, whereas a smaller window may mean that the receiving host cannot process the incoming data quickly enough to keep up with the current pace. We'll discuss TCP transmission windows below.

The TCP checksum, discussed earlier, is a two-byte field that covers the entire segment, the TCP header, and the TCP pseudo-header.

The urgent pointer field is used only when the URG flag bit is set. A common example of urgent data is the interrupt key in a Telnet session: it is used to interrupt other processes on the remote server and it should be accepted even though the server may be waiting for a process to end or waiting for some other data. The urgent pointer is used to indicate the sequence number of the last byte considered to be part of the urgent data.

The most common TCP option is to specify a maximum segment size, as mentioned earlier. Hosts can avoid fragmentation of TCP segments, which is detrimental to overall TCP circuit performance, by letting the host on the other end know the largest segment size it is willing to accept. The only other TCP options originally specified were a no-operation option, which acted as a filler to ensure that the TCP header ended on a four-byte boundary, and an end-of-option list option, which indicated that no more options were to come.

TCP has certain limitations that can pose problems when faster networks are being used. For one thing, the TCP window size has to be specified in two bytes, so it is limited to a maximum window size of 64 Kb. This may be enough for processes running on hosts connected to 10 Mbps Ethernets, but 64 Kb seems much smaller on gigabit (1000 Mbps) Ethernets. However, bandwidth as expressed in transmission speeds is not as important to the TCP window size as the latency of the network. Where bandwidth is high and latency is low, for example over a high-speed Ethernet LAN, a smaller window size will be optimal since messages can make the roundtrip between hosts relatively quickly. Given the same bandwidth, but with higher latency (for example, over a high-speed satellite link, where data must travel hundreds of miles between hosts), a larger window size is necessary to avoid long delays between transmissions.

Another issue arises from the fact that TCP sequencing numbers are limited to 32 bits, or about four billion different values. Imagine two processes communicating across a TCP circuit transmitted over a 10 Mbps Ethernet. Assuming that the processes are able to saturate the LAN, it would take close to an hour to move four gigabytes (10 Mbps is equivalent to 1.25 million bytes per second; at that rate it would take at least 53 minutes to transfer 4 gigabytes). There is little chance that a sequence number refers to anything but the current data stream.

Consider that same TCP connection running over a gigabit Ethernet. The network can move 125 million bytes per second and exhaust the sequence number space in as little as half a minute operating at top speed. Finally, if one end fails to acknowledge a segment when operating at very high speeds, the sending host has to retransmit and reduce its rate of transmission to make sure that more segments aren't lost—with the result that the hosts aren't able to take advantage of their high-bandwidth networks.

TCP options like sliding windows and time stamping make it possible to support the new faster networks by allowing larger window sizes. Time stamping segments helps to eliminate ambiguity caused by the wrapped sequence numbers, as well as improving flow control by making roundtrip time estimation more accurate.

Finally, it is worth noting that TCP segments need not be carrying data. In particular, when initiating or terminating a connection, the segments have no data other than that contained in the header to pass between hosts.

Three-Way Handshake

A TCP connection requires what is called a **three-way handshake** between the two connected hosts. The process uses the fact that all TCP segments must be acknowledged to produce a reliable link.

The three opening segments, as shown in Figure 10–3, are as follows:

1. Process A (on Host A) sends a segment to process B (on Host B), requesting process B to open a TCP circuit with process A and telling process B its opening sequence number. The SYN flag is set to on, to indicate that the circuit is in the process of being synchronized.

2. B responds to A's initial segment by sending an acknowledgment of the initial segment. It sets the ACK flag to on and takes A's initial sequence number, adds one to it (the next expected byte in the sequence), and puts that into the acknowledgment field. The SYN flag for this segment is also set, to indicate that synchronization is still not yet complete. At this point, when A receives this segment, it knows that B acknowledges the request, the connection from A to B is valid, but the link back from B to A won't be validated until B receives A's acknowledgment.

3. A acknowledges B's acknowledgment by putting the correct value in the acknowledgment field: B's sequence number plus 1. The ACK flag is also set, since A now knows the correct sequence number for the next segment from B. The SYN flag is no longer set, however, because once A sends this segment the synchronization process is complete.

Once the handshake is complete, the two processes continue to acknowledge each other's transmissions, but now they can start sending data in the segments as well, so the applications using TCP can communicate with each other.

Acknowledgment and Retransmission

Once the connection has been established, each side starts transmitting. For connections where large volumes of data are being transferred from one host to another, for instance in an FTP session, a large volume of data will move in one direction, but TCP segments will still move in the other direction (receiving host to the sending host) to acknowledge receipt of each segment being sent. While most of the application data may be moving in one direction, there is always a flow in the other direction that includes acknowledgments and any other application data (like requests for more information). The process sending the bulk of the data also sends acknowledgments along with that data—to acknowledge receipt of the other host's acknowledgments!

In a perfect world, both systems happily transmit TCP segments back and forth, receiving each other's acknowledgments and continuing to transmit new segments. In the real world, particularly across large internetworks, network traffic is delayed, fragmented, and corrupted. When that happens to UDP datagrams, not much happens because it is an inherently and admittedly unreliable delivery protocol. However, when TCP segments don't get delivered, action must be taken because TCP is a reliable protocol.

Instead of waiting for acknowledgment of receipt of every individual TCP segment before sending another one, TCP implementations determine some number of bytes (the window) they are willing to send before expecting to get back acknowledgments. Determining the size of that window depends on what the host at the other end indicates is the maximum number of bytes it is willing to accept, as well as the time it takes to move from the first host to the second host and back again: the roundtrip time (RTT). Various mechanisms are used to estimate the RTT in any given TCP circuit, and the resulting value is used to help determine how long a sending host should wait before assuming that a segment has been lost rather than simply delayed along its route. When it sends a segment, the host starts a countdown; if an acknowledgment for the segment is not received when that time is up, the segment is retransmitted.

Transmission Windows

TCP lets communicating processes determine how much data they are willing to process at any given time. Every time a segment is sent it includes a value indicating a current window size, so the host at the other end can modify the amount of data it is sending to accommodate the receiving host. This helps avoid flooding a smaller, slower computer's buffers when communicating with a larger or faster computer. The window size indicates the number of segments that can be considered to be "in transit" and the size of the window affects how fast segments are sent.

The optimal size of a transmission window depends on how fast data can be transmitted between hosts and how much latency there is in the connection. The problem is to make sure that the pipeline between hosts is always full of data, while never being too full of data. Imagine the TCP connection as a conveyor belt carrying bits of data to be processed (for the sake of the analogy, imagine that there is a second conveyor belt running in the opposite direction to carry responses and acknowledgments back to the sender).

The distance between the sender and recipient can be short, meaning that there is low latency, or it can be long, meaning there is high latency. Let's say that the conveyor belts move at four units per second, and that the two hosts are separated by ten units. Thus, it takes a little more than five seconds for a round-trip: you send an item from one host to another, it takes 2.5 seconds to arrive and some small amount of time is taken to create an acknowledgment and put it on the belt going back to the sender, 2.5 seconds later.

Five seconds is a long time to wait for an ACK without sending anything. If the receiving host can handle four units/second, the sender could actually just start sending its packages at that rate. In this case, the transmission window is about five units wide. If it doesn't start getting ACKs after five seconds, though, the sender might have to resend some or all of the packages—as well as consider making the window smaller. On the other hand, the receiving host can indicate to the sender that it can handle more segments in a given time—in other words, it wants a bigger transmission window.

Transmission windows give TCP a way to do flow control. This goes beyond the end-to-end flow possible between the two communicating processes. Transmission windows enable the connection to adapt to variations in internetwork traffic that occur within the Internet or intranet clouds. When the network link becomes congested (segments get lost), a sending host quickly can reduce the amount of data being sent. The objective is to avoid having to resend all segments and, in particular, to avoid having to slow down transmission to the point where each segment must be acknowledged individually before another segment can be sent. By backing off quickly and gradually building back up to a higher speed, the impact on throughput due to a congested internetwork will be minimized, and throughput will recover reasonably quickly. Most important, though, is to avoid getting bogged down to the point where each segment is individually acknowledged.

TCP Performance Features

RFC 2001 describes four important algorithms used for TCP performance enhancement:

♦ Slow Start
♦ Congestion Avoidance
♦ Fast Retransmit
♦ Fast Recovery

These techniques were all developed by Van Jacobson. Without them, TCP would be a considerably less powerful transport protocol, and TCP/IP would be a less useful protocol suite. The rest of this section provides brief descriptions of each algorithm as it is used for TCP.

Slow Start

In the early days, TCP implementations did nothing special for the first few segments sent after the connection was established. As soon as the connection was made, as many segments as filled the window would be transmitted down the line. Although this works when the hosts are on the same local network, it presents a problem when the hosts are connected across a routed internetwork. Since the intervening routers may have to queue the traffic carrying the segments, some part of that initial set of segments can be lost and thus cause significant performance problems.

The slow start algorithm addresses this problem of regulating the speed of transmission of segments by observing how fast the other side acknowledges the segments that have already been sent. In other words, if the ACKs are coming in very fast, then the transmission window can be made larger; if the ACKs are dribbling in very slowly, the transmission window may need to be made smaller.

With slow start, an additional window is added to the transmission window. The transmission window is set by the recipient, and the congestion window is set by the sender. The congestion window starts out at a value of one segment, and is increased every time an ACK is received. To determine the number of segments a sender can have in transit at any given time, the sender compares the values of the congestion window and the transmission window and is limited to the smaller of the two values.

With slow start, TCP implementations are able to gradually work their way up to a mutually acceptable value for the rate at which segments are transmitted, while minimizing the impact of sending too fast. In theory, the sender starts by transmitting a single segment (at which point the congestion window is set to one). When it receives an ACK of this first segment, the congestion window is increased to two—at which point it sends out two segments. When the recipient sends out ACKs for those two segments, the congestion window increases to four. Now, the sender can transmit four segments; when those are ACKed, the congestion window doubles again to eight. Eventually, if the congestion window exceeds the transmission window, the smaller value will be used to limit the window size. The other possibility is that the capacity of some intermediate system will be exceeded, in wihch case the sender will have to reduce the size of the congestion window.

Congestion Avoidance

Almost always implemented in conjunction with slow start, the congestion avoidance algorithm provides a mechanism for dealing with lost packets. Congestion avoidance acts as the brake for when the sender receives indications that packets are being lost somewhere along the line. Congestion occurs in networks for the same reasons it occurs in motor vehicle traffic: a high-volume roadway is being routed into a lower-volume roadway, two or more roadways are merging into a single roadway with lower overall capacity than the others put together, or a roadway is operating at a lower than normal capacity (a lane is blocked by a stalled vehicle, for example).

With slow start, all vehicles would come to a halt at any obstacle and then gradually speed up again until they hit another obstacle. This is not a good way to handle traffic. The congestion avoidance algorithm allows the congestion window to increase by one segment per ACK received when congestion is detected.

Congestion is assumed when a timeout occurs or when duplicate ACKs are received. A timeout means there may be a complete stop to traffic somewhere along the route; in this case the sender begins the slow start algorithm from scratch, setting the congestion window back to one. From there, slow start continues until the congestion window is half as large as it was when the timeout occured. At that point, congestion avoidance kicks in, keeping the congestion windows increase in size much smaller to avoid overloading a possibly congested link.

Duplicate ACKs, on the other hand, indicate congestion because the segments were received out of order or because a segment was lost somewhere en route. In that case, the congestion window is not reduced, but is only increased very slowly to avoid overloading the possibly congested link.

Fast Retransmit

Duplicate ACKs may be caused either by lost segments or by segments that have been delivered out of order. If the segment was actually lost, early TCP implementations had to wait for a timer to expire before retransmitting the missing segment. If the segment was delivered out of order, then it will eventually be ACKed and the sender won't have to retransmit it.

Fast retransmit is a simple algorithm: if three or more duplicate ACKs are received in a row, the TCP implementation can assume that there is a missing segment and therefore resend it. If the segment was merely delivered out of order, waiting for one or two duplicate ACKs should be enough to clear up the matter. If it takes longer, just resending the missing segment will be the right choice in almost all cases.

Fast Recovery

When a duplicate ACK is received, it means that there may be some congestion to avoid. When the fast retransmit algorithm is put into play, the fast recovery algorithm dictates that the TCP implementation invoke the congestion avoidance algorithm.

How TCP Fits In

UDP is useful for applications that rely on simple request/reply interactions and for broadcasting information to multiple hosts: because it does not place high demands on network bandwidth or performance through reliability requirements, it is ideal where reliability is not needed.

However, reliability is a necessity for providing most end user applications across an internetwork. TCP builds in the ability to communicate, as if connected with a physical circuit, between two hosts. Applications that use UDP often operate undercover and behind the scenes, but applications that use TCP are much more visible and need much more reliability. For example, Telnet and FTP both use TCP to ensure that connections are made and maintained and to make sure that data flows reliably between hosts.

Chapter Summary and References

In this chapter we examined the Transmission Control Protocol (TCP) and how it provides reliable transport services over IP to applications. Starting with a look at the properties and features of the protocol, we continued by discussing TCP connections, the TCP header, and the operation of the three-way handshaking protocol used to open TCP connections. We concluded with a look at TCP transmission windows and the algorithms used to enhance TCP performance across large internetworks.

Some useful RFCs to read in conjunction with this chapter include those listed in Table 10–1.

RFC	Title	Description
793	Transmission Control Protocol	This is the Internet standard specification for TCP.
2018	TCP Selective Acknowledgment Options	This document describes the use of selective acknowledgments to specify which segments have been lost rather than require sending processes to resend all segments since the last acknowledgment.
1323	TCP Extensions for High Performance	Describes window scaling to allow TCP windows larger than 2^{16} bytes, and a timestamping method for use with TCP. This specification has been a proposed standard since 1992, and has not advanced along the standards track since then.
2001	TCP Slow Start, Congestion Avoidance, Fast Retransmit, and Fast Recovery Algorithms	Describes the four important algorithms used for TCP performance enhancement.

Table 10–1: Useful RFCs for Chapter 10.

11

TCP/IP Host Name Resolution

Computers do well with numbers, and numbers provide a compact precision that names don't always offer, so IP addresses are quite useful for directing traffic from one host to another. However, people do much better with names and often find numbers, especially complicated ones like IP addresses that can be as long as 12 digits, hard to remember and easy to make mistakes with.

Most TCP/IP internetworks support numbers for precision and names for human convenience, both of them within systematic organizational frameworks. These frameworks were introduced in Chapter 2. Although host names and host addresses are required for each internetworked host, the TCP/IP network and transport protocols do not involve themselves with host names. They rely on IP addresses to function, so the Domain Name System must be used by the network application before any kind of internetwork transmission can take place. Discussion of how the network software applies name resolution methods to translate host names into network addresses follows.

Name and Address Resolution

TCP/IP network applications let the user identify servers by name. Web browsers accept servers by name, e-mail clients are configured to connect to servers by name, and most telnet and FTP clients will accept a host name when initiating a connection. Most of these clients will also accept IP addresses, but most users prefer to use names.

The application program may be able to accept a name rather than an address, but it must provide an IP address to the lower layer protocols if the application wants to communicate with the remote host. There are just a few ways for the application to get an IP address. The simplest (for the application) would be to get it from the user. Another approach is to use a **hosts** file, stored locally, that lists host names and their associated IP addresses. Figure 11–1 shows what a hosts file looks like. When an application needs an IP address, it compares the host name with the hosts file. If the host name matches a name in one of the rows of the hosts file, the application uses the IP address in that row.

Host files include the IP address, followed by the host name assigned to the IP address. An alias is an optional extra name for a host. This is particularly useful when a single host fulfills more than one function in a network. For example, Figure 11–1 shows several hosts with aliases: the first host is called *router* as well as *cisco*. This is probably the network's Internet router, and it is probably a Cisco router. The second host is probably an Internet server system that offers World Wide Web and FTP services on the Internet. It makes sense to use generic aliases for servers, rather than using some unrelated host name for public services, because these services are often moved from one host to another. Should a

```
192.168.127.1          router          cisco
192.168.127.2          iserver         www          ftp
192.168.127.3          mojo
192.168.127.4          maddog          fluffy
192.168.127.5          joyce
192.168.127.6          prod
192.168.127.7          fin
192.168.127.8          zeus
```

Figure 11–1: A simple host file contains IP addresses, host names, and host name aliases.

new host be purchased to act as a dedicated WWW server, the host iserver would give the www alias to the new server.

Hosts files are handy for small, closed networks that don't change very much. The hosts file is easy to understand and easy to set up, being a simple ASCII text file. Closed networks, where hosts don't need to connect with servers from the outside, can be mapped to hosts files with relative ease: you just make a list of all the hosts on the closed network. And hosts files work well with very stable networks, where there are relatively few changes in address and host name over time, and where new hosts are not added very often.

Another approach, useful for larger, more complex networks, is to store a master hosts file on a server and have all hosts download that file periodically to make sure all hosts are synchronized. In fact, this was roughly how name resolution happened in the very early days of the Internet. It worked adequately when the Internet had a few hundred hosts, but failed to scale up very well as the number of connected hosts increased by the mid 1980s. And in today's global Internet, which may have on the order of 100 million connected hosts, there is no question that a hosts file would be woefully inadequate to the task.

The Domain Name System

The Domain Name System, or DNS, was very briefly introduced in Chapter 2. DNS is nothing more than a highly distributed database of host names and addresses. The problem DNS solves is similar to the problem faced by a person who wants to make a telephone call to someone whose name is known but whose telephone number is not. This is a common problem. One solution would be to give all telephone subscribers a universal directory: a telephone book that included every single telephone number in the world, and the name of the person or entity associated with each number.

Unfortunately, this will not work very well. For one thing, if it were on paper, such a directory would be huge; even on digital media, there would be billions of entries, requiring a very large industrial-strength system to use the directory. And every directory would be constantly undergoing updates as people and businesses add lines, move, and go out of business or die.

Another option is to provide all subscribers with a local directory, and have each regional telephone service provider offer directory services for its own region. If you're in New York and want a phone number for a person in California, you would contact the appropriate entity in California to request the number. You might not know which entity (area code) in California you needed, so you might have to ask your local telephone company for that information. If you're in New York and want to call someone in Davos, Switzerland, you'd have to go through a slightly longer process: first contact your local telephone company to discover how to contact Switzerland, then some entity in Switzerland would direct you to the entity responsible for the Davos directory.

This is not really the way telephone directories work, but it gives an idea of how a distributed database can work. There is no central authority responsible for keeping track of each and every node connected to the network. DNS names are hierarchical. The root domains (.com, .org, .net, and so on) are served by root domain servers: these domain servers know everything about the domain names at the next level up. So, the .com root server will know where to find out more about any domain that takes the form *.com. For example, the .com server will be able to point you to another server that knows all about the domain loshin.com (or any other .com domain). And the domain server for loshin.com will be able to give you address information for any host or domain that takes the form *.loshin.com.

Each domain entity is responsible for maintaining a system that is always available to answer questions about the entities under it. The .com domain server knows where to send you for more information about loshin.com, but that server knows nothing about anything at a lower layer—like www.loshin.com. The DNS server for the loshin.com domain is the only place to get more information about www.loshin.com and other other *.loshin.com entity.

DNS Data

DNS servers store information in resource records (RRs). Though the most important piece of information that DNS provides is the IP address that matches a particular host name, other data is available. For example, the Domain Name System can provide a host name when it is queried with an IP address. This is useful for software that checks to make sure that clients attempting to make connections are who they say they are.

Another important use of DNS is to offer mail exchange (MX) information. MX records point electronic mail directed to some particular address to some other address. This is particularly helpful in a number of different situations. For example, not all organizations wish to make the details of their networks and e-mail systems known. They may be using a firewall, which forwards Internet traffic, or they may simply want to provide a universal, unchanging e-mail address format while allowing end users to receive e-mail on whichever host they prefer within the organization.

Setting up an MX record means that mail sent to the standard MX address will be exchanged with the real host taking that mail. MX records can be used to exchange e-mail between an e-mail gateway connected to a non-Internet network or internetwork, for example. Sending e-mail from an Internet-connected system to a system that maintains a gateway to send and receive Internet mail uses this method.

DNS can also provide a canonical host name when presented with an alias. Using the example in Figure 11–1 and assuming that the domain name for that network is starfleet.edu, a query to DNS could provide the information that the host name

www.starfleet.edu

actually refers to the host

iserver.starfleet.edu

This is not terribly exciting, but network managers more often use aliases to simplify host names to users of outside services so that, although they see something like

service.orgname.org

the actual host may be named something like

host.dept.something.orgname.org

Some DNS servers maintain host information, which may indicate something about each host (make or model of the computer or operating system), but again, some organizations prefer not to share this type of information across the Internet as it can be used by hackers to identify systems susceptible to certain types of attack.

A resource record contains the following information:

Name: This is the domain name to which the RR refers.

Type: This is a 16-bit value containing an RR type code, which specifies what kind of data is contained in the RDATA field. Some examples include A, for a host address; CNAME for a canonical address; NS for an authoritative name server; and MX for a mail exchange.

Class: This is a 16-bit value that further defines, by class, what kind of data is contained in the RDATA field. There are only a few valid values here, related to different networks. The only class value that most people will ever use (or even hear about) is the IN class—for the Internet.

TTL: This is a time to live value. This 32-bit field contains the number of seconds that the RR may be cached before it should be discarded. If this field is set to zero, it means that the RR should not be cached at all, just used for the current request and discarded immediately.

RDLENGTH: This 16-bit value indicates how many bytes long the value in the RDATA field is.

RDATA: This is the meat of the RR, containing a variable length string that will, usually, contain an IP address, host name, or mail exchange information.

DNS Queries

When an application is given a host name to send data to, it must decide whether or not to submit a DNS query. First, it has to determine whether or not it already knows about this host. If there is a local hosts file, the application might check there first. The application might also check in a cache, if the host name was resolved recently (see the next section on DNS caching).

DNS requests are sent out as UDP datagrams. Requests can pertain to a host's IP address, canonical host name, or MX information. The query format is relatively straightforward: What is the IP address of the named host? The query includes five sections:

Header: This section is present in all DNS queries, and provides information about the query itself and what else is contained in the rest of the query.

Question: This section contains the question—what information is being requested from the server.

Answer: This section contains a resource record that actually answers the question being asked. For example, if the original query was for an IP address of hostname.domain.org, the response would contain the RRs that answer that question.

Authority: This section contains RRs pointing to an authoritative name server, from which more information can be retrieved.

Additional: This section contains RRs that relate to the query, but which don't necessarily answer the question.

Domain names are expressed as character strings, with no dots or periods. Each section (part of the domain name set off by a period) is preceded by a single byte indicating its length (instead of the period). The last byte of the domain name is a 0, which represents the root node. For example, the domain name

```
www.starfleet.edu
```

would be represented within the UDP datagram as

```
3 w w w 9 s t a r f l e e t 3 e d u 0
```

The query containing this host name goes to the www.starfleet.edu's name server, which replies with the answer in a UDP datagram.

DNS servers respond to requests by repeating the question and appending the answer or answers to the question within the datagram. The answers are always one or more RRs, which include the type of information in the answer (in this case, a pointer from a domain name to an IP address), the type and class of the query, a time to live value assigned to the information being provided, the length of the reply, and the IP address associated with the domain name.

DNS Caching

If, every time a system requested a connection to some other system off the local internetwork, the DNS server had to query all the way to one of the root domain name servers and then work its way down the domain names, things would get very slow very quickly. To avoid this, DNS servers cache responses they get from other servers whenever they do a name lookup with another server.

As mentioned previously, DNS responses include a time to live value. Some DNS information is very stable: it is unlikely that the IP address of a well-known server will change over a short period. Other information is less stable: personal computers often move or drop from service without notice. The DNS servers attach some value to each response, so that remote servers can keep that information on hand for future reference. That way, the name server doesn't have to keep repeating the same queries to remote servers every time.

Chapter Summary and References

In this chapter, we examined the Domain Name System (DNS), and how it came to be the method of choice for resolving host IP addresses from host names. Starting with the basic hosts file, we looked at how DNS grew out of the need to maintain information for a huge number of different networks and hosts.

We continued with a look at DNS data, resource records, and mail exchanges, followed by an overview of DNS queries, and a brief discussion of DNS caching.

Table 11–1 lists some useful RFCs to read in conjunction with this chapter.

RFC	Title	Description
1034	Domain Names—Concepts and Facilities	This document describes the basic concepts underlying DNS, how DNS came about, and how DNS works.
1035	Domain Names—Implementation and Specification	This is the Internet standard that describes the way DNS should be implemented.
974	Mail Routing and the Domain System	Describes how e-mail routing works through DNS.

Table 11–1: Useful RFCs for Chapter 11.

12

BOOTP and DHCP

Most computers load their operating system and network configurations from their own local storage. From a technical viewpoint,
it's simpler: as long as the CPU is able to communicate with a disk
drive, the system will start. From a supportability viewpoint, however, this is a nightmare: someone must install and configure the
proper software for each system, and someone must physically
attend a malfunctioning system to determine what is wrong.

The idea of booting a system over the network is very attractive.
Loading the operating system and network configuration from
files stored on a network means users can't mess up their own configurations by mistake. It means all systems are configured according to rules set by the network manager. And it can mean that
systems can be added to the network without the explicit partici-
pation of a network engineer: true plug-and-play.

Initially, implementers deployed network booting through the Boot Protocol (BOOTP) to make smart terminals network-aware without reconfiguring them every time they boot up. The Dynamic Host Configuration Protocol (DHCP) grew out of work on BOOTP to help configure any kind of networked host, again without human intervention. Whereas BOOTP is rarely used other than for smart terminals, Internet Service Providers (ISPs) and many other organizations routinely use DHCP to configure all kinds of personal computers and workstations automatically.

Relatively new to Internet users is the concept of stateless auto-configuration. Available only under IPv6, stateless autoconfiguration has the potential to provide true plug-and-play network connectivity for all kinds of devices. As we'll see, with stateless autoconfiguration you'll be able to plug any device into any network and have immediate connectivity without the need for any human intervention—no need to notify the network administrator, no need to assign network addresses, no need to set up user IDs or passwords. Chapter 14 discusses IPv6 at length.

Configuration at a Distance

The Bootstrap Protocol (BOOTP) was specified by 1985 in RFC 951. BOOTP enables hosts without any significant computing resources in their own right to connect to an internetwork. BOOTP specifies the way the workstation can discover its own network identity (IP address) and initiate contact with a boot server. Once connected with a boot server the workstation downloads a boot file from the server using a file transfer protocol (usually the Trivial File Transfer Protocol, described in Chapter 16).

BOOTP is a simple protocol, intended for a single exchange of information between the host and boot server. The booting host tells the server what it knows about itself and its own boot process, and the server replies with whatever other information is necessary to allow the host to boot.

BOOTP's limitations became clear by the early 1990s: personal computers and workstations had more than enough disk storage to allow them to store their own operating systems as well as network configurations. However, network managers needed help allocating, configuring, and managing the IP addresses and host names of the systems connected to their networks.

Configuration errors abounded, despite the best efforts of the network management professionals. Personal computers in a large organization move frequently, and users as well as network staff misconfigure systems with alarming frequency. Tracking down problems related to misconfigured systems is very difficult, and reconfiguration sometimes exacerbates existing problems.

Even if configuration problems can be controlled, growing organizations often find that their assigned address space is being depleted. A company with a single Class C address is strictly limited to 254 simultaneously-attached hosts. ISPs must also be careful about how their IP addresses are used.

The Dynamic Host Configuration Protocol (DHCP) answers these issues by offering a mechanism that is backward compatible with BOOTP but that distributes a more complete set of network boot attributes to networked systems.

Both BOOTP and DHCP are **stateful autoconfiguration** protocols: somewhere, in a boot server connected to the network, is some configuration information related to every host authorized to be connected to the network. When a host requests configuration information, the boot server responds to the request with the information and keeps track of the status ("state") of that host's connection. Clients must be configured explicitly to use BOOTP and DHCP. The boot servers must also be configured explicitly for each host to which they are authorized to provide services.

BOOTP offers only the basic information that is absolutely necessary to initiate a TFTP connection with a boot file server, the client's IP address and a pointer to a boot file. DHCP offers more complete configuration services, including IP address, subnet mask, default gateway, and more.

BOOTP

BOOTP solves the problem of booting smart terminals or other systems with minimal storage resources. BOOTP does require that the system have local access (through a boot ROM or diskette, for example) to a minimal network protocol stack. Instead of TCP, BOOTP assumes the stack implements UDP for the transport layer and IP for the internetwork layer.

The terminal boots itself up with its minimal operating system and network configuration, and then BOOTP can get to work. The BOOTP process works in two phases. First, BOOTP discovers its own IP address, the IP address of its boot server, and the name of the file it must download from that server in order to boot. Second, the client downloads the file and loads it.

BOOTP Messages

BOOTP uses a very simple format for the exchange between host and server. Requests and replies both use the same message format. Client hosts requesting information leave blank the fields they don't know and the boot server responds by filling in those fields for the client.

When a client starts up, it sends a BOOTREQUEST message to a boot server. BOOTP may send this request as a broadcast to the local network; if there is a boot server available on the network it will respond to the request. However, broadcast transmissions are frowned upon, and BOOTP clients can be preconfigured with the IP address of their designated boot servers. If the boot server has been configured, the BOOTREQUEST message is sent directly to that server.

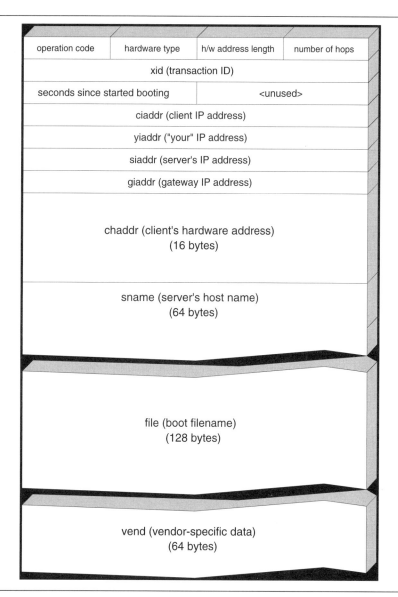

Figure 12–1: BOOTP message format.

Figure 12–1 shows the BOOTP message format. The BOOTRE-QUEST message includes the client's hardware network interface address (if present), as well as any other network boot information it already has. The client might have no other information, or it might have been preconfigured with its own IP address, a host name for a preferred boot server, and a path and filename for its boot file.

The boot server's BOOTREPLY includes the client's IP address as well as the IP address of the preferred boot server. Other information may be included in a separate vendor-specific data field. Descriptions of the various fields are in Table 12–1.

Field	Purpose
op	Operation code; requests (1) and replies (2)
htype	Hardware address type, with the same options as those available for ARP
hlen	Hardware address length in bytes; Ethernet addresses are 6 bytes long
hops	Normally zero; used for booting across routers
xid	Transaction ID number to match each boot request with its reply
secs	Number of seconds since the client started trying to boot
<blank>	This area is unused
ciaddr	Client IP address, if the client knows it
yiaddr	Your IP address; address filled in by the server, indicates client's address
siaddr	Boot server IP address, to be used by client to get boot file
giaddr	Gateway (router) address, used only for booting across internetworks
chaddr	Client hardware network interface address
sname	Server host name, may be a default server requested by the client
file	Name and path of the boot file
vend	Optional data that was originally intended to pertain to the hardware vendor, but may be used for various configuration options

Table 12–1: BOOTP message fields.

The BOOTP Process

BOOTP uses two UDP well-known ports: the client uses port 68 and the server uses port 67. This helps reduce the confusion that would occur when the server had to broadcast its response: using an arbitrary port for these responses might confuse other systems using that port.

The BOOTP process is simple. Unless the client knows the IP address of its boot server, the client broadcasts a request to the local wire for its own IP address and the IP address of a server storing its boot file. The server responds to BOOTP requests by sending them back, of course, but the server can't use ARP to discover the IP address of the destination client. The server sends its response back to the requesting client by broadcasting it—unless the server can edit its own ARP cache to add the booting system's IP and hardware addresses.

The BOOTP specification requires that clients be able to maintain at least one entry, their server's, in an ARP cache. This keeps network broadcasts to a minimum, especially if a failure occurs on the server side as a client is downloading a boot image file.

DHCP

BOOTP solves the remote booting problem for terminals that must download not only their IP address but also their operating system from the network. As network managers increasingly had to assimilate personal computers into IP networks, a different problem became apparent. Personal computers could boot themselves without resorting to network resources, but properly configuring them is much more difficult.

DHCP provides complete network configuration from the network. Hosts using DHCP configure themselves completely with all the necessary network parameters needed to perform as a normal host. DHCP is also intended to provide network configuration without human intervention.

The protocol defines two components to DHCP: delivery of specific host configuration parameters from a server to a client and a mechanism for allocating and assigning IP addresses to clients.

DHCP Messages

DHCP is a superset of the BOOTP protocol, using virtually the same message format and the same transmission mechanisms. The vend field under BOOTP is a 64-byte field, and is modified in DHCP, becoming the options field, with a variable length field of up to 312 bytes. This means that BOOTP requests can be handled as if they were DHCP requests—and DHCP servers can respond to BOOTP client requests. The name change more accurately reflects the function of the field. Also changed is the function of the two-byte unused field: this is now a flags field.

Requests from DHCP clients and responses from DHCP servers otherwise appear similar to BOOTP requests and responses.

DHCP Address Allocation

DHCP uses three mechanisms for allocating addresses:

Automatic: Hosts requesting an address are provided with a permanent IP address

Dynamic: Hosts requesting an address are provided with a temporary IP address

Manual: Host IP addresses are manually configured and DHCP just delivers these assigned addresses to hosts requesting them

Automatic allocation simply assigns the next available network address to each requester. This is simple, but it may not be effective for networks with lots of clients but not many IP addresses.

Dynamic allocation sets a time limit on the "lease" of the address, and the address reverts back to the allocation pool after that time (or after the host terminates its session). This is useful when a lot of clients connect to the network for relatively short periods or when hosts change location frequently. Manual allocation is useful when an administrator wishes to control the allocation, but not be present when a host is configured.

Figure 12–2 is an excerpt from the DHCP specification RFC 2131 showing the different network parameters that can be exchanged.

Stateless Autoconfiguration

Configuring IP hosts by hand is difficult: the network administrator must have a reliable way to keep track of which host names and IP addresses have been assigned and which are available, and a mechanism to prevent or at least avoid assigning the wrong addresses. Without a protocol like DHCP to simplify configuration, the Internet would not be experiencing continued growth as a consumer service.

However, DHCP relies on servers to maintain the state of all connections. And hosts cannot be configured unless they have been entered into a server's list of authorized hosts. As part of the IP Next Generation initiative for mobile networking, a protocol for stateless autoconfiguration was developed that allows any network-aware box to be connected to any IPv6 network and get all its configuration information automatically over the network— without the need to do any explicit configuration either by the user or the network administrator.

With IPv6, there are special addresses that can be used to communicate on the local network. These link-local addresses are used for stateless autoconfiguration, among other things. When a host connects to a network, it assigns itself a link-local address and then uses that connectivity to get an IPv6 router to respond with valid network configuration information. Stateless autoconfiguration

```
IP-layer_parameters,_per_host:_

    Be a router                     on/off                    HRC 3.1
    Non-local source routing        on/off                    HRC 3.3.5
    Policy filters for
    non-local source routing        (list)                    HRC 3.3.5
    Maximum reassembly size         integer                   HRC 3.3.2
    Default TTL                     integer                   HRC 3.2.1.7
    PMTU aging timeout              integer                   MTU 6.6
    MTU plateau table               (list)                    MTU 7
    IP-layer_parameters,_per_interface:_
    IP address                      (address)                 HRC 3.3.1.6
    Subnet mask                     (address mask)            HRC 3.3.1.6
    MTU                             integer                   HRC 3.3.3
    All-subnets-MTU                 on/off                    HRC 3.3.3
    Broadcast address flavor        0x00000000/0xffffffff     HRC 3.3.6
    Perform mask discovery          on/off                    HRC 3.2.2.9
    Be a mask supplier              on/off                    HRC 3.2.2.9
    Perform router discovery        on/off                    RD 5.1
    Router solicitation address     (address)                 RD 5.1
    Default routers, list of:
            router address          (address)                 HRC 3.3.1.6
            preference level        integer                   HRC 3.3.1.6
    Static routes, list of:
            destination             (host/subnet/net)         HRC 3.3.1.2
            destination mask        (address mask)            HRC 3.3.1.2
            type-of-service         integer                   HRC 3.3.1.2
            first-hop router        (address)                 HRC 3.3.1.2
            ignore redirects        on/off                    HRC 3.3.1.2
            PMTU                    integer                   MTU 6.6
            perform PMTU discovery  on/off                    MTU 6.6


    Link-layer_parameters,_per_interface:_
    Trailers                        on/off                    HRC 2.3.1
    ARP cache timeout               integer                   HRC 2.3.2.1
    Ethernet encapsulation          (RFC 894/RFC 1042)        HRC 2.3.3


    TCP_parameters,_per_host:_
    TTL                             integer                   HRC 4.2.2.19
    Keep-alive interval             integer                   HRC 4.2.3.6
    Keep-alive data size            0/1                       HRC 4.2.3.6

Key:

    MTU = Path MTU Discovery (RFC 1191, Proposed Standard)
    RD = Router Discovery (RFC 1256, Proposed Standard)
```

Figure 12–2: Network parameters that can be exchanged through DHCP (Appendix A "Host Configuration Parameters," RFC 2131).

also relies on the use of multicasting, using standard multicast addresses to which configuration information and requests can be sent. For more details, see RFC 2462.

Chapter Summary and References

In this chapter, we examined the two principal mechanisms for booting hosts from the network. The Boot Protocol (BOOTP) was originally developed in the mid 1980s to support not only network configuration of smart terminals and other network devices but also for network distribution of operating system images. We introduced the BOOTP message formats and discussed how those messages are used to configure hosts over the network.

The Dynamic Host Control Protocol (DHCP), a superset of BOOTP, makes it possible to configure hosts more completely with many different configuration options, as well as to control the distribution of IP addresses. We finished with a brief introduction to the concept of stateless autoconfiguration as it is specified for use in IPv6 networks.

Table 12–2 lists some usefulRFCs to read in conjunction with this chapter.

RFC	Title	Description
951	Boot Protocol (BOOTP)	The specification for the Boot Protocol, describing a mechanism that allows a diskless client work-station to boot off a network server.
1542	Clarifications and Extensions for the Bootstrap Protocol	RFC 951 left unclear some BOOTP issues. This RFC clarifies the origi-nal specification and discusses issues that arose since RFC 951 was published.

Table 12–2: Useful RFCs for Chapter 12.

RFC	Title	Description
1534	Interoperation between DHCP and BOOTP	DHCP is a superset of BOOTP. This document specifies how BOOTP and DHCP protocols interact.
2131	Dynamic Host Configuration Protocol	The current, draft standard, specification for DHCP. This RFC supersedes RFC 1541, an earlier specification for DHCP.
2462	IPv6 Stateless Address Autoconfiguration	Describes the mechanisms by which an IPv6 host can configure itself using a stateless autoconfiguration protocol.

Table 12–2: Continued

13

IP Multicast

Bandwidth is one of the most precious resources available on any network, and IP networks are no exception. Anything that can help preserve bandwidth is good, and anything that wastes bandwidth is bad. As the number of nodes on a network increases because the number of systems connected to the Internet has grown, the amount of available bandwidth for any given user decreases.

Network multicasting is an important tool for using bandwidth more efficiently, and IP multicast has long been an important part of the Internet Protocol specification. However, multicast is still not used very often for Internet transmissions. In this chapter, we examine how multicast works, why it is useful, and why organizations have been slow to deploy multicast across the Internet.

Network Multicasting

With broadcast transmission of data across a network, all nodes on the network receive the data. This is one way to get information to more than one node at a time, while sending only one copy of the message. The alternative is to send a separate copy of the message to each recipient.

Each of these alternatives has serious drawbacks. Broadcasts are very inefficient. Despite the fact that network bandwidth is conserved, overall performance of systems connected to the network is degraded because each system must accept and process each broadcast message. It doesn't take that many routine broadcasts to affect at least some systems. This is a large part of the reason that use of broadcasts is being deprecated (for example, IPv6 does not include support for broadcasts, as discussed in Chapter 14).

Sending a separate copy of the message to each recipient takes far less of a toll on the systems receiving the messages. However, each copy of the message takes up network bandwidth. For bandwidth intensive applications, it doesn't take very many duplicate data streams to overwhelm most network media.

A middle path exists in the form of network multicast. Messages sent to a multicast address are sent only once on each network link, but any number of connected nodes can listen to messages sent to that address. In that way, it is like broadcast, but unlike broadcast, only those nodes that opt to subscribe to the multicast address need to process multicast messages sent to that address. And the message needs to be sent only once.

Multicast works best on a network medium like traditional Ethernet, where all nodes are connected to the same wire and where every node can process all messages sent on that wire. Subscribing to a multicast address on this type of network is a simple matter of having the network interface card listen not only for messages sent to its own MAC address but also to messages sent to whatever multicast addresses are of interest.

When you start trying to do multicast on nonbroadcast media access (NBMA) networks, things get more complicated. The nodes can't just "listen in" for multicast messages—they've got to notify some entity to formally subscribe to a multicast address. That entity can then duplicate the multicast message for all the subscribed nodes. In this situation, multicast is not really any more efficient for delivering messages to multiple nodes than sending separate copies of the messages to each subscribing node.

Network multicast, as just described, is available at the data link layer for deliveries within the local network. It can be particularly useful for improving efficiency of Ethernet networks. Extending the multicast address to the IP layer extends its power, but can also make it more complicated to deploy. As we'll see in the next section, IP multicast has been around for a long time, but has yet to find widespread acceptance and implementation.

Understanding Multicast

Applying multicast at the network layer, across internetworks, poses a problem similar to that of using multicast in a nonbroadcast network. Routers (or some other systems) must act on behalf of subscribing nodes to accept and forward messages sent to a multicast address. To understand how IP multicast works, consider an actual application that could benefit from it.

When Pointcast rolled out its news service to Internet users, it was heralded as a milestone application. Users signed up for the news categories and sources they preferred, and Pointcast "pushed" those items out to users automatically. Users loved it, but network administrators hated it: Pointcast chewed through bandwidth faster than a school of piranha through a pound of hamburger. Dozens or even hundreds of users at corporate offices would often subscribe to the same news streams, causing Pointcast to flood the network with duplicate messages every time a news item was published. Corporate Internet connections would be flooded by

Pointcast transmissions, because Pointcast sends a separate copy of each message to each individual user signed up for the service.

One approach to reduce this waste of bandwidth using multicast would be to have Pointcast transmit its news messages to a specific multicast address and to have all the computers subscribing to the Pointcast service also subscribe to that multicast address. However, this would require that all the routers operating between the subscriber computers and the Pointcast server support multicast routing, something that is not always likely to be the case.

Figure 13–1 shows how a Pointcast-like service works—let's call it Broadcast News. Subscribers may be connected to the same local

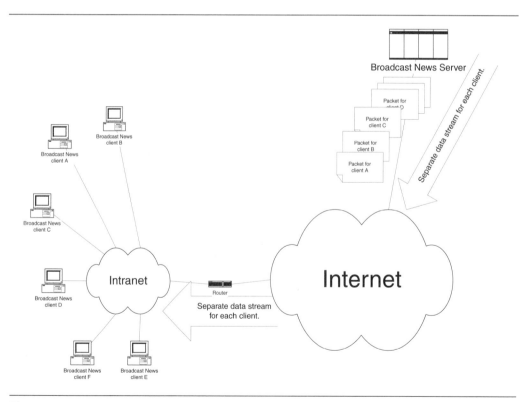

Figure 13–1: Unicast transmission can be wasteful of bandwidth when the same messages are sent out to many nodes.

networks or directly connected to an Internet service provider, but in each case every subscriber gets a direct stream of data sent to its own unicast address. This approach is expensive in terms of bandwidth: every new subscriber requires a discrete amount of additional bandwidth capacity from the Broadcast News server. Not only that, but the intranet users clog up their organization's Internet connection with duplicated inbound messages.

One way to cut down on the waste is to have organizations with many users of this service set up a system designated as a proxy or agent for internal subscribers. Rather than have a separate stream of messages for each subscriber within the intranet, the service sends a single stream of messages to the proxy agent, which distributes the messages to local subscribers. Within the intranet, the agent might make duplicates of every message and send it out individually to subscribers, or it might make use of network multicast functions to reduce the amount of internal bandwidth wasted. However, this approach reduces the wasted Internet bandwidth both for the organization receiving the messages and also for the organization sending the messages.

IP multicast offers an even better solution to this problem. Assume that all Internet routers support multicast (a big assumption, by the way). Now, our Broadcast News service sends out a single stream of messages to a multicast address. Instead of using special-purpose proxy agent systems, all IP routers act on behalf of subscribers. If a node wants to subscribe to a specific IP multicast address, it notifies its local routers. If one of a router's clients wants to subscribe to a multicast address, then the router must subscribe to that multicast address too. Once a router is asked to subscribe to an IP multicast address, it requests that the routers on the other networks to which it is connected subscribe to that address too.

Ideally, the result will be something like what is shown in Figure 13–2, where the originator of material sent to a multicast address sends only a single copy of the material to that address. Consider first the nodes on the intranet. Each of these nodes notifies its router, Router A, that it wants to subscribe to the multicast

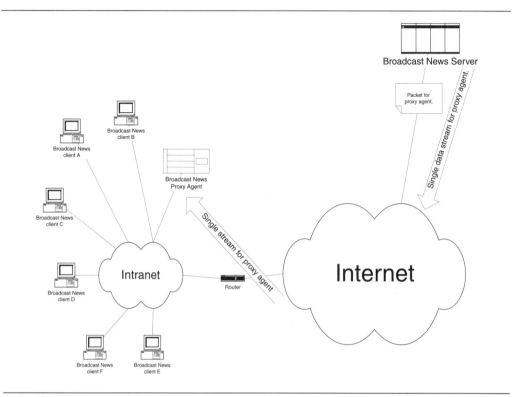

Figure 13–2: Agents can act on behalf of a service, and reduce the duplication of messages within an intranet.

address. Router A then tells Router B it wants to subscribe to that address; Router B tells Router C, which tells Router D, which is connected to the source. When the source sends out a datagram to that multicast address, Router D will send a copy to Router C, which will send it to Router B, which will send it to Router A, which will send it to the subscribing nodes.

Now something similar happens with the other subscribers connected to an ISP. Those nodes tell Router E they are subscribing, which tells Router F to subscribe, which tells Router D. Thus, Router D sends out two copies of that datagram, one to Router F and the other to Router C. Router F forwards the packet to Router E, which forwards the packet to the two subscriber nodes.

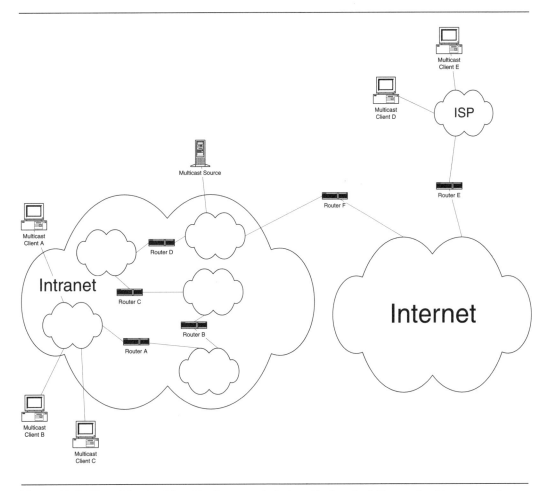

Figure 13–3: IP multicast, at least in theory, minimizes the bandwidth required to propagate a message to many destinations across the Internet.

In practice, the route that a datagram takes is likely to be more complicated than what is shown in Figure 13–3. And it assumes that all the routers in the paths between subscribers and the broadcaster are multicast-enabled—not a likely situation. Few Internet service providers routinely enable their routers and backbones for multicast, at least not so far. We'll look at the issues holding back IP multicast later in the chapter.

IP Multicast

Multicast has long been an integral part of IP, at least as far as standards go. RFC 1112, "Host Extensions for IP Multicasting," defining the use of multicast within IP internetworks, was published in 1989. RFC 1112 is considered an integral part of the set of IP standard specifications. However, when RFC 1812, "Requirements for IP Version 4 Routers," was published as recently as 1995, the authors stated "the forwarding of IP multicasts is still somewhat experimental." That document indicates that IP routers "should" implement IP multicast forwarding, but that it is not a required part of the specification. By 1999, the situation was changing, albeit slowly.

RFC 1112 specifies three levels of conformance to IP multicast. At level 0, the host has no support for IP multicast. When such a host improperly receives a datagram addressed to a multicast address, its proper response is to quietly discard the datagram. Level 0 hosts should be able to identify Class D addresses as multicast addresses, but do not have to support multicast in any other way.

Level 1 hosts are able to send multicast datagrams, but not receive them. Converting a level 0 host to level 1 conformance is relatively simple, and allows such hosts to participate in applications that require hosts to report their status or submit other information to a multicast address, but which do not require such hosts to be able to accept multicast datagrams.

To achieve level 2 compliance, a host must not only be able to send multicast datagrams but also to join and leave **host groups**, which are the sets of hosts that are identified as being associated with a particular multicast addess. By joining a host group, a host can receive multicast datagrams.

Internet Group Management Protocol (IGMP)

Earlier in this chapter, we spoke of hosts "telling" routers about which multicast addresses they wanted to subscribe. The Internet

Group Management Protocol (IGMP), specified in RFC 1112, describes the mechanisms by which hosts can notify any multicast routers that are in the immediate neighborhood of the host's multicast group memberships.

IGMP specifies two types of messages that are relevant to multicast hosts. Multicast routers send out the IGMP membership query message to a standard multicast address that identifies the all-hosts group (224.0.0.1). This address differs from the broadcast address in that only level 2 multicast-enabled hosts respond to it—other hosts ignore messages sent to this address.

When a multicast host receives an IGMP membershp query it begins to send IGMP membership replies, one for each multicast group to which it belongs. The replies are addressed to the multicast address of the group. This helps reduce traffic if there are other members of the same multicast group on the local link. Once the first member of the group responds to the IGMP query, the other members don't have to notify the router of their own memberships.

Multicast routers periodically send out IGMP membership queries to keep track of which multicast addresses they should be listening for on their other networks. Hosts usually send out IGMP membership replies in response to these queries—or as soon as the host joins the group.

As defined in RFC 1112, multicast works most effectively on network media that offer a broadcast/multicast function at the link layer. Ethernet, for example, allows a single broadcast or multicast to be received by all connected nodes. However, this can be a problem for non-broadcast multiple access (NBMA) networks like ATM, which use virtual circuits to transmit data directly from a router to a host.

As defined in RFC 1112, routers need not keep track of which hosts are subscribing to which multicast addresses—if a host is a member of a group, it simply listens to multicasts forwarded at the link layer multicast address. However, things are different for NBMA networks, where broadcast and multicast are more complicated. Such networks require some mechanism to keep track of which nodes need multicast retransmissions.

Multicast Routing

Routing multicast datagrams is more complicated than routing either unicast or broadcast datagrams. A router that forwards packets on several networks might find itself forwarding the same multicast packet on all or some of those networks—or on none, depending on whether or not hosts on those networks are members of the multicast group in question.

These protocols generally use a mechanism to discover the shortest path for multicast datagrams by looking at the source address of the datagram. If a router receives a multicast packet on an interface that is on the shortest path back to the sender, then the router can forward the packet on to other network interfaces to other group members. If the router receives the multicast packet on some other interface, then it just discards the packet because there is no need to forward it.

There are two approaches to multicast routing. Dense-mode multicast routing algorithms work on the assumption that there are likely to be multicast group members on all or most connected networks. Sparse-mode multicast routing algorithms work on the assumption that there are relatively few members of each multicast group and that most routers won't be involved in forwarding multicast packets. Each of these approaches has advantages and disadvantages, and each has specific types of situations in which it works best.

Dense-Mode Multicast Routing

Dense-mode multicast routing protocols are best suited to networks with plentiful bandwidth where most routers are connected to networks that may have multicast group members. These protocols are built on the assumptions that there will be many other multicast routers in the routing environment and that there will be many hosts that are members of multicast groups. Routers implementing these protocols use IGMP messages to build routing tables, and share their results with other multicast routers.

One dense-mode protocol, the Distance Vector Multicast Routing Protocol (DVMRP), was published as an experimental protocol in 1998, in RFC 1075. IETF members currently are engaged in work on a very different, modern version of this protocol. DVMRP routers are used to calculate multicast delivery trees that include the optimal routes to all members of the multicast group. As members join or leave the group, the routing trees are modified. As its name implies, DVMRP uses distance-vector routing and has some features in common with RIP (see Chapter 8 for more on routing protocols).

Multicast Open Shortest Path First (MOSPF) is another dense-mode multicast protocol. Described in RFC 1584, "Multicast Extensions to OSPF," MOSPF extends OSPF to enable it to forward multicast packets as well as unicast packets. (*Unicast* packets are those sent to a single IP destination, in contrast to multicast packets, which are sent to multiple destinations.)

The Protocol Independent Multicast-Dense Mode (PIM-DM) protocol is currently an IETF work-in-progress, described in Internet-drafts. In PIM-DM, it is just assumed that all downstream routes will want copies of a multicast datagram. Routes on which there are no group members will eventually be pruned off the PIM-DM routing tables.

Sparse-Mode Multicast Routing

Sparse-mode multicast routing protocols are built on the assumption that there just aren't that many multicast group members or multicast routers around. Common to sparse-mode multicast routing protocols is an approach that uses the concept of a core router or rendezvous point (RP). In each case, the core or RP acts as a reference point for multicast groups. Rather than attempt to build routing maps, as is done by the dense-mode protocols, in sparse-mode protocols the routers route multicast packets to and from the core routers or RPs. This approach reduces the overhead of keeping track of a multicast routing map.

RFC 2362, "Protocol Independent Multicast-Sparse Mode (PIM-SM): Protocol Specification," specifies (as an experimental protocol) a multicast routing protocol that is largely identical to PIM-DM, except that it uses rendezvous points through which to route packets. The Core-Based Trees (CBT) routing protocol is described in RFC 2189, "Core Based Trees (CBT version 2) Multicast Routing," and in RFC 2201, "Core Based Trees (CBT) Multicast Routing Architecture." CBT is also specified as an experimental protocol, and uses the concept of a core router from which multicast routing trees sprout. Other multicast routers must determine routes to these trees for multicast group members.

IP Multicast Applications

Multicast lends itself to applications that require the systematic transmission of identical information to many different recipients. Financial firms often use multicast to enable applications to transmit financial ticker and news information to every workstation on a trading floor.

Multicast is seen as a key enabling technology for the broadcast of audio and video over the Internet, especially for audio and video conferencing applications. These applications can withstand delivery delays or interruption in transmission of datagrams, but still require some degree of feedback from recipients as well as some kind of framework for the data being delivered. The Real-Time Transfer Protocol (RTP), described in RFC 1889, helps provide quality of service feedback to multicast originators from multicast recipients.

The Real Time Streaming Protocol (RTSP) described in RFC 2326 defines the way data is carried and controlled within the transport layer, and provides mechanisms for setting up recipients to receive multicasts.

Chapter Summary and References

In this chapter, we elaborated on the concepts of multicasting, both at the data link layer and at the internetwork layer. We examined IP multicasting both in terms of what kinds of problems multicast can solve and of the current Internet standards for multicasting. We introduced multicast routing, discussing the different approaches taken by sparse-mode and dense-mode routing protocols. Finally, we discussed the type of applications that can best use multicast.

Some useful RFCs to read in conjunction with this chapter are listed in Table 13–1.

RFC	Title	Description
1112	Host Extensions for IP Multicasting	Internet standard specification for IP multicasting.
1812	Requirements for IP Version 4 Routers	Discusses multicast router implementation.
1584	Multicast Extensions to OSPF	Extensions to OSPF to enable multicast routing.
2362	Protocol Independent Multicast-Sparse Mode (PIM-SM): Protocol Specification	Standards track specification for multicast routing protocol.
2189	Core Based Trees (CBT version 2) Multicast Routing	Specification for an experimental sparse-mode multicast routing protocol.

Table 13–1: Useful RFCs for Chapter 13.

RFC	Title	Description
2201	Core Based Trees (CBT) Multicast Routing Architecture	Describes the architecture for a sparse-mode multicast routing protocol. This RFC describes an experimental protocol.
1889	RTP: A Transport Protocol for Real-Time Applications	Describes a transport protocol for real-time applications.
2326	Real Time Streaming Protocol (RTSP)	An application layer protocol to format and deliver real-time data with minimal service interruptions.

Table 13–1: Continued

14

Internet Protocol Version 6

This chapter introduces the Internet Protocol version 6 (IPv6), the update to IPv4, the version that most people have been using for the past twenty years or so on the Internet. Starting with an overview of IPv6 features and functions and the new IPv6 protocol header and header extensions, we continue with an overview of the IPv6 address architecture. We finish up with a discussion of the transition from IPv4 to IPv6.

This chapter introduces IPv6, but is far from exhaustive. The interested reader is urged to read the RFCs cited in Table 14–1, as well as the book IPv6 Clearly Explained (Morgan Kaufmann 1999) for more information about how IPv6 works.

Why IPv6?

With IPv4, IP addresses are unique and usually persistent identifiers of all nodes on IP networks. That view of IP addresses has been changing: it may not be necessary or efficient to allocate network and node addresses as we have been doing for the past 20 years. There is no question that the IPv4 address space is being depleted—this has been clear since the late 1980s, when work started on the IP Next Generation (IPng) project.

At first, the primary objective for the IPng working group was to come up with a way to extend the IP address space so that it could support more networks and more hosts. However, it soon became clear that any modification to IP to accommodate more hosts would require an update to every node's IP networking software—and if an upgrade of that magnitude was being undertaken, the reasoning went, why not do a true upgrade to IP? Fix not just the address space problem, but also the other problems, big and little, that have become apparent after twenty years of deployment. And while we're at it, why not enhance the protocol as well?

It turns out that the address space squeeze was amenable to a variety of short-term fixes like network address translation (NAT) and Classless Interdomain Routing (CIDR). However, the way IPv4 routing is done, combined with the growth of the number of discrete IP routes, has posed an even greater danger to the growth of the Internet. Backbone routers must store all IP routes in order to forward datagrams anywhere in the Internet. As the number of routes continues to grow, it becomes more and more difficult for routers to forward packets efficiently as they must look up routes on larger and larger routing tables.

The IPng working group published their first specifications for IPv6 as standards track RFCs in late 1995: RFC 1883 decribed the protocol itself, and RFC 1884 described the IPv6 address architecture. By the end of 1998 a second wave of revised specifications was published, describing draft standards for IPv6 and related protocols. Some networking vendors have been working on IPv6 implementations since the early 1990s, and commercial implementations are available from leading vendors like 3Com and Hitachi. As issues related to IPv4 address space and other shortcomings cause increasing problems and anxiety, IPv6 deployment will grow. By design, IPv6 can coexist with IPv4, so there is no need to mandate a cutover date when all systems on the Internet must support the new protocol.

The Internet Protocol as we know it was designed during the late 1970s, when it seemed that a 32-bit address space—permitting an absolute maximum of 2^{32} (4,294,967,296) hosts—would be more than enough to address all the hosts connected to the Internet for the foreseeable future. For one thing, IP was still very much an experimental technology, of interest almost exclusively to academics and researchers. For another, the idea of ubiquitous networked personal computers was many years in the future.

IPv6 addresses are four times as long as IPv4 addresses, and at 128 bits provide an absolute maximum of 2^{128} individual hosts. This is very roughly 340 billion billion billion billion different hosts! Even if every human now living were to have a personal network, with a billion nodes on each network, the IPv6 address space is large enough to support (at least theoretically) roughly another 50 billion billion similarly wired planets.

What's New in IPv6

IPv6 improves on IPv4 in five important areas:

♦ **Expanded addressing:** Based on projections made as early as the late 1980s, the IPv4 address space would have been depleted by the early to mid 1990s without numerous stopgap measures such as network address translation (NAT) and Classless InterDomain Routing (CIDR). The IPv6 address space should be sufficient to accommodate all network growth for the foreseeable future.

♦ **Simplified header format:** In practice, the IPv4 header was found to be more complicated than necessary—and susceptible to improvement in ways that could improve routing efficiency as well as the overall performance of attached systems.

♦ **Improved extension and option support:** Header extensions and options in IPv4 required treating datagrams as special cases, thus hampering the ability of routers to process those datagrams efficiently. A design goal of IPv6 was to improve the way header extensions and options are implemented so that they don't affect network and routing performance.

♦ **Flow labeling:** Although IP is a connectionless, unreliable protocol, some applications suffer unless they can depend on the network to treat their data flows with some degree of predictability. Flow labeling provides a mechanism by which related packets can be treated as streams, improving the way IP works as a transport for real-time multimedia applications.

♦ **Authentication and privacy:** In its original incarnation as a research project, IPv4 delegated security issues to higher layer protocols. From the start IPv6 was intended to incorporate security features to make it a desirable option for business and other types of users who need assurance that the information they send is received only by authorized entities, unchanged, and unseen by unauthorized entities.

The original IPng working group charter, approved by the Internet Architecture Board (IAB) in 1991, mandated most of these areas of concern.

IPv6 Addressing

The IPv4 address space is inefficient for most networks. Although with 32 bits, over four billion individual nodes could, in theory, be addressed, the way the address space is organized means that the actual number of nodes and networks possible is considerably lower. The 126 possible Class A networks use up almost half of the entire IPv4 address space; Class B networks use up one quarter and Class C networks make up only one eighth of the space. Just increasing the number of bits in the address field goes a long way toward improving the situation, but is not sufficient to solve the problem for the long term.

IPv6 addresses are 128 bits long, but in addition to moving from a 32-bit address space to a 128-bit address space, the IPv6 addressing architecture makes some adjustments to the different types of addresses available to an IP host. IPv6 eliminates broadcast addresses but adds the concept of **anycast** addresses. Unicast addresses, specifying a single network interface, and multicast addresses, specifying an address to which one or more hosts may be listening, continue basically unchanged from their IPv4 incarnations. IPv6 addresses will be discussed in more detail later in this chapter.

Header Simplification

IPv6 headers contain eight fields, and all IPv6 headers are exactly 40 bytes long. IPv4 headers contain at least 12 different fields and may be as short as 20 bytes with no options or as long as 60 bytes with options. By making all headers the same length, routers can process the datagrams more efficiently. Figure 14–1 shows the IPv6 header.

The IPv6 header is simplified partly because the protocol has been simplified. With all headers the same length, the header length field can be eliminated. Intermediate routers are not allowed to do packet fragmentation in IPv6—fragmentation is available only on an end-to-end basis as an option, so all the header fields related to fragmentation have been removed from the IPv6 header. Finally, the IP header checksum has been removed from IPv6.

Header Extension and IPv6 Options

Unlike IPv4, in which options are appended as part of the IP header, IPv6 adds options in separate extension headers. This way

Version	Traffic Class	Flow Label	

Figure 14–1: The IPv6 header fields; compare to the IPv4 header fields shown in Figure 7-1.

routers not involved in processing the extension headers can ignore them and treat the datagram just like any other datagram.

As mentioned earlier, IPv6 doesn't allow intermediate routers to fragment packets. Communicating nodes may decide they want to fragment packets on an end-to-end basis, in which case fragmentation information is carried in a fragmentation header extension. Routers don't bother with that header; they just process the datagram based on the IPv6 header. The source node does the fragmentation, putting fragmentation information into the header extension; that extension is processed only by the node at the receiving end.

Now consider a hop-by-hop option extension header specifying something that must be done by the router every time the packet is forwarded. This option requires that every node along the packet's route process that extension header. Every router in the datagram's path has to process the hop-by-hop option as well as the main IPv6 header. The first such hop-by-hop option is defined for handling extra-large IP packets (jumbo payloads). Packets with jumbo payloads (over 65,535 bytes) require special treatment because not all links will be capable of handling such large size transmission units, and routers want to avoid attempting to send them out on networks that cannot handle them. Thus, it is necessary for the option to be checked at every node the packet traverses.

Flows

In IPv4, all packets are treated roughly equally, which means each is handled on its own by intermediate routers. Routers do not keep track of packets sent between any two hosts so they can "remember" how to handle future packets. IPv6 implements the concept of the flow, which is, according to RFC 2460, "a sequence of packets sent from a particular source to a particular (unicast or multicast) destination for which the source desires special handling by the intervening routers."

Routers keep track of flows by storing some flow information that persists from datagram to datagram within the flow. In this way the router can handle all datagrams in the flow similarly.

Authentication and Privacy

Security has long been a missing piece of the IP puzzle. The IP Security Architecture (IPsec) was first defined in RFC 1825, and updated most recently in RFC 2401. IPsec is designed to work with either IPv4 or IPv6, but because it relies on header extensions, it works best with IPv6. Two types of security extensions are defined: the IP authentication header (AH) first described in RFC 1826 and updated in RFC 2402, and the IP encapsulating security payload (ESP) first described in RFC 1827, and updated in RFC 2406. Security issues will be discussed at greater length in Chapter 24.

IPv6 Datagram Headers

The IPv6 protocol specifies the following fields for its header:

- ♦ **Version:** A four-bit value which for IPv6 must be equal to six.
- ♦ **Traffic Class:** This eight-bit value specifies what, if any, form of "differentiated service" is to be provided for the packet. Use of this field is defined separately from IPv6; see RFC 2474 for more about differentiated services. The default value for this field is all zeros.
- ♦ **Flow label:** This 20-bit value identifies packets that belong to the same flow. A node can be the source for more than one simultaneous flow. The flow label and the address of the source node uniquely identify flows.
- ♦ **Payload length:** This 16-bit field contains an integer value equal to the length of the packet payload in bytes; that is, the number of bytes contained in the packet after the end of the IPv6 header. IPv6 extensions are included as part of the payload for the purposes of calculating this field.
- ♦ **Next header:** This field indicates what protocol is in use in the header immediately following the IPv6 packet. Similar to the IPv4 protocol field, the next header field may refer to a higher-layer protocol like TCP or UDP, but it may also indicate an IPv6 extension header.
- ♦ **Hop limit:** Every time a node forwards a packet, it decrements this eight-bit field by one. If the hop limit reaches zero, the packet is discarded. Unlike in IPv4, where the time-to-live field fulfills a similar purpose, sentiment is currently against putting a protocol-

defined upper limit on packet lifetime for IPv6. This means that the function of timing-out old data should be accomplished in upper-layer protocols.

♦ **Source address:** This is the 128-bit address of the node originating the IPv6 packet.

♦ **Destination address:** This is the 128-bit address of the intended recipient of the IPv6 packet. This address may be a unicast, multicast, or anycast address. If a routing extension is being used (which specifies a particular route that the packet must traverse), the destination address may be one of those intermediate nodes instead of the ultimate destination node.

It is instructive to compare the IPv4 header fields (in Figure 7-1) with the IPv6 header fields (in Figure 14–1). Although several of the fields are similar for both protocols, the only field entirely unchanged is the version field. The version field must remain the same for IPv6 to be backward compatible with IPv4. The next IPv4 field, header length, is irrelevant to IPv6 because all IPv6 headers are the same length; IPv4 requires this field because its headers can be as short as 20 bytes and as long as 60 bytes.

The IPv4 Type of Service field is similar to the IPv6 traffic class field, but ToS is positioned later in the header than that field—and it also has not found wide acceptance from implementers. The IPv4 datagram length field evolved into the payload length field in IPv6. The IPv6 payload length includes extension headers, whereas the IPv4 datagram length field specifies the length of the entire datagram including headers. Routers can calculate the length of the IPv4 datagram payload by subtracting the header length from the datagram length; this calculation is unnecessary in IPv6.

The datagram identification, flags, and fragment offset fields in the IPv4 header all pertain to datagram fragmentation, and are therefore dispensed with in the IPv6 header.

The IPv4 time to live (TTL) field has become the IPv6 hop limit field. The IPv4 TTL value is an upper bound, in seconds, of the lifetime of a packet within the Internet cloud. When the TTL value reaches zero the packet is discarded. IPv4 specifies that routers decrement this value by the number of seconds it took from receipt of a packet until the packet was forwarded, but in practice most routers simply decrement this value by one rather than attempting to measure the actual time spent in the router. The hop limit field in IPv6 makes official this approach to limiting the lifetime of the datagram by hop count.

The IPv4 protocol field identifies the next-higher layer protocol, usually a transport layer protocol. This function is retained in the IPv6 next header field, which refers to the protocol of the next header, whether that header is an IPv6 extension header or a higher-layer network protocol like UDP or TCP.

The IPv4 checksum was deemed unnecessary to IPv6 and dispensed with. After all, many data link layer protocols (like Ethernet) apply checksums in some form or another, TCP and UDP both use their own checksums, and more serious integrity checks are available through the IP security architecture headers.

Finally, the 32-bit IPv4 destination and source address fields have been expanded to 128 bits to accommodate IPv6 addresses.

IPv6 Extension Headers

IPv4 options, as described in Chapter 7, change the shape of the IP headers. This means that optioned packets must be treated as special cases by routers, which are usually optimized to handle standard datagrams. As a result, datagrams with options tend to be delivered more slowly not so much because they require special processing as because they tend to be shunted off to the side to be handled when the router is not busy forwarding "normal" packets. IPv6 extension headers should drastically reduce, if not eliminate, this kind of performance hit on packets that use options. Except for hop-by-hop options, which by definition must be processed by each forwarding router, options on IPv6 packets are hidden from intermediate routers and thus can have no affect on how the packets are forwarded.

IPv6 Options

One of the benefits of IPv6 is that it simplifies the process of defining new options. So far, the following are the first options defined for IPv6 extension headers.

Hop-by-hop options header: This header always appears immediately after the main IPv6 header and contains optional data that every node on the packet's path must examine. So far, two hop-by-hop options have been specified: the Jumbo payload option and the router alert option. The Jumbo payload option identifies the payload of the packet as being longer than 65,535 bytes (including the hop-by-hop option header). If a router cannot forward the packet, it returns an ICMPv6 error message. The router alert option notifies routers that information inside the IPv6 datagram is intended to be viewed and processed by an intermediate router even though the datagram is addressed to some other node (for example, control datagrams that contain information pertaining to bandwidth reservation protocols).

Routing header: This header causes the packet to visit specific nodes, specified in the header, on its route to its destination. The initial destination address of the IPv6 header is not the same as the ultimate destination of the packet, but rather the first address in the list contained in the routing header. When that node receives the packet, it processes the IPv6 header and the routing header and resends the packet to the second address listed in the routing header. This process continues until the packet reaches its ultimate destination.

Fragment header: The fragment header contains all the information about IP fragments that formerly would be stored in the main IPv4 header fields. This extension includes fields for a fragment offset, a "More Fragments" flag, and an identification field; it is used to allow a source node to fragment a packet too large for the path MTU between the source and the destination.

Destination options header: This header stands in for the IPv4 options field. At present, the only destination options specified are padding options to fill out the header on a 64-bit boundary if the (future) options require it. The destination options header is meant to carry information intended to be examined by the destination node.

Authentication header (AH): This header provides a mechanism for calculating a cryptographic checksum on some parts of the IPv6 header, extension headers, and payload.

Encapsulating Security Payload (ESP) header: This header will always be the last, unencrypted header of any packet. It indicates the rest of the payload is encrypted, and provides enough information for the authorized destination node to decrypt it.

IPv6 Addressing

The IPv6 addressing architecture is described in RFC 2373. There are several facets of IPv6 addressing that are important: the structure of the 128-bit IPv6 address representation, address architecture, address space structure, and the different types of IPv6 addresses—unicast, multicast, and anycast.

IPv6 Address Representation

As explained in Chapter 2, IPv4 addresses are usually represented as a dot-delimited four-part series of values ranging from 0 to 255 (hexadecimal values of 00 through FF). IPv6 addresses, four times as long as IPv4 addresses, are not so easy to represent. The basic representation of an IPv6 address is of the form:

```
X:X:X:X:X:X:X:X
```

where X is a four-digit (16 bit) hexadecimal integer. Note that instead of being dot-delimited, IPv6 addresses are colon-delimited, for clarity. For example, the following are valid IPv6 addresses:

```
CDCD:910A:2222:5498:8475:1111:3900:2020
1030:0:0:0:C9B4:FF12:48AA:1A2B
2000:0:0:0:0:0:0:1
```

These are hexadecimal integers; decimal equivalents could also be used.

Some conventions have been designated to simplify IPv6 address representation. A series of zeros in an address can be collapsed, with a double-colon replacing the zeros. The last address shown in the preceding example would be represented as:

```
2000::1
```

In mixed IPv4/IPv6 environments, where some IPv6 addresses may encapsulate IPv4 addresses, those addresses can be represented in the form:

```
X:X:X:X:X:X:d.d.d.d
```

In these cases, the colon-delimited values are 16-bit integers (standard for IPv6 addresses), and the dot-delimited values are 8-bit integers (standard for IPv4 addresses). For example, the following is a valid IPv6 address, encapsulating an IPv4 address:

```
0:0:0:0:0:0:10.0.0.1
```

IPv6 Address Architecture

The IPv6 addressing model is similar to the IPv4 model: each address consists of two parts. The most significant bits of the address (those bits starting at the left of the address) represent the network to which the node is attached. The least significant bits of the address (those bits starting at the right of the address) represent the unique node connected to the network.

As in IPv4, the network portion of the IPv6 address is aggregatable. This is another way of saying that subnets are considered to be part of the parent network, and that to nodes outside of a subnetted network, all datagrams addressed anywhere within that network are forwarded to a single point. Consider a Class B network that has been subnetted. Routers inside that network need to be aware of routes for subnets, but routers outside that network need to know only one route for that network.

IPv4 network classes were a good idea, but the implementation turned out to be too rigid to accommodate the kind of growth in personal computers as well as networks that we've experienced since 1980. IPv6 addresses are designed to avoid the problems of running out of network node address space within networks as well as the problem of running out of organizational network addresses. At the same time, IPv6 addresses are all aggregatable, thus solving the problem of IP backbone routing.

A backbone router stores a single route for all nodes on a Class B network, no matter that there may be dozens or hundreds of subnets that are routed locally inside that network. IPv6 addresses are all aggregatable in a similar way.

IPv6 addresses are divided into two parts: the high-order 64 bits identify the network address, the low-order 64 bits identify the node. Each node address includes an **interface identifier** based on the IEEE EUI-64 format for interface identifiers. This format builds on existing MAC addresses to create 64-bit interface identifiers that can be unique across a local or global scope. This IEEE standard is available at:

```
standards.ieee.org/db/oui/tutorials/EUI64.html
```

With 64-bit interface identifiers, as many as 2^{64} unique physical interfaces (about 18 billion billion) can be addressed—on any given network. With 64-bit network addresses, the same number of different networks is possible.

So far, all IPv6 network addresses are specified to be aggregatable, either by network service provider or by some other basis. What-

```
|  3|  13  | 8 |    24     |   16    |                 64 bits                  |
+--+-----+---+---------+---------+------------------------------------------+
|FP|  TLA |RES|   NLA   |   SLA   |              Interface ID                |
|  |  ID  |   |   ID    |   ID    |                                          |
+--+-----+---+---------+---------+------------------------------------------+
```

Figure 14–2: The format for IPv6 global aggregatable unicast addresses, from RFC 2373.

ever entity provides the network address block is also responsible for maintaining the network route. IPv6 unicast addresses take the form shown in Figure 14–2, and the fields designated within the address are described next.

The IPv6 unicast address is broken down into these fields:

FP: The format prefix is the three-bit prefix to the IPv6 address that identifies where it belongs in the IPv6 address space (as shown in the IPv6 address map in Figure 14–3).

TLA ID: The top-level aggregation identifier contains the highest-level routing information of the address. This is the grossest level of routing information in the internetwork, and at 13 bits there can be no more than 8192 different top-level routes.

The next eight bits are reserved for future use. They may ultimately be used to expand the top-level or next-level aggregation ID fields.

NLA ID: The next-level aggregation identifier is 24 bits long, and is intended to be used by organizations that control top-level aggregation IDs to organize that address space. In other words, those organizations (probably to include large Internet service providers and others providing public network access) can carve that 24-bit field into their own addressing hierarchy. Such an entity might break itself down into 16 top-level routes (internal to the entity) by taking four bits for those routes and leave itself 20 bits of address space to allocate to other entities (likely to be smaller-scale, more local, service providers). Those entities, in their turn, could also subdivide the space they are allocated in the same way—if there is enough room.

SLA ID: The site-level aggregation identifier is the address space given to organizations for their internal network structure. With 16 bits available, each organization can create its own internal hierarchical network structure using subnets in the same way they are used in IPv4. As many as 65,535 different subnets are available using all 16 bits as a flat address space. Using the first eight bits for higher-level routing within the organization would allow 255 high-level subnets, each of which has as many as 255 sub-subnets.

Interface ID: This 64-bit field contains a 64-bit value based on the IEEE EUI-64 interface ID discussed earlier.

Consider a host originating a packet outside the destination's top-level aggregation entity. The host forwards the packet to its local router, which examines the destination address. It immediately recognizes a foreign top-level aggregation entity, so it can forward that packet to the route designated for all packets sent to that entity. It works similarly to postal services: consider a letter originating in Australia with a destination in the United States. The sender drops the letter off at a post office in Adelaide, where it is sorted—because it is addressed to the United States, it will probably be put in a sack with other letters intended for that part of the world. The local postal authorities don't worry too much about the rest of the address.

Datagrams that originate within the same top-level aggregation entity (or letters that originate within the same country) get forwarded based on what the next-level aggregation entity is. A letter originating in Zurich with a destination in Berne does not leave Switzerland.

With aggregation, no router—not even a backbone router—needs to know every route on the Internet. Each router needs to know detailed routes only within its own aggregation entity; outside the entity, the router needs to know only default routes to each other aggregation entity at the same level. Backbone routers can manage with no more than 8,192 routes; reports in 1998 have put the number of routes some backbone routers were storing at over 130,000. Although the 24-bit section of the address devoted to the next-level aggregation entity might seem to permit over 16 million (2^{24}) routes, in practice that section will almost certainly be subject to its own aggregation, as mentioned earlier.

IPv6 Address Space Structure

Figure 14–3 shows how the IPv6 address space is allocated. A similar breakdown for IPv4 would be considerably simpler—and would tell the story of inefficient address allocation. Fully one half of all IPv4 addresses are Class A addresses—and largely underused. One quarter are Class B, and only one eighth are Class C addresses. Class D (multicast) addresses take up one sixteenth of the address space, and the rest is either reserved or unassigned.

By contrast, only one eighth of the IPv6 address space is allocated to aggregatable unicast addresses; the vast majority of the IPv6 address space is left unassigned. Of course, this approach leaves plenty of slack in the event that the Internet and IP continue their rapid growth for the next twenty years. The new address space can accommodate all foreseen and perhaps even any imaginable growth for the foreseeable future.

Two important allocations are for link-local and site-local unicast addresses. In IPv4, the private network allocations used for network address translation (NAT) give organizations an option for setting up networks with whatever type of network address they want—datagrams sent on those networks are not supposed to be forwarded outside the private network. These addresses were added more as an afterthought, however, than as part of the original design of IPv4.

In IPv6, link-local and site-local unicast addresses are designed to function almost like private network addresses. However, there are some big differences. Link-local addresses are intended to stay

```
Allocation                             Prefix         Fraction of
                                       (binary)       Address Space

---------------------------------      ---------      -------------
Reserved                               0000 0000      1/256
Unassigned                             0000 0001      1/256

Reserved for NSAP Allocation           0000 001       1/128
Reserved for IPX Allocation            0000 010       1/128

Unassigned                             0000 011       1/128
Unassigned                             0000 1         1/32
Unassigned                             0001           1/16

Aggregatable Global Unicast Addresses  001            1/8
Unassigned                             010            1/8
Unassigned                             011            1/8
Unassigned                             100            1/8
Unassigned                             101            1/8
Unassigned                             110            1/8

Unassigned                             1110           1/16
Unassigned                             1111 0         1/32
Unassigned                             1111 10        1/64
Unassigned                             1111 110       1/128
Unassigned                             1111 1110 0    1/512

Link-local Unicast Addresses           1111 1110 10   1/1024
Site-local Unicast Addresses           1111 1110 11   1/1024

Multicast Addresses                    1111 1111      1/256
```

Figure 14–3: Allocation for IPv6 addresses, from RFC 2373.

on the physical network link—they are not to be forwarded off the link. Site-local addresses can be forwarded throughout the organizational site but not out to the public Internet.

Unlike NAT addresses, all IPv6 networks and nodes support link-local and site-local addressing. You could use the site-local address range to enumerate an entire organizational network, but one important purpose of these addresses is to help nodes that haven't yet been configured for their correct IP network address to locate various services on the link or site level.

IPv6 Address Types

IPv6 supports three types of addressing: unicast, multicast, and anycast. Unicast and multicast work much the same as they do in IPv4; broadcasts are not supported in IPv6. The unicast address is defined as an identifier for a single network interface. When a datagram is addressed to that unicast address, it is delivered to the interface identified by that address.

A multicast address is defined as an identifier for a set of one or more interfaces. When a datagram is sent to a multicast address, it is delivered to all the interfaces associated with that address.

An anycast address is, like a multicast address, defined as an identifier for a set of one or more interfaces. Unlike multicast, datagrams sent to an anycast address are delivered to only one of the interfaces identified by that address. The datagram is supposed to be delivered to the nearest interface, as defined by a measure of the distance of the receiving node from the sender.

An important use of anycast addresses is for stateless autoconfiguration. Standard anycast addresses are defined for functional categories like domain name servers and time servers. When a node needs one of these services, it can send out an anycast datagram, and it will get a response from the closest server rather than from all servers within earshot of the node.

Migrating to IPv6

It was IPv4's success that made an upgrade necessary, which means that there is a significant installed base of users to upgrade. Keeping the transition orderly was a major objective of the entire IPng program, and there are no plans for a cutover date when IPv6 would be turned on and IPv4 turned off.

The strategy chosen for the upgrade is to deploy the IPv6 protocol stack in parallel with IPv4. In other words, hosts that upgrade to IPv6 will continue to exist as IPv4 hosts at the same time. An experimental IPv6 backbone, or 6bone, has been set up to handle IPv6 Internet traffic in parallel with the regular Internet. Such hosts will continue to have 32-bit IPv4 addresses but will add 128-bit IPv6 addresses. By 1999, hundreds of networks were linked to the 6bone.

The transition can be achieved through two approaches: protocol tunneling or IPv4/IPv6 dual stack.

Protocol Tunneling

One strategy that will help facilitate the growth of the IPv6 Internet is protocol tunneling. Hosts on IPv6 intranets can interoperate fine on their own network, but if the intranets are connected to the Internet only through an IPv4 route, they cannot link to other IPv6 hosts via IPv6. The answer is to allow tunneling: the IPv6 packets are encapsulated within IPv4 packets and forwarded across the Internet to a router that can strip off the IPv4 headers and forward the IPv6 packets to their destination.

Likewise, hosts can operate on IPv4 intranets and be connected to the IPv6 Internet through a router. Data from those hosts could be encapsulated within IPv6 packets by the router and forwarded across the IPv6 Internet to a router that would strip off the IPv6 headers and forward the IPv4 packets to their destination.

Another possibility that is neither encouraged nor discouraged by the authors of the IPv6 protocol is the use of protocol translators. These take IPv6 packets and convert them to IPv4 packets, and vice versa.

The IPv6 tunneling approach makes it possible for isolated IPv6 "islands" to interoperate with each other across "seas" of IPv4 networks.

IPv4/IPv6 Dual Stack

Any node can run both IPv4 and IPv6 network stacks simultaneously. In this way, the node can send and receive both IPv4 and IPv6 packets. This approach makes possible heterogenous networks where both IPv4 and IPv6 coexist on the same network infrastructure. This makes it possible to deploy IPv6 on an organizational network without losing IPv4 connectivity for the nodes implementing IPv6.

Chapter Summary and References

In this chapter, we introduced the issues that made IPv6 necessary as well as the goals set for the next generation of the Internet Protocol. We looked first at why IPv6 was necessary, followed by an overview of the new features and functions available in IPv6.

We discussed the IPv6 protocol header fields, contrasting them with the IPv4 header fields. A discussion the IPv6 network addressing, including an overview of the IPv6 network address space, the architecture of IPv6 addresses, the address space allocation, and IPv6 address types including anycast, multicast, and unicast followed. We finished up with an introduction to the transition strategies used to migrate IPv4 populations to IPv6.

Table 14–1 lists some useful RFCs to read in conjunction with this chapter.

RFC	Title	Description
2460	Internet Protocol, Version 6 (IPv6) Specification	The most recent specification for IPv6.
1924	A Compact Representation of IPv6 Addresses	Describes approaches for simplifying the representation of IPv6 addresses.
2401	Security Architecture for the Internet Protocol	Describes the IP security architecture (IPsec) using encryption and authentication tools for IP datagrams.
2474	Differentiated Services Field	Describes the use of the quality of service/type of service field for IP.
2374	An IPv6 Aggregatable Global Unicast Address Format	Describes the aggregatable format for IPv6 addresses.
2373	IP Version 6 Addressing Architecture	Describes the IPv6 addressing architecture.
1933	Transition Mechanisms for IPv6 Hosts and Routers	Discusses how the transition from IPv4 to IPv6 can be done.

Table 14–1: Useful RFCs for Chapter 14.

Part Three

TCP/IP Applications

15

Remote Computing: Telnet and r-Utilities

Remote terminal sessions once ruled the Internet. The dominant technique for accessing computing resources remotely, terminal sessions allowed users to connect to remote hosts as if they were using a terminal connected directly to the host.

As the web and e-mail have come to dominate Internet applications, remote terminal sessions have certainly lost most of the market and mindshare. Not long ago, the only type of Internet access available to most individuals was the shell account. Users dialed into a Unix host, ran terminal emulation software, and used the Unix host's Internet access for e-mail, file transfer, and terminal sessions with other Internet hosts.

Terminal sessions remain a useful management tool for controlling many types of network device, as well as for accessing legacy mainframe and multi-user systems. Although these programs no longer are as important as they once were to users, the terminal emulation protocols demonstrate an important principle of interoperable protocol design.

This chapter discusses the most important terminal emulation protocols for remote computing, including explanations of what they are, how they work, and how they can be used.

Telnet

Long ago in the 1970s when TCP/IP was first being implemented, most computing was through a remote terminal session. Users accessed mainframes through a terminal connected to a large multiuser system. Terminals were usually cabled through a terminal server, as shown in Figure 15–1. Each computer vendor sold its own terminals, so if you wanted to connect to an IBM mainframe you needed an IBM or IBM-compatible terminal; to connect to a DEC VAX you needed a DEC or a DEC-compatible terminal.

As long as companies stuck with a single mainframe computer vendor, this worked fine. Employees who worked with the mainframe got a terminal. By the late 1970s companies increasingly had more than one computer, often from different vendors. By the 1980s it became common to see offices where workers might have an IBM terminal, a DEC terminal, and a personal computer all vying for desk real estate.

This worked as long as all the different mainframe systems stood alone. The only alternative would have been to buy universal terminals that worked with all different mainframes, and cable each one to all the firm's mainframes. Of course, this depended on being able to find such an all-purpose terminal as well as connecting each terminal to two, three, or more different computers.

As soon as MIS departments started linking the mainframes with networks, things changed. It became worthwhile to consider using

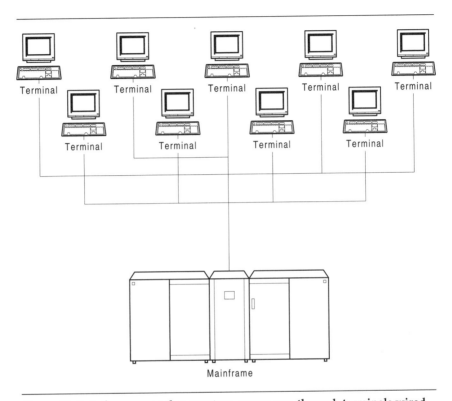

Figure 15–1: Before personal computers, access was through terminals wired directly into the mainframe.

the same terminal to connect to all the different remote computers. Telnet, short for Telecommunications Network Protocol, was intended to solve the problem of interoperating between different computer platforms. The result is that users on just about any type of system can log in remotely to just about any other type of system—transparently—across an internetwork, as shown in Figure 15–2.

The problem of standardizing on a single terminal lessened as computer vendors moved to handle input from the now-standard DEC VT-series terminals. The most important holdout, IBM, kept building mainframes that required different remote terminal emulations to handle its special terminals. Most common are the 3270 terminal and 5250 terminal emulations, both of which are widely supported in commercial telnet software implementations.

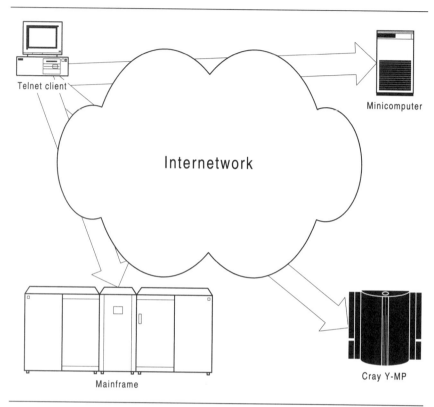

Figure 15–2: A personal computer running a telnet client can do the job of a
dumb terminal, and more, in accessing remote hosts across an internetwork.

Telnet is a straightforward application for end users who are
accustomed to using their mainframes through a hardware terminal. Users often find the most puzzling part of using telnet is figuring out how to work the remote host, rather than figuring out
how to use telnet.

Network Virtual Terminal

Interoperable terminal sessions are not a problem when all terminals use the same keyboard/mouse—and when all the computers
use the same encoding for data. Unfortunately, this is not how the

world works. There are as many as half a dozen different major variations on the DOS/Windows/Intel personal computer keyboard. Apple Macintoshes have Enter and Return keys; DEC VT terminals have a Gold key; IBM 3270 terminals have PF (Programmed Function) keys along with several other unique keys. Macintoshes use a single-button mouse, Unix boxes often use three-button mouses, and Windows/Intel PC mouses may have two or three buttons.

Data encoding poses another obstacle. Most systems use ASCII: the American Standard Code for Information Interchange. The major exception is IBM, which uses EBCDIC (Extended Binary Coded Decimal Interchange Code) for encoding mainframe data. The situation is worse than it appears, however: IBM uses several slightly different flavors of EBCDIC, and even computers that use ASCII often use it in different ways. Some systems use carriage-return/linefeed character pairings to indicate the end of a data line; for others such pairings are redundant.

So, how does one build an interoperable terminal emulation protocol? One option is to create converter modules that convert input from one terminal type into data that can be understood by another type of host. This quickly becomes unwieldy. Even if there are only ten different host types and 20 different terminal types, the protocol would have to specify converters for 200 different terminal/host combinations, with accommodation for new converters whenever a new type of host or terminal comes on the market, and support for bug-fixes and upgrades for each and every converter. These converters can be hard to build because they may require significant access both to the terminals and to the hosts for building and debugging.

Telnet uses a different approach. Rather than cross-convert every possible combination, something called a **Network Virtual Terminal (NVT)** was invented to allow different systems to interoperate through telnet. NVT allows telnet clients to convert input from users into a form usable for the remote host, and allows telnet servers to funnel output that can be made usable for display from the remote client. Each terminal type requires one converter, and each host type requires one converter. The converter interprets the key presses and mouse moves into a standard format. Pressing the Enter key on a PC or the Return key on a Macintosh converts into the same value on the NVT. And each host uses a converter that accepts NVT input and interprets it appropriately for its own type of system.

The effect is that both systems, client and server, use the virtual terminal emulation: the client generally converts keystrokes on the local system into universal keystrokes, which are then sent on to the server. The server, in turn, generally converts its output—screen output—into a standard form that could be displayed on the virtual terminal monitor.

Instead of building 200 different conversion routines for 10 different host types and 20 different terminal types, the NVT lets us get away with only 30 different conversion routines. And since those routines can all be built with access only to the seminal NVT standards, the routines will be simple and they will suffer fewer interoperability problems.

Using Telnet

In a telnet session the user initiates a connection with a remote host, the client and server negotiate a connection, the user enters user ID and password, and on successful completion the terminal session begins. From there the session will look like any terminal session with the remote host. At the end of the session, the user may have to exit the telnet client manually or the client may close automatically depending on the configuration and implementation.

By far, an overwhelming majority of user interaction with telnet will be through the process of starting or stopping it. When used from a command line, like DOS or Unix, the session begins with the command:

```
telnet [host name|IP address] [port]
```

```
IRIX System V.4 (maddog)


Welcome to MadDog - unauthorized access is prohibited


login: pql1191
Password: ******
```

Figure 15–3: A telnet session looks very much like a terminal session with a remote host using a dumb terminal wired to the host (or dialed up over a telephone line) once the connection has been made.

The destination host name or address is optional; if you don't use one, you'll simply get a telnet prompt. If a host name is used, then the name will be resolved into an IP address (by DNS or through the hosts file, if one is being used), whereas IP addresses are used directly. This probably covers about 95 percent of all telnet use—users connect to remote hosts, log in, and carry on their remote sessions. telnet connections are made, by default, to the well-known port for telnet (23) but telnet can also be directed at a non-well-known port by including the desired port on the command line. This is done occasionally for special custom applications that use the telnet protocol.

The start of a telnet session invoked from a system prompt is shown in Figure 15–3. Using telnet on GUI systems is only slightly different. GUI telnet clients tend to offer more options for display, colors, fonts used, and keyboard mappings than are available in text-only command-line implementations. Figure 15–4 shows a sample GUI telnet session, which is basically the same as the character-only implementation, just with more choices for display options.

One advantage GUI implementations appear to have over character-based implementations is the ability to multitask. However, many character-based implementations include the ability to shift from one concurrent telnet session to another.

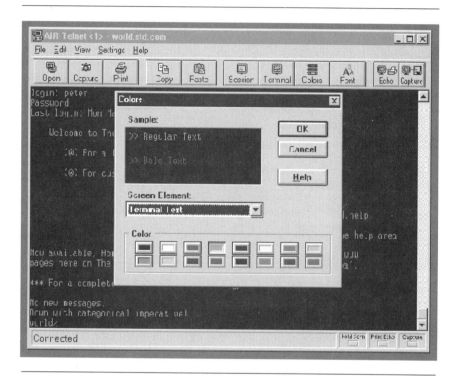

Figure 15–4: Telnet with a graphical user interface lets users modify screen appearance to integrate into the rest of the GUI desktop.

The bulk of interaction between the user and the telnet application is transparent: all the user's keystrokes are passed through the internetwork to the remote host. Network support staff often encounter calls for help with telnet that turn out to be calls for help with the remote host application that is being used as part of the remote login session.

However, many telnet options and commands control the behavior of the telnet client. The telnet command line must be invoked, usually through an escape character (most telnet clients indicate which key combination is used for escaping to the command line when first started).

Telnet Features

Most telnet implementations offer some selection of terminal emulation, usually a choice of various DEC VT terminal emulations. Most common is the VT 100/102 emulation, which is also very often the default emulation. Other common emulations include the VT 52 and VT 220/320 terminals.

The emulations mentioned so far are all for nongraphical, fairly standard (read that to mean non-IBM) terminals. Graphics terminals, as well as IBM terminal emulations, require special implementations. Despite the widespread use of personal computers and workstations, plenty of IBM mainframes are still up and running. Due to the use of a different character set (EBCDIC instead of ASCII) on IBM mainframes, the telnet implementation for 3270 terminal emulation is quite different from other, "normal," emulations and is usually written as a separate program. PC-based IBM terminal emulations, particularly 3270 emulations, are widely available, either included with vendors' TCP/IP application suites or as optional add-ins or separately available products.

Terminal emulation of IBM 5250 terminals for connectivity to AS/400 minicomputers is also widely available. Likewise, Tektronix graphics emulation is also available from a few vendors, but more should follow suit as users do more remote computing with graphics-intensive applications.

Interactive Telnet Commands

If you start telnet without indicating a remote host to log onto you will get a telnet prompt. Likewise, you can invoke a telnet prompt during an active session by pressing the Escape key combination. Commands you can enter at this point include those shown in Table 15–1.

Likewise, on command line systems that support it, the ! command invokes a subshell—another operating system command

Command	Quick explanation
!	Invoke a subshell
?	Print help information
close	Close current connection
display	Display operating parameters
environ	Change environment variables ('environ ?' for more)
logout	Forcibly log out remote user and close the connection
mode	Try to enter line or character mode ('mode ?' for more)
open	Connect to a site
quit	Exit telnet
send	Transmit special characters ('send ?' for more)
set	Set operating parameters ('set ?' for more)
status	Print status information
toggle	Toggle operating parameters ('toggle ?' for more)
unset	Unset operating parameters ('unset ?' for more)
z	Suspend telnet

Table 15–1: Telnet commands available (output from HELP command) on an average Unix implementation.

line. This is handy for running other programs or for doing other tasks on the local host while the terminal session is still live.

Telnet's implementation size is partly due to its features and configurability. For example, the commands

```
mode
send
set/unset
toggle
environ
```

Mode Option	Purpose
character	Disable LINEMODE option (or disable obsolete line-by-line mode)
line	Enable LINEMODE option (or enable obsolete line-by-line mode)

These require the LINEMODE option to be enabled:

isig	Enable signal trapping
-isig	Disable signal trapping
edit	Enable character editing
-edit	Disable character editing
softtabs	Enable tab expansion
-softtabs	Disable character editing
litecho	Enable literal character echo
-litecho	Disable literal character echo

Table 15–2: Telnet mode command options, as implemented on a typical Unix system.

all take various parameters to customize the connection. As shown in Tables 15–2 and 15–3, all drawn from an actual Unix telnet implementation, the user has lots of control over the remote connection if the user chooses to use the tools available.

Most mode command options are not relevant for everyday use, and normally would be modified only for problematic connections. For example, the character/line option enables/disables the LINEMODE option, switching between the client sending an entire line of input at a time, or sending one character at a time to the server and having the server echo the input back through the connection. By and large, this option is available to accommodate older telnet server implementations (where this was an issue), but most current implementations will negotiate the correct type of connection.

Table 15–3 shows special telnet commands that can be sent during a session. Again, sending special telnet characters is usually unnecessary during normal sessions between hosts running current software. Occasionally it may be necessary to send, for example, the "Are You There" query to determine whether a connection is still alive—lack of system response to terminal session commands may be due to the remote host being busy or the telnet connection being dropped.

Option	Meaning
ao	Send telnet abort output
ayt	Send telnet 'Are You There'
brk	Send telnet break
ec	Send telnet erase character
el	Send telnet erase line
escape	Send current escape character
ga	Send telnet 'Go Ahead' sequence
ip	Send telnet interrupt process
nop	Send telnet 'No Operation'
eor	Send telnet 'End of Record'
abort	Send telnet 'Abort Process'
susp	Send telnet 'Suspend Process'
eof	Send telnet end of file character
synch	Perform telnet 'Synch Operation'
getstatus	Send request for STATUS
?	Display send options

Table 15–3: telnet *send* command options.

The Telnet Protocol

Telnet uses the client/server model, as described earlier. As shown in Figure 15–5, a daemon program on the server listens to the network for requests to open a connection. The telnet client takes the user's input from the local computer and maps it onto the NVT; this information is passed along the connection to the server, which maps the input from the NVT onto its own terminal and sends output to the server program, which in turn maps that output to the NVT and passes it on to the client.

Telnet uses TCP as its transport protocol because it must be able to maintain a reliable virtual circuit between two hosts that will interact with each other. Servers must be able to both receive commands from the clients reliably and send system responses to the client reliably.

Opening a Telnet Session

A telnet session can be initiated by indicating the remote host's name or IP address. If the host name is used, the client system must resolve the host name (see Chapter 11) to get a valid IP address. The client system then attempts to initiate a TCP connection with the remote host (see Chapter 10). The client attempts to create a circuit by sending to the well-known TCP port number 23, for telnet, at the remote host (a telnet server can also monitor other non-well-known ports for nonstandard applications as mentioned earlier). The client assigns an arbitrary TCP port number for its own part of the connection.

If the remote host offers telnet service, it will have a special telnet daemon that accepts requests to connect over TCP port 23. When that host receives IP datagrams addressed to it from potential clients, it strips away the IP header to reveal a TCP seg-ment intended for its telnet daemon, which is listening for just such network traffic. The telnet daemon then allows a TCP connection to be established.

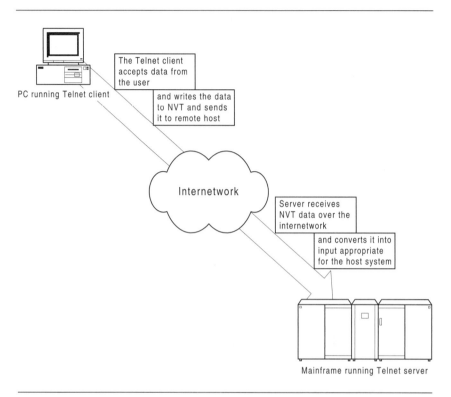

Figure 15–5: Systems that provide telnet service listen on their internetwork connection for requests to open a telnet session from remote clients.

Each host, both client and server, can maintain more than one telnet connection at any given time, as long as there are enough resources to maintain additional TCP connections. In fact, the client can activate more than one telnet session with the same remote host: although it uses the same IP address and TCP port (port 23) as destinations for the telnet traffic, the client assigns non-well-known port numbers for its side of the TCP connection. As a result, two or more different telnet links to the same server could be active on a host: the only difference between segments intended for the different sessions would be the TCP port numbers on the client host (the rest of the addressing information, IP addresses of both hosts, and the TCP port number for the server, would remain the same for all segments).

Telnet Protocol Commands

The telnet protocol itself has relatively few commands. These include options negotiation commands (see the next section), as well as a few commands regarding the flow of data. Commands are set off from the rest of the flow of data by a special one-byte character, 255 (or 0xff, in hexadecimal) that is called the *Interpret As Command* (IAC) character. The commands are also single bytes, and follow the IAC character.

Table 15–4 shows some of the telnet protocol commands. Some of these represent virtual keys on the NVT, like "Erase Character" or "Break."

Negotiating Options

One of the important features of telnet is the ability to negotiate options between the server and the client. By allowing options, telnet implementations permit either client or server programs to extend functionality between two hosts—if they both agree. Option negotiation between the telnet client and server is symmetric, meaning that either side can initiate a request to honor any option. Either side also has the authority to veto any option requested by the other side.

Negotiation begins when one participant sends a request that it wants to turn on (or off) a certain option for itself, or a request that it wants the other participant to turn on (or off) an option.

WILL means that the sending system wants to turn on a certain option; WON'T means that it will not turn on the option.

DO means the sending system wants the other system to turn on the option, and DON'T means the sending system wants the other system to turn off the option. Table 15–5 shows the various permutations for negotiating a single option.

Command	Hex value	Stands for	Command Explanation
AO	0xf5	Abort Output	Finishes process but doesn't output results
AYT	0xf6	Are You There	Requests a response from the other side, to indicate the link is still functioning
BRK	0xf3	Break	Used as an attention key on NVT
DM	0xf2	Data Mark	Used for synchronization purposes, places a mark in the data stream to allow urgent data to be transmitted
DO	0xfd	Do <option>	Announces host willingness for other host to enable <option>
DON'T	0xfe	Don't do <option>	Announces host unwillingness to permit another host to enable <option>
EC	0xf7	Erase Character	Erases the last character sent
EL	0xf8	Erase Line	Erases the last line sent
EOR	0xef	End of Record	Indicates end of data sent; part of a negotiated option
IP	0xf4	Interrupt Process	Interrupts the current process being executed on the server
NOP	0xf1	No Operation	Acts as a place holder
SB	oxfa	Suboption Negotiation	Used when options have suboptions
WILL	0xfb	Will Do <option>	Announces host willingness to enable <option>
WON'T	0xfc	Won't do <option>	Announces host unwillingness to enable <option>

Table 15–4: Some of the more important telnet protocol commands.

Request	Response	Result
DO <option>	WILL <option>	The requester wants the responder to turn on <option>, and the responder agrees
DON'T <option>	WON'T <option>	The requester wants the responder to keep <option> turned off, and the responder agrees
WILL <option>	DO <option>	The requester itself wants to turn <option> on, and the responder agrees
WON'T <option>	DON'T <option>	The requester indicates it wants <option> turned off, and the responder agrees
DO <option>	WON'T <option>	The requester wants the responder to turn on <option> but the responder refuses
WILL <option>	DON'T <option>	The requester itself wants to turn <option> on, and the responder refuses

Table 15–5: Telnet options negotiation options.

Either host can initiate a request to enable (or leave disabled) any particular option. If a host doesn't understand some option being requested, it can simply decline it. This lets newer telnet implementations, which may include support for more options, interoperate with older implementations.

Because an option request can also look like an acknowledgment of a request, no acknowledgment is required when a host receives a request for a service that is already on: it is just ignored. This avoids looping requests between the two hosts.

Telnet options vary from implementation to implementation, but some of them relate to terminal characteristics, like negotiating the size of the window represented on the terminal: how many characters wide and how many high can be represented on screen. This type of option must first be negotiated, and then the two hosts can exchange information about terminal type. Line mode or character mode is another option, which determines whether characters are sent individually or grouped together to be sent one line at a time. Other options include choices about whether or not to allow a host to echo data it receives or whether or not to use a special end of record code to indicate the end of a data transmission.

Remote Utilities

While telnet became the solution for robust, reliable, and reasonably secure remote logins across an internetwork, smaller TCP/IP networks, especially those dominated by Unix systems, were seeing development of a family of the so-called **remote utilities** or **r-utilities**. The r-utilities are generally simpler than the more general TCP/IP applications that they resemble, because they were designed to operate between Unix systems, cutting down on overhead required for negotiating connections between dissimilar systems (though most r-utilities have now been ported to other systems).

The r-utilities solve the security issue by allowing remote access based on the source system in use. In other words, remote users are given access to a host if the user ID is listed in a special file (.rhosts on Unix systems) that includes the originating host name coupled with a user ID. Although this can be sufficient for enclosed work groups of Unix hosts, many experts consider this to be an open door for serious security breaches when implemented on systems with less built-in security, like personal computers. There are opportunities for spoofing servers with forged host name/user ID combinations to enable unauthorized access to systems offering r-utility services.

These utilities offer the advantage of being simple to implement, but they generally lack the features and options that the more

Program Name	Utility	Purpose	Alternate Application	r-Utility Advantages (if any)
rcp	Remote copy	Copy a file from a remote host	FTP	Supports recursive copying of sub-directories
rexec	Remote execute	Executes a single command on remote host	telnet	
rlogin	Remote login	Remote terminal session	telnet	Simpler to implement
rsh	Remote shell	Execute commands on a remote host using shell scripts	telnet	Can execute local shell scripts remotely
rwho	Remote who	Display current users of remote host	Finger	

Table 15–6: A few of the more common remote utilities.

widely used TCP/IP applications provide. The r-login offers a basic level of remote login service with very simple terminal emulation. Telnet implementations support various different terminal emulation options as well as other amenities, particularly in GUI versions. Table 15–6 shows a list of a few remote utilities.

r-login Connections

Like telnet, r-login uses the TCP transport protocol to initiate a connection between the client and the server. However, once the connection is initiated, the client sends user information to the server. This includes the user's ID on the client system and the user's ID on the server system; the server may also prompt for a password. The password prompt and response are not handled any differently from other data passed between the two hosts. If the server gets a valid password, it continues the session; otherwise it will terminate the connection.

One feature of r-login that makes it extremely convenient is the ability to create a special file on a system that provides r-login service that includes user IDs of authorized users and the names of the hosts they connect from. When users listed in the .rhosts files connect from their regular systems, they are not prompted for a password. This feature poses a significant security threat when using r-utilities.

Remote Utility Features

Although the remote utilities seem to have some major disadvantages when compared to telnet, they do have some points in their favor. For one, they are relatively simple to implement because they have far fewer options and don't attempt to offer the level of interoperability of the more general TCP/IP applications like telnet or FTP.

The time when you could assume that a system connected to a TCP/IP network was running Unix is gone. The remote utilities do offer high levels of interoperability between Unix systems because they take advantage of some of the Unix operating system commands, but as Unix declines as the operating system of choice of internetworked hosts, these utilities are becoming less important.

Chapter Summary and References

In this chapter we examined the methods used to do remote terminal access over the Internet. Starting with an overview of the issues posed by building an interoperable terminal emulation protocol for the Internet, we described the basis of the solution: the Network Virtual Terminal.

From there, we looked at how telnet works from the perspective of the end user, followed by telnet protocol commands and options negotiation. Finally, we discuss the family of remote login programs used for terminal sessions and other purposes.

Some useful RFCs to read in conjunction with this chapter include those listed in Table 15–7. Telnet has long been an Internet standard, and the protocol has long been specified in RFCs. The most important ones are listed here.

RFC	Title	Description
854	Telnet Protocol Specifications	This is the basic telnet specification, with attention to the NVT and standard representation of control functions.
855	Telnet Option Specifications	A short document that explains how options are assigned and documented.
856	Telnet Binary Transmission	Another short document explaining the operation of the binary transmission option for telnet.
857	Telnet Echo Option	Explaining how the telnet echo option works.
1091	Telnet Terminal-Type Option	Explaining how the terminal-type option works and why it is useful.
1041	Telnet 3270 Regime Option	Discusses issues relating to implementation of a 3270 emulation for telnet.
1282	BSD Rlogin	Explains how the BSD version of rlogin works.

Table 15–7: Useful RFCs for Chapter 15.

16

File Transfer Protocols: FTP and TFTP

If the ability to control computers at a distance through telnet was a fundamental requirement for the early Internet architects, so was the ability to move data and program files from one host to another. It's fine to access a remote host to do some computing, but it can be expensive—generating data on one host and then moving it to another host helped cut computing costs. And the ability to move program files from one host to another helped improve the efficiency of networked computing.

File Transfer Protocol (FTP) has long been the standard for moving files between hosts on TCP/IP internetworks. The Trivial File Transfer Protocol (TFTP) is a simpler version of FTP used specifically for remote booting of diskless workstations. TFTP is increasingly rare, but FTP continues to be a standby on the Internet for moving files between hosts, particularly when a server is set up for anonymous transfers (anonymous FTP). And the lessons learned from designing FTP have been extended to development of other important protocols, especially the web's Hypertext Transport Protocol (HTTP).

FTP and TFTP

Typical network resource sharing applications like Novell Net-Ware and Sun's NFS (Network File System, described in Chapter 18) work by making remote network resources appear as if they are local to the user's computer. The user can view a directory listing of shared resources in the same way the user views directories of local storage. Shared files can be opened, copied, moved, and deleted just as if they are on the local computer.

FTP and TFTP are different. They are separate programs that are explicitly invoked by the user, and they allow files to be copied from one host to another. Less automatic and transparent to the end user than the resource sharing protocols; FTP offers the highest degree of interoperability between hosts. Although FTP requires that files be copied from one host to another before they can be used, it does allow any host running TCP/IP to access an FTP server and exchange data. The two hosts can exchange files regardless of their operating systems, file structure, or even character sets in use. A user can copy data files from an IBM mainframe using the EBCDIC character set, down to a Macintosh personal computer, without having to do explicit file conversions.

FTP is the full-featured version, providing a high degree of reliability and speed. TFTP is the stripped-down version, useful for nodes that have limited memory, limited file download requirements, and less need for reliability and speed.

File Transfer Protocol

The FTP protocol defines a set of file transfer commands that suffice for almost any file transfer eventuality. Commands for sending and getting files, changing current working directory, directory listings, and changing file transfer mode from ASCII to binary cover all the important file transfer functions.

FTP specifies a very basic set of commands and responses, and for many years was implemented with a command line interface that accepted those commands and displayed the responses on the command line. This was a mixed blessing: on the one hand, it meant FTP on any system used almost the exact same commands; on the other hand, it meant that FTP was equally cryptic on all systems, as Figure 16–1 shows.

As the TCP/IP market on personal computers became increasingly competitive, vendors began to submerge the FTP command set into more appealing graphical interfaces. Rather than requiring explicit commands changing directories or selecting files for transfer, developers produced interfaces that display remote hosts' directories and files and allow point-and-click file and directory selection and drag-and-drop file movement. The commands issued from the client remain the same (and some implementations include a window displaying the actual commands being issued and the responses from the remote host), but the user no longer needs to know what those commands actually are. SPRY Inc.'s AIR Network File Manager, shown in Figure 5-3, was modeled on Windows' File Manager and uses point-and-click navigation through file systems and drag-and-drop file copying.

Using FTP

A typical FTP session begins when the FTP client program is started; an FTP server must be specified and a connection initiated. Once a user ID and password are provided to the server, the user typically locates the file or files needed and gets them from the

```
ftp> ls
200 PORT command successful.
150 Opening ASCII mode data connection for /bin/ls.
total 110
drwxr-xr-x  2 root      1           512 Aug 27  1994 bin
drwxr-xr-x  2 root      1          3072 Mar 17 20:44 ddn-news
lrwxrwxrwx  1 root      1             8 Jun 29  1993 ddn-news: -> ddn-news
drwxr-xr-x  2 356       1           512 May 11  1992 demo
drwxr-xr-x  2 root      1           512 Aug 16  1993 dev
drwxr-xr-x  2 root      1           512 Mar 23 21:13 domain
drwxr-xr-x  2 root      1           512 Sep 20  1991 etc
lrwxrwxrwx  1 root      1             3 Jun 29  1993 fyi -> rfc
drwxr-xr-x  2 root      1          1024 Oct 19 20:17 gosip
drwxr-xr-x  2 root      1           512 Oct 20  1991 home
drwxr-xr-x  2 gvaudre   1          3072 Nov  9  1993 ien
drwxrwsr-x  3 gvaudre   0          2048 Feb  1  1994 iesg
drwxrwsr-x161 gvaudre   0          4608 Jun 14  1994 ietf
drwxrwsr-x  2 gvaudre   0         43008 Apr 26  1994 internet-drafts
drwxrwxr-x  2 426       1          1024 Feb 23 15:05 iso
drwxrwxr-x  2 426       1          1024 Nov  9 15:38 isode
drwxr-xr-x  2 root      0           512 Jul  1  1991 lost+found
lrwxrwxrwx  1 root      1             8 Aug 22  1994 mgt -> ddn-news
drwxrwxr-x  2 426       1           512 Sep 21  1994 namedroppers
drwxr-xr-x  3 nicdb     0          2048 Mar 28 16:30 netinfo
lrwxrwxrwx  1 root      1             7 Jun 29  1993 netinfo: -> netinfo
drwxr-xr-x  2 root      1           512 Nov 25  1992 netprog
drwxr-xr-x  2 root      1          1024 Sep 28  1994 protocols
drwxr-xr-x  2 root      1           512 Feb 18  1993 pub
drwxr-xr-x  2 postel    isi       25088 Mar 24 20:35 rfc
drwxr-xr-x  2 root      1          5120 Mar  9 19:04 scc
drwxr-xr-x  2 root      1          1536 Mar 24 20:38 std
drwxrwxrwx  2 426       1          1024 Feb 23 14:57 tcp-ip
drwxr-xr-x  2 root      1          1024 Dec  3  1993 templates
drwxr-xr-x  3 root      1           512 Oct  1  1991 usr
226 Transfer complete.
ftp>
ftp> cd netinfo
250 CWD command successful.
ftp> get ways_to_get_rfcs
local: ways_to_get_rfcs remote: ways_to_get_rfcs
200 PORT command successful.
150 Opening BINARY mode data connection for ways_to_get_rfcs (840 bytes).
226 Transfer complete.
840 bytes received in 0.37 seconds (2.19 Kbytes/s)
ftp>
```

Figure 16–1: A simple command line FTP session.

server to the local host. Less often, the user will send files from the local host to the server. Once all transactions have been completed, the user terminates the session.

Some FTP commands are listed in Table 16–1. Though most are implemented as part of GUI versions of FTP, not all FTP implementations include every defined command. Figure 16–2 shows a list of all the available commands implemented in a typical Unix version of FTP.

Command-line implementations of FTP are, depending on the users' perspective, reassuringly or frighteningly like Unix. Graphical implementations are usually considerably easier to use, though some do not implement all of the normally supported functions. The command line version is

```
ftp [host name|IP address]
```

Host name or IP address is optional; if omitted, the raw FTP prompt will be displayed (GUI versions usually require that a host be specified). The FTP client starts and attempts to connect to the selected server by opening a login dialog. The user is prompted for a user ID and a password. If the server was not specified at startup, the user must send the FTP command

```
FTP:> open <host name|IP address>
```

The login dialog then begins.

The open and close commands are important here, if only because when FTP is opened with a server specified and an initial connection fails, the user must close the attempted connection (even though it had not been actually opened) before attempting to connect to another server. Figure 16–1 demonstrates the directory command (ls), change directory (cd), and a simple copy (get) on a remote host.

As shown in the example in Figure 16–1, the command line does not offer many "ease of use" amenities, but it gets the job done.

Command	Purpose
!	Open operating system shell
?	Get help
ascii	Set file type to ASCII transfer
binary	Set file type to binary transfer
cd	Change default directory on remote host
close	Terminate connection with remote host
delete	Remove file on remote host
dir	Get directory listing on current directory on remote host
get	Retrieve file from remote host
hash	Display # (hash character) for each block of data transferred
lcd	Change directory on local host
ls	Get directory listing on current directory on remote host
mdelete	Multiple delete of files using wildcard
mdir	Make directory
mget	Retrieve multiple files from remote host
mkdir	Make directory on remote host
mput	Send multiple files to remote host (from local host)
open	Open connection with remote host
put	Send file to remote host (from local host)
pwd	Return current working directory on remote host
quit	End FTP session
quote	Execute command on server
recv	Same as get
rmdir	Remove directory
send	Same as put
type	Return current file transfer type (ASCII or binary)
verbose	Toggle verbose mode—start or stop plain-language prompts

Table 16–1: Some commonly encountered FTP commands.

```
ftp> help
Commands may be abbreviated.    Commands are:

!                 debug           mget            pwd             status
$                 dir             mkdir           quit            struct
account           disconnect      mls             quote           system
append            form            mode            recv            sunique
ascii             get             modtime         reget           tenex
bell              glob            mput            rstatus         trace
binary            hash            newer           rhelp           type
bye               help            nmap            rename          user
case              idle            nlist           reset           umask
cd                image           ntrans          restart         verbose
cdup              lcd             open            rmdir           ?
chmod             ls              prompt          runique
close             macdef          proxy           send
cr                mdelete         sendport        site
delete            mdir            put             size
ftp>
```

Figure 16–2: Available commands for a typical Unix FTP implementation.

And, by implementing (basically) the same command set, users familiar with FTP on one host can adapt easily to other implementations. The ? command returns a list of valid commands (as shown in Figure 16–2); issuing any command with a ? after it will return a one-line description of the command. For example, some systems differentiate between `ls` and `dir`, offering a simple list with one and a more detailed listing with the other, but some implementations don't.

The commands `get` and `send` are used for single files; the `mget` and `msend` commands are useful for sending groups of files using wildcards. Figure 16–3 demonstrates the use of the multiple get command to retrieve a group of files from a remote host.

Using Anonymous FTP

System administrators use anonymous FTP as a simple way to make files available to the public. Anonymous FTP servers permit

```
ftp> mget *.*
local: gnus-mime.el.shar remote: gnus-mime.el.shar
200 PORT command successful.
150 Opening BINARY mode data connection for gnus-mime.el.shar (20509 bytes).
226 Transfer complete.
20509 bytes received in 0.19 seconds (107.06 Kbytes/s)
local: msend.tar.Z remote: msend.tar.Z
200 PORT command successful.
150 Opening BINARY mode data connection for msend.tar.Z (37089 bytes).
226 Transfer complete.
37089 bytes received in 0.18 seconds (196.79 Kbytes/s)
local: msend1.2.tar.Z remote: msend1.2.tar.Z
200 PORT command successful.
150 Opening BINARY mode data connection for msend1.2.tar.Z (37089 bytes).
226 Transfer complete.
37089 bytes received in 0.17 seconds (207.52 Kbytes/s)
ftp>
```

Figure 16–3: Retrieving a group of files with a single command, using a wildcard character.

connections from anyone, whether they have an account or not, by allowing use of a standard user ID. Remote users enter the user ID *anonymous* (or sometimes *ftp* or some other standard word) and are prompted to enter their e-mail address as a password. They may then access public files on the server.

Administrators generally offer this service from secure computers and permit public read-access only to files and directories that pose no security threat if compromised.

FTP: The Protocol

Like other applications that require reliability and a virtual circuit between the client and the server, FTP uses TCP as its transport protocol. Unlike other applications, though, FTP uses two distinct circuits instead of just one: the first provides a control channel for sending commands from the client to the server and for the server to send return messages to the client. The second channel is dedicated strictly for the transfer of data, which includes files being sent from the client to the server or from the server to the client, as well as directory information from the server to the client.

Figure 16–4 illustrates how FTP uses two TCP circuits. The user sends commands through the application, which passes those commands on to the client control process, and the server receives commands through its own control process. The control circuit connects the control processes on both the client and the server. When the server receives a command, the server control process passes the request to the server data transfer process. The data transfer process on the server then sends requested data across the internetwork to the client's data transfer process. The server control process sends reply codes back to the client control process, reporting on the response to the original request.

The FTP control circuit remains active for the entire FTP session, but the data transfer circuit may exist only as long as each data transfer request. This partitioning guarantees that there is still a circuit to pass error messages across if the data circuit is lost.

Another reason for maintaining two distinct circuits comes from the use of the stream mode for sending data; rather than use an end-of-file marker when sending a single file, files are considered complete when the circuit is closed. As a result, whenever a file has been sent, the data transfer circuit closes and the control circuit opens another one. If a data transfer circuit closes unexpectedly, the FTP implementation treats that action (the closing of the circuit) as an indication of the end of the file. A fragment of the file being sent will be stored in the destination host's file system, and the file transfer must be retried in order to get the complete file.

Connecting to the Server

As with other applications that use TCP, the FTP client starts by attempting to resolve the host name of the remote server. This is unnecessary if the server is specified by an IP address. The FTP

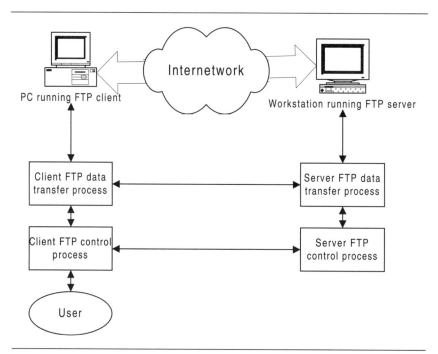

Figure 16–4: FTP partitions actual data transfer and the control functions, each into its own TCP circuit.

client initiates the control circuit to the server's port number 21, the well-known port for FTP control, assigning an arbitrary port number for its side of the circuit.

The server then prompts the client for a user ID and a password. Since a protocol already defines a set of rules for this function, the Telnet protocol, FTP uses a subset of the Telnet protocol to manage this exchange of information between the two hosts. The Network Virtual Terminal (see Chapter 15) specifications are used at either end to handle the request (sending the prompts through the server NVT) and the response (interpreting the keystrokes through the client NVT). FTP simply uses the basic NVT and includes no provisions for negotiating options, since that is outside the scope of the protocol's basic function: to provide a means for transferring files between dissimilar hosts.

When the client sends a request for data transfer (either a directory listing or a file transfer), it sends along another port number for the server to use to initiate a data transfer circuit. The server initiates the connection to transfer data using that port number on the client and its port number 20, the well-known port number for FTP data transfer. The file (or directory listing) is sent, the circuit is terminated, and the control circuit remains open for additional requests. When the session is complete, the control circuit is closed (or, to phrase it another way, when the control circuit is closed the session is over).

Reply Codes

As was mentioned previously, the FTP control circuit is used to send reply codes from the server back to the client. These reply codes can be seen in the examples shown in Figures 16–1 and 16–3. For example, the code 200 means the specified command was received and processed successfully. Each time the FTP client sends a command to the server, the server responds with a three-digit code. The first digit of the code indicates the status of the response to the command. Table 16–2 shows the meaning of the first digit of these codes. The middle digit of the reply code further specifies the meaning of the reply. Table 16–3 shows the meaning of these digits.

The third digit simply makes the reply code more specific. For example, the code 331 means that the user ID received was acceptable but a password must be sent before the server will proceed: the first digit, 3, indicates that an additional command is needed, the second 3 indicates the message is about authentication or accounting, and the 1 is simply the indicator for that particular message. Code 332 has a similar context: it indicates another command is needed, and it too relates to authentication and accounting, but it indicates that an account number is required by the server before proceeding.

The reply codes serve two purposes. The first is to keep the client informed about the status of the current transfer or connection.

Code	Meaning
1	Command was received and is being processed (not yet completed)
2	Command was received and is complete, ready for next command
3	Command was received, awaiting another command before proceeding
4	Command was received but could not be processed now (may be able to process it later)
5	Command was received but cannot be processed as received

Table 16–2: The first digit of the FTP reply code indicates status of the command.

Code	Meaning
0	Indicates a syntax message
1	Indicates an informational message
2	Indicates a connection
3	Indicates a message about authentication (password) or accounting (user ID or account)
4	Not specified
5	Indicates a message about the file system (file or directory message from operating system)

Table 16–3: The second digit of the FTP reply code indicates what the reply indicates.

This is important, as the client needs to know what responses previous commands have received before moving forward. The second purpose is to keep the user apprised of the status of the connection. This purpose is becoming less important as FTP is increasingly implemented in a GUI; but where it is implemented as a character-based, command-line application, these reply codes are associated with character strings so that the messages will have meaning for the user.

Trivial File Transfer Protocol

Trivial File Transfer Protocol is commonly used for remote booting of diskless workstations, rather than for end user interactive file transfer. It uses no security functions, offers a very limited command set (send and receive files, and a handful of connection commands; see Table 16–4 for a list of the main ones), and uses UDP for a connectionless, unreliable link rather than the TCP used by FTP. By virtue of its very limited functionality, TFTP clients, along with protocol stacks, can be small enough to load into memory on a diskless workstation from a small EPROM, thus allowing bootstrapping of more complete (and up-to-date) network software from a server.

Because of the lack of security features (even at the transmission layer), most network administrators limit TFTP servers to very limited files (usually only boot files) and some network administrators prefer not to permit TFTP at all.

Since TFTP uses UDP, files cannot be sent in data streams as in FTP, but rather one piece at a time. The client initiates a file transfer by

Command	Description
ascii	Sets file transfer type to ASCII mode
binary	Sets file transfer type to binary mode
connect [host name]	Connects to remote host
get	Retrieves a file from the TFTP server
put	Sends a file to the TFTP server
trace	Sets packet tracing on
verbose	Sets verbose mode on

Table 16–4: The Trivial File Transfer Protocol supports only a few commands, so it can be implemented in very little memory on a diskless workstation to support remote network bootstrapping.

sending a request message for a file, and the server responds by sending the first part of the file. When the client receives that first part of the file, it sends back an acknowledgment, and the server sends the next piece of the file. This continues until the file is complete; either side may retransmit a message if sufficient time has elapsed without a response for the other side. Since TFTP uses this simple method of receipt acknowledgment, there is potential for relatively long delays when sending data across an internetwork.

Security and TFTP

Most network administrators implement TFTP servers sparingly, if at all. No provision is made for soliciting a username or password from the client; although this helps make the implementation smaller, it is also necessary since systems that use TFTP to bootstrap themselves probably won't have account information available during the booting process.

Administrators usually set TFTP servers to offer access only to boot files in a specific directory, and restrict access to all other directories on the server.

TFTP: The Protocol

Because it is intended to be used mostly in situations that require minimal implementations, like diskless workstations that need to boot off a network server, TFTP is a simple protocol. The five basic types of TFTP messages are shown in Table 16–5.

Every TFTP message includes a two-byte operation code that signifies what type of message it is (see Table 16–5). Read and write requests include a filename and the TFTP mode to use to transfer the file, either ASCII or raw binary. Data messages include the operation code, a two-byte block number that corresponds to the number of the piece of data being sent, and 512 bytes of data (except for

TFTP Message Type	Op code	Purpose
Read Request	1	Requests a file to be opened on the server and copied to the client
Write Request	2	Requests a file to be written on the server and copied from the client
Data	3	Contains data to be read or written
Acknowledgment	4	Acknowledges receipt of a data message
Error	5	Indicates an error condition

Table 16–5: TFTP message types.

the last data message; see the following). Acknowledgment messages contain simply the operation code and a block number corresponding to the block number of the data message being acknowledged. Error messages occur when requested operations can't be done; there is very little error handling in TFTP, though.

When a client does a read request, the server sends back a data message containing the first part of the file and the block number 1. If the client receives this message, it sends back an acknowledgment message with the same block number. Once the acknowledgment is received, the server sends out block number 2. This continues until the file transfer is complete. The client knows when the file transfer is complete because the last data message contains less than 512 bytes: if the file size is exactly divisible by 512, the last data message contains no data to signal completion.

When a client does a write request, to send a file from the client to the server, it sends a write request message that contains the file name and transfer mode. If the server is willing to allow the file to be transferred to it, it replies with an acknowledgment message with the block number set to 0. The client then begins sending data messages to the server, waiting for acknowledgment of each message before sending the next piece of the file.

Chapter Summary and References

In this chapter we examined the File Transfer Protocol (FTP) and the Trivial File Transfer Protocol (TFTP). First, we looked at how FTP works from a user's standpoint. Next, we examined the FTP protocol, its control and transfer circuits, and the use of reply codes to indicate status of requests. Finally, we looked at TFTP: how it works, why it is useful, and how the protocol operates.

Some useful RFCs to read in conjunction with this chapter include those listed in Table 16–6. FTP has long been an Internet standard, and the protocol has long been specified in RFCs. The most important ones are listed here.

RFC	Title	Description
906	Bootstrap Loading Using TFTP	Describes the most important function of TFTP, published in 1984.
959	File Transfer Protocol (FTP)	This is the current full Internet standard specification, published in 1986.
1350	The TFTP Protocol (Revision 2)	This is the full Internet standard specification for TFTP. Published in 1992.
1635	How to Use Anonymous FTP	An information document explaining how anonymous FTP works.
2228	FTP Security Extensions	This document outlines security issues with FTP and provides some solutions.

Table 16–6: Useful RFCs for Chapter 16.

17

Internet Messaging

E-mail has long been the benchmark application that divides the Internet connected from the disconnected. Although e-mail has been common on shared systems like mainframes and dialup services for many years, interoperable messaging as provided by Internet e-mail applications provides almost universal connectivity.

Internet e-mail is based on an architecture devised in the late 1970s and early 1980s. This basic structure has changed little since then, although new functions and features as well as new applications have been added. In this chapter, we outline the basic structure of the Internet messaging architecture as well as the foundations of related Internet messaging protocols.

Messaging Applications and Standards

E-mail is the most important Internet messaging application, and was the first messaging application to be widely implemented. Very simply, e-mail allows entities to send and receive messages. Each entity has an e-mail address which, when appended to an e-mail message, provides enough information to deliver the message to the recipient. All Internet e-mail messages conform to a standard format, with specific rules defining what kinds of information are to be included in the message headers as well as how the information in the body of the message is to be formatted.

Although e-mail is fine for communicating with known entities, there are times when you want to share information with a group of interested entities. In some cases, you won't know who, exactly, is a member of the group; in other cases, not every member of the group actually will be interested. The concept of a bulletin board, where people can post electronic or physical messages, provides a foundation for the network news application. Using many of the same standards for new postings as those used for e-mail messages, and building delivery protocols that are similar to those used for e-mail, the network news application provides a forum for sharing information among anyone who might be interested.

Internet standards define how the e-mail and news applications themselves work, as well as how the messages are transmitted from one entity to another. Internet standards also define how end-user applications are able to download and manage messages. Finally, Internet standards define how nontext data can be incorporated into Internet messages and seamlessly transmitted across the Internet.

There are several new areas of Internet messaging, developed since the mid 1990s. With the commercialization of the Internet, businesses clamored for ways to extend their network applications outside their organizational borders. New standards have been published or are being developed to support calendaring and scheduling applications, use of digital business cards, and entity identification.

Electronic Mail

E-mail is now as common a business tool as the telephone, pager, and fax machine. For proof, simply look at the increasing number of business cards that list one or more e-mail addresses alongside the fax, phone, and pager numbers of the bearer of the card. E-mail is a very simple application so most users get the idea quickly about how to read incoming messages and generate outgoing messages.

Most Internet standard e-mail clients perform the same basic functions: read e-mail, reply to e-mail, and file e-mail messages. Implementations vary, of course, and many proprietary e-mail clients will also do Internet standard e-mail. The most basic e-mail implementations do little more than display character-based messages, allow users to edit outgoing messages, and list filed messages by topic. Full-featured implementations provide graphical interfaces, quick searching and sorting of filed messages, insertion of graphics and message formatting, simultaneous display of different messages, lists of messages, and other information in separate windows, and more.

The most basic electronic mail client can

- Receive e-mail messages
- Read e-mail messages
- Address e-mail messages
- Send e-mail messages
- Reply to received e-mail messages
- Forward received e-mail messages to others

In general, e-mail clients also offer additional functions pertaining to management of sent and received messages, as well as more complicated e-mail functions, like the ability to:

- Store e-mail messages that have been sent out
- Store e-mail messages that have been received and read
- Manage address lists
- Attach raw files to e-mail messages being sent
- Detach raw files from e-mail messages being received

All e-mail clients can send and receive basic e-mail messages.

There are four basic protocols that define Internet e-mail. The Simple Mail Transfer Protocol (SMTP) defines how e-mail messages are forwarded across the Internet from their source to their destinations. The Post Office Protocol (POP) defines how client machines retrieve messages from e-mail servers. The Internet Mail Access Protocol (IMAP) provides tools for managing e-mail accounts on e-mail servers through client systems. The Multipurpose Internet Mail Extensions (MIME) defines methods for encapsulating various types of data files in a format that can be transmitted across the Internet, and, for example, attached to an e-mail message. Though not strictly speaking, a protocol, e-mail headers must conform to a standard format, as defined in RFC 822, "Standard for the Format of ARPA Internet Text Messages."

Internetwork E-Mail Model

Internetwork e-mail is based on a simple model: e-mail users interface with **user agents** (UAs) for sending and receiving e-mail. The program used for reading and sending e-mail, which has been referred to as the *e-mail client* or *e-mail reader,* is actually a UA. The UA runs on the user's local host and communicates with a **message transfer agent** (MTA) on a mail server. The MTA interacts with each user's UA and also connects with other MTAs over TCP links to exchange e-mail. The entire system of interacting MTAs is sometimes referred to as the **message transfer system** (MTS). This model is represented in Figure 17–1.

The e-mail client software acts as the UA. The e-mail server acts as the MTA. There is no technical reason that the UA and MTA could not be part of the same system—that would mean the same machine on which a user reads and writes e-mail would also serve as the machine that transmits and receives those messages across the Internet. However, a system that hosts both the UA and the MTA would always have to be up and running to accept messages from other MTAs; this is impractical for most end-user systems.

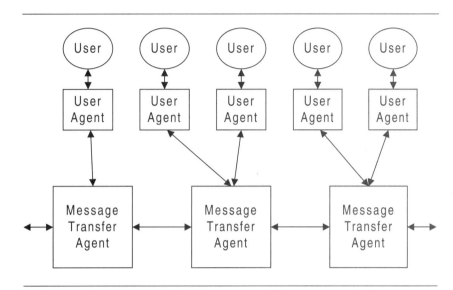

Figure 17–1: TCP/IP e-mail is delivered by message transfer agents, which connect with user agents to deliver mail to recipients and receive mail to be delivered across internetworks.

By separating the UA from the MTA, the client becomes responsible only for supplying the correct e-mail address for any outgoing e-mail. No other information is required from the user. The MTA takes care of e-mail transmission, transparently to the end users.

> *NOTE: Basic e-mail does not provide any mechanism for security or for delivery guarantees. Messages are sent in plaintext, and the route taken by any particular e-mail message can traverse any number of systems over the Internet, over which neither the sender nor the recipient has any control. This means that e-mail users should assume that their messages can be read by anyone with access to one of those systems. Likewise, there is no mechanism by which delivery of a message can be guaranteed, nor is there any mechanism by which a sender will always be notified in the event that a message is not properly delivered. Although e-mail is convenient, fast, and cheap, it should not be used to convey sensitive information without proper encryption, nor should it be used as the only channel for transmitting urgent or critical information.*

E-Mail Addresses

At one time e-mail addresses could take several different formats, depending on how the messages were delivered and what network the user was connected to. Internet e-mail now almost universally is of the form

```
userID@domain.name
```

where `domain.name` refers to a valid domain in the Domain Name System (see Chapter 11). As explained there, mail exchange records can be used to point e-mail destined for a particular e-mail address to a particular host and account.

E-Mail Message Structure

The e-mail message itself consists of three parts: an envelope, the headers, and the body of the message. Working from the inside out, the message body is simply what the sender wants the recipient to receive. It has no relevance to any of the e-mail systems other than as payload to be delivered. The message body is an optional part of the e-mail message.

The headers of the message include various information about the message (when it was sent, who sent it, what the topic is) and who sent it (sender's name, an e-mail address to reply to, and other optional information), and to whom it is being sent (recipient). The information in the header is put there by the user agent (e-mail client) on the sending side and is interpreted and output for the person receiving the message by the recipient's user agent.

All of this is wrapped up in the envelope: the e-mail addresses of the source of the e-mail message and the recipient of the message. This is the part that the message transfer agents use to determine what action to take with messages they receive from user agents.

The envelope itself consists of the e-mail address of the user who created the enclosed e-mail message, the e-mail address (or addresses for multiple deliveries) of the recipient(s), and the delivery mode (virtually always specified to send to a recipient's mailbox; other available modes relate to options for sending the message to the recipient at a terminal session instead of, or in addition to, sending to the mailbox—these modes are largely obsolete).

The headers, as might be expected, are at the head of the mail message. Headers consist of a header title immediately followed by a colon. A space follows the colon, followed by the value of the header. Figure 17–2 shows a sample e-mail message with headers, in raw form. Some e-mail clients reformat the headers, or hide some of them, to make the message easier to read. The body of the message comes after the headers and is separated from them by a blank line.

```
Received: from kermit.acme.com (ppp1.acme.com [199.0.65.52]) by zork.tiac.net
        (8.6.9/8.6.6.Beta9) with ESMTP id QAA15049 for <ploshin@tiac.net>;
        Tue, 28 Mar 1995 16:50:52 -0500
Received: from bert (bert.acme.com [198.69.147.3]) by kermit.acme.com
        (8.6.10/8.6.9) with SMTP id QAA22785 for <ploshin@tiac.net>; Tue, 28
        Mar 1995 16:51:17 -0500
Message-Id: <199503282151.QAA22785@kermit.acme.com>
Sender: <rhj@kermit.acme.com>
From: "Robert H. Jones" <rhj@acme.com>
Organization:  acme, inc, Anytown, MA   USA
To: ploshin@tiac.net
Date: Tue, 28 Mar 1995 16:48:24 -500
Subject: Thanks!
Reply-to: rhj@acme.com
Priority: normal
X-phone: 1+617 555-4549
X-mailer: Pegasus Mail/Windows (v1.21)


Bob, thanks for the proposal.  I'll be in touch.

-Pete
```

Figure 17–2: A sample e-mail message with headers.

The Received header indicates the mail transfer agents involved in delivering the mail, as well as time and message ID for those transfers. When the message has passed through multiple MTAs to get to its destinations it can have multiple Received headers. The Message-ID assigns an ID number to the message. Although it might seem that the Sender, From, and Reply-to headers are redundant, this is not the case. Organizations are increasingly using aliases and mail forwarding to make e-mail addressing within the organization uniform and transportable. For example, in Figure 17–2, the Sender address,

`rhj@kermit.acme.com`

refers to an account on a host named "kermit." However, the From header, which includes a person's name and e-mail address, as well as the Reply-to header, which shows the e-mail address to use when replying to the message, both show the address:

`rhj@acme.com`

which is more generic. By assigning these more generic e-mail addresses, organizations are able to keep the e-mail addresses shorter and easier to remember. More important, though, users retain the flexibility of being able to receive e-mail on any host they want simply by having a network manager change a mail exchange record to forward e-mail received at the generic address to their host of choice.

The Reply-to header may be different from the other two headers under certain circumstances: the person sending mail is temporarily using a different host, or for some reason wishes the recipient of the e-mail message to reply to some other e-mail account.

The other headers are fairly self-explanatory: To, Date, Subject, and Priority mean exactly what they say. Headers starting with X are, technically, defined by the user; for example, listing a telephone number to reach the user. However, they are usually inserted by the application program (as in the example, the name of the e-mail client program is included).

When headers take up more than one line, they wrap to the next line, but start several spaces in on that line. Headers are separated from each by a line feed/carriage return pair.

E-Mail Functions

E-mail is simple to understand, conceptually, since it so closely mirrors the function of that other kind of mail. Users receive messages in their mailboxes; they can choose which to read (and which to discard unread) by looking at the subject lines and sender that the e-mail client displays. Users can reply to e-mail messages, forward them to other users, print, save, or delete the messages. They can send copies of the same message to additional recipients and can even use a "blind carbon" option to send a copy of a message to additional recipients without those recipients appearing in the original message. Files can also be attached to e-mail messages, offering a simple means of file transfer.

Once a message has been received by a single recipient, the recipient can elect to discard the message unread on the basis of the Subject line (the subject is not of interest to the user) or the Sender (the recipient does not wish to read any messages from the person or entity sending the message). If the recipient does read the message, it can be deleted from the mailbox or saved.

Recipients can take further action on any message received by replying to the message or forwarding the message to some other recipient(s). Often, e-mail clients offer an option to include the message being replied to, and usually set off the original message from the new message by either including "begin" and "end" lines, indicating where the original message starts and ends, or by indenting the original message and putting special characters at the start of each line. Figure 17–3 shows a sample message where both approaches are used.

As may be apparent, the original sender of a message loses control over its distribution once it is sent. Unlike regular mail, e-mail can be duplicated simply and easily and often is sent mistakenly to the wrong recipient or even to public forums like Internet news groups. Similarly, messages can be forwarded much more simply than any hard-copy message. Users are well advised to consider the content of their messages before posting e-mail and assume that just about anyone might ultimately get to see a copy. Forwarding e-mail without permission is frowned upon, but it still happens, which brings up the next point: recipients should ask permission before forwarding messages to third parties.

```
Received: from kermit.acme.com (ppp1.acme.com [199.0.65.52]) by zork.tiac.net
        (8.6.9/8.6.6.Beta9) with ESMTP id QAA15049 for <ploshin@tiac.net>;
        Tue, 28 Mar 1995 16:50:52 -0500
Received: from bert (bert.acme.com [198.69.147.3]) by kermit.acme.com
        (8.6.10/8.6.9) with SMTP id QAA22785 for <ploshin@tiac.net>; Tue, 28
        Mar 1995 16:51:17 -0500
Message-Id: <199503282151.QAA22785@kermit.acme.com>
Sender: <rhj@kermit.acme.com>
From: "Robert H. Jones" <rhj@acme.com>
Organization: acme, inc, Anytown, MA  USA
To: ploshin@tiac.net
Date: Tue, 28 Mar 1995 16:48:24 -500
Subject: Re: Re: lunch appointment
In-Reply-To: bob's message of Wed, 29 Mar 95 07:16:33 -0800.
        <9503291516.AA12300@kermit.acme.com>
Reply-to: rhj@acme.com
Priority: normal
X-phone: 1+617 555-4549
X-mailer: Pegasus Mail/Windows (v1.21)


How about noon?
>What time?
><— Begin Included Message —>
>Pete, how about lunch tomorrow?
>
>-Bob
><— End Included Message —>
```

Figure 17–3: E-mail clients may use one of several methods of setting off the text of an original message from the text of the reply to that message.

Mailing Lists and Automatic Reply

Another set of functions involves the use of mailing lists and automatic mail responders. Individuals can create lists of e-mail addresses for groups of recipients to which they would like to send messages. For instance, a manager may have one list that includes all employees reporting to the manager, another list of all people to whom the manager reports, and a third list including all managers at the same organizational level. When sending a message, the user specifies the list name to the e-mail client software, which then exchanges the name of the list for the list of addressees on that particular list.

A different type of mailing list is often encountered that fills a function similar to that fulfilled by network news groups. Special mailing list software is configured to accept messages to a special list address (also called an *alias*) and then to create new messages that are sent to subscribers of the list. Users subscribe or unsubscribe to the list by sending an e-mail message with a special format to a list administration address (the format usually requires a one-line list command as the body of the message) and can submit to the list by sending e-mail to the list address itself. The personal mailing list is converted into individual messages by the e-mail client software itself, whereas the formal mailing list is exploded by a program running on a system acting as a message transfer agent (a mailing list can also be configured directly through the message transfer agent itself, but this can be very complicated, and list management software is readily available).

Another e-mail service is the automated reply. Organizations that receive many queries by e-mail about their products or services often set up automated reply addresses. These addresses, which frequently take the form info@company.com, are sent to a program that responds by automatically replying to the sender with the requested information. A similar mechanism can be configured to distribute a selection of data files on demand and is called an **e-mail archive**. Messages are directed at an automated reply address that usually returns an index to available files and instructions. The person seeking information can then send another message that includes one or more commands in the body indicating the desired files.

The Postmaster

The only address required at every domain connected to the Internet is the postmaster. Because there is no central and authoritative directory to find users' e-mail addresses or to connect to an administrator or manager at any given site, every domain must support at least one e-mail address and forward messages to that address to a human. The postmaster addresses all take the form

```
postmaster@<domain.name>
```

where the <domain name> is a valid Internet domain name. This ensures that there is a point of contact at every domain to handle incoming messages about e-mail coming from that domain. This is important, because it means that if message software at a particular domain is generating network errors or excessive traffic, someone can be notified to correct it.

E-Mail Protocols

The Simple Mail Transfer Protocol (SMTP) defines the way message transfer agents exchange e-mail with each other (see RFC 821, "Simple Mail Transfer Protocol"). Figure 17–1 showed a simple model for the movement of e-mail: the end user interacts with a user agent, which in turn interacts with the message transfer agent. The message transfer agent then forwards e-mail to other message transfer agents for delivery and receives messages from other message transfer agents to deliver to the end user (through the user agent). In practice, this model originally called for implementation of user agents and message transfer agents on the same host: the user interacts with the UA, the UA then passes the e-mail commands through the MTA.

Network managers prefer to have a single **relay MTA** that acts as an e-mail gateway for e-mail going in and out of an organization, to simplify e-mail account management. As a result, the model looks more like Figure 17–4. This is especially true when individuals receive e-mail on their personal computers or workstations. The Unix `sendmail` program implements SMTP for each Unix workstation and interacts with the various Unix e-mail clients to receive mail and commands, then passes them on to the relay system for e-mail.

E-Mail Headers

RFC 822 defines the rules for e-mail headers. These include some standard headers that appear at the start of any e-mail message as well as potential for user- or application-defined headers. There is no set order in which headers must appear, as long as all headers

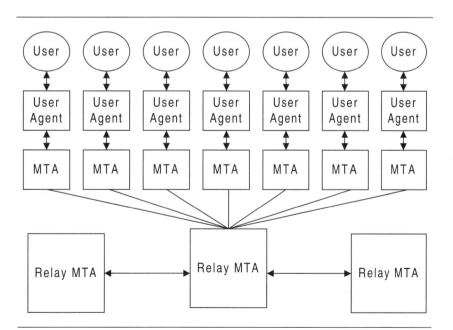

Figure 17–4: E-mail model, modified to reflect use of relay message transfer agents.

of any given message appear before the body of the message (any content appended to a message below the first blank line is considered part of the message body). The envelope of the message is of importance to its processing through SMTP (the recipient and the sender are used with the MAIL FROM: and RCPT TO: commands described previously); the headers are the concern of the user agents involved (the e-mail client being used to compose the message and the client used to receive the message).

It is possible to deliver an e-mail message with only three headers: Date:, From:, and To:. These and other important e-mail headers include

To: Indicates the recipient(s) of the e-mail message by spelling out the recipient's e-mail address(es).

cc: Indicates recipient(s) of copies of the e-mail message by spelling out e-mail address(es). Similar to the cc: line in hard-copy mail, indicating a list of people who get (carbon) copies of the original.

bcc: Like cc: except that it indicates recipients of copies of the message whose names and addresses are not included in the original message.

From: Indicates the e-mail address of the entity causing the message to be sent. More than one entity may be indicated and may be different from the Reply-To: or Sender: headers.

Reply-To: An address to which message replies should be addressed; when this header is present, it should indicate an e-mail address different from the From: header.

Sender: Indicates the e-mail address from which the message is actually being sent.

Subject: Usually a short description of the topic of the message.

Date: The date and time the message being sent was created.

Keywords: A list of words or phrases that pertain to the topic of the message and that may be used for sorting or searching by the recipient.

Comments: Another descriptive header that may include comments about the message.

References: Used to refer to previous correspondence, particularly if the current message is a reply to a previous message. Uses the message ID of that message.

Message-ID: An identification string that combines the domain portion of the originating message with a locally assigned combination of numbers and letters.

Simple Mail Transfer Protocol

Clients initiate an SMTP session by opening a TCP circuit to the server's port 25; the SMTP server then responds with a server ID and a status: it is either available to transfer mail or it is not available. If it is available, the client can continue the session and transfer mail. SMTP uses only a few commands, and most e-mail can be transferred with just five.

Communication between client and server uses the same NVT ASCII as Telnet and FTP and, like FTP, SMTP has three-digit reply codes (with optional human-readable explanatory strings) that are issued in response to each command. The format of these reply codes is very similar to that of the FTP reply codes.

Once the TCP connection has been initiated, the client sends the HELO command along with its fully qualified domain name. This identifies it to the server, which (if the command is accepted) will reply with its own fully qualified domain name.

The client then sends the MAIL FROM: command, with the full e-mail address of the sender enclosed in angle brackets (< and >). If the server is able to accept the mail, it sends back a reply code indicating it is ready for the e-mail address of the recipient.

The next command from the client is the RCPT TO: command, also with the full e-mail address of the recipient of the message enclosed in angle brackets. When the same message is being sent to multiple addresses, this command is repeated until all recipients have been identified to the SMTP server.

Once recipients' addresses have been sent to the server, the client sends the DATA command; if the server answers with the reply code that indicates it is ready to receive the content of the message, the client starts sending the message. When finished, the client indicates completion of the message by sending a period (".") on a line by itself; the server then sends back the reply code indicating that the previous message was accepted and the client can either start another message transfer or end the session with the QUIT command.

Error messages generally indicate either that the server is not available, in which case the session is terminated and the client tries again later, or else that there is a syntax error in a command.

Once the SMTP server has an e-mail message, it either delivers the message—it has direct access to the host on which the recipient has his or her e-mail account—or forwards the message to another SMTP server. SMTP servers pass messages back and forth for each other. Generally, the SMTP server forwarding a message tries to open a connection with the appropriate SMTP server for each recipient. The server in this case then has the option of accepting the message and forwarding it directly into the recipient's mailbox. However, the server can also notify the remote SMTP server that the message should be forwarded to a different SMTP server.

SMTP relies on constant connectivity, as well as availability of resources to maintain message databases as well as to process all incoming requests. Most personal computers and individual workstations don't have these resources, nor are they capable of guaranteeing round-the-clock availability and connectivity. As a result, implementing SMTP on every personal computer attached to the Internet or to an organizational internetwork is not practical.

As we'll see in the next section, the Post Office Protocol (POP) was developed as a means of offering access to a user's mailbox from a system that doesn't fully implement SMTP. POP lets users check for new mail, read, and delete mail. Where the client host uses POP to download mail from an SMTP server, the client is usually set up to transmit outgoing messages to the SMTP server using SMTP commands—the client needs only to implement enough of SMTP to be able to submit outgoing messages.

Post Office Protocol

The Post Office Protocol, version 3 (POP3), is an Internet standard specified in RFC 1939. It provides a simple service: a mechanism for client systems to download mail being held by a mail server for the user. The protocol is straightforward, with the POP server listening to port 110 for client requests. Once a request is received and authentication has been completed, the session begins. The client requests messages, and the server sends them.

In most cases, the client system uses POP to download messages from the server and then delete those messages from the server. The only other option with POP is to download messages and not delete them from the server. This provides an approximation of one of the services that the Internet Mail Access Protocol (IMAP) was designed for: a semi-permanent e-mail repository. POP is intended as a basic service for e-mail, rather than a more full-featured application like that provided by IMAP, as described next.

Internet Mail Access Protocol

Proprietary e-mail products, designed to be implemented on an organizational LAN and served from a single organizational server, offer some useful functions and features to the end users. Storing all messages on a central server means that those messages can be backed up centrally and made accessible at a later date. It also means that users can access their mailbox from any network-connected system, not just from their own "home" system. SMTP and POP simply don't offer these amenities to users, so the Internet Mail Access Protocol (IMAP) was developed.

IMAP, specified in RFC 2060, "INTERNET MESSAGE ACCESS PROTOCOL—VERSION 4rev1," defines a protocol that allows users to access and manipulate their messages stored on a remote server. By design, it allows users to read, delete, file into folders, and otherwise manipulate messages stored on a server as if they were stored on the user's own local system.

Multipurpose Internet Message Extensions (MIME)

Standard Internet e-mail assumes that all data in the e-mail message, from the header to the body, consists of ASCII text characters. The Multipurpose Internet Message Extensions (MIME) structure and encode other types of data into a form that can be attached to e-mail messages. MIME uses two sets of headers to do most of its work. The `content-type` header identifies what kind of material is being enclosed. The `content-transfer-encoding` header identifies how the content is encoded.

MIME content types consist of a type, which provides a general description of what kind of data is enclosed; and a subtype, which provides a more specific description of what kind of data is enclosed. Parameters may be present to provide additional customization for the content description. Valid types include application, text, image, audio, video, message, and multipart. Each different type has its own set of valid subtypes. For example, a Microsoft Word document MIME enclosure would be identified with the content-type header value of application/MSWord. The type is application, the subtype is MSWord. A text file would be identified with the value of text/plain, where the type is text and the subtype is plain.

MIME multipart enclosures are worth mentioning as they enclose more than one item in a single enclosure. Multipart enclosures are used to include security data related to the message, for example a multipart enclosure might include an encrypted file and a digital signature for that file.

MIME offers a set of three encoding mechanisms for the representation of the data included in the enclosure. Although all systems process e-mail messages as if they are ASCII text, other types of data can become mangled if treated as seven-bit ASCII characters. Binary data or non-ASCII text (for example, character sets for non-English languages) tends to be difficult to transmit in e-mail bodies, unless MIME is used to enclose the data.

One of MIME's three encoding mechanisms is **7bit**, which is used to indicate that the content can be treated as standard ASCII text. Another encoding mechanism is called **quoted-printable**, which is used to indicate that the content is mostly ASCII, but may have some non-ASCII characters included. Quoted-printable enclosures retain the non-ASCII characters so that the recipient can use the data as originally sent.

The **base64** encoding mechanism is used for binary data. The danger with sending binary data through e-mail is that e-mail processing systems treat all messages as if they were ASCII text; the characters are treated as if they are seven-bit characters even though the binary data uses all eight bits of each available byte. The binary data would often have the last bit truncated, and would appear at the receiving end as nonsense streams of ASCII characters. The base64 encoding mechanism avoids this problem by mapping 24 bits (three bytes) of binary data onto four ASCII characters. When a MIME enclosure is received, the recipient determines whether it was encoded with base64, in which case the ASCII characters are converted back into binary data.

There are many RFCs that describe how MIME works, as well as defining different mechanisms related to and working with MIME. RFC 2045, "Multipurpose Internet Mail Extensions (MIME) Part One: Format of Internet Message Bodies," is the first of a series of five RFCs (2045-2049) that document how MIME works.

Internet News

USENET, or User's Network, was a loosely bound "network" for distributing USENET news. It provided the basis for an Internet standard protocol, Network News Transfer Protocol (NNTP), which carries one of the more popular Internet applications. USENET news and NNTP were originally intended to be vehicles for the dissemination of information between individuals with access to the Internet or USENET, particularly announcements regarding research results and other relevant news like bugs, fixes, and new products. They have come to a vehicle for discussion groups about virtually every topic imaginable.

News is grouped with Internet mail for a number of reasons. First, it performs a similar function as e-mail and partially grew out of the e-mail mailing list function. It is more economical of network resources (bandwidth, storage, and processing) to store messages intended for a group on a central server rather than sending each participant his or her own copy of the message. Second, news postings have a structure similar to e-mail messages: headers, indicating information about the posting, and a body for the contents of the posting. In fact, the network news message uses RFC 822-compliant headers.

Most important, though, the news function allows an individual to communicate ideas across an internetwork to others. The primary difference, as noted before, is that although e-mail is directed to a limited group of recipients by the author, news postings are directed to (usually) public forums whose readers can be anyone with access to the Internet.

The Network News Transfer Protocol is specified in RFC 977, "Network News Transfer Protocol: A Proposed Standard for the Stream-Based Transmission of News." This specification has been a proposed standard since 1986, when it was published; despite the fact that it has not advanced toward full Internet standard status since then, it is still widely used and implemented.

Making network news a service, accessible through TCP using a news reader client program, has advantages over using e-mail. First, Internet traffic is reduced, since each message is repeated only once to each site receiving it and then propagated locally to all interested parties. Transfer of news articles is done interactively between news reader clients and servers, so hosts that have already received an article do not need to have that article sent again. Finally, news can be retrieved interactively between news servers and news feeds, so that existing articles received from one feed are not duplicated when sent over another feed.

News Groups

Just as the Domain Name System uses hierarchical naming conventions, so does network news. There are a handful of major news hierarchies, with others distributed locally or regionally. Some of the most popular and common hierarchies include

alt   Alternative; just about any topic is covered here, particularly topics that may not be sanctioned by administrative authorities; these news groups are very heavily used and include many relating to sex, drugs, and conspiracy theories

biz   Business-related topics; also, some news groups permit commercial content

comp Topics relating to computers, such as computer science, programming, software and hardware, etc.

misc A catchall hierarchy; includes news groups like misc.kids

news Topics pertaining to the use of network news and network news software; these groups are not intended for the distribution of news items

rec   Recreational topics, covering all types of hobby and leisure activities and interests; typical groups include rec.pets.cats and rec.tv.simpsons

sci   Topics pertaining to science and research

soc   "Social" or "socializing" news groups, relating to social interaction in various situations or regions

talk   Open forums for never-ending discussions of particular topics; typical topics might be religion, politics, and other issues whose adherents rarely change their positions based on discussion with nonbelievers

News group names use the same type of representation as domain names, with each layer name separated by a period (pronounced "dot"). News group names are generally pronounced as spelled, with "dot" separating each hierarchy layer: rec.pets.cats is pronounced "rec dot pets dot cats." News group hierarchies can go fairly deep, though after a point there is little added value to the creation of "pinpoint" groups. The alt.* hierarchy, on which virtually anyone can create a new list, is famous for being the source of "tongue in cheek" news group names like "alt.barney.die.die.die".

News Posts

Network news posts are comparable to e-mail messages: they consist of headers separated from the body of the post by a blank line, and when transmitted they are terminated with a period and a blank line. Headers use the same format: the header name, colon, and a space followed by the header content. A header can wrap beyond the first line if it is too long, as long as at least one space is left at the start of the additional line. Some headers are required, and others are optional. These are the required headers:

From: E-mail address of the person sending the post

Date: Date and time the post was submitted to the network

News groups: Name or names of news groups to which the post is being submitted; multiple news groups are permitted if they are separated by a comma

`Subject:`	A brief description of the content of the post
`Message-ID:`	A unique identifier for the post, which includes an arbitrary sequence of characters and the full domain name of the host from which the post originated
`Path`	The names of the hosts (routers) that have transmitted the post

Some of the optional headers include

`Followup-To:`	If the poster wishes to redirect response to the post to another news group (e.g., if another news group seems to be a more appropriate forum), that news group is indicated here
`Reply-To:`	Similar to the e-mail header; indicates an e-mail address to send replies to that is different from the address in the `From:` header
`Sender`	Similar to the e-mail header; indicates that the message was actually transmitted from a different host than the host in the `From:` header
`Expires:`	A date at which the post should expire; intended to allow posts with short-lived purposes to expire quickly, but it is not usually recommended
`References:`	Message-ID values for previous messages relating to the current one
`Distribution:`	A regional distribution that is less wide than the normal distribution for the news group, used when posting about regional topics
`Keywords:`	Words or short phrases that pertain to the topic of the post and can be used for searching

Much more can be said about the topics, content, and protocol of actually participating in Internet news groups, but those topics are beyond the scope of this book and are handled competently and voluminously elsewhere.

Network News Transfer Protocol

Just as the format of the network news post resembles that of the network e-mail message, so does the Network News Transfer Protocol resemble the Simple Mail Transfer Protocol. Both use TCP as a transport protocol: NNTP uses well-known port 119. Both also use three-digit reply codes to respond to NNTP commands, and both handle transmission of post or messages in much the same way.

Hosts acting as clients initiate a TCP link to a host acting as a server. Once the connection is established (with the server indicating that it is ready and able to respond to requests) the client can issue a series of commands:

NEWGROUPS   Asks the server if any new news groups have been set up since the date and time indicated in the command; the server returns newly created news groups in a list. The date and time are required, and an optional "distributions" parameter can be added to narrow the lists of groups (within hierarchies) that are being sought.

NEWNEWS   Asks the server if there have been any new postings received at the server since the indicated date and time; new postings are listed by Message ID number. The date and time are required, as is at least one news group name—wildcards are permitted, so all news groups or some subset of selected hierarchies may be specified. Multiple news groups can also be listed, separated by commas. A distribution parameter is optional, limiting retrieval to the specified geographic distribution.

IHAVE   Indicates that the client has news posts to transmit to the server. This command is used by hosts that are collecting news from other news feeds to provide news service to regular clients. The server offers a copy of the news post to its server; if the feeding server already has a copy of the post it can decline to receive that post. Individuals posting to a news group generate a different command through their network news client when they submit a new post: POST.

POST   Indicates that a news user intends to submit a news posting, and the news server is obligated to receive the transmission for forwarding (as long as it is available and able to do so).

There are several other commands, providing capability mostly for the news client to point at a desired news group, to list available news postings, and to retrieve the contents of desired news postings for local display.

Network News Client Functions

News clients usually offer functions that parallel, and in some cases duplicate, e-mail functions. The primary functions are the ability to display lists of available news groups, list posts in any given news group by a subject line, display an individual news post, post a reply to any given news post, and submit a post on a new topic to the news group. The news client also keeps track of the news groups to which the user subscribes, or follows, and makes sure that new posts in these subscribed news groups are presented to the user for reading. Another important function is to list only those news posts that are new and to drop from the list of unread posts those already seen by the user.

Most news readers also offer a way to generate e-mail sent directly to the author of a given post. This function is intended as a way to cut down on Internet traffic by taking public interactions (which require higher bandwidth to reach all parties who may be interested) into the private realm where the two individuals can communicate.

The daily volume of news generated across the Internet is staggering: not long ago it was possible to manage a full news feed with two-week expiration dates on all posts on a system with as little as a few hundred megabytes of free disk space. By 1995 it was over a gigabyte, and continues to expand. This is a problem not just for the administrators of the systems acting as news servers, but also for the users who need or want to read news. Many news clients offer a "kill file" that allows the user to specify certain topics they do not wish to read about or certain individuals whose posts they do not want to read. This helps to cut down on the volume.

Also helpful is the use of "threads" to identify ongoing conversations on the same topic. Some news clients are programmed to group together posts that have the same topic and refer to the same chain of previous posts (using the Topic and References headers). The user can select whether or not to follow any particular news thread.

As with e-mail clients, news clients come in all shapes and sizes. Some, like the Unix `trn` (for "threaded read news") shown in Figure 17–5, are character-based. Though they do not offer the ease of use of graphical applications, the Unix-based news readers are more likely to implement kill files and other Unix-oriented features. Other news readers are implemented as graphical applications and permit point-and-click access to news groups and news posts.

Other Internet Messaging Protocols

Workgroup software provides an important collaborative tool for Internet users as well as corporate users. Calendaring and scheduling tools have long been a part of the workgroup software toolkit, but these tools have not been a traditional part of most TCP/IP application suites. That is changing, as the iCalendar and related

```
33736 comp.protocols.tcp-ip.ibmpc Frequently Asked Questions (FAQ), 1 of 3
33737 comp.protocols.tcp-ip.ibmpc Frequently Asked Questions (FAQ), 2 of 3
33738 comp.protocols.tcp-ip.ibmpc Frequently Asked Questions (FAQ), 3 of 3
34487 Re: TCP/IP over Arcnet on a Windows NT system
34488 Re: Looking for DNS server s/w for non-UNIX OS
34489 Fastest PC -> UNIX backup utility?
34490 Re: Telnet with Zmodem
34491 Slugish network—any suggestions
34492 Re: Help on Minuet: Name or pwd failed on server
34493 Re: Printing from SunOs to HPlaserjet
34494 Re: Looking for DNS server s/w for non-UNIX OS
34495 How much work is in TIA?
34496 Re: What X Servers exist for MS-Windows PC with dial up PPP or SLIP?
34497 Re: What X Servers exist for MS-Windows PC with dial up PPP or SLIP?
34498 Making a PC talk to SVR4 lp
34499 Re: WfW over PDETHER?
34500 Re: Fastest PC -> UNIX backup utility?
34501 Novell ODI to UNIX
34502 Re: Many people want DOS TCP/IP clients!
34503 Esker Looks pretty good
34504 tcp/ip slip
34505 Re: Telnet with Zmodem
34506 Re: Novell ODI to UNIX
[Type space to continue]
```

Figure 17–5: **trn** is a threaded news reader implemented on Unix, shown here browsing articles by subject line.

protocols have been published as proposed Internet standards late in 1998. iCalendar, defined in RFC 2445, specifies a special MIME content type/subtype called text/calendar and specifies how that MIME type is used to carry calendar and scheduling information across network transports.

iCalendar specifies how the text/calendar MIME enclosure can be used to carry information necessary to perform calendaring and scheduling activities like setting up appointments, checking for free time, notifying participants of upcoming meetings, notifying participants of cancellation of a scheduled meeting, and other related functions.

Published as proposed standards at about the same time as iCalendar are the iTIP (RFC 2446) and iMIP (RFC 2447) protocols. iTIP, which stands for iCalendar Transport-Independent Interoperability Protocol, defines a protocol for using iCalendar data with any calendaring or scheduling system. iMIP, which stands for iCalendar Message-Based Interoperability Protocol, specifies how iCalendar and iTIP data is to be bound into Internet e-mail messages for delivery. Together, these three protocols make it possible for software developers to permit users of personal productivity tools like PDA organizers as well as more sophisticated proprietary workgroup tools to interoperate with each other, independent of the proprietary products each is using.

Chapter Summary and References

This chapter introduced the concepts of Internet messaging, including e-mail as well as network news and other, newer, Internet messaging applications like Internet collaboration and scheduling.

We started by examining what e-mail is and how it works, followed by a discussion of the most important e-mail protocols including the Simple Mail Transfer Protocol (SMTP), the Post Office Protocol (POP), the Internet Mail Access Protocol (IMAP), the Multipurpose Internet Message Extensions (MIME), and the RFC 822 header structure.

Next, we discussed network news, including what it is and how it uses Network News Transfer Protocol (NNTP) to distribute bulletin board-style messages to news groups around the world.

Finally, we summarized the new proposed Internet standards for iCalendar, iTIP, and iMIP scheduling and calendaring protocols.

Table 17–1 lists some useful RFCs to read in conjunction with this chapter.

RFC	Title	Description
821	Simple Mail Transfer Protocol	Internet standard for moving messages.
822	Standard for the Format of ARPA Internet Text Messages	Defines formats for headers and bodies of text messages over the Internet.
1939	Post Office Protocol—Version 3	Standard protocol for downloading e-mail from a server's mail-drop.
2045	Multipurpose Internet Mail Extensions (MIME) Part One: Format of Internet Message Bodies	First in series of five RFCs that describe how MIME works.
2060	INTERNET MESSAGE ACCESS PROTOCOL—VERSION 4rev1	Specifies the IMAP protocol for remote e-mail management.
977	Network News Transfer Protocol: A Proposed Standard for the Stream-Based Transmission of News	Specifies how network news messages are propagated across the Internet.
2445	Internet Calendaring and Scheduling Core Object Specification (iCalendar)	Defines a MIME type and representation for calendaring and scheduling events.
2446	iCalendar Transport-Independent Interoperability Protocol (iTIP) Scheduling Events, BusyTime, To-dos and Journal Entries	Specifies how iCalendar data can be used by any scheduling or calendaring system for interoperable scheduling.
2447	iCalendar Message-Based Interoperability Protocol (iMIP)	Specifies how iCalendar and iTIP data is transported over the Internet within e-mail messages.

Table 17–1: Useful RFCs for Chapter 17.

18

Resource Sharing

File and resource sharing, unlike file transfer, don't require the user to do anything explicit to access the resource—they appear as if they are connected directly to the client computer, once the initial network connection is made. This has long been the primary function of network operating systems like Novell's NetWare and Microsoft's Windows NT server. The Network File System (NFS) provides access to remote file systems over TCP/IP networks, and in that way offers similar functionality to that offered by commercial LAN products.

Sharing Resources

The TCP/IP protocol and application suite define network applications and implementations to operate within internetworks. The objective is to ensure that different hosts can communicate with each other despite being separated by different types of network media, different types of computer software and operating systems, and different types of computer hardware.

These applications also tend to stress the type of task that organizations want to be able to do across internetworks, particularly those that may cross organizational and geographic boundaries. This usually means applications that have very definite start and end points (defined by making a connection, getting a response, and ending the connection), and boundaries defining the functions available (a specific set of commands relating to particular functions: sending or receiving a data file, e-mail message, or news posting).

Resource sharing, most often defined by file sharing (though printers and other devices like fax machines or modems are frequently included as network resources), is usually considered on a more local basis: resource sharing is usually defined by the needs of the organizational local area network. The local network operating system has usually been specified, bought, and installed long before the organization decides to link the network to a larger internetwork or to the Internet.

Network operating systems like Novell's NetWare, Microsoft Corporation's Windows NT server, and others can all be implemented on top of a TCP/IP network. Discussion of these products is beyond the scope of this book: in general, these products do not operate any differently when they use TCP/IP network protocols than when they use some other transport or network layer protocols. In addition, these products are usually implemented and intended for use within individual local area networks or organizational internetworks. Most organizations do not want to make their corporate file servers, which may contain sensitive or proprietary information, available across a public internetwork like the Internet. Likewise, most of the other types of network resources that are shared through this type of network operating system, like printers, are not considered open for sharing across even many organizational internetworks: most users prefer local printers.

The Network File System (NFS), originally developed by Sun MicroSystems, Inc., is widely implemented and has a long history paralleling the use of TCP/IP networks to connect Unix workstations and other types of systems. In 1989, Sun published a specification for NFS in RFC 1094; NFS version 3 is specified in RFC 1813, published in 1995. Both these RFCs were published as information specifications because they reflected work done solely by Sun on its proprietary NFS protocol—they were released so that other implementers could build their own versions of NFS software that would interoperate with Sun's version.

However, in 1998 Sun and the IETF came to an agreement to open up the NFS protocol and bring it into the IETF standards track process. RFC 2339 is the agreement entered into by Sun and the IETF, under which the IETF can develop the next version of the protocol. Shortly after the agreement was signed in May 1998, an IETF working group was formed to develop NFS version 4 as a fully-open Internet standard. Their work is expected to be finished by the end of 1999, and their work is currently documented in Internet-drafts (and eventually in RFCs as more work is completed on the project).

Like other network applications for resource sharing, NFS provides transparent access to network resources: files and directories stored on remote hosts can be made to appear as if they are local to the client and can be manipulated (if the user has authorization) as if they are files and directories on the client host.

However, like other network operating systems, NFS was originally intended to provide a tool for network resource sharing on local networks. Like other network resource sharing specifications, implementations of NFS are currently available for a wide range of different systems, both client and server. Also like other resource sharing specifications, NFS can be used across internetworks. NFS differs from the other available products, however, in that it was originally designed for use in TCP/IP networks and that it is quite often distributed as a part of Unix operating system implementations as well as an integral part of personal computer TCP/IP software products.

NFS was originally intended to operate transparently not just to the end user but also to a great extent to the programmer implementing it. The objective was to provide a very fast way to share data across a network, while providing robustness of service.

Network File System

Network File System implementations are very straightforward for the end user: the personal computer or workstation runs a program (usually) at startup, usually called `mount`, to connect to network resources like an NFS server. This initiates a connection with the server and points the operating system at the mounted resource. The result is very similar to that of network redirectors, network operating system software that redirects local logical drive and port names (e.g., drive names like G:\ or lpt3 on DOS or Windows systems). The operating system treats the resource as if it were local, using a drive or path name functionally equivalent to drives or path names of local resources.

Access and authentication are similar to those used by the r-utilities (see Chapter 15): access is determined by lists of approved users and hosts. Security is an issue with NFS and various options are available to make NFS more secure. However, NFS was originally designed as a resource-sharing protocol for a local Unix network, where system security may have been less of a priority than it currently is in enterprise networks.

Although most of the other applications discussed here use TCP as their transport protocol to ensure that exchanges are reliable and robust, Sun used a different approach to reliability, robustness, and performance when designing NFS. Instead of relying on the network protocols to provide reliability, NFS uses two network programming constructs, the Remote Procedure Call (RPC) and the External Data Representation (XDR), to handle reliability issues. This leaves NFS free to be a relatively simple implementation (by itself) and keeps open the option to use UDP as a transport protocol in many cases. Reliability and recovery from failure are provided by the RPC and XDR. RPC and XDR are both proposed Internet standards; RPC is documented in RFC 1831, and XDR in RFC 1832.

NFS is intended to be a stateless protocol, meaning that interactions between the server and client are not being tracked or managed. A server receives a request and responds to it. The same request from the same client could be received immediately after, and the server will (ideally) respond in exactly the same way—that the request was just made from the same client does not change the response. When dealing with reading or writing data to a file, this is perfectly acceptable (although the file and directory manipulation commands, like removing or creating files or directories, would not necessarily be repeatable in that way).

> NOTE: NFS itself is simple, but the details of how it is implemented, as well as the theory and practice behind the use of RPCs and XDR, are complicated and well beyond the scope of this book. This chapter offers a highly simplified overview of the issues involved.

Sun Remote Procedure Call

Most of the network applications presented in this book call for a client application running on the client host, sending requests to a server application running on the server host, which in turn sends back replies to those requests. Remote Procedure Calls operate differently: the client that needs something from the server just calls up a procedure on the local host. This procedure, in turn, puts the request together in the proper form and sends it out to the server, which executes the procedure and returns the response back to the client.

RPCs are implemented in the context of an RPC package implementing the various different functions that can be called up as remote procedures. Since network requests don't have to be processed through an actual application but can be passed directly through the operating system (because NFS in effect redirects network connections through the operating system), NFS can offer good performance over a local network. Likewise, since the RPC implementation can handle issues like retransmission of requests for data, it is possible to use UDP as a transport protocol.

External Data Representation

Not all computers represent data in the same way. Issues range from the ASCII versus EBCDIC dichotomy (most computer systems vs IBM mainframes) to other less dramatic differences in the way information and numerical data is encoded on different systems.

Since NFS offers a way to share information across different systems, it needs a special universal format for all data to be shared across systems with differing data representation methods. The XDR is a specification for such a format. All data being sent from an NFS server is converted into this standard format; all data received by an NFS client is converted from this format to the local host's format.

How NFS Works

An NFS daemon program running on a server waits for RPC requests from clients. These requests are made to port number 2049, usually using UDP. Although TCP connections are also supported, UDP is usually preferred as it offers better performance. When an RPC request is received, the server passes the request on to its own internal operating system to do the requested procedure on the (server's) local file system. When the procedure is accomplished (usually a request for a file stored on the server), the server sends back a reply to the original request, containing the requested data.

It should be noted that NFS uses RPCs to request some portion of a file. No explicit command is available to NFS that opens a file; instead, the client request would be of the form, "read N bytes of the file, starting from offset X." The number N represents how much data is to be sent in the datagram, and the number X indicates how many bytes from the beginning of the file to begin reading the requested number of bytes.

This is in line with a stateless protocol: the server does not need to know whether some or all of the file has already been read; it simply gets requests to send some specific part of a file. Since NFS does not use an open command to change the state of the server (*open* refers to the state of a particular file on the server), the same request can be made more than once with exactly the same response. The request is for a specific number of bytes, from a specific place in the file, not the next group of bytes.

By avoiding state, NFS also avoids some of the problems that can arise when network traffic is not delivered immediately or when requests are delivered out of order. For example, a client may have out more than one read request at a time (to improve performance, the client may anticipate additional reads). If the second request arrived at the server first, it is simply another request and the server can, correctly, do the requested file read and send back the data before getting any previous read request.

Chapter Summary and References

In this chapter, we introduced the basic concepts of the Network File System (NFS) protocol. Integral to understanding NFS are the Remote Procedure Call (RPC) and External Data Representation (XDR), also discussed here.

Table 18–1 lists some useful RFCs to read in conjunction with this chapter.

RFC	Title	Description
1813	NFS Version 3 Protocol Specification	Specification for the proprietary Sun NFS protocol.
2339	An Agreement between the Internet Society, the IETF, and Sun Microsystems, Inc. in the matter of NFS V.4 Protocols	The agreement by which Sun turned over future development of NFS to the IETF.
1831	RPC: Remote Procedure Call Protocol Specification Version 2	Specification of the RPC protocol used by NFS.
1832	XDR: External Data Representation Standard	Specification for the XDR standard for data representation.

Table 18–1: Useful RFCs for Chapter 18.

19

The World Wide Web

When the first edition of this book was written, the World Wide Web was just one of several important Internet applications. This is no longer the case. Gopher, a text-only, menu-based, pseudo-hypertext application, no longer has relevance except as a precursor to the World Wide Web. The web is even perceived as the sum total of the Internet, the most important aspect of TCP/IP networking.

The web is based on a set of protocols that define how web data is transmitted across the Internet, how web data is formatted for display, and how web resources are identified and addressed. In this chapter, we introduce these protocols: the Hypertext Transfer Protocol (HTTP), which describes how servers and clients exchange web information; the Hypertext Markup Lanugage (HTML), which defines how data is represented for storage and retrieval from the web; and the Uniform Resource Locator (URL) and related specifications that define how resources are located on the web.

We'll touch on related protocols and technologies, even though most of these will be beyond the scope of this book. We'll even briefly describe the Gopher application, highlighting how it differed from the web and why it failed to capture users' imaginations in the same way the web has.

The World Wide Web

There are several ways to define the World Wide Web:

♦ A simple (graphical) interface to Internet resources
♦ A highly-distributed multimedia database
♦ A global hypertext mega-document

The operative word here is "hypertext," discussed next. The World Wide Web provides its users with a simple graphical interface to access data stored virtually anywhere in the world, all made possible by the use of hypertext techniques.

The web is defined by its use of marked-up hypertext formatting, identifying hypertext resources through a universally accepted resource-naming syntax, all presented to the user in an easy-to-use graphical front-end.

Hypertext

Hypertext is a method of creating online documents that contain active links to other parts of the same document (for instance, linking a word in the main text of a manual to its definition in the document glossary), to other documents (linking a name with a related article in an encyclopedia maintained separately), or to other resources (linking a name with a scanned photograph of the named person or place). Hypertext links traditionally have been cited as nonlinear reading tools, but they can also be used to present a document as it was written, one page at a time.

Though available on a wide range of computers for many years, hypertext systems had not been widely accepted in the marketplace until they were implemented as internetwork resources. One of the stumbling blocks had been how to reference information stored and managed elsewhere short of making a copy and storing it on the local (standalone) system. Unless a wide range and depth of information was made available, the task facing a hypertext document creator was daunting: to locate and assemble all relevant information and incorporate it into a document at a single site.

The WWW protocols offer a way for hypertext implementers to locate relevant information online, and rather than assemble it and incorporate it into their own site, they add pointers to the off-site information to their own documents.

Hypertext, particularly as implemented in the World Wide Web, relies on visual cues to indicate "active" parts of the document; for example, a mouse pointer may change shape when it is placed on a section of a document that points to another resource.

Markup Language

There are two basic approaches to creating computer-generated documents: the traditional approach, used by word processors, defines the document's appearance strictly through setting format indicators. For example, you could specify that a block of text be italicized, formatted flush left, and indented half an inch. This gives the author complete control over how every part of a document appears, but this is not always desirable. For example, the author of a long document may not remember the exact formatting for third-level headings. This drawback can be resolved by using style sheets that define different document part functions, and associate a set of formatting commands for each function. For instance, chapter titles can be defined as using a certain size font, so the document author can just specify that a section of text is to appear formatted as a chapter title.

Another approach to document authoring is the use of tagging. Rather than specifying exactly how a block of text is to appear, either manually or with the use of style sheets, the author simply identifies blocks of text as having a particular function within the document. This identification is done with tags placed before and after text blocks. For instance, the start of a chapter title might be indicated with a text string "[start chapter title]" and the end of the title might be indicated with another string, "[end chapter title]." As will become apparent later in this chapter, tags used for World Wide Web documents don't look like that, but tags could (theoretically) be expressed in any agreed-upon format.

The tagging approach differs subtly from the use of style sheets in that the exact form in which the document is output is not determined until it is processed by an interpreter, appropriate to the output medium. For example, a chapter title might be formatted and sent to be printed in large black letters from a laser printer, but the same title might be formatted in a multicolor font for output to a computer screen.

The big advantage to document tagging is that the author need not be concerned with the exact output formatting, just with identifying the functional parts of a document. Formatting is done appropriate to the output form.

There are reasons tagging languages are preferred for hypertext (and even regular) document creation. Tags ensure uniformity of appearance throughout the document. Documents of all types often include lists; in long documents, each list should have the same appearance (use the same type of bullet or number, be indented the same amount). List element tags free the author from having to decide how to format each list.

Although uniformity of appearance is important, the ability to deal with functional elements of a document is more important. The use of tags means that the same document can be produced several different ways, for different methods of transmission. Consider a user's instruction manual that has been tagged. The document can be printed with the tags interpreted appropriately for a user manual. The document might also be produced for on-line review, interpreting the tags appropriately for display on a screen instead of on a printed page.

Finally, tagged documents can be retrieved by a client and interpreted appropriately for the local host running the client. Parts of the document that require special interpretation, like hot areas or buttons, can be displayed most appropriately for the local system—and the end user can customize the way documents are displayed. Some obvious choices would be to use reverse video instead of changes in color to indicate active links to the user who cannot discern colors (or who is using a monochrome monitor); the option to increase the size of all display fonts for users who find the default fonts too small; and the option to use character attributes (bold, reverse video, underline) instead of different size fonts to indicate that parts of an online document have different functions.

Locating Internet Resources

Attempting to create a framework for uniform and easy access to network resources requires a syntax for identifying those resources. The Uniform Resource Locator syntax was developed to provide just such a set of conventions. Though URLs appear to use a relatively simple and straightforward syntax, RFC 1738 requires 25 pages to define it. Two other specifications, for the Uniform Resource Name (URN) and the Uniform Resource Identifier (URI), have been defined to help standardize methods for naming and identifying things—resources—on the web.

Graphical Client

There is no requirement that World Wide Web clients use graphics, and there are character-only Web clients available. In fact, for users who are vision-impaired, graphical Web clients are largely unusable. However, the graphical nature of the World Wide Web has unquestionably been vital in its success. The fact that users can navigate documents quickly and easily, by pointing and clicking, makes the web seem much easier to use than other Internet applications.

World Wide Web Protocols and Standards

The IETF defines most Internet standards. For a while, this included web standards like HTTP, HTML, and URLs as well. However, the World Wide Web Consortium (also known as W3C) has taken over much of the standards development process for web-related protocols. The result is that the IETF (in cooperation with W3C) still does the bulk of the standards development work for HTTP, which is a network transfer protocol, whereas W3C concentrates its efforts on issues that relate more to web representation like HTML, and to issues related to resource identification like URI, among many other issues.

For more information about the W3C's activities and related standards, see their Web site at:

```
http://www.w3c.org
```

Meanwhile, the IETF has published a specification for HTTP version 1.1 in RFC 2068; HTML has been documented in RFC 1866. The IETF URL syntax specification is published in RFC 1738, the URI syntax specification is published in RFC 2396, and the URN syntax specification is published in RFC 2141.

Other standards and tools are used for programming more elaborate web documents, with more functions. For example, the Common Gateway Interface (CGI) provides a standard interface from web documents to other computer resources like databases. Programmers can use the CGI standard to create web documents that can incorporate pointers to data stored on legacy mainframes, or other types of databases.

Java is a specialized language designed for creating small applications, or applets, that can be downloaded from a web server and can run on the remote client, instead of requiring that the client acquire larger pieces of software, or requiring the client to request the server to execute the program. Developed by Sun, Java has quickly gained many adherents. Netscape has also produced a programming language based on Java called JavaScript. Unlike Java applets, which are compiled and downloaded to the client system for execution, JavaScript programs are interpreted by the Netscape Navigator browser.

In 1996, Microsoft introduced Active X as an alternative to Java and JavaScript, but required that users use the Microsoft Explorer Web browser rather than the Netscape Navigator browser. The intent was to provide further incentive for users to switch from the Netscape browser to the Microsoft browser.

Web Resource Identification

Central to the concept of the World Wide Web is the idea that there is a way to retrieve any resource that can be identified. Identifying web resources is not a trivial matter, even though the Uniform Resource Locator (URL) format is widely used and apparently intuitively understood by most users. The specification for URL syntax, published in RFC 1738, defines a format for locating a particular resource on the web—but this syntax is revised by that specified in RFC 2396, which describes the Uniform Resource Identifier (URI). URI provides a system for specifying any type of resource, including URL as well as the Uniform Resource Name (URN).

A URL locates a resource, and a URN names the resource. The URL of a particular resource might change over time as the resource moves from one host to another, or is moved from one directory to another on the same host. However, the intention of the URN syntax is to provide a namespace in which resources are identified with a specific, unchanging, globally unique name. If you have a URN for a particular resource, you can retrieve that resource only if you are able to map the URN to a URL. Without a mechanism to resolve URNs into URLs, the URN is not useful.

Although the URI syntax includes both URN and URL, it is more useful to focus on the URL syntax for several reasons. First, by far URLs are the most common implementation of URI. Second, the URI specification is highly technical and focuses on discussion of syntax to the exclusion of specific applications. Finally, the URL specifications provided in RFC 1738 provide specific examples and syntax for web resources currently in use.

Universal Resource Locator (URL)

The objective of the URL is to have a single format in which to express any kind of Internet resource, whether it is a web document, an FTP file archive, a telnet server, an e-mail address, or any other type of service available through TCP/IP.

A URL uses only ASCII characters; only lowercase characters are specified, but uppercase characters are permitted and interpreted as lowercase. RFC 1738 specifies that the URL is to be used to locate network resources and may be reproduced in print ("ink on paper") or digitally in different formats. The purpose of the URL is to unambiguously specify a location for a particular network resource.

Web clients use URLs to locate network resources; the URL may contain special port numbers to direct a TCP connection to a port other than the well-known port for a particular service. Services, like FTP or telnet, are called **schemes**, which are referred to by a field in the URL.

In general terms, a URL consists of a service identifier, followed by a colon, followed by the source of the service. For the most part, the source is a complete host name, followed by a file and path; other services use different locations. For instance, the `mailto` resource targets electronic mail to an Internet address specified in the URL. Table 19–1 shows some of the most common service types. The generalized representation of a URL is

```
<scheme>:<scheme-specific-part>
```

Scheme ID	Service type
`ftp`	File Transfer Protocol (FTP)
`http`	Hypertext Transport Protocol
`gopher`	Gopher protocol
`mailto`	Electronic mail address
`news`	USENET news
`nntp`	USENET news using NNTP access
`telnet`	Reference to interactive sessions
`wais`	Wide Area Information Servers
`file`	Host-specific filenames
`prospero`	Prospero Directory Service

Table 19–1: Service identifiers used in URLs (from RFC 1738).

Table 19–2 shows the format templates for creating URLs for the more common network resources referenced by web documents.

Scheme	URL format
WWW	`http://<host>:<port>/<path>?<searchpart>`
E-mail	`mailto:<rfc822-addr-spec>`
Gopher	`gopher://<host>:<port>/<gopher-path>`
Network news (by message ID)	`news:<message-id>`
Network news (by news group)	`news:<news group-name>`
Network news (using direct NNTP access)	`nntp://<host>:<port>/<news group-name>/<article-number>`
Telnet	`telnet://<user>:<password>@<host>:<port>/`
Local HTML file	`file://<host>/<path>`

Table 19–2: Formats for creating URLs for different network resource types (from RFC 1738).

HTTP

HTML defines how World Wide Web documents are formatted and displayed, and the URL specification defines how Internet resources are uniquely identified. The actual business of requesting and moving web documents from a server to a client is defined by the Hypertext Transport Protocol (HTTP). RFC 2068 specifies HTTP, version 1.1. HTTP provides mechanisms for clients and servers to ask for and transmit web resources, though it also provides a sort of application transport over which other types of Internet applications can be executed. HTTP can carry telnet, FTP, and other application session information as well as web data. Thus, HTTP provides a front-end application for any conceivable Internet application.

Protocol Summary

HTTP is specified as an application-level protocol. As summarized in RFC 2068, it is:

> ...an application-level protocol for distributed, collaborative, hypermedia information systems. It is a generic, stateless, object-oriented protocol which can be used for many tasks, such as name servers and distributed object management systems, through extension of its request methods. A feature of HTTP is the typing and negotiation of data representation, allowing systems to be built independently of the data being transferred.

HTTP is a request/response protocol: nothing happens until someone asks for something to happen. HTTP servers listen for requests on port 80. HTTP requests and responses can consist of two parts: the basic request/response information, and message bodies that use a MIME-like format (see Chapter 17 for more about MIME). This approach allows interoperability between any systems using any MIME-encoding method, as well as the ability to build complex messages relating to client and server capabilities for the negotiation of data delivery.

HTTP requests include a request **method** to signify what the client wants from the server, a Uniform Resource Identifier to signify what resource the clients wants to manipulate, a protocol version to indicate what version of HTTP is being used, and a MIME-like message that carries additional request information. The MIME-like message may have request modifiers, client information, and may even contain some content data to be transmitted to the server.

HTTP server responses contain a status line that includes the protocol version of the message as well as a success or error code, similar to those described for FTP (see Chapter 16). Following the status line, the server's response includes a MIME-like message that may contain server information, entity metainformation, and entity-body content. The **entity** is whatever information is being transferred within the MIME-like message; it consists of entity-header fields (this is the **metainformation**, data that describe the information contained in the entity) and the content of the entity. In simpler terms, the entity is just the information, usually web content, carried in the HTTP request or response.

A few HTTP requests are specified in RFC 2068, including GET, which clients use to request web content; PUT, which clients use to submit material to a specific web URI; and POST, which clients use to add material to an existing URI. Most web activity is in response to GET requests, where clients request a particular piece of web content from a server. POST requests are often used to submit material for web discussion groups, for exampe, and PUT requests are used by people with write-access to web sites to submit material to be published on the web server.

Other defined request methods include OPTIONS, HEAD, DELETE, and TRACE; these may be used for a variety of web entity maintenance or testing. Other methods may be defined as extensions, so more functions can be supported through HTTP.

HTTP 1.1 Protocol Improvements

Although a specification for HTTP 1.0 was published in RFC 1945, implementers were found to be building their own versions of HTTP 1.0 that didn't always interoperate completely or correctly. As a result, the IETF (Internet Engineering Task Force) decided to respecify HTTP with a version revision so that servers and clients could more explicitly determine protocol capabilities through version number. At the same time, HTTP 1.1 addressed some problems identified through extensive use of HTTP 1.0.

As web pages became more complex, consisting of many different resource entities, web browsing performance took a hit because most HTTP 1.0 implementations are based on the assumption that every time a resource is requested, a separate TCP session is set up—only to be taken down as soon as the request is fulfilled. For a web page consisting of a single text file, this is not a problem. However, for a web page consisting of a few dozen different text and graphics files, the cost in time and bandwidth of setting up and tearing down a few dozen TCP circuits becomes significant. To solve this problem, HTTP 1.1 specifically allows clients and servers to keep TCP circuits open so they can send and receive more than one request/response pair.

Another problem that HTTP 1.1 addresses is the use of a variety of different types of systems to deliver web content. The concepts of **request chain** and **response chain** are introduced in RFC 2068. Most HTTP interactions occur between a **user agent** (a client) looking for a resource on an **origin server**. In these cases, the request chain is described by a link from the user agent and the origin server; the response chain is a link from the origin server and the user agent.

However, there may be other systems interposed between the origin server and the user agent. A **proxy** acts on behalf of the origin server, accepting the user agent's request, rewriting it and resubmitting it to the server identified by the resource identifier. Organizations may use proxies to give outsiders access over the Internet to internal resources. A **gateway** acts as a receiving agent for the resource identifier, and may function as a protocol gateway as well. Organizations may use gateways in cases where it wants to publish on the web resources that are stored in a variety of different systems; for example, database information stored in legacy mainframes. A **tunnel** acts as a relay system, passing messages unchanged from one point to another through some intermediary like a firewall.

A gateway or a proxy may also use **caching**, the storage of recently or frequently requested resources in memory. These resources can then be transmitted to clients more quickly because they do not have to be retrieved from the origin server.

Unlike HTTP 1.0, HTTP 1.1 provides facilities for clients and servers to identify when more complex architectures are in use and to take advantage of them, or at least to gracefully deal with failures in the different parts.

HTML

Web documents are created using the Hypertext Markup Language (HTML). HTML, a markup language based closely on the Standard Generalized Markup Language (SGML), is used to functionally differentiate between different sections of a hypertext document. SGML actually specifies how tags and related output rules are created and used. Another SGML-compliant specification, the eXtensible Markup Language (XML) is rapidly gaining acceptance as a tool for building self-describing documents for interoperable processing of electronic commerce transactions over the Internet. XML is discussed in more detail in Chapter 21.

HTML is described in RFC 1866, though further developments may be described more accurately in W3C documentation. This section is intended to introduce you to the most basic concepts of HTML.

Web document authors can specify the way certain parts of their documents appear by identifying how they fit into the document.

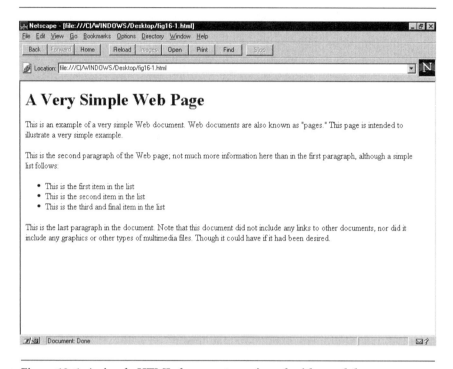

Figure 19–1: A simple HTML document, as viewed with a web browser.

For example, a simple document might consist of a first-level heading at the top, followed by several paragraphs of text, with a numbered list included somewhere in the document. Figure 19–1 shows a very simple HTML document, as viewed with a web browser.

HTML documents are simply text files, with all the parts of the text identified by tags. The tags themselves are usually very short and always enclosed in angle brackets. The source text used for the document shown in Figure 19–1 is shown here:

```
<h1>
A Very Simple Web Page
</h1>
```

```
<p>
This is an example of a very simple Web
document. Web documents are also known as
"pages." This page is intended to illustrate a
very simple example.
</p>

<p>
This is the second paragraph of the Web page;
not much more information here than in the first
paragraph, although a simple list follows:
</p>

<ul>
<li>This is the first item in the list
<li>This is the second item in the list
<li>This is the third and final item in the list
</ul>

<p>
This is the last paragraph in the document. Note
that this document did not include any links to
other documents, nor did it include any graphics
or other types of multimedia files. Though it
could have if it had been desired.
</p>
```

The HTML tags themselves appear inside angle brackets (<>), and usually occur in pairs, one tag to indicate the start of a functional block and another (with an added slash (/)) to indicate the end of the block. Tags can be inserted anywhere in the document, and there are no rules calling for them to be separated from other text, although for clarity many HTML authors use extra spacing.

Some of the most basic HTML tags are shown in Table 19–3.

In theory, at least, it would be possible to create a document and publish it as both a printed document and an online document. In

Tag	Purpose
`<p>`	Paragraph marker (does not require an end paragraph marker)
`<h1>`, `</h1>`	Level-one heading and end of level-one heading
`<h2>`, `</h2>`	Level-two heading and end of level-two heading
`<dl>`, `</dl>`	Definition list start and finish
`<dt>`	Definition term (required in definition list)
`<dd>`	Definition of definition term
`<li>`	Indicates a list item element
`<ol>`, `</ol>`	Ordered list (items are numbered) and end of ordered list
`<ul>`, `</ul>`	Unordered list (items are bulleted) and end of unordered list

Table 19–3: A few of the tags defined for use with HTML.

practice, most web documents are designed specifically as online documents. Graphic and other multimedia elements are included by using links that refer to data files. Companies like Netscape and Microsoft add other features to their web clients that allow documents to include special formatting features. For example, tables have been widely supported. The Netscape frame option has proven to be less popular: it allows the document author to split the client window into several frames that can all simultaneously display different HTML documents, independent of each other.

A slightly more complicated web page, incorporating graphics, tables, and links to other web resources, is shown in Figure 19–2.

Some of the source code of the web document shown in Figure 19–2 appears as follows:

```
<html>
<title>
```

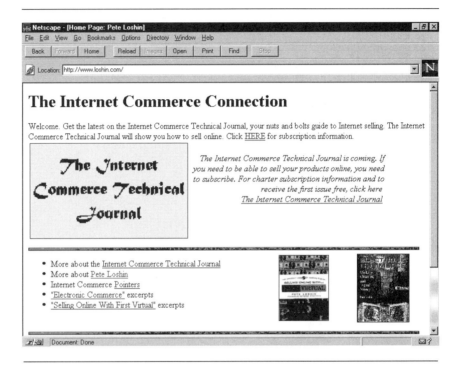

Figure 19–2: A more typical web page, incorporating graphics and links (copyright 1996, Pete Loshin).

```
Home Page: Pete Loshin
</title>
<h1>
The Internet Commerce Connection
</h1>
<p>
Welcome. Get the latest on the Internet Commerce
Technical Journal, your nuts and bolts guide to
Internet selling. The Internet Commerce
Technical Journal will show you how to sell
online. Click <A HREF=newslett.html>HERE</A> for
subscription information.
<Table Border=0 units="relative">
<TR>
```

```
<TD Align=right Valign=top width=300>
<A HREF=newslett.html>
<IMG BORDER=1 SRC="newslett.gif"
WIDTH=300 HEIGHT=175 ALT="The Internet Commerce
Technical Journal cover"></A>
</td>
<TD ALIGN=right VALIGN=TOP width=375>
<br><em>The Internet Commerce Technical Journal
is coming. If you need to be able to sell your
products online, you need to subscribe. For
charter subscription information and to receive
the first issue free, click here
<br><A HREF=newslett.html>The Internet Commerce
Technical Journal</A>
</TD>
</TR>
</table>

<img src="div2.gif" alt="[HRule Image]"
align=bottom width=750 height=6>

<Table border=0 units="relative">
<TR>
<TD align=left width=450>
<ul>
<li>More about the <A
HREF=newslett.html>Internet Commerce Technical
Journal</A>
<li>More about <A HREF=publ.html>Pete Loshin</A>
<li>Internet Commerce <A
HREF=pointers.html>Pointers</A>
<li><A HREF=ec.html>"Electronic Commerce"</A>
excerpts
<li><A HREF=fv.html>"Selling Online With First
Virtual"</A> excerpts
</ul>
</td>
<TD align=center width=150>
<A HREF="fv.html">
<IMG BORDER=1 SRC="virtual2.gif"></A>
```

```
</td>
<TD align=center width=150>
<A HREF="ec.html"><IMG BORDER=1
SRC="ecsmallx.gif"></A>
</td>
</tr>
</table>

[and so on...]
```

Althought it is possible to create very simple documents using the most basic HTML tags, more complicated documents may take longer. There are many books as well as Internet resources for those seeking more information about creating web documents. One of the best ways to learn to create these documents is to browse many different web documents and look at the source text for those documents with features you would like to emulate (many web browsers include an option to "view source" of the current document). This method can help you learn how other authors use HTML tags—remember, however, to respect copyrights and not to "borrow" chunks of code (or text or graphics) directly from other Web sites.

As a result of the web's dizzying success, a wealth of HTML translation and authoring software products is available. Though these products are usually enough to author most web documents, at times it is still worthwhile knowing how to tag a document manually.

Gopher

By the late 1980s, it was clear that the Internet would not grow beyond technical users without an improved user interface. From our perspective, the answer clearly was the World Wide Web. However, at that time networked personal computers with reliable graphical user interfaces were not the most common systems used to connect to the Internet. Most connections were through character-based terminals, so at the time it seemed an application that could offer users detailed and nested menus to choose network resources and applications would be the way to simplify the Internet. Thus, Gopher was born.

Gopher offers a framework in which users can select network resources from a series of menus. Gopher servers are usually set up, with a series of submenus accessible through a root menu. Each menu item refers to either another menu or some kind of network resource: a file, an index, a Telnet connection to another host, an FTP session with another host, and so on.

Gopher servers can still be found on the Internet, though they are usually accessed through web clients. Gopher no longer provides many important Internet resources, though gopher servers are helpful for users who don't have access to systems capable of running graphical Web browsers and for administrators who don't want to upgrade existing systems based on gopher.

Gopher is strictly menu driven: each resource is connected specifically with some menu item. Gopher links are simple: select the menu item, and the resource to which it points is returned. The gopher framework is simple: present users with a list of resources and when one is selected, return that resource. Adding to the appropriateness of its name, gopher in effect acts as a "go-fer," retrieving pointers to network resources on demand.

As shown in Figure 19–3, Gopher menus are usually terse. The user commands available at any given time usually appear at the bottom of the screen, and the cursor arrow keys usually will (intuitively) navigate the menus: left to go back to the previous menu, up and down to change the selection on the current menu, and right to select a menu option. Other Gopher commands may be entered with one or two characters.

Gopher lost its market to the World Wide Web largely because it is not a hypertext-based application but a men-based application. There is no way to traverse menus quickly, nor are there any navigation mechanisms to bypass menus. The lack of graphics hurt Gopher, but not as much as the lack of dynamic content. Gopher sites are more difficult to keep current and up to date than web

```
Internet Gopher Information Client v1.13

                    Root gopher server: gopher.acme-amalg.com

        1.  Information About Acme Amalgamated/
        2.  The ClariNews AP OnLine Newswire Index/
        3.  OBI The Online Book Initiative/
        4.  Internet and USENET Phone Books/
        5.  Shops on The World/
        6.  Commercial Services via the Internet/
        7.  Book Sellers/
   ->   8.  Bulletin Boards via the Internet/
        9.  Consultants/
        10. FTP/
        11. Government Information/
        12. Internet Information and Resources/
        13. Libraries/
        14. Membership and Professional Associations/
        15. Metropolitan and Community News/
        16. News and Weather/
        17. Non-Profit Organizations/
        18. Other Gopher and Information Servers/

Press ? for Help, q to Quit, u to go up a menu          Page: 1/2
```

Figure 19–3: A sample root menu from a Gopher server, retrieved with a character-based Gopher client.

sites. And Gopher's ability to front-end other Internet applications did not turn out to be such an asset, since it didn't make FTP or telnet any easier—it only made it easier to connect to hosts using those applications.

Chapter Summary and References

In this chapter, we examined the World Wide Web and the principal protocols on which it depends. First we defined what the web actually is. Next, we examined the Uniform Resource Identifier

(URI) and related syntaxes for identifying network resources. We followed that with a description of the Hypertext Transfer Protocol (HTTP) and the Hypertext Markup Language (HTML). We concluded with a brief look at Gopher, a considerably less successful Internet application that, like the web, offers a platform through which network resources can be published.

For a list of useful RFCs to read in conjunction with this chapter, refer to Table 19–4.

RFC	Title	Description
1738	Uniform Resource Locators (URL)	Describes the syntax for URLs as used on the World Wide Web to identify and locate network resources.
2396	Uniform Resource Identifiers (URI): Generic Syntax	Describes the generic syntax for resource identifiers, which include URLs and URNs.
2068	Hypertext Transfer Protocol—HTTP/1.1	Specification for HTTP.
1866	Hypertext Markup Language—2.0	Specification for HTML.
1436	The Internet Gopher Protocol (a distributed document search and retrieval protocol)	Specification for the gopher protocol.

Table 19–4: Useful RFCs for Chapter 19.

20

Distributed Computing

Proprietary product differentiation was one of the forces that long drove computer industries. Computer hardware vendors liked to piggyback sales of proprietary disk drives and terminals to the same customers who bought their mainframes. Operating systems vendors like to sell their own application software as well. However, standardization of interfaces, particularly networking interfaces, means that proprietary products lose most of their shine. Why should users settle for proprietary document formats when open formats exist? If open standards exist for data representation and data transmission, why not for data processing as well? Distributed computing is a logical outgrowth of the success of open Internet standards as well as the ubiquitous deployment of relatively powerful personal workstations. Distributed computing enables the intelligent and adaptive distribution of computing tasks and responsibilities across networks as well as across operating systems and hardware platforms.

Interoperability and Distributed Computing

In the very early days of computing users composed their programs and submitted them to the white-coated technician who actually entered the program into the computer. Hours or even days later, the user could collect the results of the program from another white-coated technician. In those days, all the computing was centralized: users might write their programs on special programming forms to be entered into punchcards by clerks, or the user might go to a data entry room where he or she would type in the program for later submission.

Time-sharing and terminals introduced the concept of remote computing. As we discussed in Chapter 15, a terminal connected to a computer gives the terminal user access to the computer's resources. However, having remote access to a computer does little more than give all users with a terminal the same access that the white-coated technician had, more or less.

The computing is still done at the central location, and the user must still write and submit the programs to be processed by the centralized mainframe computer. The terminal contributes nothing more than a convenient interface to the mainframe. If the mainframe goes down, the terminal is useless. If the mainframe is too busy to accept more jobs, the terminal is useless. If the connection to the mainframe is broken, the terminal is useless.

And with remote computing, all the computing is done by the mainframe. No matter that the mainframe manages multi-megabyte record databases—it must also be available to a programmer who needs to code a program, or to print out a report, or to deliver an e-mail message.

By the late 1980s and early 1990s, the concept of client/server programming came into vogue. The servers managed the data, and client software written for personal computers acted as the interface for users: accepting input and formatting output. However, client/server has been found lacking because it requires custom programming for every pairing of client and server—and because it doesn't go far enough in distributing the computing chores. Mainframe servers still manage the databases and accept queries and input. Clients are barely more intelligent than the terminals, though perhaps easier to use.

A different client program has to be written for every different client platform, which means a different program for Macintosh, Windows 3.x, Windows 95/98, Windows NT, DOS, and Unix. Any change in the user interface requires a change in every copy of the client software—making every upgrade, bug fix, and patch a major project. Likewise, any changes in the platform hosting the server precipitate changes in the server programs. Moving the server from one system to another also becomes a major project.

Distributed computing, unlike remote computing or client/server computing, depends on connectivity as well as on interoperability. Distributed computing applications are based usually on an open standard that allows any standards-compliant client to access the application. Using the interoperable standard as the basis for the application, even if that standard is simply HTML, allows any system that supports that standard to use the application—without any need for pre-installing software.

Distributed computing takes in a lot of ground, but includes approaches like those used by the X Windows system, Microsoft's Terminal Server, and Citrix's WinFrame products. These all build on a concept of a network computer, a simple system that is capable of enough processing to format and display graphics. In this case, the NC (or network PC, as Microsoft terms it) may be capable of some limited computing, with its own disk and peripherals, but most of the actual data processing occurs elsewhere. Java, a programming language developed by Sun Microsystems and eventually offered as an open standard, allows development of small applications (applets) that may be running on one system but whose results are reported to another system. Microsoft's ActiveX and COM/DCOM architectures provide similar capabilities.

Network Computing

The X Window System, more commonly referred to as X, was developed at MIT as a graphical user interface for Unix. It is now the most popular Unix GUI, implemented widely and inexpensively through a liberal license structure provided by the X Consortium. What makes X so interesting for distributed computing, however, is the way it works. Each desktop runs an X server process, which acts on behalf of the desktop's hardware. All keyboard and mouse input are handled through the X server process; all graphical monitor output is rendered by the X server process.

In X, the client is actually the process running the application. An application behaves as the client by requesting keyboard input from the X server and by requesting that the X server render output on the desktop's display. For a standalone system, the power of this arrangement is not immediately apparent. However, an application can be running an X client on a remote host while the X server runs locally. The intuitive client/server relationship is usually reversed in X, where the X client is running on the system that is actually serving the application, while the X server is running on the system that is behaving as the client.

X has great potential, for more than traditional client/server applications. For one thing, interoperability issues are reduced to a single question: do both the end-user workstation and application server support X? If so, then the end-user can use the application; if not, then the end-user cannot use the application. Unlike client/server applications, once it is set up with X server software an end-user system can access resources on any remote system with an X client running. Each and every new client/server application requires a separate client program.

Since the application is running on the remote system, with X it is not necessary to be upgrading end user systems constantly (as it is with client/server). When the application is upgraded on the application server system, all end user systems simply execute the upgraded application—remotely. As long as the remote user is running X windows, it doesn't matter what operating system or hardware is being used—X is available for Unix, Linux, Macintosh, as well as Windows platforms.

X has been around for a while; commercial X products have been widely used since the 1980s. However, it has never gained much ground on the Windows/Intel platform. Considering that Microsoft's Windows is already a graphical user interface, there has never been that much demand for X on Windows other than from niche markets that already use X on other platforms. X has been hobbled by performance issues as well. Though not usually a problem on fast LANs, X can be bandwidth intensive as well as sensitive to high-latency links.

That is not to say that Microsoft does not offer a network computing alternative. First developed as WinFrame by Citrix, Microsoft licensed technology from Citrix to develop Windows Terminal Server (WTS) in this market. Designed to allow any Windows desktop to display programs that are actually executing on a remote server, WTS does many of the same things that X does, but differently.

Whereas X is an entirely open architecture, WTS is a Microsoft product. Microsoft makes available open interfaces for programmers building WTS applications as well as client software that allows WTS applications to be run on Macintosh and other platforms. However, WTS incorporates Microsoft Windows as its operating system, and competitors may not simply build their own implementations of a WTS-compatible server—though Microsoft would probably not mind if developers wrote WTS-compatible client software for otherwise unsupported platforms.

Neither X or WTS represents a highly scalable solution to distributed computing. A single high-end server, with fast processor and much memory, still can support only in the neighborhood of (very roughly) 10–20 concurrent users, depending on the application being distributed. X servers are capable of supporting more concurrent users, but not significantly more. In general, both X and WTS are useful for providing application services to end users working on relatively weak workstations. WTS is aimed at a segment of the market that may be using otherwise obsolete hardware that is capable of displaying graphical content but that has minimal RAM and low-powered CPUs.

There are other approaches to distributed computing, including Java and ActiveX.

Java and ActiveX

Web developers building interactive web sites in the mid 1990s soon discovered an inherent limitation in the tools then available: lack of flexibility in program execution. With HTML, developers could build pages that displayed graphical and multimedia information, as long as the data was stored on the web server and retrieved by the client browser. With CGI, developers could use forms to gather information or requests from users and then submit that data to another system. This approach provides greater interactivity, but is still largely based on a client/server model: the browser acts as a dumb terminal, allowing the user to enter information which is then submitted to the server. The server processes the information and then sends it back to the client.

The client/server model inherent in CGI may be acceptable for applications like database queries, but it is not acceptable if you want to provide graphical interactivity with the user. A web publisher might want to publish a three-dimensional graphic image and let the end user manipulate the image, to view it from different vantage points. One solution is to add some buttons labeled "rotate up/down" and "rotate left/right" to the web page, and have the user click on them to change the view. When the browser sends a click to the server, the server responds with a new view of the image. This solution may work, but it takes a lot of network bandwidth for resending the image. It also becomes a very high-latency application, because each time the user clicks to change vantage point, the request must be submitted to the server and an entirely new—and only slightly changed—version of the image is downloaded.

Another approach is to build a little program that can be downloaded over the Internet along with the 3D image. The program can do the manipulations on the same system as the browser, thus cutting out all network delays (other than the original download) from the image manipulation process. This is a good answer, but before Java and ActiveX it would not have been practical. Building such an image manipulation program usually means knowing something about the system on which the program is to run. Developers would have to build separate versions of the program to run on Windows, Macintosh, Unix, and other systems. They might even have to build different versions for different versions of each operating system—and perhaps even different versions for every different browser (and browser version). Even if you're dealing with four different OS platforms, each of which has three different major versions, with two browsers on each system, and three versions of each browser, that is 72 different versions of the image manipulation program.

Java

Java originated at Sun Microsystems as a solution to this problem. Rather than building different versions of each program, the objective of Java is to provide a "write once/run anywhere" programming environment for the web. Java introduces the concept of a **Java virtual machine** (JVM), a software construct that behaves like an idealized, universal computer. Rather than require developers to build their specific programs for multiple platforms, browser developers simply need to build a JVM in each browser. The JVM can then seamlessly execute any Java program as if it were written specifically for that platform. The JVM interprets the Java code, and displays results appropriately.

Java programs are usually called **applets** because they tend to be smaller in scope than full-grown applications. An applet might be written to provide local control to a GUI, or to play a game, or to do simple processing of information before it is submitted to a server.

In much the same way that telnet uses the network virtual terminal (see Chapter 15), the end user platform systems use the JVM as a least common denominator for interpreting the Java code. The JVM interprets the Java code and implements it appropriately for the platform on which the JVM is running. That means it renders images appropriately for the platform, painting in full color on full color monitors or in black and white on a celullar telephone's LCD display. Likewise, the JVM accepts inputs from the appropriate input devices, whether a stylus input on a handheld PDA or a keyboard for a desktop computer.

Security presented a major obstacle to deployment of Java. The problem was how to prevent code downloaded over the Internet from unknown sources from doing anything harmful to the client computer or device. Harmful code could be anything from malicious programs written to steal sensitive data from hard drives to buggy code that just happens to trash hard drives by mistake. At first, the solution was the Java sandbox concept. The idea was to create an area within the computer in which the Java applets could run without harming anything else—sort of a sandbox in which the applets could play safely.

Inside the sandbox, the Java applet is not permitted access to the local filesystem, either to write data or to read data. Likewise, access to system and process information is also restricted, so applets should not be able to affect other programs running at the same time, or to bring the operating system down. However, this approach so severely limits the ability of Java applets to do anything useful that later revisions of the JVM specification allow applets more lattitude in what they can do as long as the applets have a digital signature authenticating their source.

ActiveX

In keeping with its general strategy of building in advanced features to its proprietary operating system, Windows, Microsoft provides ActiveX as a capability roughly comparable to Java. ActiveX programs, also called **controls**, operate within the Windows framework in a way that allows Windows desktops to execute ActiveX programs across networks. Unlike Java, which is designed for interoperability, ActiveX is designed specifically and integrally as part of the Windows architecture.

Microsoft designed an architecture for Windows programming called Component Object Model (COM) that allows Windows applications to request services from other Windows applications; Distributed COM (DCOM) is the networked version. ActiveX controls operate within this architecture, accepting services from some Windows applications and providing services to others.

Unlike Java, ActiveX controls can access any system resource, so malicious controls could conceivably damage systems. However, Microsoft uses its Authenticode protocol to specify how controls (and other software) can be digitally signed to provide a trail back to the software authors.

Chapter Summary and References

In this chapter, we briefly introduced some of the important concepts of distributed computing, as currently implemented on the Internet. Starting with a discussion of how improved interoperability enables distributed computing, we went on to the specifics of the X Windows System and Microsoft's Windows Terminal Server. From there, we looked at Java and ActiveX as programming environments for distributed computing.

Table 20–1 includes pointers to URLs related to distributed computing issues rather than pointers to IETF RFC documents. Distributed computing over the Internet and other TCP/IP networks is not directly related to TCP/IP itself, so there are no RFCs specifically addressing these issues.

Organization	Description	URL
The Open Group	Vendor-neutral technology consortium that owns the X Windows System.	http://www.operngroup.org
X11.ORG	Provides information and community for the X Windows System.	http://www.x11.org
Microsoft	All about the Windows Terminal Server.	http://www.microsoft.com/ntserver/terminalserver/default.asp
Citrix	All about Citrix WinFrame.	http://www.citrix.com
Sun Microsystems	All about Java.	http://www.sun.com
Microsoft	All about ActiveX and COM.	http://www.microsoft.com/com/default.asp

Table 20–1: Useful Web sites relevant to Chapter 20.

21

Internet Commerce

Until the mid 1990s, the Internet (and precursor networks) were off-limits to commercial activity because they were all sponsored by research grants, mostly through the United States government. Acceptable use policies (AUPs) that forbade even the posting of an announcement of a new product to relevant newsgroups kept most commercial companies that were aware of the Internet from attempting to promote business on it. As the government got out of the Internet business, businesses flocked to the Internet to attempt to make their fortunes there. By 1999 the success of companies like Amazon.com, eBay, CDNow, and others makes it clear that the Internet is fertile ground for commerce, even without the widespread use of special-purpose commerce protocols.

This chapter introduces the technical issues involved in doing business on the Internet, as well as some of the solutions currently in use, though it only scratches the surface of the topic.

Introduction to Internet Commerce Issues

TCP/IP networks are open networks: all the protocols are publicly specified, all the data transmitted across them is vulnerable to interception and forgery. The openness of the Internet is in large part the reason for its success, but commerce requires a covert channel to prevent losses due to data interception. Many of the obstacles to Internet commerce are similar to those encountered with doing business by credit card, check, or charge card in person or by telephone.

Secure Transmission of Confidential Information

Transacting a purchase often requires a significant quantity of sensitive or personal information. Although cash purchases are often quite anonymous, when payment is made by credit card or personal check there is much more information at stake. In addition to account information (credit card number and expiration date or checking account number), merchants frequently ask for additional information, including telephone number, address, and driver's license number.

Although consumers can judge matters of personal privacy for themselves, the banks that issue credit cards (as well as other participating organizations like charge card companies and credit card associations) are very much interested in keeping credit card account information out of the wrong hands. Even the merchants should be concerned about keeping transaction information private because increased fraud rates increase the cost of processing all credit and charge card transactions.

Accountability

More important to the consumer is a degree of accountability from the merchants. When a transaction occurs in person at a point of sale, the consumer gets a hard-copy receipt from the merchant.

Telephone orders are made to a specific telephone number, and the consumer is well-advised to avoid giving out credit card numbers to cold-calling sales people. Similarly, mail orders can be sent to well-known catalog merchants. Assurance of Internet transactions still requires a mechanism that allows the consumer to be confident that a product has been ordered and that the merchant cannot deny having taken that order.

Building In Security

Since 1994, many organizations have attacked the problems of Internet commerce. The potential rewards are huge, so contenders range in size from small startups to the likes of Microsoft, IBM, VISA, MasterCard, and American Express. To date, however, approaches to the security problem can be broadly categorized as belonging to one of three options: secured procedures, secured channels, or secured applications.

Secure Procedures

It is possible to design a payment mechanism simply using secure procedures. However, if such a mechanism allows plain-text transmissions over an open network (the Internet), then the sensitive information needs to be transmitted off-line, over a more secure link. This is the premise behind the First Virtual Holdings, Inc., payment system, as well as other offerings: use the Internet to carry nonsensitive transaction information, and get payment information like credit card numbers off-line through a telephone connection. This approach appears to be flawed, or at least not yet practical: First Virtual withdrew its commerce offering in 1998, and few other similar schemes have achieved any significant degree of success.

The objective of these methods is to eliminate the possibility of large-scale, automated, credit card theft without resorting to encryption schemes, which some consider costly, complicated, and vulnerable to being cracked eventually. Credit card numbers never appear on the open network, so they cannot be stolen. Consumer account information is transmitted over the Internet, but First Virtual requires that all transactions be verified by the consumer by e-mail. This combination of safeguards, along with other techniques, makes the First Virtual approach safe for the credit card issuers, for First Virtual, and for consumers. Merchants have less protection, though for information sales (where virtually no physical cost is attached to each new sale) the risk is low, too.

Procedural security schemes tend to be cumbersome, or at least appear to be cumbersome, requiring telephone calls, e-mail confirmations, and often entailing the use of yet another password/ userID combination.

Secure Channels

A different approach is one taken by Netscape, designing and implementing a protocol that creates a secure channel between two processes. The two communicating hosts negotiate an encrypted channel, carried over TCP. A large part of Netscape's early success can be attributed to its inclusion of support for the Secure Sockets Layer (SSL) in its browsers, which quickly gained as much as 80 percent of the browser market by 1996. Merchants wishing to sell on the Internet could do so relatively securely, merely by installing the Netscape Commerce Server, a web server that also supports SSL.

Drawbacks to the secure channel approach include all the same vulnerabilities that any encryption method carries with it. In particular, if the encryption used is not sufficiently strong or if the implementation is done poorly, the scheme is vulnerable to attack.

More problematic is that encrypted channels protect the data only while it is en route from one computer to another. Viral or trojan-horse programs on the consumer's personal computer could potentially steal credit card keystrokes and send them over the Internet to a thief. A bigger risk, however, is that the merchant's server may be vulnerable to various types of attack, either by insiders or outsiders. If security on the server is lax, outsiders can fairly easily recover data transmitted securely; in any case, insiders might also be tempted to steal credit card numbers from the server.

SSL serves as the basis for the Transport Layer Security (TLS) protocol, an Internet standards track protocol specified in RFC 2246 and published in January 1999. The secure channel approach has proven itself sufficiently robust to serve for most commercial Internet transactions, provided the encryption keys are sufficiently secure.

Secure Applications

Security, like reliability, is a function that is best built into Internet applications at a higher, rather than lower, network layer. Thus, it makes more sense for developers to create applications that handle security rather than expecting to find security features at the network (IP) or transport (TCP) layers. This allows the developers to create end-to-end security for Internet transactions. The result is that the sensitive transaction information can be encrypted at the source in such a way that only the intended recipient can decrypt it—even bypassing the merchant, so that only the credit card processor can decrypt the credit card account.

This is the approach used by CyberCash since 1995, and is similar to one proposed by Netscape in the same year ("Digital Envelope"). The Secure Electronic Transaction (SET) specification, backed by VISA and MasterCard, as well as virtually all other serious contenders in the market, also uses a similar approach.

Although this approach is acknowledged to be a better response to the problem than the purely procedural or secure-channel approaches, it requires the widespread deployment of consumer software capable of performing digital commerce functions. Likewise, merchant servers need to be able to accept and/or forward payments. These approaches have yet to prove themselves. Despite considerable expenditure of time, energy, and money, ultimately SET was too complicated while not providing enough additional functionality to provide sufficient incentive to implementers. At the same time, the secure channel approach provided everything that most implementers really needed for Internet commerce; likewise with most digital wallet, digital cash, and other commerce applications.

Internet Commerce Security Mechanisms

Some solutions for Internet commerce rely on a handful of technologies and constructs to solve the problems raised by the need for security and the need for authentication and authorization of transactions. For the most part, these tools have been developed through the science of cryptography, and this section can serve only as a very brief introduction to these tools. We caution you that strong cryptographic tools are almost always published and subject to peer reviews: creating tools that cannot be broken is not something that can be done in isolation. To a lesser extent, implementers of cryptographic algorithms need a high level of quality assurance to avoid weakening secure techniques with insecure implementations.

Encryption

Data can be protected by encryption: the process of taking plaintext data and converting it, using a specific and reversible sequence of operations, into a ciphertext that appears to be random. One of the simplest examples of an encryption algorithm is the substitution cipher in which each character is substituted by another character, using the key to act as an offset from the plaintext character. For instance, using a key of 3 in a simple alphabetic replacement algorithm, the letter "A" would be replaced by the letter "D," and the word "CAT" would be encrypted as "FDW."

> NOTE: This replacement algorithm is trivial, though it has been used widely with an offset of 13 to obscure text from casual viewing. Known as ROT-13 (for rotate by 13), it is used commonly in public forums like USENET news for items that may offend some readers (e.g., controversial remarks and lewd jokes).

Encryption algorithms require a key to seed the encryption process: this lets many different entities use the same encryption algorithm while keeping data protected from those who do not share the same key. Secret key cryptography is also known as symmetric cryptography because the same key is used for both encryption and decryption. This means that if the secret key is compromised, any and all ciphertexts created with that key can be decrypted.

Secret key cryptography requires that all parties to communication share a secret, and that all parties sharing that secret have to trust that the other parties will not divulge the secret to, or allow it to be stolen by, any unauthorized parties. As the number of parties involved increases, either more keys will be generated for each pair of communicating parties (thus increasing the need for storing and keeping track of keys), or one key will be shared among more parties (thus increasing the risk that one of those parties will divulge the secret or allow the secret to be stolen).

Secret key encryption tends to be fairly easy and efficient to implement on most computers, and algorithms like the Data Encryption Standard (DES) from the U.S. National Institute of Standards and Technology (NIST) are widely used for most business needs.

Public Key Cryptography

Mathematicians have found that it is extremely hard to factor very large numbers; this turns out to have very important implications for cryptography. It is possible to create pairs of keys using large prime numbers, with the property that messages encrypted with one of the keys can be decrypted only with the other key of the pair. It is extremely hard to factor very large numbers created by multiplying two large prime numbers together—this is why public key encryption works. Public key cryptography is also called asymmetric cryptography, because an operation on data using one of the keys of a pair can be reversed only with the other key of a pair.

*NOTE: This is a very simplified version of how public key cryptog-
raphy works. The interested reader is referred to **Personal
Encryption Clearly Explained** (Morgan Kaufmann 1998), for
more detailed discussions of public key cryptography.*

The most obvious application of public key cryptography is for an
entity to publish a public key that other entities can use to encrypt
data to be sent in confidence to the entity. Assuming that the entity generated its own key pair, and that it has not disclosed the private key of the pair to anyone else, that entity is the only one
capable of decrypting any messages encrypted with the public key
of the pair.

So far, public key cryptography has proven to be more resistant to
attack than secret key cryptography, but it is also more inefficient:
although secret key encryption can be done in real-time, public key
encryption can use enough computing cycles to cause noticeable
time lags on most personal computers. As a result, public key
cryptography is often used to encrypt secret keys to be used for
individual transmissions or interactive sessions. This allows entities to exchange keys securely, with public key cryptography, for
more efficient one-time use.

Digital Signatures

Another implication of public key cryptography is that it provides
a mechanism for an entity to digitally sign data, thus assuring that
data originated from that entity. Keeping in mind that all data
encrypted with a public key can be decrypted only with the match-
ing private key, the reverse is also true: any data that is encrypted
with the private key can be decrypted only with the public key.

The process of encrypting and decrypting entire messages or data
files can be very costly in compute cycles, and is unnecessary if the
data author wants only to assure its audience of the data's authen-
ticity. The entity can therefore create a message digest, or hash, that
is a sort of mathematical summary of the data. As a summary, it is
much easier to encrypt and decrypt.

Such digests can be used for digital signatures: the originator of the data runs a hash function over the data, and then encrypts that data using its private key. The encrypted hash is the digital signature. Recipients can affirm that the entity indeed did sign the data by running the same hash function on the message (or data) and then decrypting the signature with the sender's public key. If the two match (decrypted signature and message hash), the message was received as it was sent. If the two don't match, it indicates that the message received was not the same as the message that was sent: it may have been altered in some way in transit.

Certification Authorities

Individuals and organizations can generate their own public key pairs, but distributing and validating public keys and connecting them with known entities has so far been done at a relatively personal level. For instance, the "web of trust" approach is for individuals to sign the public keys of entities they feel comfortable trusting. This means that an individual might sign a key they received personally from a friend or colleague. That person, in turn, might sign someone else's key. The theory is that such chains of signatures can provide other users with a certain degree of comfort accepting an unknown entity's public key as valid—as long as they personally know (and trust) one of the signatures on the chain.

This approach does not scale well as the number of public key users increases to the degree required by Internet commerce. One alternative is to use a certification authority (CA) with which entities can register their public keys, and from which you can retrieve the public keys of desired entities. Verisign, Inc. was one of the first companies to offer this type of service, with varying levels of assurance for individuals and organizations. CA services are now available through other third-party vendors as well as through industry organizations. Organizations can also set up CA systems to offer certificates to their own employees, customers, and vendors.

Internet Open Trading Protocol (IOTP)

Despite many contenders, no generalized trading protocol has yet been adopted and deployed widely. The Internet Open Trading Protocol (IOTP), first published in 1998 as the Open Trading Protocol (OTP), may change that. IOTP became a task of an IETF working group, and is currently (1999) documented as a work in progress in Internet-draft documents. Its status as a potential Internet standard may provide the impetus to firms to build online business around the IOTP model.

IOTP is based on XML (see Chapter 19), the Extensible Markup Language. IOTP supports a mechanism for two (or more) parties to a transaction to completely negotiate an online transaction. As an XML application, IOTP does not bind parties into using any special client software, or setting up accounts with special servers ahead of time. The parties use IOTP to negotiate the terms of the transaction as well as how the transaction will be settled: whether payment will be immediate or upon receipt of shipment; what type of payment method will be used; how the purchase will be shipped; and how the transaction will be documented.

Though IOTP certainly has applicability to consumer transactions, it is also expected to be useful for business-to-business commerce, with potential to replace EDI entirely.

Electronic Data Interchange (EDI)

Although most companies have been using computers for years to handle things like purchase orders, invoices, product deliveries, collections, and billing, relevant data formats vary so widely that not only can they rarely be exchanged easily between companies, they often don't translate well from one departmental system to another. For example, systems may use different field sizes for common data like names and addresses, or they may permit or exclude special characters in those fields. In addition, much of the data used by one system may not be relevant to other systems with which it interacts.

Electronic data interchange, or EDI, represents a structured approach to the problem of automating transactions between companies. One common definition of EDI is that it is the direct transfer of business documents between computers by one application to another.

EDI offers businesses a framework for defining common fields between different systems and producing a method of "mapping" it between systems. This makes possible the automation of many business processes. EDI mapping software automatically translates data from each business partner into a form accessible to the other partner. In addition to handling data stored in different formats on different systems, this mapping can include the use of bar coding schemes for more comprehensive uses of EDI, as well as e-mail and other methods of communication.

The U.S. EDI standards body is known as ASC X12, which stands for Accredited Standards Committee X12, and was chartered in 1979. EDIFACT (Electronic Data Interchange for Administration, Commerce, and Transport) is the international EDI standards body established in 1985 by the United Nations. The standard transactions that these bodies define are used by EDI implementers for translating their own internal data into a format that can be used by their trading partners.

EDI is usually represented as a business-to-business solution, and until the mid 1990s, such transactions were conducted over private value-added networks (VANs) run by EDI providers like GE Information Services and others. EDI vendors are increasingly using public key cryptography to allow secure EDI transactions to be passed across the Internet.

Chapter Summary and References

In this chapter, we first discussed the issues involved in Internet commerce, including why Internet commerce is complicated by the openness of the TCP/IP protocol suite as well as how Internet commerce can be enabled through different strategies. We continued with a brief introduction to the mechanisms used to add security to Internet transactions, including public key and secret key encryption, and digital signature. We concluded with an introduction to the Internet Open Trading Protocol (IOTP) and electronic data interchange (EDI), and how they apply to commercial transactions over the Internet.

Refer to Table 21–1 for some useful RFCs to read in conjunction with this chapter.

RFC	Title	Description
2246	The TLS Protocol Version 1.0	Specification for successor to SSL, providing a secure transport layer channel suitable for commercial transactions over the Internet.
1898	CyberCash Credit Card Protocol Version 0.8	An informational RFC describing CyberCash's credit card payment protocol.

Table 21–1: Useful RFCs for Chapter 21.

Part Four

Internetwork Implementation and Management

## 22

TCP/IP Internetwork Management

Managing networks of any size calls for the use of computer-based tools, and TCP/IP internetworks are no exception. However, internetworks require additional tools to cope with their special needs and problems.

Managing Networks

Network management covers a lot of ground: anything from workstation configuration and assignment of IP addresses through network design, architecture, and topologies can be considered within the scope of the network manager. Network management functions can be broadly considered as falling into one of the following categories:

♦ Providing network service without interruption

♦ Resolving network service interruptions

♦ Avoiding network service interruptions or degradation

♦ Deploying and maintaining network systems, hardware and software

Network security is another area that falls within the scope of network management, but discussion of that topic will be deferred to Chapter 24.

The principles of network management are reasonably uniform, whether the network being managed is a high-speed Ethernet running TCP/IP, a token-ring network running Novell NetWare, a DECnet network, or an AppleTalk network. However, when managing an individual network, the manager has the benefit of a uniform network medium over which network management tools can operate at the data link layer.

Managing a network of networks—an internetwork—poses some special problems, though the internetwork manager still has to be able to provide consistent, reliable, and efficient network services with minimal interruption, and to be capable of handling increasing or changing network demands.

Any protocol or mechanism for managing internetworks must allow network devices and systems of virtually any type to communicate statistics and status information to network management stations, with minimal impact on the networks being monitored, and independent of the underlying network transmission medium. Network management workstations need to be able to request management information from remote managed nodes, and they must be able to make changes in the way the remote node handles network traffic—without knowing anything about the particular node itself.

The standard TCP/IP network management protocol, Simple Network Management Protocol, provides a simple and elegant framework in which internetwork management tools can be designed. Vendors design SNMP support in their network devices like routers, bridges, and network servers, so those devices can be monitored and managed from network management stations. These network management stations implement SNMP with a user interface, usually a graphical one, that makes management tasks simple. The SNMP protocol itself is not always easy to describe, particularly since it uses formal constructs and tools from the discipline of computer science to define a set of tools usable across a wide range of systems and devices.

Internetwork management, through SNMP implementations, relies largely on the ability of the protocol to monitor network statistics, modify network routing tables, and change the status of network links and devices. The framework in which all this information is gathered and stored is called a Management Information Base (MIB). This is a hierarchical representation of data that offers a standard representation of information across all network and vendor boundaries.

Other tools in the internetwork manager's toolbox, some discussed earlier, relate to management issues on a smaller scale. For example, ping and traceroute (Chapter 8) are both excellent diagnostic tools for troubleshooting connectivity problems. Even the use of some standard TCP/IP application, like FTP or telnet, can offer insight into connectivity problems. Likewise, use of the loopback interface (Chapter 6) can help pinpoint problems as well. To these can be added the network traffic analyzer, a device that connects to a network and collects network traffic flowing on the wire. By carefully filtering out unwanted types of traffic, it is possible to diagnose network problems and verify that hosts are sending and receiving properly.

Netstat is another program often included with TCP/IP application suites to provide information about the host and its TCP/IP connections. A brief description of netstat and its output follows the sections on SNMP.

Simple Network Management Protocol

The whole idea behind the Simple Network Management Protocol (SNMP) is to specify a mechanism for network management that is complete, yet simple. Essentially, information is exchanged between agents, which are the devices on the network being managed, and managers, which are devices on the network through which the management is done. The terms *agent* and *manager* are operative when discussing network management rather than *client* and *server*—just as a client can also be a server, so an agent can also be a manager. Since clients and servers may also be, at times, agents and managers, the more general terms are usually avoided when discussing network management.

Items of interest to the manager include things like the current status of a network interface on a router, the volume of traffic being passed by a router, how many datagrams have been dropped recently, or how many error messages have been received by a router. The network manager may want to disable a network link, or reroute traffic around a downed router, or even reboot a router or gateway.

There are a lot of possible transactions between the manager and the agent, and they may vary widely with the different possible types of devices that can be agents. Attempting to implement all the different commands that a manager could possibly send to an agent would be very difficult, particularly for new devices. Instead of attempting to recreate every possible command, SNMP simplifies matters by forcing different commands to be expressed as values that are stored in the device's memory. For example, instead of including a "down link" command to close a network link on a router, SNMP agents maintain a variable in memory that indicates whether a link is up or down stored along with information about each of the router's network links. To down any given link, a manager simply sends the value corresponding to "down" into the link status variable.

Possible transactions between agent and manager are limited to a handful: the manager can request information ("get" and "get-next") from the agent or it can modify information ("set") on the agent. Under certain specific circumstances, the agent will notify the manager of a change in status ("trap") on the agent.

Some of the data to be retrieved or changed are stored as simple variables, like error message counters, but other information is stored in tables, like interface data that include hardware addresses, IP addresses, hardware type, and more, for each network interface.

By keeping the implementation of the protocol fairly simple through limited commands, the barriers to implementing SNMP on a device are kept low—which also means that it can be implemented widely, thus making it more useful.

Another implementation issue for any network management protocol is whether to have agents be *active* and transmit updates about their status on a regular basis or have them be *passive* and polled periodically by the manager to check on their status. Each has its own drawback. When agents are passive, major problems may not be detected in a timely way if the manager doesn't check frequently enough, and undue load on the network may result if the manager checks too frequently. On the other hand, forcing agents to report status changes puts pressure on the network device's computing resources and can stress the network further when a problem occurs.

SNMP permits the use of traps from agents to signal changes to managers, but the model encourages the use of a single trap to be sent when an important event occurs and relies on the manager to request further relevant information from the agent.

Reliability is another issue for network management. It might seem that a reliable protocol like TCP should be specified to make sure that management information gets passed reliably between agent and manager. However, UDP is the TCP/IP protocol used for SNMP, for reasons that go beyond the fact that most SNMP exchanges are request/response pairs. One of the most important functions for network management is to resolve problems that occur with transmitting or routing network traffic. Network management information is more important at times of network failure or reduction in service than at any other time—which also happens to be the time that reliable protocols like TCP are more likely to fail to connect. These are also the times when any extra load on the network is least welcome. Finally, it should be recalled that a protocol may be reliable, but if the link over which it is being sent has been severed, no data will get through.

SNMP Commands

Five different messages are possible with SNMP. Three cover transactions initiated by a manager (read and write an individual variable on an agent; read a group of variables on an agent), the fourth defines the response from the agent to any of these requests from a manager, and the fifth defines the reporting of an extraordinary event (a trap) by the agent to the manager. Table 22–1 shows these commands; SNMP agents listen to UDP port 161 for requests from SNMP managers, and the SNMP manager listens to UDP port 162 for traps from agents.

By encoding device status within variables, rather than implementing network management commands, SNMP makes it possible to manage many different types of devices with a minimum command set.

By using two separate ports for SNMP, one for sending management requests and one for sending agent traps, network devices can function as both an agent (reporting traps and processing requests from managers) and as a manager (making requests of and receiving traps from agents) without confusion.

Structure of Management Information

The methods for representing managed information objects—the data items that network management is concerned with, like network traffic counters and interface addresses—are relatively com-

Command	Description
get-request	Retrieve the value of a specified variable on the agent
get-next-request	Retrieve the value of a specified variable on the agent after the one indicated in the request, used for traversing tables where there are multiple "rows" of information; for example, when getting information about a router's network interfaces
set-request	Change the value of a specified variable
get-response	Respond to manager requests with the value of the item being queried
trap	Notify the manager of a change in status or some event on the agent

Table 22–1: SNMP commands.

plicated and strictly defined by sets of formal rules. A basic understanding of how managed information is stored is useful, but few people other than those responsible for designing SNMP management software need more than that.

The Structure of Management Information (SMI) is a framework within which management information can be named and referenced authoritatively. One way to think about the SMI and MIBs is to imagine that TCP/IP networks are simply vastly distributed databases, containing nothing but network management information stored in network devices like routers and servers. These bits of the database may be stored in various different forms at the different network devices, but using a standard schema for organizing the data means the devices that store the data know they are required to report that data in a particular form when asked for it, and to store it locally in a form that they can interpret according to this standard.

Object identifiers for management information are organized like the Domain Name System, with an unnamed root parenting three nodes: itu(0), iso(1), and joint-iso-itu(2). Each node has a name and a number: the name is for people; the number is used by computers for simplicity of computing. These top nodes represent the partitioning of the management information space and allocation of a section for joint use by the International Telegraph and International Telecommunications Union (ITU) and the International Organization for Standardization (ISO).

Beneath iso(1) are four more nodes used by the ISO to assign standards, for use by OSI (Open Systems Interconnection, an effort underwritten by ISO in support of open network standards) registration authorities, member organizations of ISO, and other organizations that ISO identifies. TCP/IP management information falls under the last category, and it is listed under the Department of Defense (DOD). As shown in Figure 22–1, the MIB (version 2) is listed as a node six layers down in this structure. (Figures 22–1 and 22–2 show some of the relevant nodes in this framework for simplicity.)

The use of this system ensures that each managed item can be uniquely identified as well as related to its parent nodes, just as the Domain Name System does for domain and host names. Also like DNS, items in this framework have no inherent way to determine whether or not an identifier is a "leaf" node (a node actually referring to an item of management information rather than containing other nodes).

The labels are generally used to make the management object identifiers easier to deal with for people, whereas computers use the numbers, which are easier for them to deal with. So, the representation of the MIB itself within this framework is, more formally,

iso.org.dod.internet.mgmt.mib

and can be expressed for use by computer as

1.3.6.1.2.1

Figure 22–2 shows the main groups in the MIB. Other structures for managing network information that aren't listed in the MIB can

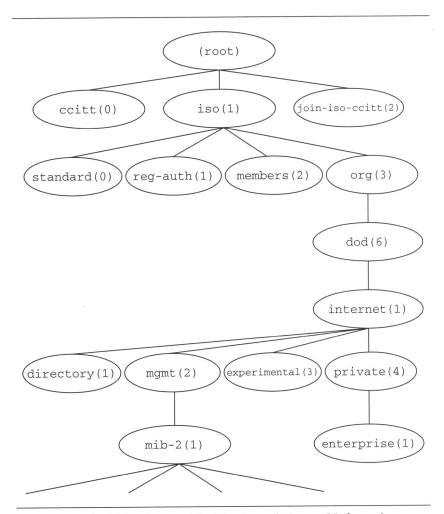

Figure 22–1: The higher layers of the Structure of Managed Information framework, above the Management Information Base.

be listed under other nodes; for instance, vendors can set up product specific information bases under the hierarchy represented by

```
iso.org.dod.internet.private.enterprises
```

Each item of management information within this framework can be very specifically identified and therefore requested by a

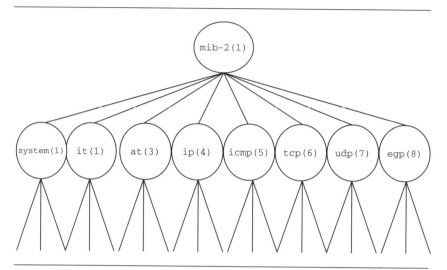

Figure 22–2: The structure of management information for the TCP/IP Management Information Base.

manager. Not all managed nodes will be able to, or even want to, maintain all the defined information items, but whatever they keep track of can be requested by a manager by specifying the item number. The next section looks at the MIB itself.

Management Information Base

Several basic categories of managed information are listed beneath mib-2(1) in the SMI. They correspond to various different categories of information relevant to TCP/IP networking. Not discussed here are the Transmission Group, where management information for devices relating to network medium protocols like Ethernet, IEEE 802, and other network hardware is stored, and a special group used for managed information relating to the first version of SNMP. Table 22–2 shows the main groups and the types of information they contain.

Network information may be maintained as single units of information; a counter, for example, indicating the number of UDP

MIB Group	Description
system(1)	Information about the device itself, including a description, what network services it provides, the contact person, the location, and the name of the device
it(2)	"Interfaces" group: basic information about the network interfaces on the device, including hardware address and statistics on transmissions sent and received on the interface
at(3)	"Address translation" group: information that relates the hardware addresses of the device's network interfaces with their IP addresses (this group is currently "deprecated," meaning that with the shift from the first to the second version of SNMP, the functions this group fulfills have been shifted to the IP group)
ip(4)	IP specific information including statistics about IP datagrams sent and received, and tables that include IP addresses and associated hardware interfaces, IP routing and forwarding information
icmp(5)	Tracks ICMP messages sent and received and statistics on the different types of ICMP messages generated and received
tcp(6)	Tracks TCP statistics, including the volume of TCP segments sent, received, and retransmitted; error messages and types; and a table that tracks current TCP connections (which ports and interfaces are in use, connecting to which remote IP address and port)
udp(7)	Tracks UDP statistics, as well as current UDP ports being used
egp(8)	Used on routers using the Exterior Gateway Protocol

Table 22–2: Management Information Base groups used for TCP/IP network management.

datagrams sent out by the device. Other types of information require a tabular approach: a router will have at least two network interfaces (and often more) to manage. Tables are used to represent this type of information; for instance, in the IP address translation table, each network interface gets a single row in the table, including values for network interface number, a hardware address, and an IP address for each interface.

As an example, the first object in the IP group is ipForwarding. There are two valid options: if the value is 1 then the system is configured to forward IP datagrams, to act as a router; if the value is 2 the system is not forwarding datagrams (is not acting as a router). Not all variables can be modified by a manager, but this one can be, which means that a network manager can effectively take a router out of service by changing this variable from 1 to 2, or put a router in service by changing this value from 2 to 1.

Another similar example is the ifAdminStatus column within the ifTable in the interface group. Each network interface has a row of various entries in this table, and the ifAdminStatus object can be changed to change the status of any particular interface: the interface can be "up," "down," or "testing."

By and large, however, MIB objects can't be reset by a manager when they contain network statistics. For example, within the ifTable are other columns like ifInOctets and ifOutOctets, which reflect (respectively) the total number of bytes received and transmitted over each network interface.

Network devices keep track of all these variables and more, and make them available to managers upon request. The network management stations collect this information from the different agents (usually routers and other critical network devices) and build a picture of where network traffic is being passed. With this information, the network administrator is able (in theory) to avoid or fix problems due to down systems or interfaces and to improve network performance in some cases.

Remote Network Monitoring

In larger internetworks, some value can derive from configuring network devices to gather network management information remotely, including setting up packet filters for gathering network traffic and analyzing results. A separate MIB has been defined for this function, the Remote Network Monitoring (RMON) MIB. Remote network monitors can be used to gather data link layer network data, which is inaccessible to remote network managers connected across an internetwork: routers screen out all that information when they forward IP datagrams.

SNMPv2

The first version of the Simple Network Management Protocol proved to be a little too simple for some. A handful of major problems and shortcomings flawed SNMPv1, so a second version called SNMPv2 was first issued in 1993 and updated with various flavors in 1996.

SNMPv1 Problems

Authentication in SNMP is trivial, based as it is on a simple, unencrypted community name—this field is included with all SNMP messages, and if the agent's community name is the same as the community name sent out from a manager, then the agent will respond. This presents security issues, to say the least. Anyone can monitor a TCP/IP network and "sniff out" SNMP packets, determine a valid community name, and perform any SNMP management function available, including bringing the network to its knees. In fact, the default community name for many devices, "public," is sufficiently often left unchanged so that a criminal could easily bypass network monitoring and perform management functions.

SNMPv1 can generate very high network traffic overhead. Getting a single piece of network information from a managed device is relatively easy, but getting complete routing tables, network statistics, or even just interface status from routers requires a seemingly endless procession of "get-next" requests. Monitoring agents on remote sections of an intranet can also generate a lot of traffic as messages may need to be relayed across many routers. Even the most basic network management tools can generate huge volumes of traffic from simple maintenance functions and can adversely impact network function during peak periods.

Another cause of high network management traffic is the need for network management nodes to send and receive SNMP requests and responses across large intranets. There is no way for network manager nodes to share management information: each manager must gather information independently. This can mean additional traffic, either from having multiple network management workstations monitoring the same TCP/IP intranet, or from a single management workstation monitoring a large intranet.

SNMPv2 Solutions

SNMPv2 adds two new commands, `GetBulkRequest` and `Inform`, to address the problem of high traffic overhead.

The `GetBulkRequest` command allows an SNMP manager workstation to get the entire contents of a part of the MIB, like a routing table, with a single command rather than with a continuing stream of get-next requests. The result is that instead of dozens of requests and responses, the manager workstation can send a single request and the agent device can send a single response.

The `Inform` command allows remote network manager workstations to notify other network manager workstations of the status of network agents that they are monitoring, thus reducing the amount of network traffic while monitoring a large intranet.

SNMPv2 does not address the security issue quite as comprehensively or completely. There are at present three "flavors" of SNMPv2, each offering a slightly different approach to security. Community-based SNMPv2, or SNMPv2c, uses the same trivial authentication scheme as SNMPv1. SNMPv2u, or the User-Based

Security Model for SNMP, adds authentication, whereas more complete security is provided by the SNMPv2* approach. Since a general consensus on what approach is most useful, it is widely believed that this issue will be dealt with more adequately by IETF workgroups in the future.

TCP/IP Network Management Tools

Network managers can use all the tools they can find, and these include formal products like network protocol analyzers as well as less formal ones like ping and traceroute. Brief descriptions of how some of the more common tools are used follow. Interested readers may find RFC 1470, "FYI on a Network Management Tool Catalog: Tools for Monitoring and Debugging TCP/IP Internets and Interconnected Devices" useful as well.

Ping

Ping is most often used as a connectivity verifier, although it can verify only that there is connectivity; failure is not an infallible indicator of lack of connectivity. Network software installers often ping a remote host from a newly installed workstation to verify that the host is truly connected to the internetwork. Pinging a host by name rather than by IP address adds the ability to check that name resolution is being done correctly. When ping fails in these instances, the problem is almost as likely to be with the configuration of the host as with connectivity.

Ping is much more useful as a diagnostic tool when used from a host suffering from a problem connecting to some other host or hosts. For an example, look at Figure 22–3. A user attempts a telnet session with remote host A but fails to connect and gets an error message that indicates the host is down.

Depending on the result, different actions may be taken:

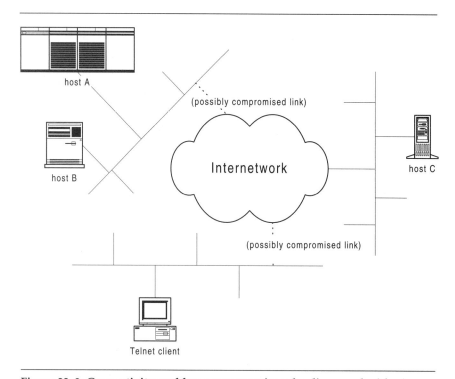

Figure 22–3: Connectivity problems can sometimes be diagnosed with ping.

1. If the user's system is not properly configured to resolve host names, connecting to Host A by its IP address should work.

2. If attempting to connect by IP address instead of host name still doesn't work, the telnet server may not be running, the host may be down, or the host's network may be inaccessible (its link to the internetwork is down).

3. If after sending a ping to host A (by its IP address) the local host gets a response from host A, then the remote host's telnet server may not be running, or it may have been temporarily down, or the local host's telnet client may not be working properly. The user can verify that the telnet client is working by initiating a telnet session with another host, perhaps a local one.

4. If host A doesn't respond to the ping, it may mean that host A is down or that the network is temporarily inaccessible. To find out, the user could attempt to connect to another host on the same network as host A (for instance, host B) or send another ping to host B. If the client cannot connect to any host on host A's network, the user could check on connectivity to other networks, which can help determine if the local network is disconnected from the internetwork or if it is the remote network that has connectivity problems.

Ping is also useful for generating traffic on a network between two hosts. Many ping implementations permit the user to specify a size for the packet, a delay between packets sent, and the number of times to retry the remote host. This controlled transmission can help the administrator identify problems, like systems that can't handle lots of traffic, or hosts that have sporadic outages, that could not be diagnosed with a single ping.

It should be clear that ping can be a helpful diagnostic, as long as the user understands all the different variables that may be at work. By itself ping may sometimes be sufficient to indicate that a problem exists, but it is not always sufficient to pinpoint problems.

Traceroute

As shown in Chapter 8, traceroute offers an ingenious use of the ICMP echo message to determine the route taken between a client and a server. The output from traceroute includes the names of the different routers forwarding packets between the two hosts as well as the round-trip time for the messages from source to router.

Network managers may use traceroute to diagnose slow response time between a client and a server: by checking what path network traffic is taking from one host to another it is sometimes possible to identify bottlenecks (routers that are responding very slowly) or instances where traffic is being routed over an unnecessarily long path.

Like ping, however, traceroute cannot be regarded as a formal and infallible management solution but rather as a useful diagnostic tool and guide.

Netstat

Netstat is another useful utility, originally implemented on Unix systems and now generally provided in some form or another with most TCP/IP application suites. Executed on a Unix workstation with the proper program parameters, netstat will return information about the network interfaces, protocol statistics for the host, active communications links, status of data buffers, or the contents of the local routing table.

As with the other tools mentioned here, netstat can help diagnose problems by checking network statistics for a given host, including things like the volume of network traffic being sent and received, network errors, and collisions. However, netstat should still be considered just another helpful tool that can be useful when evaluating a problem.

Network Traffic Analyzers

There are times when nothing beats actually looking at the traffic being exchanged between two hosts to identify a network problem. Network traffic analyzers come in all shapes and sizes and are implemented both as hardware and software, but generally share the same approach: connect to the physical network, listen to network traffic, and collect the traffic desired by the manager. Network administrators can specify what type of network traffic they want to monitor by protocol type (IP, TCP, UDP, broadcast, unicast, multicast, and so forth) as well as by source and destination, so even on a busy network it is possible to capture the exchanges between two hosts.

Although some analyzers are easier to use than others, they are rarely the first tool the network administrator reaches for.

Although highly versatile and adaptable, LAN analyzers are pointless if the administrator has no idea of the general outline of the problem. Network managers need to attempt to diagnose the problems with the more general tools so they will know what to look for—what types of interactions between which hosts—before hooking up a specialized tool like a LAN analyzer.

Chapter Summary and References

In this chapter, we introduced TCP/IP internetwork management issues as well as TCP/IP network management solutions. From a general discussion of network management issues, we first looked at the Simple Network Management Protocol (SNMP) including SNMP commands, the Structure of Management Information (SMI) and the Management Information Base (MIB). We continued with a brief discussion of SNMPv2 and its relation to SNMPv1. The chapter concluded with a discussion of specific TCP/IP network management tools including ping, traceroute, netstat, and protocol analyzers.

Table 22–3 lists useful RFCs to read in conjunction with this chapter.

RFC	Title	Description
1157	Simple Network Management Protocol (SNMP)	Specification for the first version of SNMP.
1155	Structure and Identification of Management Information for TCP/IP-based Internets	Discussion of information used for Structure of Management Information (SMI).
1156	Management Information Base for Network Management of TCP/IP-based Internets	Specification of Management Information Base (MIB) for SNMP.

Table 22–3: Useful RFCs for Chapter 22.

RFC	Title	Description
1757	Remote Network Monitoring Management Information Base	Specification for RMON.
1905	Protocol Operations for Version 2 of the Simple Network Management Protocol (SNMPv2)	Specification for the SNMPv2 protocol; there are other, related RFCs published approximately the same time that describe other aspects of SNMPv2.
2151	A Primer on Internet and TCP/IP Tools and Utilities	Good source of information about ping, traceroute, and other tools.

Table 22–3: continued.

23

TCP/IP Internetwork Troubleshooting

TCP/IP network administrators and engineers must know how to troubleshoot their networks. They can manage their networks reactively, responding to every network problem as it manifests itself, or they can manage networks proactively. Proactive network management means anticipating problems and solving them before they occur. Proactive network management requires proper network design, management, and configuration. However, even when you plan for all eventualities, there will always be the unplanned-for event that you cannot anticipate. This chapter points out some basic issues and techniques that can be used for troubleshooting any TCP/IP networks.

413

The Scope of TCP/IP Troubleshooting

Troubleshooting a TCP/IP network can be as simple as identifying those problems relating specifically to TCP/IP and solving them, or as complicated as fixing any problem with any device connected to a TCP/IP network, whether the problem is related to its networking functions or not. In theory one might imagine that TCP/IP network troubleshooters could limit their scope to TCP/IP problems, but in real life, network administrators often find themselves responsible for fixing everything, especially problems that stump everyone else. Support people often consider networking a black art so they often blame problems they cannot solve on networking issues they don't understand. The result is that network engineers are often required to prove that a problem does not originate from the network by solving it—which tends to expand the arena that is considered "network responsibility" by defining it as "those problems that the network people can fix."

Network engineers must have excellent general system management and troubleshooting skills, so they can quickly determine the cause of a system problem and solve it.

Some of the typical problems TCP/IP network engineers are called upon to solve include

♦ Lack of network connectivity
♦ Network application performance problems
♦ Network outages

This chapter highlights some of the techniques used to locate problems at different layers of the reference model.

Troubleshooting the Hardware/Link Layer

Network problems of all kinds can originate at the hardware or link layers. If anything interferes with a system's ability to send or receive data over its network interface, there will be connectivity problems. Whether the system is attempting to communicate using TCP/IP network protocols or some other protocols, the attempts will fail if the network hardware fails.

A complete discussion of network hardware troubleshooting is clearly outside the scope of this book, but it is worthwhile to mention some basic network hardware troubleshooting issues and techniques, as well as a basic introduction to configuring network interfaces.

LAN Troubleshooting Issues

Problems that can bring down a network link include, but are not limited to

♦ Faults in wiring
♦ Faulty cable connections
♦ Power failure in network devices
♦ Failure of network interface hardware
♦ Exceeding specifications of network medium
♦ Hardware address problems
♦ Network device configuration problems

The magnitude of a network problem can range from inconvenience to a single user as when connectivity to a PC is lost, to major impact on an entire organization as when connectivity to an important gateway or server fails.

Faults in wiring. Whether caused by a user inadvertently pulling a network cable out of its proper place or a backhoe digging in the wrong place and severing a network cable, a wiring fault can bring down any network. If you subject a cable to excessive twisting or put too much pressure on a wire it is also possible to damage it. Wiring faults on obsolete single-cable networks such as those that use coaxial or thick-wire Ethernet can cause a LAN to fail. In networks that cable each system directly to a central hub or switch, as in 10-baseT Ethernet, problems with individual wires will generally affect only the system it directly connects.

This type of problem can be hard to identify since it may require checking and/or replacing a significant length of wire. Diagnostic tools for testing the integrity of a network cable often will be used to identify this type of problem.

Faulty cable connections. When cables aren't properly connected, a system may seem to vanish from a network. It is usually a relatively simple matter to make sure that all network cable connections are correct. This type of problem is more or less common depending on the type of network medium in use. For instance, early Ethernet cabling used a connector with a "sliding lock" device to keep it in place on the network interface device or card, but which tended to fail. Likewise, network media that rely on twisted-pair wiring and modular telephone-style jacks sometimes need an extra push before they engage in their receptacles. Improperly terminated cabling can also cause problems like echoing on Ethernets.

Checking network cable connectors is easy to do, and may be especially productive when the system having problems has recently been moved or has had service done that may have required breaking the network connection.

Power failure in network devices. Some LANs rely on powered devices, such as thin wire Ethernet, which depends on hubs for connectivity. When a hub goes down, it can cause the entire LAN to fail. Failure of other network devices may bring down the network or simply interrupt service sporadically, depending on what the device is and what it connects. For example, if a bridge or repeater fails, local traffic may continue but traffic may fail to cross from one segment to another.

Network management workstations are often used for keeping track of the status of network devices, and generally will alert the authorities when a network device fails.

Failure of network interface hardware. When the actual device that connects a system to the network—a network interface card, for example—fails, the system may lose connectivity completely or sporadically. You can identify this type of problem with diagnostic software that ships with the network device; if that software is unavailable, it may be necessary to replace the suspect network card with another one (hopefully, one that is known to work).

Exceeding specifications of network medium. You can't put 10 pounds of flour in a five pound bag any more than you can put 100 nodes on a network medium that can support only 50. Exceeding network medium specifications may result in sporadic connectivity or performance problems.

Exceeding the specifications might be the result of making a wire too long, or adding too many nodes, or attempting to transmit too much traffic. You may need to monitor network traffic or use a diagnostic device to verify that the cable is not too long; these types of problems may be a bit harder to identify immediately without special tools.

Network device configuration problems. As system software and hardware are upgraded or repaired, configurations change. Network devices configured through software cause trouble when software or documentation are unavailable. Devices that are configured through hardware switches and jumpers require that the system be opened and boards be removed and replaced.

Configuring Network Interfaces

Network interface cards may require configuration, depending on what kind of computer is being used and what operating system software is being used. Network interface cards for personal computers generally use a hardware interrupt, a memory address, and an I/O address. Typically, modern network cards are entirely plug-and-play, and require no explicit configuration on the part of the user (or engineer). The computer senses and sets all configuration items. Most network interface cards use software configuration interfaces, though many older network cards were configured by setting hardware switches.

Network connectivity problems often arise from misconfigured cards, particularly when the network adapter is replaced, when new cards are added to a system, or when an adapter configuration changes. Diagnostic and system software is often needed to display the current system configuration. Conflicts in hardware interrupt level, I/O address, or memory address can sometimes be discovered using diagnostic programs. Diagnostic software included with the network card can also be used to verify that the network card itself is running. Some products include diagnostics modules that allow another attached host to direct LAN traffic to the system being verified; if that system is able to receive the traffic, it proves that the network adapter card is fully functional.

Complete testing of the network interface device usually includes some configuration tools and may include host to host connectivity tests. Once system connectivity is verified, meaning that confirmation is received that the system can send and receive data through its network interface and network medium, a network configuration problem usually can be confidently ruled out. Chances are that the problem is caused by something wrong either on some other network device (like a LAN bridge or internetwork router), or else at a higher layer in the protocol stack.

Using Protocol Analyzers

Protocol analyzers are important for troubleshooting many different network problems ranging from the link layer to the application layer. However, they are especially useful at the link and internetwork layer where there is less likely to be a human user interface generating understandable error messages.

Implemented either as dedicated hardware devices or as software that can run on any connected system, protocol analyzers simply listen to the network traffic on the local area network. They can then either store the most recent traffic in a memory buffer or write all traffic to a disk file for analysis.

Protocol analyzers are usually capable of translating all encapsulation schemes, as well as displaying them appropriately on a screen, showing Ethernet addresses as well as IP addresses and TCP socket information. From this information, the network engineer can determine what kinds of messages systems are sending and receiving. Network engineers scrutinize these messages to determine whether or not systems are responding, and if so, whether they are responding appropriately. From protocol analysis logs network engineers determine whether or not data is being received by destination hosts and whether or not the software sending and receiving the messages is working properly.

Filtering capability is an important feature for protocol analyzers since huge volumes of data may be moving across a LAN, only a small portion of which is of interest to the network engineer. Most protocol analyzers are able to filter based on source and recipient address, protocol types, and other criteria. The filters are used to target messages going to or from specific hosts, or to listen only to messages using particular protocols. For example, an engineer may look only at frames being broadcast on a LAN, or only at datagrams exchanged by an FTP server and client.

Troubleshooting the Internetwork Layer

IP problems can arise from a variety of causes. Often, they are caused by incorrect or poorly tuned system configurations. Other times they arise from problems in TCP/IP implementations, such as when one vendor's version of TCP/IP responds in an unexpected way to another TCP/IP implementation. Although the network software will often return error or status messages when a connection fails, those messages may not always be accurate or useful. As a result, the network engineer learns to interpret these messages, as well as to use various network troubleshooting tools to evaluate problem situations.

System Configuration

Incorrectly configured systems can produce three results:

♦ Complete system connectivity failure
♦ Sporadic system connectivity failure
♦ No apparent system connectivity problems

A system that has not been configured correctly may work all the time, sometimes, or not at all. There is often no way to determine whether a system is misconfigured based simply on symptoms. The configuration needs to be verified as correct since symptoms of misconfiguration can vary so widely.

Complete connectivity failure can ensue when the system's IP address has an invalid network address, or when a system connected to the Internet through a point-to-point link is configured with the wrong router address. Pointing a protocol to an invalid network interface device can also cause a failure to communicate.

Sporadic problems can occur in many circumstances, and can be very difficult to observe, let alone identify. If primary routers or DNS servers are configured correctly but secondary systems are improperly specified, failure to route to (or resolve host names for) remote hosts can occur when the primary systems are unavailable. Other sporadic problems can be related to high traffic periods or remote system failures.

Finally, a system can be misconfigured with no apparent ill effects. For example, an incorrect subnet mask may not cause any problems for a host that connects only to systems on the same network segment. Likewise, hosts with duplicate IP addresses can coexist happily for long periods of time as long as the systems do not attempt to connect to the intranet simultaneously.

Duplicate IP Addresses

Part of the great appeal of DHCP (Dynamic Host Configuration Protocol) is that it allows a computer to manage the distribution of IP addresses. Computers are much better at this kind of task than people are, and they are better able to keep track of which network interface is linked with which IP address.

Without DHCP, resolving duplicate IP addresses can range from difficult to almost impossible. On coaxial Ethernets, for example, you could use ARP to determine whether more than one host responded to a request for a particular IP address, and you would get hardware addresses for the systems configured with that address. However, you would still not have any idea of where on the network those hosts were located. On the other hand, ARP is a much better tool for resolving that type of problem on 10BaseT networks using hubs, where traffic can be traced to a particular connection to the hub.

One good approach is to maintain detailed records that link not just each IP address to a specific network interface MAC address (as with DHCP), but also to a location and system manager, with access to historical information through backups and dates of assignment. Ideally the system would record the hardware address of the network interface as well. With this database, a network engineer can easily link addressing problems to changes in systems, for example, when one user replaces a system and hands down the old system to a coworker.

Tools for IP Troubleshooting

Many products are available for network management that use the Simple Network Management Protocol (SNMP—see Chapter 22) to manage and monitor network devices. For more basic connectivity troubleshooting tasks, however, ping and traceroute may be just as useful. As we discussed earlier (in Chapters 8 and 22), these applications use ICMP to determine whether or not there is connectivity between two points, and just what the route between two hosts is.

In the event that a host may have a connectivity problem, ping might be used first on the host itself as a quick and dirty test of its network software installation and configuration. The command issued for a host with IP address 10.0.0.1 would be

```
ping 10.0.0.1
```

If the network software is configured properly and the network hardware connection is installed correctly, the system should identify the request as one that should go through the loopback address (the software should be able to identify its own IP address, so that no traffic should be sent over the network). If the network card is configured properly, it will write the ping request to its output buffer, read it into its input buffer, and then pass the data back to the network protocol stack.

If the ping attempt to itself fails, then the problem is very likely caused by a problem with the network card or the network software. If the host responds to its own ping request with a message saying that it is "alive," then a ping request to an IP address of a host on the same network segment can be attempted next (the host should be one that is known to be up and running and able to respond to a ping request). This should not fail if the host successfully pinged itself, but if it does fail double-checking, the network configuration may help and it may be necessary to use a protocol analyzer to trace the ping and any responses.

The penultimate test for connectivity and configuration is to ping a host (by IP address) known to be up and running and responding to pings that is not on the local network segment and that requires forwarding by a router. If this fails, it may indicate that the router is configured improperly for the host. If it succeeds, the final test is to ping a remote host by its host name; this verifies that the host is configured correctly to use its domain name system (DNS) server.

Troubleshooting the Transport Layer

Assuming that there is internetwork level connectivity between two hosts, as demonstrated by successfully pinging each other, network problems may be attributable to problems occurring at the transport layer. Performance problems may be soluble through fine-tuning of transport layer variables; more catastrophic failures may be attributed to implementation problems, timing problems, or improper use of ports.

In general, solving problems that have been traced to the transport layer often require close sifting of protocol analyzer trace files and significant network experience and expertise. This section merely outlines a handful of issues that can cause problems at the transport layer.

Because TCP is a connection-oriented protocol, problems associated with it traditionally have tended to affect only the source and destination hosts. However, if there is a problem with a system providing services over TCP, that problem could impact on all systems attempting to connect to that server.

TCP Timing Issues

As a reliable protocol, TCP relies on timers to ensure that data is received in a timely fashion. TCP implementations must maintain four timers for each connection as follows.

The **retransmission time** is the length of time that a host will wait when it is expecting an acknowledgment from the remote host before it retransmits a segment. In other words, if a host sends a segment at time 00:00:00 and expects an acknowledgment within 30 seconds, that segment will be retransmitted if an acknowledgment has not been received by 00:00:30.

A **persist timer** is used to query the other end of a TCP connection periodically to make sure that the window size has not unexpectedly changed.

A **keepalive timer** is used to nudge periodically the other end of a TCP link that appears to be idle. The purpose is to detect when a remote host has crashed or been brought down, or when the logical connection has been broken.

The **2MSL timer** is used to make sure that segments from an old connection are not misinterpreted as part of a new link between the same two hosts over the same two ports. MSL stands for maximum segment lifetime. The 2MSL timer is also used to keep the sockets from a connection from being reused.

SYN Flooding

One problem that can cause disruption in services, called SYN flooding, is invariably the result of a denial of service attack. Although the theory behind this attack had been public knowledge, in the summer of 1996 an implementation was published and malicious attackers actually deployed it against various targets. The essence of the attack is to generate over a short time a large number of requests (SYN, or synchronization, segments) to open TCP connections with a server. The server then has to allocate system resources to attempt to open all the connections, which, being spurious, it cannot do. The result is that the server can quickly and effectively be brought down and rendered unavailable to real users.

Troubleshooting the Application Layer

You can determine that there is connectivity up to the application layer if you are able to attempt to use a network service but are denied access through the application itself. Usually the server will return an error or status message generated by the service application. This type of problem is often due to an improperly configured client or server program, or to a lack of proper user authentication. One common access problem comes from users not using the correct case when entering case-sensitive users IDs and passwords.

Application Settings

Application settings, particularly at the client end, are usually easily accessible and are also often the cause of problems. They can control how data is displayed, how data is transmitted, and how the client host interacts with the remote host.

File Transfer Issues

It is important when doing file transfer to use the correct file transfer modes. For example, choosing ASCII mode for text files stored on an IBM mainframe with the EBCDIC scheme will cause the files to be transferred correctly to a non-EBCDIC computer.

Additional troubleshooting information can be gathered by reviewing the status messages (described in Chapter 16) sent from the server during the session. These messages are readily available from sessions conducted on command line interfaces, as with Unix or DOS, but may call for opening a special window or a log file under graphical interfaces. Different FTP implementations have different features and functions, and a graphical FTP implementation may not provide access to these messages.

Telnet Issues

As transfer mode is important to file transfer sessions, so is the terminal emulation to be used for Telnet connections. For example, using a VT-100 emulation to attempt connecting to an IBM mainframe that requires 3270 emulation probably will not succeed. Display options can also be critical, particularly if the Telnet implementation allows the user to select foreground and background colors for the terminal emulation window. For example, the terminal session can be rendered invisible by setting the foreground and background to the same color. Although this might at least theoretically be appropriate under certain circumstances, as when running a batch file for a Telnet session on an unprotected workstation, it is more likely to cause problems.

World Wide Web Issues

There are the same opportunities for display and transfer problems with HTTP servers and clients, but more often problems arise when HTTP clients are unable to decode the HTML code of documents stored on a Web server correctly. This is largely due to the tendency of vendors to differentiate their product by writing it to support the Internet standard, plus their own proprietary standard. Thus, it is not unusual for certain Web sites to be unviewable with one or more vendors' browser, or to be viewable only with one vendor's browser. Web site authors are urged to use human testers as well as software tools for verifying that all links and objects within a Web site are functional, as well as that the Web site is viewable with the most popular web browsers.

Chapter Summary and References

In this chapter, we discussed some of the methods and tools used for TCP/IP network troubleshooting. We started with an overview of techniques ranging from the simple "is it plugged in?" test for problems at the data link layer, to protocol analysis for data link and internetwork layer protocol problems. Moving up the protocol stack, we discussed some of the issues and answers for finding and fixing problems at the transport layer, especially for TCP, and at the application layer.

Table 23–1 lists RFCs that can be read in conjunction with this chapter.

RFC	Title	Description
1470	FYI on a Network Management Tool Catalog: Tools for Monitoring and Debugging TCP/IP Internets and Interconnected Devices	A catalog of tools for troubleshooting networks.
2151	A Primer on Internet and TCP/IP Tools and Utilities	Good source of information about ping, traceroute, and other tools.

Table 23–1: Useful RFCs for Chapter 23.

24

TCP/IP and Internetwork Security

Security was not part of the original mission of those who developed the TCP/IP protocol suite. At first, TCP/IP was largely an academic exercise, an experiment to see if it was possible to create networks of networks. Deployed largely on networks and computers in educational and research institutions, and used mostly by researchers and their students, TCP/IP networks did not need to be all that secure.

This is no longer the case. Rather than research and development, TCP/IP is now being used around the world for production business systems—and for transmitting sometimes sensitive business data. Security is very much a problem. Organizations need to protect their systems and networks from unauthorized attacks that affect the organization's ability to use its own network resources, and they need to keep their own data private.

Internetwork security includes several distinct topics, including:

♦ Restricting unauthorized access to networks through firewall technology
♦ Using encrypted tunnels to build virtual private networks over the Internet
♦ Using encrypted channels to transmit sensitive information across the Internet
♦ Monitoring network security with intrusion detection technology
♦ Protecting against denial of service attacks

In this chapter, after a brief introduction to network security issues and cryptography, we look at the IP security architecture (IPsec), a framework designed to build security services—encryption and authentication—into IP. It may seem odd that IPsec has relatively little to do with many of the issues we discuss in this chapter, but then IPsec is designed strictly to provide security for individual IP datagrams. Securing datagrams is only one part of the overall task of the IP internetwork security manager. The rest of the chapter covers firewalls, virtual private networks, the Transport Layer Security (TLS) protocol, intrusion detection, and protecting against denial of service attacks. We finish the chapter with a brief introduction to the Kerberos authentication service.

Network Security Issues

When a network is connected to the Internet, everything on that network is potentially exposed to the world: the Internet link is an open door to the organizational network. The good news is that members of the organization can now receive e-mail from anyone else connected to the Internet, as well as exchange information with any other host (for which they are authorized) connected to the Internet. The bad news is that, because of the openness of the TCP/IP protocols, everyone knows how they work. This includes the ability to impersonate other users and systems.

Everyone has access to well-known security holes, but not everyone exercises that access. Computer criminals are more likely to know that some TCP/IP applications and implementations have bugs or features that make them likely targets for breaking into the systems running them. Computer users, particularly those who administer systems in their spare time, in addition to their regular duties, often miss out on security warnings.

Adding security measures almost always seems to add cost to maintaining the system by the organization and to make the system harder to use. For example, frequent backups and off-site storage of historical backup tapes is necessary for easy recovery from data loss (whether malicious or accidental) but requires the organization to budget staff and equipment for the backup and secure storage space for the tapes. Likewise, truly secure computer passwords (sequences of unrelated characters) are much harder to remember than the user's birthdate, should never be written down, and should be changed frequently—all of which mean the user has yet another bit of meaningless information to remember.

Of course, the apparent security costs (to both user and organization) are dwarfed when compared to the cost of simply losing information stored on a computer, the cost of business lost when a network running essential corporate applications goes down, and the cost of having an eavesdropping competitor intercept confidential business plans sent across an internetwork.

Though it is relatively easy to make a single computer completely secure—simply isolate it physically, say, by putting it in a sealed room—it loses much of its utility. This approach, modified slightly to allow users to go in and out of the room, will protect data on the computer (or local area network) only as long as users are trustworthy. If it weren't for users, systems would be much more secure: dishonest users often take revenge on or steal from employers, and criminals often convince less-informed users to reveal passwords.

These issues not only don't go away in an internetworked environment, they are amplified by the much larger user base, using so many more systems. However, finding solutions to problems like password selection, user authentication, data backup, and emergency reaction planning requires essentially the same steps whether the system in question is a personal computer used by three people in a shared office, a financial transaction network, or a code-breaking system at the National Security Agency.

TCP/IP internetworks pose some special security problems, however. Since TCP/IP has been developed as an open system, and for much of its existence used primarily as a research tool, it is designed for openness rather than security. This means that villains with access to a network over which internetwork traffic is routed can monitor that traffic for "interesting" data: unencrypted passwords, credit card numbers, terminal sessions, and file transfers. They can also use the internetwork to attempt to access remote systems to steal data, subvert systems, and attempt to access other systems.

In a perfect world, every computer on the network will be properly administered by a knowledgeable user or system manager: all of its users will use secure passwords and other security measures to prevent unauthorized access; all of the data on the system will be properly backed up and verified to prevent accidental or intentional loss or damage; any confidential or sensitive data will be encrypted strongly to prevent it from falling into the wrong hands; all systems maintain detailed logs (with frequent human reviews) that record attempts to access or modify data stored on the system. Unfortunately, in the real world most networked systems are personal computers, and many more are departmental servers that aren't professionally managed, with the result that most organizations are quite vulnerable to attacks through their internetwork connections.

Internetwork security, strictly speaking, requires stronger security on individual systems and in local area networks, but some tools can be applied to strengthen protection on internetworks, particularly those connected to the Internet. Fundamental to almost every type of network security are the cryptographic functions introduced next.

Cryptography

Cryptography is the study of ciphers and encryption—techniques for taking data and information that is understandable (**plaintext**) and turning it into what appears to be random data (**ciphertext**). Encryption is often described as a way of scrambling data, but most encryption **algorithms** (the actual instructions for how to encrypt data) use a combination of methods to make orderly, understandable information into what appears to be random.

Randomness is essential for encryption because any kind of order that carries over into the ciphertext from the plaintext offers attackers a way to attempt to break the encryption. Data is encrypted by using a function (the algorithm) with another piece of data called a **key**. If an attacker can figure out a way to decrypt the ciphertext without access to the key, the algorithm is probably not that secure. If the attacker can't easily break the encryption, the algorithm is probably secure—but the more attackers who try to break the encryption algorithm and fail, the more likely the algorithm is secure.

Cryptographic functions are indispensible for making data sent over a network secure. Encryption, of course, helps prevent anyone but the intended recipient from being able to read or interpret the encrypted data. There are three categories of encryption that are relevant to network security. Probably the most familiar is that of **secret key** encryption. With secret key encryption, the key is kept secret because if you know the key you can decrypt any plaintext encrypted with that key. This is equivalent to a safe combination, for example. If you know the combination, you can open the safe. And if you tell your friend the combination, your friend can open it too.

Simple substitution ciphers (for example, where A=C, B=D, and so on) are the most obvious specimen of secret key encryption algorithms. If you know that the key is to offset each letter of the alphabet by two characters, then you know the key. Secret key encryption has been in use for hundreds, if not thousands, of years. Adding computer power allows far more intricate and secure secret key algorithms, that use much longer keys and much more complicated calculations to produce plaintext from ciphertext. Reversing the encryption is simple: it is generally a matter of running the same algorithm on the ciphertext using the same secret key. Thus, decrypting the simple substitution cipher cited at the start of this paragraph would be a matter of offsetting all the ciphertext letters by –2 (making D=B and C=A). Secret key encryption can be said to be reversible or **symmetric**, because encryption and decryption use essentially the same process and the same key.

Secret key encryption tends to be used a lot: when used properly it is reasonably secure, and there are several highly secure algorithms that provide good performance when implemented in software. However, the problem with secret key encryption for network security is that you need to have a way to distribute the keys. Unless you can distribute the keys in person or over some other secure channel, secret key encryption can be complicated to implement (see the section on Kerberos, at the end of this chapter).

A better way to protect information transmitted over an open network like the Internet is to somehow build an encryption algorithm that uses two keys: one for encrypting data and another for decrypting data. You keep the decrypting key secret and share it with no one. The other key, used for encrypting data, can be made as public as you like since it would be used only for encrypting data.

In the late 1970s, such **public key encryption** algorithms were first discovered. Diffie-Hellman and RSA are the two most widely used public key algorithms. With a public key algorithm, the sender encrypts data with the recipient's public key. In this process, a function uses the key to generate ciphertext from the plaintext, but a different key is needed to decrypt that ciphertext. Unlike symmetric encryption algorithms, public key encryption algorithms are not reversible, and are thus also known as **asymmetric**. The details of these algorithms are not important for this discussion, but they can be found in *Personal Encryption Clearly Explained* (Morgan Kaufmann 1998).

Public key encryption to a great degree makes possible Internet commerce as well as any type of security for data over the Internet. Its value is not just for encrypting data, but also for **digital signatures**. Consider what happens when you encrypt some data using your secret key rather than a recipient's public key. Now, anyone can decrypt the message using your own public key. This turns out to be a valuable function. If a message can be decrypted with your public key it means that the only entity who could possibly have encrypted it—with your secret key, the one you don't tell to anyone—is you.

Because public key algorithms tend to be rather slow, even on computers, most encryption is done using a secret key algorithm but with the secret key being transmitted only after it is encrypted using a public key algorithm. And because performance is usually so poor, most digital signatures are done not on entire messages but on what is called a **message digest**.

A message digest (sometimes called a **hash**) algorithm accepts as input a plaintext and sometimes a key and produces as output a value of fixed length that represents a sort of digital summary of the original plaintext. In other words, a message digest will always produce a result that is 128 bytes (or 256 bytes, or some other value), whether the original message is 10 bytes long or 10 million bytes long. A message digest is a type of encryption that takes plaintext as input and produces a message digest that cannot be turned back into plaintext. And hashes are very fast, much faster even than secret key encryption and much, much faster than public key encryption.

Message digests are valuable for authentication purposes. Let's say you want to prove that you know a password, but you don't want to tell me the actual password (just in case I'm not who you think I am). You can hash the password, and I can hash the password, and if the results are the same then we both know the same secret. Message digests are also used to make digital signatures: the message to be signed is hashed, and the result of that hash is encrypted with the signer's secret key. When the message is to be certified, the recipient takes the signer's public key and decrypts the message digest, then hashes the message. If the two values are the same, the message is authenticated.

Cryptographic functions such as these are integral to almost every type of network security there is.

IP Security Architecture

It used to be a truism that guarantees and security should be provided at a higher network layer than the internetwork layer. Applications should provide their own security, and transport layers could provide guarantees about the data being transmitted across the Internet. Many contended that IP should remain open and simple and that security issues should be handled elsewhere. This is no longer the case, as, after many years of debate and development, the IP security architecture is gathering support.

First defined formally in RFC 1825 and revised in 1998 as RFC 2401, "Security Architecture for the Internet Protocol," describes the mechanisms by which IP datagrams can be kept secure. Security, in this case, means:

♦ Protecting the contents of the datagram from unauthorized access through encryption.
♦ Protecting the contents of the datagram from unauthorized modification through the use of message digests and digital signatures.
♦ Providing a mechanism by which the recipient of the datagram can prove that the datagram was actually sent by the entity claiming to have sent it, through the use of digital signatures.

This may sound relatively straightforward, but network security is far from simple. Table 24–2 at the end of the chapter lists some of the documents that describe current proposed Internet standards for IPsec. The following is excerpted from section 3.1 ("What IPsec Does") of RFC 2401:

IPsec provides security services at the IP layer by enabling a system to select required security protocols, determine the algorithm(s) to use for the service(s), and put in place any cryptographic keys required to provide the requested services. IPsec can be used to protect one or more "paths" between a pair of hosts, between a pair of security gateways, or between a security gateway and a host. (The term "security gateway" is used throughout the IPsec documents to refer to an intermediate system that implements IPsec protocols. For example, a router or a firewall implementing IPsec is a security gateway.)

The set of security services that IPsec can provide includes access control, connectionless integrity, data origin authentication, rejection of replayed packets (a form of partial sequence integrity), confidentiality (encryption), and limited traffic flow confidentiality. Because these services are provided at the IP layer, they can be used by any higher layer protocol, e.g., TCP, UDP, ICMP, BGP, etc.

There are several important areas that IPsec must address, including:

♦ **Encryption of packets.** The Encapsulating Security Payload (ESP) protocol is defined in RFC 2406, "IP Encapsulating Security Payload (ESP)" to provide a way for two devices to send and receive IP packets that have been encrypted to keep the contents secure.

♦ **Authentication of packets**. The Authentication Header (AH) protocol is defined in RFC 2402, "IP Authentication Header," to provide a way for two devices to use digital signatures or message digests (or some other cryptographic technique) to authenticate packets.

♦ **Security associations.** The Internet Security Association and Key Management Protocol (ISAKMP) is defined in RFC 2408, "Internet Security Association and Key Management Protocol (ISAKMP)," to provide a framework within which security parameters can be exchanged between entities using IPsec. ISAKMP defines what information is needed to set up a security association (associating a network entity with some security information) as well as how that information should be handled.

♦ **Key exchange.** The Internet Key Exchange (IKE) protocol is defined in RFC 2409 "The Internet Key Exchange (IKE)." Based on ISAKMP, which defines how key exchange protocols must behave, the IKE is an example of a key exchange protocol. IKE specifies how cryptographic keys are to be transmitted from one network device to another for the purpose of doing any IPsec function (encryption or authentication).

IPsec can be used by higher-layer protocols to transmit application data securely, but is more often used to allow two entities to communicate securely across the Internet. By encrypting and authenticating datagrams, data can be transmitted securely across the Internet through **virtual private networks** (VPNs). Firewalls and IP network devices can use the authentication header (AH) protocol to make sure that only authorized users access their services. Firewalls will be discussed in the next section, followed by a section on VPNs.

Firewalls

To address the Internet security situation, most organizations do well to consider implementing a selective barrier at their point of connection to the Internet: a firewall. Although TCP/IP internetworks can have many points of contact between linked networks, most organizations connecting to the Internet do so through a single link. This makes it much easier to manage, as well as police, the Internet connection. Firewall gateway systems are intended to be the single point through which all Internet traffic, both incoming and outgoing, is passed. The system (or systems) examines every piece of network traffic and determines the proper course of action: either pass it along to its intended destination or not.

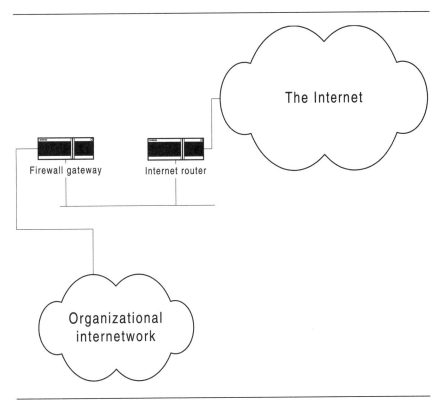

Figure 24–1: A firewall gateway system separates an organizational internetwork from the Internet.

Figure 24–1 shows a representative architecture for an Internet firewall gateway system. Internet access is provided by a router connected to the Internet and a small network it shares with the firewall gateway. The Internet router forwards traffic intended for the organizational internetwork to the firewall, which forwards approved traffic on the organizational internetwork.

By choking all access to and from the Internet through a single point, the firewall system can be used to restrict access to services and systems—and can also be a monitoring station, keeping logs of attempts to access services and systems from off-site. Firewalls usually use one or more of three approaches to protecting networks: packet filtering, application gateways, and circuit-level gateways.

A formal Internet firewall uses a separate system or systems, sometimes using their own separate network, to buffer between the Internet router (or gateway) and the organizational network. Depending on the level of need for security, the organization may use more or less extravagant methods. The degree of openness for any given organizational internetwork depends on the organization's security policies, goals in connecting to the Internet, and corporate culture.

Some organizations are by their nature more open: universities are often cited as organizations more likely to allow free access to and from the Internet from internal systems; banks are organizations that would be less likely to expose operational systems to the Internet. The validity of these generalizations is open to question: university administration systems are not likely to be exposed, and banks are starting to make information resources available through the World Wide Web. However, they illustrate the point that corporate culture affects Internet access.

Each organization must make a decision about security policies: whether to be permissive or strict. A permissive policy can identify certain activities, services, systems, and users that are not allowed—and everything else is permitted. This "tree of life" approach (Adam and Eve were permitted to eat anything they wanted, except for the apple) assumes that the network policymakers can identify the sources of potential danger and screen them out, while permitting all other types of access.

A strict policy identifies certain activities, services, systems, and users that are permitted—and everything else is forbidden. This more restrictive approach assumes that the network policy makers can identify the services and uses that are safe (or absolutely necessary) and screens out all other uses as potentially dangerous.

Since it is often hard to identify potentially dangerous applications in advance and reports of unsafe implementations are frequent occurrences, it isn't surprising that many organizations prefer to take a stricter policy stance for their Internet security.

Packet Filtering

The job of a router is to accept network traffic (packets) to be forwarded to another network. A router filters packets it receives on the basis of their ultimate destination: an Internet router accepts packets destined for the Internet from an organizational internetwork and forwards them to the Internet.

It might not always be prudent to allow the router to accept all the packets it receives from the Internet. Whether the organization decides to follow a permissive or a strict policy, the Internet gateway can be configured to implement the chosen policy.

Packet filters use tables configured on the firewall gateway to test network traffic against. Table 24–1 is a very rudimentary packet filtering table: it allows Internet e-mail traffic destined for the mail server (MAIL) from anywhere through SMTP through port 25; it allows UDP DNS traffic from the Internet to MAIL through UDP port 53; it allows a secondary name server from off-site (DNS-2) to access the mail server with DNS traffic over TCP port 53; it allows the organizational internetwork to send TCP segments off-site and permits TCP acknowledgment segments back in; and it allows an external time server (TIME) to send UDP datagrams through port 123 to a local time server (TIME1). The asterisk (*) specifies that all values of the variable are indicated.

Packet filtering is a very inexpensive method of protecting an organizational network because it can be implemented in software on the router used to connect directly to the Internet. It is also the weakest of the firewall gateway strategies, since it relies on applications playing by the rules. If traffic to a vulnerable host is permitted in any form, even if it is just through a single well-known port, computer criminals may be able to use that as a point of entry to the system.

Action	Source host	Source port	Dest host	Dest port	Flag	Notes
Allow	*	*	MAIL	25		In-bound e-mail
Allow	*	*	MAIL	53	UDP	DNS service is required
Allow	DNS-2	*	MAIL	53		Secondary DNS server access
Allow	TIME	123	TIME1	123	UDP	Network Time Protocol service
Allow	local-net	*	*	*		Local network TCP segments will all be forwarded
Allow	*	*	local net	*	ACK	TCP acknowledgments will be forwarded
Block	*	*	*	*		No other TCP is allowed
Block	*	*	*	*	UDP	No other UDP is allowed

Table 24–1: An extremely simple packet filter table.

Application Gateways

Using an application gateway firewall takes another step to increase security (and decrease ease of use). Rather than permit direct access between hosts in the organizational internetwork and hosts out on the Internet, which might allow an outsider to gain unauthorized access, all Internet traffic is directed through a single application gateway. As shown in Figure 24–2, the application gateway shares a "no-man's land" network with two firewall routers.

Users on the inside who want to make a connection with the Internet must log onto the application gateway and use the applications on that system to connect. Users on the outside who want to make a connection with this organization, for example, to

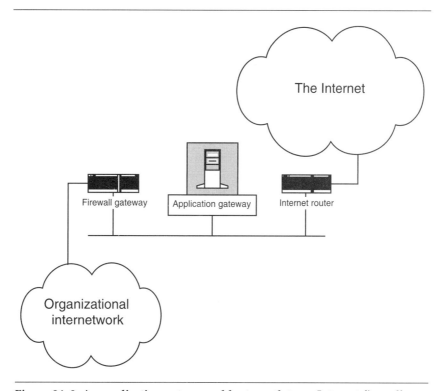

Figure 24–2: An application gateway adds strength to an Internet firewall.

retrieve files or to use a World Wide Web document, would connect to the application gateway.

The two firewalls are configured to forward packets only to the application gateway; neither will transmit to the other. The only packets the internal firewall will forward to the organizational internetwork are those originating from the application gateway; the only packets the external firewall will forward are those intended for the application gateway.

When there are many different systems in an organization, each running its own operating system, network software, and client and server implementations, there is a significant risk that some of those implementations will have security bugs. This is a particular problem when systems are administered by end users who may not have the time or training to determine whether an implementation is safe. Application gateways reduce this risk significantly by reducing the number of versions of network servers and clients that need to be certified "safe."

Users don't always like this approach because it is inconvenient; for instance, transferring files requires a two-step process, first from the remote system to the application gateway, then from the application gateway to the internal system. Another problem is that only one version of each application is implemented, which usually disappoints users who want to be able to use their favorite client.

Circuit Level Gateways and Proxy Applications

Another level of security, as well as added convenience, can be attained by implementing network applications that work only through the gateway. The clients are modified to connect only to the firewall gateway, which in turn connects to the remote system. The firewall mediates the connection, acting simply as a conduit for data passing between the client and server after the initial connection is made. The applications are sometimes called proxies, because they act on behalf of the end user, managing the connection with the remote host securely on the outside part of the gateway, while relaying data from the remote host to the system inside the gateway.

Security is achieved through the control the firewall has over all connections. It can mediate very strictly which ports, both source and destination, are used for any given links. Other possibilities for achieving security include requiring the internal user to be authenticated before initiating a connection and using lists of restricted or permitted external hosts.

Protocol Gateways

For many organizations, linking to the Internet means adding a new set of protocols (the TCP/IP suite) to existing LAN protocols;

in particular, IPX as used by Novell NetWare and other popular networking products. Some vendors have begun offering these organizations an alternative in the form of protocol gateways. These systems are usually nothing more than small computers with two network interfaces: one for the LAN and one for an Internet connection. They act as protocol translators, allowing users inside the firewall to use IPX as their network protocol to carry application information rather than IP.

Virtual Private Networks (VPNs)

The term **virtual private network** (VPN) refers to a construct in which data communication takes place over public channels but the result is something that functions like and appears to be a private network. Figure 24–3 shows a large organization with several branches separated geographically. This organization creates its own VPN by linking each network through IP tunnels across the Internet. Intranets A through D are all connected to the Internet, and each intranet's security gateway creates an encrypted tunnel with each of the other security gateways.

Each security gateway creates a connection with each other security gateway using IPsec protocols. When a host on Intranet A sends data to a host on Intranet C, the data is packaged up into an IP datagram addressed to the destination node. The sending host sends the datagram to its local router, which determines that the datagram is intended for a destination outside the local intranet but still within the organizational VPN, so it forwards the datagram to the security gateway. The security gateway then uses the appropriate combination of ESP and AH to protect the datagram.

At this point, the original datagram is encapsulated into a different datagram which is addressed to the security gateway for Intranet C and addressed from the security gateway for Intranet A. This is what is known as tunneling: the actual data is being passed through a separate set of communications between the security gateways. When the security gateway for Intranet C receives the

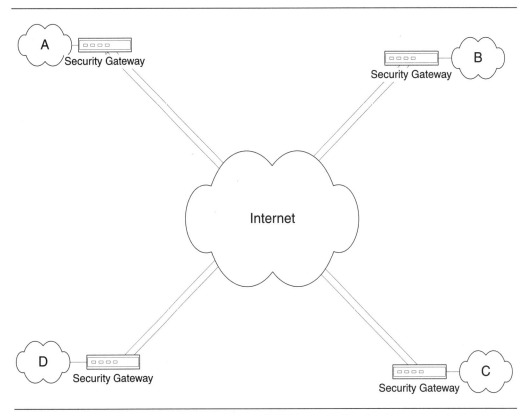

Figure 24–3: An organization can create its own VPN by tunneling its data across the Internet.

datagram, it decrypts and authenticates (as appropriate) the *origi-nal* datagram—the message being sent from the host on Intranet A to the destination host on Intranet C. At this point, the security gateway passes the decrypted and authenticated packet to the appropriate router on Intranet C, which then forwards the packet on to its destionation. Figure 24–4 shows how the VPN shown in Figure 24–3 appears to its users in terms of its function.

In general, security gateways use encryption to prevent unautho-rized access to data, and digital signatures to provide some degree of authentication services. VPNs are the most obvious and most common use of IPsec protocols to date.

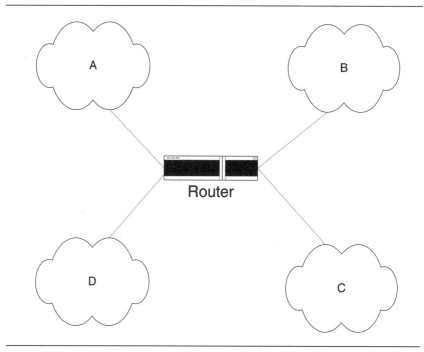

Figure 24–4: The VPN in Figure 24–3 creates a logical architecture that looks like this to its users.

Transport Layer Security (TLS)

The Transport Layer Security (TLS) protocol, specified in RFC 2246, "The TLS Protocol Version 1.0," defines a mechanism for processes to interoperate securely over the Internet. Based on the Secure Sockets Layer (SSL) protocol that was originally published by Netscape as an enabling technology for Internet commerce, TLS is a new protocol and does not interoperate with SSL.

The stated goals of TLS are as follows:

1. Provide cryptographic security for connection between two parties. The parties should be able to send and receive encrypted and/or digitally signed material.

2. Provide interoperability, so that any programmer can develop applications that use TLS and that can interoperate securely with other such applications.
3. Provide extensibility, so that existing TLS implementations can accept new public key, secret key, and other encryption methods as they are needed or as they become available.
4. Provide efficiency, so that network cryptographic interactions are kept to a minimum.

According to RFC 2246, the "primary goal of the TLS Protocol is intended to provide privacy and data integrity between two communicating applications." This goal is achieved through a pair of protocols, the TLS Record Protocol and the TLS Handshake Protocol. The TLS Record Protocol operates just above TCP, and can use symmetric encryption algorithms to do bulk encryption of data generated by an application. The TLS Record Protocol may also (or instead) use message digests to insure the integrity of the data being transmitted.

The TLS Handshake Protocol operates just above the TLS Record Protocol, and can be used by the server and client to negotiate how the secure connection is to be set up. For example, the server (or client) may use the TLS Handshake Protocol to solicit authentication information from the client (or server). The TLS Handshake Protocol can also be used for the client and server to negotiate what encryption and integrity algorithms are to be used, and even to exchange keys for use with the TLS Record Protocol.

The TLS Protocol can be used by any higher-level application protocol, whether that protocol is HTTP, FTP, telnet, or anything else.

Intrusion Detection

Network managers can hide their networks behind firewalls and can tunnel their network data through the Internet with VPNs, but these methods don't always protect against unauthorized intrusions into organizational resources. Despite the widespread use of firewalls, attackers can still get through in some cases, and network managers need mechanisms that will notify the manager of these attacks.

Intrusion detection is the practice of building systems that can be made aware of unauthorized accesses, and notify the authorities when they happen. Most intrusion attempts, we hope, are rebuffed by firewalls and other security measures (like pass phrases and user authentication mechanisms). Simply relying on these measures and assuming that they will work all the time is an invitation to disaster.

Intrusion detection practices rely on a variety of mechanisms that identify problems and alert the appropriate authorities. These mechanisms include

- Tools for tracking system logs and identifying suspicious activities like repeated failures at logging in or logging in from unusual locations.
- Tools for monitoring the status of sensitive resources. For example, some of these set off alarms when certain system files are modified.
- Traps for attackers. A honeypot system is one that is sufficiently wide-open to attract most attacks once the attackers are inside. These systems offer a tempting target, but at the same time occupy the attackers' interest while the network administrator has time to call the police.

Though important for IP networks, intrusion detection strategies are necessary for any kind of network. Methods for intrusion detection are being borrowed from other areas, notably from cable television providers who have long battled attackers trying to steal cable services and from the telecommunications industry where attackers attempt both to invade sensitive systems and to steal services where they can.

Denial of Service Attacks

Some attacks against network resources are made with the intention of stealing or modifying information. Encryption and authentication technologies are useful for preventing these attacks, but there is another category of attacks that can often be as costly to the victim as losing information. **Denial of service attacks** can be defined as any type of attack that causes (or could cause) the loss of access to a network resource by an authorized user.

Denial of service attacks may cause mere inconvenience, simply slowing down a resource for a moment, or they may disrupt an organization's operations for hours or days and cost thousands of dollars in lost revenues or increased operating costs.

Some people consider **spam** or unsolicited e-mail, usually carrying an advertisement or solicitation of some sort, to be a denial of service attack. After all, the person receiving an unsolicited message must pay for his or her connect time while that message was downloaded, and must expend some effort (though usually minimal) to identify the junk e-mail and then delete it. More serious are the computer viruses and other malicious code that are often incorporated into files that are attached to e-mail messages. However, these attacks may be carried out over any transmission medium from a network to a shared diskette.

There are far more malicious denial of service attacks, especially those that take advantage of features of TCP/IP protocols and the way that these protocols are implemented. Two important such attacks that have surfaced over the past few years are the **Ping of Death** and **syn flooding**.

It is a basic requirement that all TCP/IP nodes respond to pings from other nodes. If they don't, they cannot be considered to implement IP properly. Ping requests use a message format that includes not only the requesting node's IP address but may also include a payload of data. The purpose of this data payload is to permit troubleshooting of the route from pinger to pingee, including the maximum transmission unit size. However, the Ping of Death takes advantage of the ability to attach a data payload by using a data payload that is too large. Some implementations of IP properly ignore and discard such ping messages, but some attempt to process the data payload and subsequently may crash.

Another protocol-related attack is syn flooding. As discussed in Chapter 10, the TCP protocol uses a three-way handshake protocol to set up a TCP circuit between two nodes. Usually, the node requesting the circuit sends a SYN message to "synchronize" the two nodes and start setting up the connection. The response of the second node is to allocate system resources to set up a new circuit and respond with an ACK. In the syn flooding attack, however, the attacker merely sends a stream of SYN requests to the victim node. Again, some implementations are able to resist the attack, but others find themselves allocating all their resources trying to set up new circuits and subsequently are not able to provide any services to any other users.

Kerberos

Named after the three-headed dog guarding the gates of hell, Kerberos was developed at the Massachusetts Institute of Technology as a method of authenticating users through user IDs and passwords without exposing those passwords on an internetwork. This is a real danger, particularly since users tend to reuse their passwords: capturing a user's password, which is very often transmitted across internetworks in plain text, means gaining access to at least one system.

Under Kerberos, when a user initiates a network session, a request on behalf of the user (as specified by a user ID) is transmitted to a Kerberos security server by the system the user is attempting to log into. This Kerberos server is also called the *Key Distribution Center* (KDC) because it distributes session keys to be used when attempting to connect to network resources.

The KDC verifies that the user is, in fact, known to be an authentic user, and it replies with session credentials: a session key and a *Ticket Granting Ticket* (TGT), all encrypted with the secret key assigned to the individual specified by the user ID (which is a secret key derived from the user's password). The TGT includes the session key, an expiration time, and the user's name, which are all encrypted with a key assigned to the Kerberos server, so that no other system or person other than the KDC can read it.

The system being logged into prompts the user for a password once it receives the session credentials. It then derives the secret key from the password, decrypts the credentials to get the TGT and the session key, and if it succeeds, allows the user to initiate the session.

Once the session is initiated, the user can access other network resources similarly. To connect to or use resources of some other host, the user executes commands normally while the workstation negotiates authentication issues with the KDC.

For example, if the user wants to initiate a Telnet session with host X, the user's workstation sends a request to the KDC for a session key to communicate with that host. The request includes the TGT that was sent when the session was first started. The KDC decrypts that TGT, checks to make sure it hasn't expired, and replies by sending back a ticket to connect to host X. This ticket includes a session key encrypted with host X's secret key and also indicates the user who wants to log in. The workstation then sends this on host X, and a session can be started after host X decrypts the ticket.

Kerberos makes it possible to avoid transmitting any passwords in plain text across a network. All sessions require a session key and authentication before allowing any access at all.

Although it does address some of the problems inherent in communicating potentially sensitive data across a network that is known to be susceptible to eavesdropping, Kerberos requires a high degree of cooperation between network resources and the security servers to make sure that passwords and secret keys are known to the security servers and are not compromised.

Chapter Summary and References

In this chapter, we took a fleeting glance at some of the most important topics related to Internet security. We began with an introduction to network and Internet security issues, followed by a brief introduction to cryptography and cryptographic functions like secret key encryption, public key encryption, message digests, and digital signatures.

In the next section we looked at the IP security architecture, also known as IPsec, and discussed briefly what it includes and what it is used for. Next came an introduction to firewall technologies and techniques, followed by an introduction to virtual private networks (VPNs).

We introduced the Transport Layer Security (TLS) Protocol, providing a successor to the Secure Sockets Layer (SSL) long used in most web browsers and servers to set up secure channels for the secure exchange of information over the Internet. The last sections of the chapter introduced intrusion detection, denial of service attacks, and the Kerberos authentication protocol.

Table 24–2 lists some useful RFCs to read in conjunction with this chapter.

RFC	Title	Description
2196	Site Security Handbook	An informational RFC providing important guidance on building a secure site.
2401	Security Architecture for the Internet Protocol	Defines IPsec.

Table 24–2: Useful RFCs for Chapter 24.

RFC	Title	Description
2411	IP Security Document Roadmap	Describes the various documents that describe the Internet Protocol security architecture.
2406	IP Encapsulating Security	Specifies how IP datagrams can be encrypted for security.
2402	IP Authentication Header	Specifies how IP datagrams can be digitally signed for authentication.
2408	Internet Security Association and Key Management Protocol (ISAKMP)	Specifies what data is needed to set up IPsec interaction.
2409	The Internet Key Exchange (IKE) ISAKMP.	Provides a specific protocol for Internet key exchange, based on
2246	The TLS Protocol Version 1.0	Specification for a protocol that defines a secure channel between processes running on clients and servers.

Table 24–2: continued

25

Intranets

What do you call a network that uses the TCP/IP protocol suite, but that isn't the Internet? In the mid 1990s, the Internet became famous but the Internet Protocol did not. Up to about 1995, the standard term for a network that used IP was an internetwork or internet, with lowercase i. For the sake of clarity when speaking about internets and the Internet, apparently, the term **intranet** came into vogue.

Very simply, an intranet is a TCP/IP internetwork. It might (or might not) be connected to the Internet, and it probably uses web servers and clients for distributing information throughout the organization it serves. Intranets can do anything traditional LANs can do, and then some. One can argue that a special chapter on intranets is unnecessary in a book about TCP/IP internetworking, but there is a growing sense that TCP/IP intranetworking is a special area of corporate and business networking expertise.

The Intranet Story

Typical corporate networks include products from dozens, if not hundreds, of different hardware, software, and networking vendors. Likewise, there are invariably many megabytes of corporate data stored in legacy mainframe systems as well as on personal computer LANs and various other systems. Even where some degree of interconnection exists between and among personal computers, workstations, departmental computers, and corporate mainframes, without a common, nonproprietary set of protocols supported by all systems there can be no simple sharing of data across certain boundaries.

As the rest of this book made clear, TCP/IP represents a platform-independent set of protocols that can facilitate sharing of data across virtually all vendor and operating system boundaries.

Although network engineers previously were content to differentiate between the global Internet and corporate or campus internets simply by using an upper- or lowercase i as appropriate, by about 1995 a new term started gaining currency to describe a network within an organization that used TCP/IP: **intranet**.

The actual term can be found in very early RFCs, including RFC 791, which specifies the Internet Protocol in 1981. The earliest instance is in RFC 753, in a reference to an individual network. In RFC 791 the term is used while discussing fragmentation across local networks, and describes fragmentation that is invisible to external IP modules. In other words, whatever happens "intranet" is private. In these early uses, "intranet" seems to be used as an adjective, meaning "what happens inside a network," rather than as a noun.

However the term initially migrated from its technical meaning to its popular meaning, intranet has almost entirely replaced internet and internetwork as the word describing organizational TCP/IP networks spanning multiple LANs.

Intranet Features and Benefits

As long as major network software product vendors ignored or provided minimal support for TCP/IP, their customers were unable to take advantage of the platform-independent interoperability provided by TCP/IP. As the products started arriving on the market in the early to mid 1990s, however, TCP/IP intranets came to be viewed as an excellent way to break down the walls of proprietary solutions.

Interoperability

As more application, workgroup, and networking products are made TCP/IP-friendly, more end users can participate in corporate intranets without being required to adopt and invest in undesirable new software and hardware. The previous history of computing had been marked by a tendency for organizations to attempt to standardize their computing and networking platforms at the expense of users' desires. Although a mainframe may have been the correct solution for most computing needs in an organization, it was far from correct for all of them. As departmental computers, workstations, and personal computers became available, companies were hard pressed to impose some order on the products being used, if only to simplify interoperability between corporate computing resources and to keep support costs down. As corporations came to wire their computers into LANs, they fought the same battles over standardization of network operating systems as were fought over which PC operating system was to prevail.

Implementing intranets means that each and every user can use the platform they prefer, no matter what (as long as there is a usable TCP/IP stack available for it). This means that platforms from handheld PDAs to mainframes can all participate as peers on a TCP/IP network. If data is maintained in a format accessible through a TCP/IP application, for example as HTML documents, then accessing that information is no longer limited to users of certain systems, with certain software installed. And no longer is it necessary to evaluate, buy, and install a new piece of software every time a new use for the network is cooked up.

Scalability

Another benefit of intranets is that they scale to larger sizes much more easily than most personal computer LAN products. Not all such products handle network segmentation well, and some may have inherent or explicit limits on the number of systems that simultaneously can be connected, logged on, or actively using the network. IP networks, on the other hand, are designed to scale to much larger size: the earliest recognizable versions of the Internet were quite small, with only a handful of networks connected; the current version of the Internet connects hundreds of thousands of networks and millions of hosts.

Intranets can be used to manage many of the applications typically deployed on LANs, like sharing data, distributing file storage, e-mail, and software. More important is deployment for elimination of the difficulties posed by heterogenous computing environments. By publishing corporate data using a Web server, incompatibility between platforms is eliminated and the need to develop different interfaces for those platforms is also eliminated. This means that adding support for a new computer platform does not require development of yet another version of some in-house or proprietary product—it simply means that a TCP/IP Web client must be located for the platform in question.

Improved IP WAN Performance

Many network administrators find that IP routing across WANs is more robust and requires less bandwidth than typical PC network protocols like Novell NetWare or Banyan VINES. Routing is necessary to ensure that hosts can interoperate even without direct connections to the same networks.

Performance is an important feature for organizations implementing intranets to link remote offices with each other and with headquarters. An important part of that performance is the efficient use of telecommunications resources. Properly designed, a WAN linking dozens of remote locations does not require each location to maintain a direct link to every other location: organizations can maintain their own intranet backbones to carry all their network traffic.

Access to Legacy Systems

There are two dimensions to the issue of accessing legacy systems. The first is that corporate data may be stored in databases that were designed ten or twenty years before, using technology that is at least that old, and requiring significant programming effort to modify existing data reports and formats or to extract different types of information. The second is that providing access to legacy data for new platforms or new users is costly and time consuming. Intranets can help reduce the expense of maintaining, upgrading, and migrating such systems.

A continuing issue related to legacy systems arises every time two companies merge. TCP/IP intranets are much simpler to combine than networks using proprietary network protocols.

Defining an Intranet

The Internet is defined as a network of networks; an intranet can also be a network of networks, though the big difference is that the intranet is internal to a single organization, and the Internet connects many organizations and individuals. Intranets can be connected to the Internet, but usually are defined as organizational networks that run TCP/IP protocols.

Although companies that offer intranet products tend to focus their efforts on World Wide Web-based applications, any TCP/IP application can be used within an intranet. This means that main-frame terminals can be replaced with terminal emulation services; FTP servers or NFS services can supplement existing network file servers. Internet-compatible e-mail that uses SMTP, network news that uses NNTP, and many other services are available for a broad range of platforms.

However, the focus for many vendors remains Web-based tools. In particular, Web servers and tools that can be used to create links between Web servers and legacy systems are in high demand, as are development tools that can be used to create simple network applications that can be used from any compatible Web browser program.

Intranet Deployment

Organizations interested in deploying intranets tend to develop them gradually, often developing them around core applications. If these are standard applications, like e-mail, that have already been implemented using proprietary protocols, the intranet may be replacing an outdated application or it may be implementing an improved or value-added version. Other organizations take advantage of updates to existing systems to replace entire propri-etary networks; still others use other excuses, like mergers or divestitures, to convert to TCP/IP networking.

Workgroup applications as well as corporate bulletin boards are popular intranet applications. These may use standard TCP/IP applications, particularly Web servers and clients, or they may use special workgroup servers along with standard Web browsers or other types of client software.

Intranet software vendors promote their products as ideal tools for sharing corporate computing resources, and provide a wide range of case studies in support of intranets. Some applications cited include managing sales contacts, providing human resources information services, and MIS support functions.

Intranet Design

Common wisdom says that intranet design includes both the creation of a TCP/IP network architecture, as well as the creation of the organization's specific TCP/IP network applications.

Intranet designers also must often contend with blending existing network technologies and protocols into the new intranet. The result is that intranet designers need to be conversant not only in TCP/IP but in other network protocols, applications, and protocol architectures.

Even though IP provides a more efficient internetworking solution, many organizations still want to retain their commercial networks based on IPX or other network layer protocols. With careful use of protocol gateways, it is possible to use TCP/IP applications on local area networks that do not support IP. This may be a preferred solution for intranets (or portions of intranets) where the mission critical application resides on a proprietary LAN server, but where the intranet application is a vital secondary application.

Intranet Security

Organizations approach intranet security differently, depending on a number of variables. For example, some intend to deploy TCP/IP for their internal networks only, with no thought of connecting to the global Internet in any way. Others plan to use some form of security, whether it be a firewall gateway, proxy servers, protocol gateway, or some combination to protect internal data and systems.

As TCP/IP software has become increasingly easy to install and configure, one security problem that arises often is the use of dial-in services on personal computers. For example, Windows 95 users can configure their systems to allow dial-in access so the system can be accessed when the user is off-site. This presents a major security problem since this connection can allow the remote user the same access and privileges that are allowed when the user is logged on to the intranet locally. Intranet administrators should be aware of this issue, and should educate users in proper use of the network. More important, intranet designers should provide alternate, and secure, remote network access facilities to their users.

Potential security problems for intranets are otherwise quite similar to those of any other organization system or network.

Chapter Summary

In this chapter, we discussed what an intranet is, and how it is used. In particular, we looked at the benefits intranets offer to organizations including improved interoperability, scalability, IP WAN performance, and access to legacy systems. We also looked at how an intranet can be differentiated and defined in terms of applications and scope. Finally, we introduced issues related to the deployment, design, and security of intranets.

Inasmuch as intranets are simply another type of TCP/IP network, most of the documents relevant to the Internet are also relevant to intranets—thus, no need for a special reading list on intranets.

26

Extranets

If the term intranet refers to an IP network that links nodes only within the borders of an organization, what do you call it when you create a network that links nodes inside and outside the organization? Simply saying that the intranet has now been linked to the Internet may be accurate, but lacks zip. If intranets are IP networks on the inside, well then, when you open up the intranet you've got an **extranet**. Is the term nothing more than marketing gibberish? In some ways, the functions and features associated with extranets are largely equivalent to the functions and features implied by any widespread, ubiquitous, and interoperable network.

In common parlance, extranets are what happen when organizations offer access to some or all of their network resources to users not physically connected to the organizational network and not physically located on organizational turf. In this chapter, we'll see what technologies are required to set up an extranet and what kind of applications can be supported with an extranet.

Extranets, Defined

In 1996, when the term extranet first started creeping into the general consciousness, anything that used the Internet as a conduit for organizational activities might be identified as an example of an extranet. One common definition of extranet identified this as what you get when you built a network that linked geographically distributed intranets—expecially when those intranets were linked through VPN connections across the Internet. In these cases, the term extranet was used to mean an internetwork (network of networks, remember?) that crossed organizational boundaries. Thus, building an extranet was just a matter of setting up VPN links between the different branch offices of a large organization. This seemed somewhat interesting but not an entirely radical concept.

Far more exciting was the image of the extranet as a means of directly sharing resources across organizational borders. Prior to the extranet, all resource sharing across organizational borders is done through intermediaries. A customer in a bookstore who wants to know whether or not a volume is in stock must ask a bookstore clerk, who checks the store's inventory through a terminal. A receiving clerk who wants to know whether a particular package has been shipped by an overnight delivery service would have to call a toll-free number. A clerk employed at the delivery service would solicit package information, enter it into a mainframe system, and read back the result of the query to the receiving clerk. A purchasing agent who wants to know the status of an order from a supplier must contact a sales representative at that supplier, who must check the vendor's database for the purchasing agent.

In each of these cases, the customer must wait until someone is available to query the system for them. This is the way customer service was performed hundreds of years ago—you didn't let customers into the back of the store to rummage around for themselves, and you didn't let them check your books. In any case, none of these queries can be answered easily without a computer. With or without computers, each query uses up resources—the time and effort of the bookstore clerk, delivery customer service agent, or sales representative—that could be used more productively (we hope).

The more exciting extranet vision removes the intermediary from the picture. Federal Express at some point decided to put a web front-end on its package tracking system, and it was rolled out as early as 1994. Now, customers don't have to make a telephone call, wait on hold, and then tell someone else some data which is then entered into the mainframe. They only need to enter their package shipping date and tracking number into a simple web interface, and they get the status of the package.

The Federal Express package tracking service is often cited as one of the earliest extranet applications. It opens up a network resource—the FedEx package tracking system—to individuals and organizations outside FedEx. You don't need a pass phrase, and you don't need to set up an account with them to do package tracking. You don't need any special software, just a web browser and Internet access. And if you wanted to build your own application that checked on the status of important packages for your company, using the FedEx web site, you could automate the queries and accept as input the results of each request. Those inputs could be formatted as a special report, funneled into e-mails to the shipping department, or even dumped into a voice-mail message or turned into an urgent alphanumeric pager message.

Most customer service requests are relatively straightforward: you enter some kind of identification (whether for an account or an item or a book) and you get back information and more options. Most customers could actually manage to enter the data themselves, and if they can do that, the organization being queried saves itself the cost of answering that query with a person.

Extranet applications share several features:

♦ **Interoperability.** Extranet applications can be accessed through open standards rather than through proprietary standards. The objective is to make the resources available to anyone who wants access and has authorization, so most allow access through any web client.

♦ **Distributed object architectures.** Extranet application hosts must make information available from within an organization through a web interface. This means that the service interface developers need to be able to refer to internal resources as objects that are distributed within (or sometimes outside) the organization.

♦ **Security.** Extranets expose some or all of an organization's network resources. Measures must be taken to protect these resources, including encryption to protect sensitive material being transmitted over the Internet (or any other open network), authentication of users to protect against unauthorized access to resources and services, and data integrity to prevent counterfeiting and malicious attacks.

It should be clear by now that the term extranet is simply a label for a special type of network application. You do not need to use the TCP/IP protocol suite to implement an extranet—any open and widely used internetworking protocol suite will do. Which means that extranets by default will use TCP/IP protocols, as TCP/IP is the only suite that fills the bill.

Special care must be taken to provide interoperability at a much higher level than usual for TCP/IP networking. Extranet users are not just using a web server to retrieve information, they are actually using an Internet-based front-end to applications that are running behind firewalls in one or more different organizations. Consider the example of the package-tracking application offered by Federal Express. If FedEx were to modify their output data formats, any application written by a client organization that used those data formats would have to be revised as well.

Distributed object architectures, like those offered by the Common Object Request Broker Architecture (CORBA) or Microsoft's Distributed Common Object Model (DCOM), allow programmers to build data constructs that can be referred to by virtually any kind of program running on any kind of system.

Ultimately, extranets have more to do with networked application development than with TCP/IP networking. For more information about extranets and how they are structured, consider *Extranet Design and Implementation* (SYBEX 1997).

Chapter Summary

In this chapter, we introduced the concept of the extranet. Extranets are primarily sophisticated networked applications that interoperate, securely, across open networks. Although extranets depend on the TCP/IP protocol suite and related protocols for their ability to interoperate, extranets merely use these protocols to accomplish their application objectives.

Inasmuch as extranets are simply another type of TCP/IP network, most of the documents relevant to the Internet are also relevant to extranets—thus, no need for a special reading list on extranets.

Part Five

Appendices

A

Internet History and Organizations

The Internet is far from a monolithic entity, but rather an agglomeration of people, machines, and organizations, often working together for seamless and global connectivity. What ties it all together are members of the mostly voluntary organizations who cooperate, using time-tested procedures, to develop new protocols and adapt existing protocols to new uses.

Although the focus of Internet implementation is rapidly moving from the research community to the commercial arena, the focus of Internet technology remains with the research community—at least for the moment. The Internet has proven remarkably resilient and adaptable during its first generation. Drastic changes in organization over the next few years are just as unlikely as no change. Internet organizations tend to evolve to meet new needs, eliminating the wasteful and adding complexity only as needed.

Two notable changes occuring in the last days of the 20th century include the move to support for IPv6 (see Chapter 14) and changes in the way Internet domain names, IP addresses, and Internet standards are assigned and administered. The Internet Assigned Number Authority (IANA) is being replaced by the Internet Corporation for Assigned Names and Numbers (ICANN), as discussed later in this appendix.

A Brief History of the Internet

As previously mentioned, the rapid success of the Internet is closely related with the widespread use of inexpensive personal computers and workstations connected across Ethernet LANs. Funding for the original research into packet switching data communications between computers, back in the late 1960s, came from the Department of Defense's Advanced Research Projects Agency (ARPA). The original intent was to develop methods of reliably transmitting data across unreliable links using *packet switching*, meaning that each packet is sent via the best available route, independent of any other packet in the data stream.

Although the first few years saw much development of the intellectual underpinnings of the Internet, not the least of which was a sort of Internet culture of cooperation and excellence, connectivity was limited largely to systems being used by the research and defense communities. ARPANET was the result. Originally a sort of laboratory for internetwork experimentation, in 1983 the military decided ARPANET had passed beyond the stage of experimentation, and split it in two. One part, MILNET, was a functional internetwork to be used for military purposes; the other part, ARPANET, continued to be used for research and development.

By the mid-1980s, the National Science Foundation (NSF) was looking for a way to distribute access to its five national supercomputing centers. Using the protocols being developed for ARPANET, NSF connected the five centers to each other to form the NSFNET backbone. Regional networks were formed in the late

1980s to provide access to this backbone, to which universities and research organizations attached their networks.

By the late 1980s, the people who were connected to one of these wide-ranging internetworks might refer to the ARPANET, DARPANET, NSFNET, or Internet, as the network they were on. By the early 1990s ARPANET had disappeared as a separate entity and the Internet appeared, linking many of the different internetworks that had been springing up. A common link was that most of these internetworks were largely government funded. Government funding meant that traffic over the networks had to meet certain *acceptable use policies.* For the most part this meant that organizations could use the Internet for promotion of research and education but not for promotion of commerce. This meant no advertising and no promotion of commercial products, and it resulted in further ingraining the Internet culture of impartiality and disclaimers.

As government agencies moved out of the internetworking business in the 1990s, businesses moved in to provide Internet service to businesses and individuals. As more and more Internet traffic was routed away from the restricted networks onto commercial networks, businesses and individuals increasingly came to see the Internet as a vehicle for commerce. More important, the success of the World Wide Web as an entry point for unsophisticated users, along with the development of protocols supporting secure commercial transactions over World Wide Web links, is accelerating the Internet's transition from an educational and research resource to a commercial medium.

Internet Organizations

No single, central, authoritative organization oversees all Internet activities and connections. Various functions are performed by different types of organizations. If you want to get connected to the Internet, you contact a local or national Internet service provider. These companies sell connectivity to the Internet, very similar to the way telephone companies sell access to the international telephone network.

However, the only really global organization is the Internet Society, or ISOC. ISOC is a nonprofit professional society, but some of its most important functions relate to the development of Internet standards and the allocation and assignment of Internet resources. The standards, for the most part, are reflected in implementations of TCP/IP and can be found in RFCs, or *Requests for Comments*. The resources allocated and assigned are mostly informational and include things like IP addresses and host names, well-known ports, and codes used by the protocols.

ISOC bodies that handle these tasks include:

- *IAB:* The Internet Architecture Board (formerly the Internet Activities Board) is responsible for overseeing all technical development and standards for the Internet. This is an executive committee that oversees many other Internet-related groups, including those listed next.
- *ICANN:* The Internet Corporation for Assigned Names and Numbers manages the assignment of numbers for protocol-related codes as well as administering domain registry services for the Internet. ICANN takes over this task from the Internet Assigned Number Authority (IANA), which also used to manage the lists of well-known ports, the values assigned to different protocols for use in header protocol fields, and RFC numbers, among other numbers.
- *IETF:* The Internet Engineering Task Force produces new Internet standards and revises existing ones to meet current and expected needs. The IETF is divided into work groups, each of which addresses specific needs. For example, an IP Next Generation work group is working on producing the standards for the next version of IP. The IETF is an open organization, and anyone who wants to participate is considered a member.
- *IESG:* The Internet Engineering Steering Group provides supervision and oversight to IETF activities, as well as offering guidance to IETF working group agendas.

B

References and Selected Bibliography

Information about the Internet and TCP/IP is available both in printed form and online. The bookstores are full of texts introducing the various Internet applications and resources, although there are fewer resources explaining the protocols and applications in depth. Likewise, many sources of information are on the Internet itself, but some are unedited and some are unreliable. The most important online resources are current RFCs and IETF drafts, which detail the current and future Internet standards. This appendix refers the interested reader to books for further study of TCP/IP and related topics. Also included are instructions for locating and retrieving IETF documents.

Annotated Bibliography

Cheswick, William R. and Steven M. Bellovin. *Firewalls and Internet Security.* Addison-Wesley Publishing Company, 1994).

An introduction to Internet security issues by two firewall pioneers. Despite a high-tech content, this volume is also accessible to nontechnical readers. A revision is expected in the year 2000.

Comer, Douglas E. *Internetworking with TCP/IP,* vol. 1. Prentice-Hall, 1995.

The seminal work on TCP/IP internetworking, this volume rigorously introduces TCP/IP concepts. This is the third edition, updated with information on IPv6 and other more current issues.

Cronin, Mary J. *Doing Business on the Internet.* Van Nostrand Reinhold, 1994.

An introduction to business uses of the Internet.

Huitema, Christian. *IPv6 The New Internet Protocol.* PTR Prentice-Hall, 1996.

An account of IPv6 by one of its primary architects: what it is and what it will become, how it came to be that way, and what can be expected from it in the future.

Hunt, Craig. *TCP/IP Network Administration.* O'Reilly & Associates, 1998.

An introduction to TCP/IP internetwork Unix node and server administration. Particularly useful for Unix novices.

Kaufman, Charlie, Radia Perlman, and Mike Speciner. *Network Security.* PTR Prentice-Hall, 1995.

A comprehensive and technical introduction to network security issues and solutions, including public and private key encryption, firewalls, and more.

Krol, Ed. *The Whole Internet User's Guide*. O'Reilly and Associates, 1994.

The original "guide to the Internet," it offers a basic introduction to using Internet applications and locating Internet resources.

Liu, Cricket, Jerry Peek, Russ Jones, Bryan Buus, and Adrian Nye. *Managing Internet Information Services*. O'Reilly & Associates, 1994.

A guide for network managers who must publish information over the Internet using Gopher, the World Wide Web, an anonymous FTP, or any type of e-mail responders.

Loshin, Pete. *Extranet Design and Implementation*. SYBEX, 1997.

A complete discussion of extranet theory, architecture, and implementation.

Loshin, Pete. *IPv6 Clearly Explained*. Morgan Kaufmann, 1999.

A readable yet complete introduction to the next generation of the Internet Protocol suitable both for novices and experienced network professionals.

Loshin, Pete. *Personal Encryption Clearly Explained*. Morgan Kaufmann, 1998.

A comprehensive introduction to the use of authentication and encryption over the Internet and other networks.

Miller, Mark A. *Troubleshooting TCP/IP*. M&T Books, 1996.

A solid overview of the TCP/IP protocols, along with helpful information about troubleshooting and analyzing TCP/IP network problems. The second edition includes information on IPv6 as well as IP over ATM and Frame Relay. Included is a CD-ROM containing RFCs, which makes an excellent research resource for tracking down original specifications for Internet standards.

Musciano, Chuck *et al. HTML Definitive Guide.* O'Reilly & Associates, 1998.

A comprehensive guide to creating web documents using the Hypertext Markup Language (HTML).

Quarterman, John S. and Smoot Carl-Mitchell. *The Internet Connection.* Addison-Wesley Publishing Company, 1994.

Useful information for managers who must connect their organization to the Internet, including references to procedures and organizations.

Rose, Marshall T. *The Internet Message.* PTR Prentice-Hall, 1993.

A complete description of the theory and practice of the use and implementation of TCP/IP and Internet electronic mail.

Rose, Marshall T. *The Simple Book.* PTR Prentice-Hall, 1994.

A detailed introduction to the concepts and theories behind the Simple Network Management Protocol (SNMP).

Stevens, W. Richard. *TCP/IP Illustrated,* vol. 1. Addison-Wesley Publishing Company, 1994.

An indispensable aid to internetwork implementers, this book explains TCP/IP applications and protocols through the use of specific examples.

Online Resources

The Internet itself offers a vast repository of resources pertaining to the Internet and the TCP/IP protocols. However, many of these resources are subject to rapid and unexpected change, so only a handful of web resources are cited here.

The Internet Engineering Task Force publishes current working documents, RFCs, and pointers to other relevant entities, as well as information about its activities online. It can be reached at:

http://www.ietf.org

The Internet Society web site offers information about ISOC activities as well as many other relevant links:

http://www.isoc.org

Finally, you can get information about Internet standards as well as errata about this book, pointers to other good books about TCP/IP and related topics, and more at the author's web site:

http://www.internet-standard.com

Glossary and Abbreviations

- **10Base2.** One part of the IEEE 802 specification using coaxial cable, also called *thin wire Ethernet*. The *10* indicates 10 Mbps transmission, *base* indicates that it is a baseband medium, and the 2 indicates that segments can be (almost) 200 meters in length.

- **10Base5.** One part of the IEEE 802 specification using thicker coaxial cable, also called *thick wire Ethernet*. The *10* indicates 10 Mbps transmission, *base* indicates that it is a baseband medium, and the 5 indicates that segments can be up to 500 meters in length.

- **10BaseT.** One part of the IEEE 802 specification using twisted pair wires, also called *twisted pair Ethernet*. The *10* indicates 10 Mbps transmission, *base* indicates that it is a baseband medium, and the T indicates twisted pair wiring.

- **ACK.** The name given to network traffic that acts as an acknowledgment, or the field in a network transmission unit that indicates it is an acknowledgment.

- **acknowledgment.** A response from a host indicating that a previous transmission has been received. See also **ACK**.

- **address.** A number or group of numbers that uniquely identifies a network node within its own network (or internetwork).

- **address resolution.** The process of relating a logical address (like an IP address) to a physical address (like the MAC address of a network interface).

- **Address Resolution Protocol.** See **ARP**.

- **agent.** A system that acts on behalf of another system or individual.

- **anonymous FTP.** An instance of the File Transfer Protocol application that permits individuals who do not have explicit authorization to perform file transfers with a host anonymously by using a generic user ID to log in and (usually) their e-mail address as a password.

- **API.** Application Programming Interface; a standardized set of routines that make system functions available to programmers.

- **application.** A program that provides functionality to end users or systems.

- **application layer.** The layer in network conceptual models where interaction between the end user and the application takes place.

- **architecture.** The structure of a system, a description of which can be used to recreate the system; for example, the way the TCP/IP protocols interact can be considered an internetwork architecture; a physical network's architecture is defined by the systems and components that make it up (routers, servers, cabling, and attached hosts).

- **ARP.** Address Resolution Protocol; the protocol used in TCP/IP networks to relate IP addresses with physical network addresses of network interfaces.

- **ASCII.** American Standard Code for Information Interchange; generally refers to standard 7-bit text with a limited number of nontext characters.

- **asynchronous.** A method of transmitting data that does not require synchronization between hosts; instead, data must be "framed" with extra bits to identify the beginning and end of each byte sent.

- **backbone.** Usually a high-speed, high-performance network that links together other networks into an internetwork.

- **bandwidth.** The volume of data that a communications link is capable of carrying, usually measured in bits; typical telephone links provide up to 28.8 Kbps (thousand bits per second), typical Ethernet links provide up to 10 Mbps (megabits per second); see also **latency**.

- **baseband.** A method of transmitting data on a network that uses the entire bandwidth of the network for any individual transmission; Ethernet is a baseband standard, with only one transmission possible at any instant.

- **BGP.** Border Gateway Protocol; a routing protocol.

- **BOOTP.** Boot Protocol; a protocol used for booting systems remotely to the network.

- **Border Gateway Protocol.** See **BGP**.

- **bridge.** A device that connects two networks, using the same protocol (e.g., two Ethernet networks), receiving network transmissions on one network, processing them, and recreating the transmissions on the other network.

- **broadband.** A method of transmitting data on a network that subdivides the available bandwidth and allows multiple simultaneous transmissions between different hosts.

- **broadcast.** The sending of a single message intended for all connected nodes on a network, addressed to a special address intended for such transmissions.

- **bus.** A type of network layout that uses a single cable to which all networked nodes attach.

- **Carrier Sense Multiple Access/Collision Detection.** See **CSMA/CD**.

- **cache.** An area of computer memory allocated as a temporary storage space for incoming data.

- **CIDR.** Classless InterDomain Routing; a method that assigns network addresses and modifies routing tables to avoid routing tables getting too large while using IP network addresses efficiently.

- **circuit.** A communications link between two systems.

- **Classless Interdomain Routing.** See **CIDR**.

- **client.** A system or computer that requests network services from some other system or computer (called a server).

- **collision.** The result when two systems on a baseband network attempt to use the network medium at the same time.

- **Compressed SLIP.** See **CSLIP**.

- **connection.** The link between two entities; connections can occur between networked hosts, between programs running on networked hosts, and between programs running on the same host (between entities at different network layers).

- **connectionless.** A type of network service that does not depend on connections between hosts, but rather exchanges requests and replies between connected hosts (as with UDP).

- **CRC.** Cyclic Redundancy Check; a technique used to calculate the contents of a network transmission unit, add the resulting value to the unit, and allow the receiving system to verify that the contents of the network transmission have arrived uncorrupted.

- **CSLIP.** Compressed SLIP; see also **SLIP**.

- **CSMA/CD.** Carrier Sense Multiple Access/Collision Detection; CSMA provides a means for all hosts on a baseband network to be able to access the network medium in turn; CD is a method each host uses to determine when another host is attempting to use the network.

- **Cyclic Redundancy Check.** See **CRC**.

- **daemon.** A program running on a system providing network services; the program "listens" to the network for requests to use that service.

- **Data Encryption Standard.** See **DES**.

- **data link layer.** The layer in network models that handles communication between physical hosts.

- **datagram.** A network transmission unit used with connectionless services; see also **IP datagram**, **UDP**.

- **default router.** A router to which a network node is configured to send TCP/IP traffic to when it doesn't know where else to send it.

- **DES.** Data Encryption Standard; approved by the United States National Bureau of Standards for encrypting data.

- **destination.** In a network, the host or system for which network traffic is finally intended by the originating system.

- **DHCP.** Dynamic Host Configuration Protocol; designed to allow networked hosts to access configuration information across the network, rather than having to be configured by hand directly.

- **DNS.** Domain Name System; a distributed database system that allows TCP/IP applications to resolve a host name into a correct IP address.

- **domain.** An organizational unit with administrative responsibility for naming networks or hosts.

- **domain name.** A name assigned to a domain.

- **Domain Name System.** See **DNS**.

- **dotted decimal notation.** A means of representing IP addresses using decimal numbers (instead of binary or hexadecimal), with periods (.) separating each eight-bit portion of the address.

- **Dynamic Host Configuration Protocol.** See **DHCP**.

- **e-mail.** Electronic mail; an application that allows individuals to exchange messages across a network.

- **EBCDIC.** Extended Binary Coded Decimal Interchange Code; describes the eight-bit character set used in IBM mainframe computers.

- **EGP.** Exterior Gateway Protocol; a routing protocol that was once used on the Internet.

- **emulation.** The process of imitating a device or service; for example, Telnet client implementations allow the hosts running them to emulate terminals.

- **encapsulation.** The process of transmitting network traffic that uses one network protocol by enclosing (encapsulating) it in another network protocol.

- **ephemeral port.** A port chosen by a host to be the destination for transport layer network traffic, intended for use only during the duration of the communication and then discarded (see also **port, well-known port**).

- **Ethernet.** A baseband network medium.

- **Ethernet address.** A unique 6-byte (48-bit) address assigned and hard-coded into each Ethernet network interface card.

- **Exterior Gateway Protocol.** See **EGP**.

- **FDDI.** Fiber Distributed Data Interface; a standard for network transmission over a fiber optic medium.

- **file server.** Usually a computer attached to a network with the sole purpose of providing network access to shared files.

- **File Transfer Protocol.** See **FTP**.

- **forwarding.** The process of accepting network traffic on behalf of some network entity and retransmitting it as an intermediate step in the delivery of the traffic.

- **FQDN.** Fully Qualified Domain Name; the complete host name and domain name of a network host.

- **fragmentation.** The process of breaking network transmission units into smaller units for more efficient transmission by another protocol.

- **frame.** A network transmission unit at the data link layer, usually refers to the unit sent out onto a physical network (e.g., Ethernet frame).

- **FTP.** File Transfer Protocol; defined in the TCP/IP suite for transferring files from one host to another.

- **Fully Qualified Domain Name.** See **FQDN**.

- **gateway.** A multihomed host used to route network traffic from one network to another; also used to pass network traffic from one protocol to another (see also **router**).

- **gigabit.** 1 billion bits.

- **gigabyte.** 1 billion bytes.

- **Gopher.** A character-based information publishing protocol using menus to access text files.

- **handshake.** The process of negotiating a connection between two hosts, particularly used with TCP.

- **hop.** A unit of distance used when comparing internetwork routes; usually a single hop is the distance from one router to another, crossing a single network.

- **hop count.** The number of hops between two hosts, based on the number of different routers needed to traverse the distance between the two hosts.

- **host name resolution.** The process of determining a network address when presented with a network host name and domain name, usually by consulting the Domain Name System.

- **HTML.** Hypertext Markup Language; a specification for creating World Wide Web documents by adding tags to plain text files; based on the Standard Generalized Markup Language (SGML), tags indicate different functional portions of the resulting document.

- **HTTP.** Hypertext Transfer Protocol; a specification used for World Wide Wide services to provide a simple, seamless, and graphical method of publishing and accessing data on an inter-network.

- **HTTPD.** Hypertext Transfer Protocol daemon; a name given to the program that acts as a World Wide Web server.

- **Hypertext Markup Language.** See **HTML**.

- **Hypertext Transfer Protocol.** See **HTTP**.

- **ICMP.** Internet Control Message Protocol; used to exchange routing and reachability information between hosts and routers on the same local network.

- **IEEE.** Institute of Electrical and Electronics Engineers; a professional standards body.

- **IEEE 802 standards.** A body of specifications pertaining to Ethernet networks, based on work begun in February 1980.

- **IESG.** Internet Engineering Steering Group; a steering committee of the Internet Engineering Task Force (IETF).

- **IETF.** Internet Engineering Task Force; a standards-oriented group that works on specifying and developing Internet standards.

- **IGMP.** Internet Group Management Protocol; a routing protocol.

- **Internet.** The name generally given to the worldwide network of networks that uses TCP/IP protocols.

- **internet.** A network of networks; internets can be differentiated from the Internet by their lack of connectivity with the global Internet; internets do not necessarily have to use TCP/IP protocols, either; shortened form of *internetwork*.

- **Internet Control Message Protocol.** See **ICMP**.

- **Internet Engineering Steering Group.** See **IESG**.

- **Internet Engineering Task Force.** See **IETF**.

- **Internet Group Management Protocol.** See **IGMP**.

- **Internet Protocol.** See **IP**.

- **internetwork.** See **internet**, **intranet**, and **Internet**.

- **intranet.** A term for an organizational TCP/IP internetwork introduced around 1995 (possibly by marketing specialists) to differentiate closed, internal networks using TCP/IP from the global Internet.

- **IP.** Internet Protocol; the dominant network layer protocol used with the TCP/IP protocol suite.

- **IP address.** Internet Protocol address; a 32-bit network address that uniquely locates a host or network within its internetwork.

- **IP datagram.** Internet Protocol datagram; the network transmission unit used by IP.

- **IPX.** Internetwork Packet eXchange; an alternate network layer protocol used by Novell NetWare and other commercial products.

- **ISDN.** Integrated Services Digital Network; a type of telephone service that offers high-speed digital service for any digital device connected to the telecommunications network.

- **Kerberos.** A method for authenticating users to hosts securely, developed at MIT and widely implemented.

- **LAN.** Local area network; usually refers to a network connecting users in relatively close physical proximity (e.g., the same floor of a building) to a single physical network.

- **latency.** The delay between the time that data is sent from its origin and received at its destination; latency and bandwidth determine the limitations on a network connection: the bandwidth determines how much data can be transmitted in a period of time, and the latency determines how responsive the link will be; see also **bandwidth**.

- **learning bridge.** A device that connects two networks using the same protocol (e.g., two Ethernet networks), receiving network transmissions on one network, processing them, and recreating the transmissions on the other network; the learning bridge differs from ordinary bridges because it "learns" which hosts are on which network and repeats only traffic intended to cross that bridge; the ordinary bridge repeats all traffic whether it needs to be transmitted to both networks or not.

- **link.** A connection between two network entities.

- **LLC.** Logical Link Control; part of the protocol defined by the IEEE 802 standards governing data exchange between two network nodes.

- **local area network.** See **LAN**.

- **MAC.** Media Access Control; part of the physical layer of a network that identifies the actual physical link between two nodes.

- **Mail Exchange.** See **MX**.

- **mail exchanger.** A system that acts as a gateway for Internet electronic mail addressed to a local network or internetwork.

- **MAN.** Metropolitan Area Network; usually refers to a network that links network users within a physical area up to the size of a metropolitan area.

- **Management Information Base.** See **MIB**.

- **Maximum Transmission Unit.** See **MTU**.

- **MBONE.** Multicast Backbone; a special network backbone used to transmit multicasts.

- **Media Access Control.** See **MAC**.

- **Message Transfer Agent.** See **MTA**.

- **Metropolitan Area Network.** See **MAN**.

- **MIB.** Management Information Base; a database used by the Simple Network Management Protocol to check network statistics and configurations.

- **MIME.** Multipurpose Internet Mail Extensions; a specification for the transfer of nontext files with regular Internet e-mail.

- **MTA.** Message Transfer Agent; a generic term for a program that transfers and forwards electronic mail between hosts and networks.

- **MTU.** Maximum Transmission Unit; the largest size network transmission unit possible between a source and a destination, depends on the network media used by both hosts as well as the topology and architecture of the intervening internetworks and devices.

- **multicast.** A transmission of network traffic intended for multiple hosts, but not all connected hosts, within a network or internetwork.

- **multihomed host.** A host with network interfaces on more than one network; such a host will have an IP address for each network interface.

- **multiplex.** To transmit more than one signal over the same circuit. Multiplexing can also be applied to layered data, that is, to indicate data that is encapsulated within other types of network layer protocols.

- **Multipurpose Internet Mail Extensions.** See **MIME**.

- **MX.** Mail Exchange; a Domain Name Service record type that associates an electronic mail address with a host accepting e-mail for that address (and with a different domain than the e-mail address).

- **name resolution.** See **host name resolution**.

- **National Science Foundation.** See **NSF**.

- **NetBIOS.** Network Basic Input/Output Operating System; a network file sharing application defined for use with PC-DOS personal computers, usually implemented under TCP/IP at the application layer.

- **NetWare.** A commercial network operating system sold by Novell Inc. that offers network resource services using the IPX network protocol.

- **network.** A system of interconnected systems; the system defined by interconnection to the same medium of two or more computers, which enables the connected computers to communicate with each other.

- **network address.** A unique identifier of an entity on a network, usually represented as a number or series of numbers.

- **network interface.** The hardware device through which a computer or networked device is connected to the network.

- **Network File System.** See **NFS**.

- **Network Information Center.** See **NIC**.

- **Network Information Service.** See **NIS**.

- **network layer.** The layer in the OSI or TCP/IP network conceptual model at which data is transferred between hosts across networks; also referred to as the *internet layer*.

- **Network News Transfer Protocol.** See **NNTP**.

- **Network Time Protocol.** See **NTP**.

- **Network Virtual Terminal.** See **NVT**.

- **network traffic.** Data transmitted on a communications medium for the purpose of sending information from one networked system to another.

- **NFS.** Network File System; a network resource sharing protocol developed by Sun MicroSystems, Inc. for sharing file systems between networked workstations; currently widely implemented on many different hosts using different operating systems.

- **NIC.** Network Information Center; the sum of resources, usually aggregated into a single area that is allocated by an organization for the purpose of providing network information to users and others with a need for it; also, Network Interface Card, a board used to connect a computer to a network.

- **NIS.** Network Information Service; a distributed database application developed by Sun MicroSystems, Inc. to provide network address and name resolution; though similar in function to DNS, it does not provide the same level of function, nor is it is universally implemented as DNS.

- **NNTP.** Network News Transfer Protocol; a TCP/IP application protocol designed to allow the exchange of network news between news servers (for the propagation of the news) and clients (for the distribution of news to end users).

- **node.** A system or device connected to a network.

- **NSF.** National Science Foundation; a primary organization involved in the early development and funding of NSFNET, which ultimately became the Internet.

- **NTP.** Network Time Protocol; a TCP/IP network application protocol that defines the exchange of requests and replies to requests for the correct time.

- **NVT.** Network Virtual Terminal; a logical construct of a generic terminal used to simplify exchange of keystrokes and data by both the client and the server implementations of several TCP/IP network applications (may also refer to NetWare Virtual Terminal, a Novell program).

- **octet.** A single eight-bit unit of data; refers to the presence of eight bits; often used to refer to parts of an IP network address; also commonly used to refer to network data of other types.

- **Open Shortest Path First.** See **OSPF**.

- **OSPF.** Open Shortest Path First; a routing protocol used inside autonomous systems.

- **packet.** A unit of network transmission; more properly, the unit of data transmitted across a packet switched network.

- **Ping.** Packet internet groper; a network application that uses ICMP requests to verify reachability of another host on the internetwork.

- **Point-to-Point Protocol.** See **PPP**.

- **port.** A convention used by network applications to direct responses to network requests to multiple destinations on the same computer; ports are specified as destinations for network transmissions at the transport layer; some applications use "well-known ports" to listen to the network for requests, other connections may use "ephemeral ports" that are assigned by each individual host to be used for the duration of the exchange and then discarded.

- **PPP.** Point-to-Point Protocol; specifies the establishment of a link between a remote host (usually over a telephone line) and another host acting as a gateway to a remote network.

- **PROFS.** Professional Office System; an integrated software product from IBM for use with the VM mainframe operating system and used largely for its e-mail services.

- **protocol.** A set of rules that specify the behavior of interacting systems, particularly as characterized by the rules used to exchange information.

- **proxy ARP.** The use of a designated system to respond to ARP requests on behalf of other systems that are not physically on the same cable but may appear to be on the same network segment (they are separated by a router).

- **r-login.** Remote login; a remote utility used to do remote terminal sessions.

- **r-shell.** Remote shell; a remote utility that presents the user with a shell session on the remote host.

- **r-utility.** Remote utility; one of several applications originally implemented for use between Unix workstations, currently widely implemented.

- **RARP.** Reverse Address Resolution Protocol; a protocol designed for the data link layer that allows hosts to associate a network hardware address with an IP address.

- **rcp.** Remote copy (from the Unix cp command); a remote utility used to copy files between two hosts.

- **Remote Procedure Call.** See **RPC**.

- **repeater.** A network hardware device that connects two segments of a physical network and extends the size of the resulting network segment; repeaters simply repeat on one connected segment the signals they receive on the other side (they do not process the signals).

- **Request for Comments.** See **RFC**.

- **resolver.** A network name resolver; a mechanism or process to correlate a network host name into an appropriate network address in support of network applications.

- **resource.** Any device, accessory, or process that can be used in support of network functions.

- **Reverse Address Resolution Protocol.** See **RARP**.

- **rexec.** Remote execute; a remote utility whose function is to execute a single command on a remote host.

- **RFC.** Request For Comments; the official designation of Internet standards documents.

- **RIP.** Routing Information Protocol; a routing protocol used inside autonomous systems.

- **roundtrip time.** See **RTT**.

- **router.** A multihomed host that forwards network traffic from one connected network to another (see also **gateway**).

- **Routing Information Protocol.** See **RIP**.

- **routing table.** A list maintained by hosts and routers connected to an internetwork that includes the most recent information on proper routes for different destinations.

- **RPC.** Remote Procedure Call; a method of programming network applications that implements commands from the client as procedures called locally on the server.

- **RTT.** Roundtrip time; a variable computed during TCP sessions that indicates the total time required to send a TCP segment to the remote host and receive a reply to that segment.

- **segment.** The network transmission unit used by TCP; also may refer to a single LAN that connects to an organizational internetwork.

- **Serial Line Internet Protocol.** See **SLIP.**

- **server.** A system that receives requests for a network service from a system running a client program; the system may be dedicated only to providing a network service or services; the program running on a system that offers a network service.

- **Simple Mail Transfer Protocol.** See **SMTP.**

- **Simple Network Management Protocol.** See **SNMP.**

- **SLIP.** Serial Line Internet Protocol; designed to allow a host to connect to a TCP/IP internetwork over a telephone connection.

- **SMTP.** Simple Mail Transfer Protocol; designed for the seamless transmission of electronic mail across an internetwork using e-mail servers and clients.

- **SNMP.** Simple Network Management Protocol; designed to monitor and manage network devices (particularly routers and servers) from across an internetwork.

- **socket.** The combination of port and IP address that uniquely defines the destination of network traffic being sent at the transport layer.

- **source.** A network device that generates or initiates network traffic.

- **subnet.** A physical or logical subdivision of a TCP/IP network; usually a separate physical segment that uses a subdivision of the site's IP network address to route traffic within the organizational internetwork.

- **subnet mask.** A method of representing the portion of the IP network address that is devoted to subnet addresses (as opposed to the portions of the address that refer to individual hosts or to the organizational network overall).

- **synchronous.** A method of transmitting data across a connection controlled by a timer, requiring that each participant be synchronized; beginning and end points of transmitted data are indicated by elapsed time rather than by the use of special headers and trailers.

- **TCP.** Transmission Control Protocol; a transport layer protocol that offers connection-oriented, reliable stream service between two hosts; the primary transport protocol used by TCP/IP applications.

- **TCP/IP.** Transmission Control Protocol/Internet Protocol; the name usually given to the collection of network protocols used by the Internet protocol suite from the two primary network protocols of the Internet protocol suite.

- **Telnet.** Remote Terminal Protocol; the application protocol that defines remote network connections between any client and any server across an internetwork.

- **TFTP.** Trivial File Transfer Protocol; a simple file transfer protocol that uses UDP for unreliable, connectionless file transfer; usually used (if at all) for network booting of diskless workstations.

- **throughput.** The amount of information (usually measured in bits per second) that a communication medium delivers in a given time; with latency, it determines the level of performance of the network medium.

- **time to live.** See **TTL**.

- **Token Ring.** A local area network architecture that uses a "token," passed from one network node to the next, to grant permission to transmit on the network, which daisy-chains nodes together to form a ring topology.

- **topology.** The architecture of a network; the way a network links networked nodes, usually described in terms of its shape.

- **traceroute.** A program that traces the route between two hosts using ICMP error messages to identify the routers forwarding network traffic from one host to the other.

- **traffic.** Signals transmitted by a networked system that carry encoded information for other hosts, requests for information from other hosts, or responses to requests from other hosts (including error messages and other control information).

- **transceiver.** A device used by networked systems to act as a transmitter of signals onto the network medium and to receive incoming signals; usually refers to an Ethernet device.

- **Transmission Control Protocol.** See **TCP**.

- **transport layer.** The layer at which network traffic is passed between an application on one host and an application on another host.

- **Trivial FTP.** See **TFTP**.

- **TTL.** Time To Live; a counter field used in IP datagrams to indicate the length of time (generally, represented by how many different routers have handled it) that the datagram can continue to be forwarded to other routers before it will be discarded because it has expired.

- **UDP.** User Datagram Protocol; a connectionless, unreliable transport layer network protocol for the exchange of requests and replies between networked hosts.

- **unicast.** Refers to the transmission of data to a single host; in contrast to broadcast and multicast.

- **Uniform Resource Locator.** See **URL**.

- **URL.** Uniform Resource Locator; the address that uniquely locates and identifies a particular network resource by the type of resource it is and the host, path, and filename it is located in; used most often to refer to resources accessible via HTTP (World Wide Web browsers).

- **User Datagram Protocol.** See **UDP**.

- **virtual circuit.** A network connection between two network nodes that functions as if there is a direct link connecting them.

- **WAN.** Wide area network; generally refers to a network that connects users and systems across large distances and usually employs telephone or other long-range communications medium.

- **well-known port.** A port number assigned for use by a specific network application for connections made with UDP or TCP.

- **wide area network.** See **WAN**.

- **World Wide Web.** See **WWW**.

- **WWW.** World Wide Web; the global network of interconnected systems offering HTTP services to users with appropriate browsing software.

Index